Jack the Ripper—
Case Solved, 1891

Jack the Ripper—Case Solved, 1891

J.J. Hainsworth

McFarland & Company, Inc., Publishers
Jefferson, North Carolina

LIBRARY OF CONGRESS CATALOGUING-IN-PUBLICATION DATA

Hainsworth, J. J., 1963– author.
Jack the Ripper : case solved, 1891 / J.J. Hainsworth.
    p.   cm.
Includes bibliographical references and index.

ISBN 978-0-7864-9676-1 (softcover : acid free paper) ∞
ISBN 978-1-4766-1913-2 (ebook)

1. Jack, the Ripper.   2. Serial murders—England—London—
History—19th century.   I. Title.
HV6535.G6L653496 2015   364.152'32092—dc23   2015036951

BRITISH LIBRARY CATALOGUING DATA ARE AVAILABLE

© 2015 J.J. Hainsworth. All rights reserved

*No part of this book may be reproduced or transmitted in any form
or by any means, electronic or mechanical, including photocopying
or recording, or by any information storage and retrieval system,
without permission in writing from the publisher.*

Cover image: A never before published picture of Montague Druitt
(the Warden and Scholars of Winchester College); Ripper silhouhette
(Alan Cotton/123RF Stock Photo)

Printed in the United States of America

*McFarland & Company, Inc., Publishers
Box 611, Jefferson, North Carolina 28640
www.mcfarlandpub.com*

To Christine,
whose affection, encouragement, research skills,
ruthless editing and discovery of several definitive
primary sources made this book possible

Acknowledgments

I wish to thank the following people for their indispensable help and support: my companion and research assistant, Christine Ward-Agius; my daughter, Victoria Hainsworth; my father, Dr. D. Roger Hainsworth (for his proofreading and advice); my friends Tony Agius, for his assistance with the illustrations and I.T. support; Sarah Agius, for her I.T. assistance, publicity and photography; Matthew Agius, for his media advice, publicity and Web site assistance; Richard, Margaret, Patrick and William Widdess; Irene and Bert Newbery; Brenton Ward; Cynthia Gillies; Dino Di Rosa; Sam Cooper; James Tonkin; Chris Perry; Jenni Laritza; Sister Jillian Havey (principal of St. Dominic's Priory College); Andrew J. Forder; John Warren and Tony Stimpson (both former principals of Eynesbury Senior College); and various students in a succession of Year 11 classes at Eynesbury between 2007 and 2010.

I wish to gratefully acknowledge the following for the material and assistance they have provided: Mr. Christopher McLaren, Roger J. Palmer, Paul Begg, Michael Hawley, Simon Wood, Don Souden, Chris Phillips, Debra Arif, Howard Brown (and his Jack the Ripper Forums Web site, JTRForums.com), Jonathan Menges (and his Casebook: Jack the Ripper Web site, casebook.org), Tom Wescott, Hermia and Tischler, Stewart P. Evans, Joe Chetcuti, Jan Bondeson and Amberley Publishing, Suzanne Foster, archivist of Winchester College, Adam Neil Wood, editor of *Ripperologist* magazine, Ancestry.com, the British Newspaper Archive, the National Archives U.K. West Sussex Record Office, the National Portrait Gallery U.K., Phil Hoffman Travel and Jackie Pool, and the timeless music of The Beatles, which helped us to continue writing this book during a particularly long, hot Australian summer.

Table of Contents

Acknowledgments vi
Preface 1
Introduction: A Gentlemen's Agreement 2
Prelude: Montie Is Missing 12

I. Boys' Own 17
II. Sent Down 27
III. Custard and Mess 36
IV. Terror Strikes London 45
V. Fiend in Flight? 55
VI. Man's Man 64
VII. The "Last" Victim 74
VIII. A Ghost Laid to Rest 86
IX. Scion of the Bourgeoisie 97
X. Well-Dressed Corpse 106
XI. The Priest's Secret 115
XII. Chief of Spin 128
XIII. Hidden in Hyde 141
XIV. From Montague to Mortemer 154
XV. Doubles and Deflections 165
XVI. Ripper Remystified 177
XVII. Jack the Oxonian 192

Chapter Notes 203
Bibliography 215
Index 217

Preface

Oh no! Not another book on "Jack the Ripper"! What could possibly justify the further sacrifice of the rain-forests for yet another tome on this well-worn subject? The short answer is that this book looks at the "mystery" from a fresh and original perspective, unique in the thriving sub-genre of true-crime nonfiction known as "Ripperology" (if you've come to gawk at autopsy pictures or to be beguiled by dodgy DNA results, you will be disappointed).

The longer answer is that it came about due to the enthusiasm of a handful of high school students. As a South Australian history teacher I was searching for a fresh topic to inspire a passion for the past. I hit upon the Jack the Ripper murders of 1888 because this tabloid-driven "reign of terror" provided a handy entry-point into studies of industrialism, imperialism, colonialism, capitalism, socialism—and maybe a couple of other "isms." As for "Jack," I assumed he was some anomic psychopath whose identity was unknown then and certainly unrecoverable now. To my surprise (and my students' delight), extensive research revealed an inescapable conclusion. The case was solved at the time and, what's more, the solution was broadly shared with the Late Victorian and Edwardian public. Newly discovered sources and the analysis of old ones—some documents as cruelly neglected as any waif in a Charles Dickens novel—reveal how and why a highly regarded police chief believed he had identified the Whitechapel assassin, albeit posthumously, and why he partly disguised that solution (the murderer was related to the family of a distinguished friend of the top cop). It is the disguise that has misled people for a century.

All historical arguments are provisional and this book is no exception. The certainty of that police chief—and the claim of parallel certainty by the alleged killer's own nearest and dearest—is as close as we can ever get. An absolutely final and definitive answer to the identity of "Jack the Ripper" is not possible. Even if the chief suspect had not killed himself and instead gone on trial, he might have been acquitted by a jury. (One of my students asked whether, since the likely killer was a barrister, he would have defended himself.) Consider that in 1893 an American society lady was quickly acquitted of double homicide because a remarkably similar crime happened on the first day of her trial, a relentless newspaper campaign trumpeted her innocence and the sympathetic judge summed up in her favor. As she left the courtroom, a free woman, a relieved crowd cheered her—yet hardly anybody does not think Lizzie Borden brutally axed to death her father and stepmother!

Introduction:
A Gentlemen's Agreement

The Chief Inspector of Explosives was Sir Vivian Majendie, one of the most delightful personalities I ever came across, and a very loyal friend. —Sir Melville Macnaghten, 1914

Detectives are only human, you know, and, like the rest of the world, they frequently go looking about in every direction for something that lies close to their hand all the time. —George R. Sims, 1897

Was he a prosperous London surgeon? Perhaps a member of British royalty? Well, our Bullshit team has unearthed spectacular new evidence which suggests that Jack the Ripper was in fact the Loch Ness Monster! —Amazon Women on the Moon, 1987

Eric Blair, better known to his readers as George Orwell,[1] wrote a much celebrated essay, "Decline of the English Murder," published in the *Tribune* on February 15, 1946, in which the author affectionately satirized tabloid culture. On behalf of the average working man relaxing on a Sunday afternoon with his *News of the World*, Orwell lamented the lack of a "good murder." He defined such a crime as a killer who was above suspicion; a "little man" of suffocating respectability who was motivated by money or lust, or both, and committed a domestic murder, preferably with poison, because "this seems less disgraceful, and less damaging to his career, than being detected in adultery." The average citizen could empathize with both the victim *and* the perpetrator because the culprits were ordinary people

The unknown link—Colonel Sir Vivian Majendie (1836–1898) was chief inspector of munitions for the Home Office from 1871. He was also close friends with Chief Constable Melville Macnaghten and the popular writer and journalist George R. Sims. Although this was unknown for 124 years, Sir Vivian was also related—by the marriage of a cousin's daughter—to the family of the chief Jack the Ripper suspect.

that had slid almost furtively into suburban horror. Often they were caught only by a chance mistake while the sums involved were, more often than not, pitifully small. But now, Orwell argued, murders had become acts of sheer anomic brutality reflecting the global mass slaughter just extinguished. Orwell listed some infamous British murderers, including the elusive assassin of poor prostitutes in London's impoverished East End in the Late Victorian Era: "Jack the Ripper." Writing a few years before the advent of television, Orwell was bemused by the mass saturation of the popular media by these notorious murderers (one can only imagine what the great writer would have made of today's global glut, encompassing as it does cyberspace too):

> Of the above-mentioned nine cases, at least four have had successful novels based on them, one has been made into a popular melodrama, and the amount of literature surrounding them, in the form of newspaper write-ups, criminological treatises and *reminiscences by lawyers and police officers*, would make a considerable library. ... In considering the nine murders I named above, *one can start by excluding the Jack the Ripper case, which is in a class by itself*. ... [The traditional murderer] should be ... chairman of the local Conservative Party branch.... [He] should only bring himself to the point of murder after long and terrible wrestles with his conscience.... He should plan it all with the utmost cunning [my italics].

What Orwell did not know was that most of his criteria for the classic British killer *did* apply to the likeliest Jack the Ripper suspect; the outward, professional respectability ("a barrister of bright talent"), the inexorable exposure by nosy neighbors or concerned relatives (a Scotland Yard file records that the suspect's immediate family were the first people to believe in their member's culpability), the links to the ruling Conservative (Tory) Party (the suspect's uncle was a mayor and a Tory, as was a local member of Parliament who learned the family's terrible secret, probably along the local constituency grapevine). And "Jack" certainly planned his bloody sorties with "utmost cunning." Perhaps the chief suspect still ultimately fails to qualify, as his victims were both heartbreakingly squalid and total strangers to their executioner—and of course "Jack the Ripper" was never caught. Orwell was a graduate of the private boys' school Eton College (1921) and, overall, the socialist gadfly judged it to be a positive experience because, despite all its born-to-rule elitism, it had inculcated in him the capacity to think as an individual, even to be receptive to progressive ideas. Ironically, Blair/Orwell never realized as he composed his brilliant essay that another Old Etonian, one who had graduated half a century before the creator of "Big Brother Is Watching You," had used Eton's "Old Boy Network" to discover the true identity of "Jack the Ripper."

It is a persistent myth or, to be precise, a modern misconception that the Jack the Ripper mystery is a mystery at all; while the Ripper was certainly never caught, this does not mean he was not identified (though this revelation was missed by even a commonsense genius such as Orwell, despite his penchant for trash culture). The Jack the Ripper mystery was in all probability solved at the time of the murders by a highly regarded police sleuth—who was as sure as he could be about a prime suspect who was already deceased—and what's more, this solution was shared with the Late Victorian and Edwardian public. Future generations of researchers, however, have been confounded by the same police chief's having clothed the killer's true identity in a discreet, even cheeky fictional shield (as the exact identity threatened to tarnish the reputation of an Establishment worthy—and law enforcement official—who was both a close friend of the police sleuth and also distantly related to the Ripper). It is this knotty aspect of the tale, the mystery *inside* the mystery, which this book attempts to untangle.

At the turn of the previous century a definitive resolution to the Jack the Ripper case was announced in the press. Initially this was done on a semi-official basis and then officially—or at least *by* an official—in 1913. In subsequent years this alleged solution was forgotten, then revived, but only in fragments; and this caused it to be eventually discarded all over again for the wrong reasons. The year before the start of the First World War, a conflagration that would transform entire regions of Europe into something like the charnel house of Whitechapel, this solution was announced in the *Daily Mail* of June 2, 1913:

SECRET OF SCOTLAND YARD.
THE END OF "JACK THE RIPPER."
INTERESTING DISCLOSURE.

It was repeated by many newspapers in the U.K. and across the world, for example in the *Evening Telegraph and Post* of the same date (see below). However, in no account was the probable murderer named. But then how could he be, as "Jack," long dead, could not enjoy the protection of due process. Instead, readers were informed of the identity of the Scotland Yard official claiming to have solved the case, "at one time or another," Sir Melville Leslie Macnaghten, who was no less than the retiring head of the Criminal Investigation Department:

"JACK THE RIPPER"
COMMITTED SUICIDE SAYS
HEAD OF CID
WHO REVEALS SCOTLAND YARD'S SECRET

The fact that "Jack the Ripper," the man who terrorised the East End by the murder of seven women during 1888, committed suicide is now revealed by Sir Melville Macnaghten, head of the Criminal Investigation Department, who retired after twenty-four years service.

"Frankly," he said, "I am sorry to leave the Force. I love the work and it will be a wrench to give it up," but [he] said when one reaches sixty it is time to make room for others.

NO REMINISCENCES

There was *no case of murder and no important burglary during his time which he did not personally investigate.* Sir Melville confessed that the greatest regret of his life was that he joined the force six months after "Jack the Ripper" committed suicide. *"That remarkable man,"* he said, "was one of *the most fascinating* of criminals. Of course he was a maniac but *I have a very clear idea of who he was* and how he committed suicide, but that with *other secrets* will never be revealed by me."

DESTROYED SECRETS

"I have destroyed all my documents and there is now no record of the *secret information which came into my possession* at one time or another" [my italics].

Following his firm declaration that there were "secrets" he would never reveal, Macnaghten implies that nobody else at the Yard would be able to do so either, due to his having destroyed the pertinent documentation that named the Whitechapel fiend. If this was true, surely it must mean that the material in question belonged to him and not to Scotland Yard. By implication they were not official documents—this alleged solution must be the chief's own private bit of sleuthing and not necessarily a collective opinion at the Yard. At the same press conference, Macnaghten spoke with pride about the police officers whom he had mentored and was becomingly modest about the role chance plays in solving cases (perhaps he was still thinking of the Whitechapel crimes) as he says none could be solved without the assistance of "Detective-Inspector Luck" and "Detective-Sergeant Chance." This Scotland Yard administrator conceded that he never had any formal training as a policeman, but he implicitly defends this gap in his resume on the basis that sleuths are "born not made" (the upper class Macnaghten also seems blessedly free of ingrained snobbery; he remarked, "One of the finest detectives I ever saw was at one time a farm hand"). He pointed to his role in helping with the greatest breakthrough in crime detection up to that time—fingerprint identification—as his "most notable achievement."

After Macnaghten passed away eight years later, the *London Times* published on May 17, 1921, an "Appreciation" by some anonymous chum of the late chief's. This gentleman wanted to put it on the record that the upper crust Macnaghten (the son of one of the last chairmen of the East India Company) was a veritable Renaissance Man, while stressing the latter's infatuation with his years at the exclusive boys' school, Eton:

> There never was a keener Old Etonian, or one more constant in his visits to his old school. He himself wrote "To know Eton is to love her, and that love lasts as long as life itself." ... For 24 years he served ... and the Force has never had a servant more devoted to the interests of the police and public. ... The interest he took in his work and his men was enormous. All his men admired and respected him, and he infused them with his own spirit of industry and devotion. ... A man of many and diverse interests; in his early years an amateur actor of no mean ability, he was a constant and enthusiastic theatre goer; always a considerable reader he never lost his love of the classics, and on a long voyage to Australia in the last 10 years of his life made a translation of the *Ars Poetica* into English verse ... fond of shooting.... He was an ardent admirer of the boxing ring, and was often to be seen at the National Sporting Club in the old day; he was also a good speaker and a delightful raconteur. Sir Melville was knighted in 1907 and received the C.B. [Companion of the Order of the Bath] in 1912.

Tall, handsome and charm personified, Melville "Mac" Macnaghten was a self-invented super-cop. What's more, he was a fascinating character, as if the indulgent satirist of upper class eccentricities P. G. Wodehouse had dreamed him up (and with words complimenting the Ripper—"remarkable" and "fascinating"—maybe there is a dash of Monty Python–style absurdity thrown into the mix too). With his overgrown-adolescent personality, one forever seeking to recreate the happiness of his school days, combined with a celebrated compassion for people of all classes and infused with a capacity for prankish deceit, "Good Old Mac" was, to borrow John Le Carre's phrase, something of an "honourable schoolboy."[2]

The Register of December 19, 1914, in my home city of Adelaide, South Australia, favorably reviewed Sir Melville Macnaghten's memoirs, highlighting the author's humane approach to crime-fighting, his joyful times at Eton and his claim to know the likely identity of the Ripper: "A kindly point view of his fellow mortals is indeed one of the most striking features of the book. He is so much occupied in praising those who worked with him that neither space nor time is left for lauding of himself. No wonder that Sir

Melville Macnaghten was prominent among the most popular of the highly placed officers who have filled responsible posts in the great Criminal Investigation Department of London." The assistant commissioner was also acclaimed in his own day for his almost miraculous powers of recall, as for example by his successor at CID, Basil Thomson, who wrote in his memoir, *My Experiences at Scotland Yard* (Doubleday, Page, 1923): "[Macnaghten] had an astonishing memory both for faces and names; he could tell you every detail about a ten-year-old crime, the names of the victims, the perpetrator and every important witness."

In so many Jack the Ripper books, however, this same jaunty charmer is depicted as little more than a cipher; a bland, bumbling know-nothing blighted by an atrocious memory. His opinion that the case was solved is universally rejected as either not what he was [plainly?] saying or a hideous mistake. The specific suspect that Macnaghten believed "in all probability" was the killer has been known by name since 1965. It is generally believed by many writers on this subject that Sir Melville shanghaied into the mystery a tragic and innocent figure.[3] After all, Macnaghten's only "evidence" against this poor fellow—or so we are smugly assured today—was that the suicide in question had the bad luck to drown himself in the River Thames soon after the Ripper's final murder. Whitechapel buffs are often at each other's throats about their pet suspects, but when it comes to Macnaghten's alleged incompetence and the lack of viability of his suspect there is a near-Stalinist consensus. (Actually, Macnaghten's suspect died two years *too early*. Consequently, the police chief had to exonerate him of Jack the Ripper murders that post-dated his suicide while pretending that Scotland Yard had never thought the subsequent homicides were by the same hand—a short-term ruse that bamboozles researchers to this day.)

Why is there such a Grand Canyon–sized gap between the positive—even affectionate—assessments of Melville Macnaghten in one contemporaneous source after another, and the almost universal disdain and derision with which he is treated in modern accounts of the Victorian hunt for "Jack the Ripper"? It is mainly due to Macnaghten's writing an internal report in which he seems to think that the likeliest suspect was a middle-aged, English physician who committed suicide within hours of the most ghastly murder—whereas we have known since 1959 that this man was in fact a young barrister (who, what is more, drowned himself in the River Thames three weeks after the climactic bloodbath). By the late 20th century a police chief praised in his own time for his formidable powers of recall and meticulous attention to detail was being crucified for not accurately remembering—or maybe ever knowing—the most basic facts about his chosen "Jack."

In the rush to discredit this primary source too many authors have not paused to consider the entirety of the available record involving Sir Melville Macnaghten—material either by him, about him, or composed on his behalf by proxies—which when examined as a whole shows that the Scotland Yard sleuth was engaged in a public relations campaign via the most famous writer of the day, George R. Sims (a close friend of the police administrator). The pair shared with the public that the case was solved while semi-fictionalizing some of the data to hide the real suspect, mostly by plagiarizing Robert Louis Stevenson's *Strange Case of Dr. Jekyll and Mr. Hyde* (1886). Hence a young barrister who killed himself on about December 1, 1888, became a middle-aged physician and asylum patient who took his life on November 9, 1888.

Hiding the murderer in *Hyde* was done for solid Victorian reasons of propriety and discretion. By acting deceitfully Macnaghten and Sims shielded the dead killer's respectable relations from social disgrace. The police chief knew that an accurate leak—even just "barrister" plus "Thames suicide" plus "Ripper"—would have inevitably identified the madman's brothers, sisters, uncles and cousins among their middle class peers. As a consequence the suspect's family would have been shunned on the street as if they were typhus carriers, their various careers in the military, the law and the church ruined. Macnaghten through Sims also hustled a myth—to put it politely—that super-efficient detectives were poised to arrest the "Mad Doctor" but he had already hurled himself into the river. We can see the hustle's exposed mechanics; between Macnaghten's reports and Sims' writings the killer's family have been disguised as friends. This begs a previously unasked question: since *they* are hidden, why not their maniacal member too?

This is the nub of our historical dilemma regarding "Jack the Ripper": the tension between primary sources that tell us the facts but not the truth versus ones that tell us the truth but not the facts. Thankfully there is one surviving document, Sir Melville Macnaghten's autobiography, that bridges this divide. When it came time to write his reminiscences about his life and career—and for the first time his own knighted name was on the line—Macnaghten became much more candid, up to a point, about what had really happened and not happened between 1888 and 1891. Yet even relatively respectful and sober works on this subject in effect emasculate Macnaghten by totally excluding his autobiography, despite its being the only document the chief ever produced under his own distinguished name on the subject of the Whitechapel murders, at least for the public record. In his chapter 4, "Laying the Ghost of Jack the Ripper," the "shape-shifting" murderer is not described as either a doctor or middle-aged.[4] Furthermore, it is specifically denied that the suspect had ever been "detained" in a madhouse, or had taken his own life immediately after the final murder. Most striking is Macnaghten's humiliating admission that police were unaware of this man until "some years after" he had destroyed himself. To soften this failure the ex-chief hyperbolically characterizes the "Protean" killer as virtually omnipotent against the forces of the state, but due to overdosing on post-mortem horror he suffered some kind of breakdown and took his own life. According to Sir Melville only the Ripper could stop the Ripper.

Is there a "smoking gun" that arguably proves that Macnaghten had to know more about his preferred suspect than what was in his spin-driven "memo"? The answer is yes—in fact, there are enough such weapons for an arsenal. For example, missed by all previous researchers is the textual evidence that provides a through-line strongly arguing in favor of Sir Melville Macnaghten's being well-informed about his Ripper's particulars (it was missed partly because it was not fully appreciated to what extent George Sims' writings about "Jack the Ripper" are a Macnaghten source, albeit at one remove). In the January 5, 1889, issue of the *Acton, Chiswick and Turnham Green Gazette* reporting on a suicide in the River Thames, we are informed that the deceased's older brother searched for his missing sibling: "Witness heard from a friend on the 11th of December that deceased had not been heard of at his chambers for more than a week. Witness then went to London to make inquiries." The data was altered by Macnaghten to become a "Mad Doctor" who had vanished from his home and was frantically being searched for by his anxious "friends," as we see in Sims' widely read column in the *Referee* of February

16, 1902: "At the time his dead body was found in the Thames, his friends, who were terrified at his disappearance from their midst, were endeavoring to have him found." In his 1914 book Macnaghten further revised this element into a mentally unstable yet high-functioning recluse who lived with his nearest and dearest and only went out on the nights of the Whitechapel murders (wholly lifted from a popular novel): "I incline to the belief that the individual who held up London in terror resided with his own people; that he absented himself from home at certain times."

Despite the fictitious bends, this remains as tough as nails because for Macnaghten to be cognizant of the older brother's quest, even if from newspapers alone, he would also have to have been aware from the same articles that his chief suspect was a 31-year-old barrister who took his own life in early December 1888. Once the suspect's true identity (though not name) was revealed in 1959 and it was at last known that he was a legal advocate and not a medical man, this "Mad Doctor" shell-game was unfortunately not simultaneously rediscovered. In a fateful moment for this subject, the police chief was assumed to have had an unreliable memory and/or to have been poorly informed. His memoir's preemptive apology for any "inaccuracies" because he could only rely on his memory when in reality he had not one but two copies of his "memo" to reference has been, illogically, taken at face value.

Even a writer as brilliant and canny as Tom Cullen plunged down this particular rabbit hole, lamenting in 1965, "It is perhaps unfortunate that the CID chief did not keep a notebook, for, relying upon his memory … he has allowed a number of errors to creep into his discussions of the Ripper case."[5] The long-term consequence was that the almost-certain fiend was thrown back into the river like so much inedible cod. New researchers headed off in different directions in the wake of the "debunking" of Melville Macnaghten, some chasing a few genuine police suspects (an unforgettable Irish-American eccentric was a major police suspect in 1888, yet he had been forgotten until 1993). Others have stuck a bloody knife into the hands of innocent celebrities from the Victorian era,[6] while a tiny few were involved in outright hoaxes (e.g., a fanciful royal conspiracy).[7]

A notable exception is the journalist-writer Paul Begg, who is itchily unsatisfied with both the modern caricature of this police chief as "Constable Magoo" and with the latter's strange errors. He wondered if perhaps Macnaghten should not be taken too literally.[8] Since the 1960s, if a tenured academic historian—with the patience and resources that only a college can provide—had taken on this subject, a whole mass of vital primary sources would have been found in one hit, rather than being stumbled upon at the glacial pace of about one a decade. The Irish-American suspect, for example, lay dormant because no researcher on this subject had checked U.S. newspapers' coverage of the Whitechapel murders. Even the most cursory glance would have swiftly revealed that this flamboyant suspect's arrest and flight from British justice was reported in one salivating American tabloid after another.

The emergence of alternate theories, fakes and an ever-increasing number of suspects (many painfully ludicrous, such as Lewis Carroll and Vincent Van Gogh) was perhaps best lampooned by a short segment in the hit-or-miss sketch movie *Amazon Women on the Moon* (1987), stitched together by film-makers in love with B-movies and junk culture: John Landis, Joe Dante and Carl Gottlieb (who co-wrote *Jaws*). One of the hits was a send-up of the 1970s show *In Search of...* It purported to investigate U.F.O.s, Bigfoot, missing persons, and so on, and was hosted by a portentous Leonard Nimoy between *Star Trek* gigs. In *Amazon Women* we see a third-rate set meant to be foggy Whitechapel, circa 1888. Into the frame steps a candidly jaded host (Henry Silva) of *Bullshit or Not?* solving the mystery of "Jack the Ripper"—it was the Loch Ness Monster! Sure enough, a huge animatronic puppet of "Nessie" in oversized Victorian attire, including a wide-brimmed hat, slithers away to slaughter an unwary prostitute.[9]

Whether B.S. or not, every alternate Ripper resolution hangs from the same very slender thread—that the amiable but dim Melville Macnaghten did not know much pertinent about his chosen suspect, not even his true vocation. In 2014 there appeared a stunning tabloid headline, along the lines of "DNA proves Ripper was Polish madman." Allegedly human material had been recovered from an alleged Whitechapel artifact, allegedly once touched by both a victim and a suspect and, allegedly, matched against their remote descendants. I fully expected to see Henry Silva looming into view asking: "Is it bullshit, or not?" This book will show that this suspect was a red herring, a harmless lunatic dangled by Sir Melville to deflect his indiscreet boss away from the real "Jack." The artifact in question—a shawl, or tablecloth, that was too expensive to belong to an East End prostitute, and was not listed among the pertinent victim's effects by the police—was in the possession of a family whose ancestor was, indeed, a policeman in 1888. The trouble is, he had nothing to do with the Whitechapel investigation. Rather than a scientific breakthrough, this was a couple of enthusiasts getting carried away.

The DNA "solution" has caused much gnashing of teeth and rending of garments, but this will pass. What sends the Whitechapel cognoscenti into permanent apoplexy is the indestructible, iconic pop image, repeated by one illustrator after another unto the end of the age, of the fiend sporting a top hat, opera cloak and black bag and sinisterly vanishing into the London fog. Ironically, the much despised image of the Top Hat Toff *does* accurately reflect Sir Melville Macnaghten's sleight-of-hand that hid the real "Jack": an English gentleman who psychologically imploded and became his own final victim (actually the killer probably dressed down in Whitechapel, as a drab sailor). Despite his sunny disposition, his need to maintain a "kindly point view of his fellow mortals," Sir Melville Macnaghten came to believe that a fellow Anglican who was so quintessentially British—a graduate of Winchester and Oxford, a barrister, schoolmaster and accomplished cricketer—was at other times the vilest of monsters. This was a conclusion that spectacularly defied the same police chief's formidable class and religious prejudices, which were *not* to believe such a hideous accusation against a fellow professional (and a chappie who was hardly in a position to defend his good name).

Another reason—or compelling bias—for the chief constable to reject this suspect's guilt is that it meant embracing Scotland Yard's total failure to identify "Jack" while he was alive, or even for some years after he was dead (the public relations campaign via Sims strenuously denied this failure for fifteen years). Yet the Scotland Yard sleuth found that the evidence, even posthumously, left no room for serious doubt (it had previously convinced the drowned man's own family and later a local member of Parliament).

What was this evidence, apparently so compelling that to only *hear* of it leaves the listener convinced forever? This book reveals for the first time why all these English gents believed something so ghastly about somebody from their own class: the killer had likely confessed his crimes to an Anglican clergyman. The latter tried to publish this story on the tenth anniversary of the death of the drowned suspect—though he candidly admitted it was "substantial truth under fictitious form" to protect the innocent. It is hard to conceive of a better summing-up of the wares Macnaghten and Sims were selling, though unlike the vicar this pair of gentleman-propagandists never admitted to mixing fact and fantasy. Since the vicar's confession-scoop would do nothing to help Scotland Yard's already dented image, the police chief got in first with his own "true lies" (i.e., that super-efficient detectives were so close to apprehending the villain, who had no time to confess anything to anybody, that they practically pushed the maniac into the river).

I believe the police chief met the suspect's relations—at least once—and that Sir Melville would have felt considerable compassion for their justified distress at the prospect of being outed. Yet would a career bureaucrat have risked his job and his own reputation to protect strangers who were hardly his burden? Another smoking gun is a previously unknown personal dimension to the Ripper tale involving Sir Melville Macnaghten—revealed here for the first time. My researcher, Christine Ward-Agius, was curious about a mutual close friend—and law enforcement colleague—of Macnaghten's named Sir Vivian Majendie. A very distinguished military officer, he was the Victorian era's chief bomb disposal expert. Genealogical detective work led Ward-Agius to discover that Sir Vivian was also connected—by a relative's marriage—to none other than Macnaghten's likeliest suspect. Thus the police chief and the famous writer had a compelling private motive to disguise the killer's true identity; they were both determined to prevent a social catastrophe for another prominent family, one with whom Macnaghten (and Sims) enjoyed a close relationship.

This recent discovery is the strongest circumstantial evidence as to just how compelling must have been the case for the dead man's guilt, how lucid and credible was that clerical confession—or else Sir Melville would have reassured his friend, Colonel Majendie, that there was nothing to the allegation. He did not because he judged he could not. As Sims puts it in one of his short stories, alluding I think to the Ripper solution: "Detectives are only human, you know, and, like the rest of the world, they frequently go looking about in every direction for something that lies close to their hand all the time." The police chief must also have been fearful as to what certain unscrupulous, radically inclined tabloid newspapers would do with a "Jack" who had been related, albeit at several removes, to a high-ranking Home Office official. No wonder that after Sir Vivian passed away, Macnaghten and Sims assumed a defensive crouch about CID's supposedly *almost* arresting the fiend. It is the contention of this book that these two gentlemen could not simply keep mum about the whole scandalous business as the aforementioned vicar—as this book will show, he was very likely Sir Vivian's cousin's son-in-law—was going to reveal the truth anyhow, and they had to be ready to quash it with their own "substantial truth in fictitious form." On that score, mission accomplished, but in the long run it was, inadvertently, at the cost of Sir Melville's rightful place in history as the sleuth who likely solved the greatest mystery in the annals of crime.

As far as knowing the identity of "Jack the Ripper," this is as close as we are ever going to get: the certainty of this competent police administrator despite countervailing pressures on him not to choose *this* tragic figure as the assassin. Much of what has passed for in-depth analysis since the 1960s has denied not only Macnaghten's professional acumen, not only the veracity of his solution, but also one of his greatest cultural achievements. This was the Tory police chief's using the famous writer George Sims—though upper class, he was a liberal progressive—to force the so-called better classes to confront a most distasteful and unwanted truth: that the Whitechapel assassin was not some convenient poor, foreign *other* from that vile swamp but "one of us"—top hat or not.

This book attempts a comeback: to restore the battered and bruised reputation of Sir Melville Macnaghten, revealing the personal motive driving him to disguise and deflect others away from the killer's true identity—at least until his memoirs. It celebrates Sir Melville's warmth and charm towards all classes of people, acknowledges his successful law enforcement career, and attempts to show why he was so convinced of the drowned barrister's guilt. This means painstakingly peeling back the layers of disguise that the police chief and the famous writer, as close pals of the heroic military officer, had created to hide the name of "Jack the Ripper," a boyish sleight-of-hand which, though essentially wound back by the retired Macnaghten in 1914, is still fooling people one hundred years later.

Prelude:
Montie Is Missing

Montague John Druitt ... was found drowned in the Thames.... A barrister of bright talent, he had a promising future before him, and his untimely end is deeply deplored.
—The Southern Guardian, 1889

"Jack the Ripper" committed suicide.... The police conclusions were given in the report to the Home Office.... The genuine "Jack" was a doctor. His body was found in the Thames.—George R. Sims (Dagonet), *The Referee*, 1903

December 31, 1888

A little after midday a local waterman named Henry Winslade was rowing across the Thames River near the Thorneycroft torpedo works at Chiswick, about half a dozen miles from the City of London—the bustling epicenter of the world's mightiest imperial monopoly. All of a sudden Winslade spotted the ghastly sight of a corpse bobbing up and down in the notoriously polluted waters. He dragged the body to shore and a local police constable, George Moulson, was quickly summoned. The bobbie investigated the remains of a well-dressed gentleman who looked about forty and, judging by the considerable decomposition, had been in the river for a month or more. Out of the pockets spilled four large stones. The drowned man had taken his own life, and perhaps by weighting down his body he had hoped his corpse would never be found. P.C. Moulson found that some material he retrieved from the pockets, while soggy, had survived better than the body: a first class season train pass from Blackheath to London and two substantial checks (along with a silver watch, a pair of kid gloves and a white handkerchief). The checks suggested that the deceased was connected to a man named W. H. Druitt who resided in the thriving, picturesque southwest coastal town of Bournemouth, Dorset.

Less than a month before, William Harvey Druitt, 32, a staunch member of the Church of England and the Conservative (Tory) Party, was basking in the afterglow of the legal coup he and his brother Montague, younger by one year, had pulled off in the High Court. In the nearby town of Christchurch a hardy Tory voter had been cheated of his voting rights because local Liberals had complained that the renter had not sufficiently contributed to the local rates—or so they had convinced a partisan magistrate.

This ruling had been justly overturned by the nimble advocacy of William's silver-tongued sibling before the chief justice, Lord Coleridge, himself a former Liberal politician. It was the kind of case that got a young man noticed by the respectable press and older grandees of the Tory Party, then the incumbent government.

Montague (Montie) John Druitt was a handsome, athletic young man whose career as a London barrister was, as one newspaper would later lament, "full of bright promise." The Druitt brothers had been born to an affluent, surgeon father in the small town of Wimborne-Minster in western Dorset and were both bachelors (and had two other brothers and three sisters). Montie was a product of the exclusive boys' school Winchester, and a graduate of New College, Oxford. To supplement the hard slog to establish a winning reputation as a special pleader (defense lawyer), he had been for some years an assistant master at a small cramming school for boys in the suburb of Blackheath, where the young man also had his "digs." He was a keen cricketer for two clubs patronized by many well-connected gentlemen. Montie was more proficient with the ball than the bat. He still parted his hair in the dead center, as he had since he was a small boy, but his neatly trimmed, fair moustache provided the necessary gravitas to reassure clients. Now it was all ashes. Arriving at the Chiswick mortuary, William gazed at what was left of the face on the slab and positively identified the corpse as his missing younger brother.

"A promising future before him"—In the center is Montague John Druitt (second from left, with hair parted), aged about 12 in the year 1871, attending his exclusive boys' school (published for the first time with the permission of the Warden and Scholars of Winchester College).

This suicide in the Thames River created not even a ripple in the bustling capital's media. Only local and regional newspapers mentioned Mr. M. J. Druitt's death at all. By contrast, the tabloids and broadsheets regularly headlined any crumb of information or rumor regarding the spate of mutilation murders of prostitutes which at that moment so riveted the attention of all the classes, upstairs and downstairs. The horrific crimes, committed presumably by some blood-lusting lunatic, were all concentrated in London's East End, specifically Whitechapel, itself a foully congested slum deformed by chronic unemployment, poverty, disease, famine, violence and simmering sectarian tension. On one night the "fiend" had infamously despatched *two* women and yet still eluded the police patrols. A letter supposedly sent by the taunting, gleeful killer—whether authentic or a hoax—had provided the indestructible nickname: "Jack the Ripper."

The Whitechapel assassin's most recent—and most audacious—atrocity had transfixed not only London, but the entire world. In the early morning hours of the just-passed November 9, "Jack" had methodically torn to pieces the dead body of a young unfortunate, Mary Jane Kelly, in her pitiful, one-room hovel. The full details were not released to the general public, as they were too gruesome. What was known was disturbing enough. As usual the police were without a clue, though to be fair fingerprint identification and the capacity to differentiate blood types, human or animal, were still out of reach by many years. The one potential clue was an alleged sighting of the same woman, earlier that evening, with a client who sounded like a well-to-do, foreign Jew. Many of the respectable class, like the upwardly mobile Druitt clan, assumed that the vile killer was probably some "foreign swine," for surely no Englishman could ever stoop to such savagery.

January 2, 1889

An inquest into Montie's death was held in Chiswick at the Lamb Tap public house, presided over by Dr. Thomas Diplock, a local coroner. It lasted all of an afternoon. Both Winslade and P.C. Moulson testified, but the star witness was William Druitt, the older brother's grief under disciplined check as he assisted the court in trying to discover the catalyst for the unexpected tragedy. William cut a lonely figure at that inquest because the Blackheath school's headmaster, George Valentine, did not testify, nor did any other member of the Druitt clan—in fact nobody from his London life designed to appear. A local newspaper reporter who covered the events at the Lamb Tap that afternoon recorded William Druitt testifying that, apart from himself and their mother, the deceased had no other living relatives. (Did the reporter perhaps mishear the witness?)

William Druitt said he had been informed—by an unnamed "friend"—that Montie had vanished, and the solicitor consequently came to London to ascertain his sibling's whereabouts. The experienced advocate produced for the inquiry nothing less than the missing piece in the tragic puzzle. It was a note left by Montie alluding to suicide, which William said he had found among the former's effects at the school—at which his younger brother had got into some sort of serious trouble and been dismissed. Why was Druitt not allowed the face-saving dignity of a resignation? Is that because he was A.W.O.L? Was his vanishing act, in fact, the trigger for his firing? The content of the note was summarized by Dr. Diplock as follows: "Since Friday I felt I was going to be like mother, and the best thing was for me to die." The Druitt father, a very distinguished Dorset doctor, was deceased, while their mother, William divulged, had been institutionalized the previous July due to a progressive mental disease. Did Montie kill himself because he feared he too was crossing the borderland of sanity, or did he mean he knew, for some reason left unexplained, that he was also inevitably headed for his own madhouse cell—and preferred death to that unappetizing fate?

Based on what was purported to be the deceased's own anguished sayonara, Dr. Diplock tidily and swiftly found that Montague Druitt had taken his own life while in an "unsound" state of mind; that he had become suddenly and fatally deranged. What other explanation could there be for this act of self-destruction? A verdict of temporary insanity would also help shepherd a respectable gentleman's burial into hallowed ground, mitigating the sin of suicide.

After burying Montie in Wimborne, Dorset, in a service attended by only a few family members including William but none of his sisters and, once more, nobody from the capital, the various members of the clan dispersed to continue on with their respectable and prosperous trajectories. One who did show for the funeral but not the inquest was the deceased's first cousin, an Anglican vicar named Charles Druitt who had married the daughter of the first cousin of Her Majesty's chief inspector of munitions, Colonel Vivian Majendie.

In the middle of 1889 there was another murder of an East End prostitute, suggesting that the Ripper was still active, if far less frequently. That same year a woman's torso was discovered in the East End; this might also have been a victim of the same fiend but, then again, who could be sure? In early 1891 some politician who represented a western district was shooting his mouth off, saying that he knew the killer was dead— he had been a surgeon's son who had taken his own life. Within a couple of days this "curious story" was debunked in the most spectacular fashion—by yet another grisly death of a young unfortunate in Whitechapel. Frances Coles was found with her throat cut—but not mutilated—by a young bobbie on his beat who had apparently disturbed her killer. After a massive police search of docks, ships and houses, this time a prime suspect was arrested; a drunken, violent sailor who had been carousing with the victim that night. Yet after much ballyhoo in the press he was discharged and the case, as they would later say, went cold.

A Decade Later

In the Edwardian era grown-up graduates of a small, private school for boys in the middle-class suburb of Blackheath would inevitably still vividly recall the reign of terror of "Jack the Ripper." For one thing, the ghastly murders coincided with the sad day when the headmaster, George Valentine, had to gravely inform the students that their young, popular and athletic classics master, Mr. Druitt, who had mysteriously vanished towards the end of 1888, had been found drowned in the River Thames. The subsequent inquiry judged that the poor man had become temporarily insane and killed himself.

By the 1900s such a grown-up graduate perusing the newspapers—actually the musings of just a single columnist, George R. Sims (a.k.a. Dagonet), who was nevertheless England's most famous writer of fiction and true crime—could not have helped but notice that the Ripper and Mr. Druitt shared some attributes: both were English gentlemen and educated professionals, and both had resided in the suburb of Blackheath.

Thankfully the resemblance ended there.

The foul murderer had been a middle-aged, wealthy, semi-retired surgeon who was by 1888 a recluse cohabiting with his very prominent West End family. A year before, he had placed himself in voluntary care, telling his own physicians of his desire to savage East End harlots. It was an outrage to common sense that he had ever been released back onto the streets! By contrast, the part-time school master was a country doctor's son, a successful barrister, and a noted local cricketer. The Ripper took his own life in the early hours of November 9, 1888, hurling himself from London's Embankment to a watery grave, according to Sims, a "shrieking, raving fiend." By contrast, the lawyer had calmly filled his pockets with rocks and waded into the same river, a few miles outside the city limits, destroying himself several weeks later.

It was not appropriate for Sims to reveal the name of the lucid maniac as he could never have his day in court (apparently a police dragnet was fast closing to arrest the "Mad Doctor," missing him by mere hours), but he did inform readers as to what "Jack" had looked like; amazingly, he was Sims' double. With his naval beard and rotund, middle-aged girth, Sims rather resembled the sovereign, King Edward VII, at least in the latter's heyday as the rakish, playboy Prince of Wales. What a decidedly repulsive visual parallel for Dagonet's millions of readers!

Speaking of parallels, that postulated grown-up graduate might have paused to wonder if the unemployed surgeon-maniac and the young barrister-teacher had known each other in 1888? If not, had they, irony of ironies, bumped into one another in a Blackheath street, or perhaps sat opposite each other on an omnibus—two very different Englishmen who ended up at the same tragic destination?

I

Boys' Own

The hours he spends at the old school are not only the happiest in his life, but that he is conscious of this at the time. —Sir Melville Macnaghten, 1914

Were I to deduce anything from my feelings on leaving Eton, it might be called "The Theory of Permanent Adolescence." The experiences undergone by boys at the great public schools are so intense as to dominate their lives and to arrest their development. —George Orwell, 1940

In December 1898 as the Jack the Ripper murders receded into recent history, Major Arthur Griffiths (1838–1908), the well-respected prisons inspector and true crime chronicler, published *Mysteries of Police and Crime* (2 vols., London-Cassell) a two-fisted tome comprehensively covering Britain's history of tackling murderers, thieves, gangs, terrorists, anarchists, rioters, and so on. Oddly, the infamous Whitechapel murders, which had never led to even a single suspect being charged, were pointedly not included in the chapter on Scotland Yard's bungles. Instead they were covered with blink-and-you'll-miss-it brevity in the book's introduction; yet here the sober Griffiths provided something like a scoop. He claimed that far from being clueless in 1888, the police did have some prime suspects on their radar after all, and one of them, an insane English doctor, may well have been the Whitechapel assassin. It could only remain a speculative solution, Griffiths cautioned, because the suspect took his own life in the River Thames before he could be arrested—or cleared. The major's caution notwithstanding, this Tom Thumb–sized glimpse into a side of the police investigation previously unknown to the general public and press caused a minor sensation—to the point that a few commentators were openly skeptical (examined in-depth in chapter 13). Yet little more than a month after Major Griffiths' book's debut, the famous writer and self-styled criminologist George R. Sims confirmed this Ripper revelation without qualification (and would continue to do so, well into the second decade of the new century).

This was the first entry into public consciousness of the alleged definitive solution to the Ripper mystery; the "Mad Doctor" super-suspect that would dominate popular culture until the aftermath of World War I (from the 1920s the doctor element would persist while the tormented suicide would fade away—see chapter 16). But where had the supposed scoop come from? Who was Griffiths' authoritative source for this complete upending of the public understanding of the case? Major Arthur Griffiths was known to have access to the top police administrators, among them the chief constable of the

Criminal Investigation Department (CID), Melville Macnaghten (as did Sims). In his book the major wrote this glowing thumbnail sketch of the police chief:

> Mr. Macnaghten, the Chief Constable, or second in command of the Investigation Department, is essentially a man of action. A man of presence is Mr. Macnaghten—tall, well-built, with a military air, although his antecedents are rather those of the public school, of Indian planter life, than of the army.

Griffiths provides us with a wonderfully panoramic description of Macnaghten's cluttered yet homely office, which sounds like nothing so much as a fan boy's basement:

> His room, like his chief's, is hung with speaking tubes, his table is deep with reports and papers, but the walls are bright with photos of officials, personal friends and of notorious criminals which Mr. Macnaghten keeps by him as a matter of business.

And then the major links Macnaghten with "Jack the Ripper." This at least hints that it was this official who might be the source of his Whitechapel revelations:

> Some other and more gruesome pictures are always under lock and key, photographs, for instance, of the victims of Jack the Ripper, and of other brutal murders, taken immediately after discovery, and reproducing with dreadful fidelity the remains of bodies that have been mutilated almost out of human semblance.

The author provides a vital insight into this boyish desk-jockey; he escaped his office every chance he could to hurtle to the scene of a crime—the more sensational the better:

> It is Mr. Macnaghten's duty, no less than his earnest desire, to be first on the scene of any such sinister catastrophe. He is therefore more intimately acquainted, perhaps, with the details of the more recent celebrated crimes than anyone else at Scotland Yard.[1]

Major Griffiths had written that Macnaghten's "antecedents" are "rather those of the public school" meaning the police chief was the product of an exclusive *private* school for boys. This is something of an understatement.[2] For to solve the mystery inside the mystery of "Jack the Ripper"—why the drowned, young barrister suspect transformed into a middle-aged "Mad Doctor"—one has to solve the riddle of this "honorable schoolboy" who orchestrated a propaganda offensive on behalf of a close friend, fellow gentleman, pillar of the establishment and fellow law enforcement official. To do that we have to understand the Jupiter-sized gravitational pull that Macnaghten's school days at Eton College exerted on him over the course of his entire life. For example, in 1914, the by-then-retired chief wistfully wrote:

> I don't know whether all old Etonians think of their school as often and as lovingly as I do; but it is an undeniable fact that a boy, on going to Eton, becomes, intuitively and instinctively, imbued with the spirit of the place.... To know Eton is to love her and that love lasts as long as life itself.[3]

It would be hard to imagine a greater contrast to the sheer hell of London's East End than the lovingly tended sporting grounds and majestic spires of Eton. By the Victorian era the college was dominated by the scions of privilege, who outnumbered the boys of merit—King's Scholars—who were not from titled or moneyed families. The Duke of Wellington, victor of Waterloo, a prime minister and an Eton graduate was alleged to have said that the British victory at Waterloo was "won on the playing fields of Eton."⁴ The story is almost certainly apocryphal. George Orwell added that Britain had since *lost* all its battles thanks to the same playing fields. Nonetheless, Eton's legendary mystique was such that it could intimidate people from afar. Upon visiting Adolf Hitler at Berchtesgaden in 1938, Foreign Secretary—and Old Etonian—Sir Antony Eden discovered that when they were anonymous soldiers on the Western Front meat-grinder they had fought quite near each other. With war clouds once more menacing the peace of Europe, the British minister hoped to break the ice by indulging in some reminiscing, one trench-veteran to another. Instead Eden was startled by the Fuhrer's declaration that Eden's country had been victorious because of his alma mater's military ethos; this seemed to be the only way to explain the defeat of Prussian military might. Eden politely demurred; the Eton College Corps was actually an under-equipped "shambles." Characteristically, Hitler would brook no contradiction and the meeting continued in a glacial state.⁵

The fox in winter—A handsome, twinkly-eyed portrait (c. 1913) of Sir Melville Leslie Macnaghten, reproduced from an edition of his 1914 memoirs which I located at the University of Adelaide, South Australia. Prematurely retired due to suffering from Parkinson's disease, "Mac" still reveled in memories of his idyllic boyhood at Eton College (Christopher McLaren).

In an article for the *Guardian*, November 23, 2005, the year before the publication of an entertaining book on his old school, author Nick Fraser wrote that many foreigners still regarded Etonians as "gods sent to walk on earth," whereas to unimpressed locals they appear to be "pricks, raving snobs, closet homosexuals, members of a closet Masonic order ... beyond the immediate comprehension of lesser mortals educated at a state school." There is an undeniable oddity about certain Old Etonians that helps us to understand why Scotland Yard sleuth Sir Melville Macnaghten acted in the idiosyncratic way he did when he stumbled upon the Ripper's identity, probably in 1891.

Famous graduates of Eton apart from Wellington and Orwell include the poet Percy Shelley, the influential economist John Maynard Keynes, the backbench M.P., historian and notorious philanderer Alan Clarke, the Anglo-French tycoon Sir James Goldsmith, the versatile actor Hugh Laurie (he was Bertie Wooster to Stephen Fry's Jeeves, as well as the brilliant but ornery Dr. House on American television) and the vanished peer Lord Lucan, the last person in Britain to be convicted in absentia of murder: he bludgeoned his family's nanny, having apparently mistaken the victim for his wife (whom he also assaulted). The classical scholar and ghost story writer M. R. James, though not an Old Boy, was provost of the school in the early 20th century (and entertained students by reading his latest chillers to them in his study). Along with Wellington, Eton has produced eighteen other prime ministers of Great Britain including William Pitt the Elder, Sir Robert Walpole, the Liberal lion William Gladstone, and the Conservative stalwart Robert Gascoyne-Cecil, the 3rd Marques of Salisbury, who was succeeded by his nephew, Old Boy Arthur Balfour. Future Etonian premiers included Sir Antony Eden, Harold Macmillan (later Earl of Stockton) and Sir Alec Douglas Home—though he was the last, in 1964, until David Cameron ended a very long dry streak in 2010.

Somewhat embarrassed by his privileged pedigree, "Dave" Cameron downplays being an Old Etonian, whereas Boris Johnson, London's flamboyant Tory mayor, is much more popular partly because he has shrewdly embraced his background as a toff, portraying himself as a lovable, overgrown schoolboy (his well-known peccadilloes apparently forgiven). As of writing, thirteen members of the current British prime minister's front bench are Old Etonians, about a third (it was over half of Balfour's 1904 cabinet), though not the unpopular chancellor of the exchequer, George Osborne, whose toff credentials are, nonetheless, not in doubt as he is a graduate of St. Paul's College and the heir apparent to a baronetcy.[6] Old Etonians are not, in general, ideologically driven; their only agenda is to serve the public interest (which they have conflated with their own elite class). But exactly whose public have some of them served? In the *Sydney Morning Herald* of February 12, 1963, there was this truly Pythonesque headline:

GUY BURGESS STAYS "TRUE BLUE ETONION"

While visiting the Soviet Union on business, the deputy chairman of Rolls Royce, Whitney Straight, ran into an old school friend he had not seen since they graduated. They spent an hour chatting and reminiscing in Straight's Moscow hotel room:

"I was delighted to see him," Straight is reported to have said, "I thought he looked very well. I found [Burgess] in cracking form ... as usual wearing his Old Etonian tie."

Guy Burgess was also in Moscow because he was a traitor and a defector. Along with Donald Maclean, Harold "Kim" Philby and Anthony Blunt, Burgess was one of the infamous Cambridge ring of Soviet spies who had helped cause the deaths of many British agents behind the Iron Curtain, and who had played—especially Maclean—a not insignificant role in the Russians' acquiring the secrets of the atomic bomb. Yet here was Burgess, in 1963, popping up without exhibiting a scintilla of shame and even wearing his old school tie. The automobile executive assured Reuters, "I think [Burgess] really loves his country: whatever has been said about him and whatever he has done, I think he has a fundamental interest in England." Did they also sing the grand old boating ballad? Mr. Straight reportedly thought Burgess looked healthy. In fact the former mole died a few months later, a pathetic alcoholic unwilling to learn Russian, refused re-entry to England to see his dying mother, while above his deathbed apparently hung a fading sepia picture of Eton.[7]

To return to Old Etonian Sir Melville Macnaghten, whose loyalty to the realm is not in question, his beloved and decidedly iconoclastic second daughter, Christabel the Lady Aberconway, paid tribute to her late father in her own entertaining memoirs:

My father was learned, gay and intelligent and had an admirable memory: he made friends easily and with every sort of person, and never, I think, lost a friend. Also he was courageous and gentle and good company. I think that he had loved almost every day of his life, and he was always as much interested in what he had not done as in what he had achieved.[8]

Upon reaching 60 and facing the ordeal of debilitating illness that would end his once active life, Macnaghten longingly wrote:

> At the age of thirteen I went to Eton, and it was really as if one had been translated to heaven.... To Eton I owe very much the happiness of my whole life, and not one hour of misery can I recall during the whole six years there spent. There are in this world no friends like old friends, and no old friends quite like old Eton friends.[9]

Known at Eton as Old Mac, he would in 1891 solve the Ripper mystery partly via this elite network of school chums. Like an overgrown adolescent, Mac would cheekily disguise that solution to both reveal and yet hide the murderer's true identity from his own bureaucratic rivals and colleagues at Scotland Yard, from the byzantine politics of the Home Office and from the public, as if smuggling booze into his dorm room under the nose of a cane-wielding master. The Eton school may have been the greatest infatuation of the police chief's life, for despite enjoying a happy marriage, a cozy family life, and a successful career, his post-graduate years were—by his own account—overshadowed by his idyllic school days. Furthermore, the ex-chief confesses he knew life would be, to some extent, downhill after Eton before he graduated:

> The hours he spends at the old school are not only the happiest in his life, but that he is conscious of this fact at the time; that throughout life, he is proud of having been at Eton, and that, whenever and wherever hears our grand old boating ballad sung, he chimes in with, "And nothing on earth shall sever the chain that is round us now" with a truthful intensity that comes straight from his heart.[10]

For all his capacities and successes as an adult, Macnaghten seems to have been intoxicated by a kind of immature nostalgia for the past. In Orwell's 1940 essay "Inside the Whale," which is partly devoted to exposing the soft-headedness of middle-class, English writers who fell in love with a criminal despot such as Stalin, he quotes from a book by Cyril Connolly in which the latter writes words that fit Macnaghten like a silk glove: "Were I to deduce anything from my feelings on leaving Eton, it might be called 'The Theory of Permanent Adolescence.' It is the theory that the experiences undergone by boys at the great public schools are so intense as to dominate their lives and to arrest their development."[11] Another writer, Hargrave L. Adam, a crime journalist of the Edwardian era who knew all the significant figures at Scotland Yard, also made note of this unusually juvenile aspect of Macnaghten when recalling the late chief in 1930:

> It is in a lofty, spacious room at the "Yard" ... [Macnaghten] invites me to be seated, making the quaint observation, "Would you like a warm chair or a cold chair?.".. Neither in appearance nor manner was he the least suggestive of the fictional idea of a "sleuth." He had a curious flippant way of talking of crime. He wrote in the same way, as his very interesting book on reminiscences proves.[12]

Exactly one hundred years before Christabel wrote her words of praise about her father in her memoir of 1966, a new group of wide-eyed boys arrived at Eton. They were a mixture of King's Scholars, who lived in the school's somewhat spartan boarding facilities, and the much larger group of Oppidans (from the Latin, "in the town") whose families paid full fees and lived in red-brick houses in the village surrounding the school. Oppidans tended to be more snobby and fanatical about sports, while the scholars were more intellectual—even progressive—in their attitudes. Among the intake that year for the "in the town" group was Melville Leslie Macnaghten. Born on June 16, 1853, Macnaghten was the youngest of fifteen children of an upwardly mobile, interbred clan of Irish and Scots. He was the progeny of giants of the British Empire: his father, Elliott Macnaghten, was one of the last chairmen of the East India Company, and his grandfather had been governor of Bengal. He admits to an early fascination with the macabre and the gruesome (he also started his own crime archive by collecting six-penny catalogues about the latest outrages against the law):

> I remember full well that, arriving at home, about two o'clock on the Saturday, I used to hurry over lunch, and almost invariably make my way to Madame Tussaud's ... and revel in the Room of Horrors till hunger and tea-time called me home. The boy, seemingly, was to be father to the man—Crime and Criminals had a weird fascination for me at a very early age.[13]

In his memoir's second chapter, "Eton Memories"—by far the book's longest—Macnaghten brusquely described his leave-taking at Windsor's South-Western Railway Station as he, a little Oppidan in his Eton hat and jacket (and embarrassed by his father's unstylish, no-nonsense chimney-pot hat), kissed his mother and father goodbye. Next to him was a larger boy, a King's Scholar, who was also taking leave of *his* parents. Macnaghten's father provided his fifteenth child with the following somewhat hair-raising admonition: "to try and avoid doing anything of which I should be ashamed to let my mother and sisters know."[14] His chapter on his school days is like finding the fragile, yellowing pages of a Victorian public school-boy's diary in which the various scrapes and misadventures over trying to decipher Latin verses, or memorize a part in a public speaking assignment, or unfairly doing lines as punishment, or noting who scored what winning run in a sporting match against a rival public school, have all been diligently and tediously recorded. They are nothing more than trivial juvenilia and would be usually judged as such by its author once he had graduated and was making his way in the real world. Instead we have here in a mature man's autobiography these disintegrating vignettes, breathlessly related to us as if they are an Aladdin's cave of treasures—which to the author they surely were. There is not the slightest sense of adult reflection on or reassessment of his school days, or about Eton, or the "putting away of childish things" as the Apostle Paul—a founding saint of Macnaghten's religion—puts it in his famous epistle. "Old Mac" seems to be reliving his adolescence in all its glory as he, in 1914, lovingly composed this chapter dedicated to Etonian minutiae. His boyishly cheerful temperament (reminiscent of Hugh Laurie's manically cheerful, super-patriotic though thoroughly dim-witted Tommy in *Black Adder Goes Forth*) is relentlessly positive; everybody must have a good word said about them. As for the game of cricket, Macnaghten becomes swoony with adoration: "I was always passionately fond of cricket.... The cricket-field and the playhouse have given me more pleasure than anything else in life, and, so far as I can judge, their joys do not wither, nor stale, with advancing age."[15]

This aging cricket-tragic gushes over the legendary batsman Charles Inglis Thornton (1850–1929), nicknamed "Buns," who was in the elite Eton Eleven in 1866, 1868 and 1869. Thornton is alleged to have hit a ball the jaw-dropping distance of nearly 160 yards and was largely responsible for creating the Scarborough festival. The athlete himself claimed that his striking power came partly from freeing his body from impedimenta such as leg-padding and batting gloves. Macnaghten's gushing description of his boyhood hero is, frankly, beyond parody: "I can see the loose figure now coming down the pavilion steps, cool as an iceberg, firm as a rock.... Perhaps no human being has ever given me quite the same amount of pure delight as did 'Buns' Thornton, by his mammoth hitting, in those days."[16]

About the frequent hitting by older boys of the younger boys–disdainfully called "fags"—or by the masters, usually in public on Fridays with the victim bending over a wooden structure, nicknamed the Block, to be caned or birched, there is almost nothing (just a passing reference about a cheating boy who was *spared* such punishment by his kindly tutor). It is possible that "Old Mac" was rarely caned because he discovered that his likeability acted as a protective buffer. Christabel's account of her father's narrow escape from punishment is instructive:

> I remember he told me his tutor at Eton, to whom he was devoted, once showed him a report that he was proposing to send to [my] grandfather. This happened, I think, in my father's last half at Eton, when he was in the sixth form. The report read: "This boy could have done anything and has done nothing." "If second thoughts are good third thoughts are better, send not until next day that angry letter," seems to have applied to my father's tutor; for twice he came into my father's room, saying, the first time: "Don't worry, Mac, I'm thinking it over." And on the second visit he said: "I have decided to, um—er—relent." That, I think, was characteristic of the way people treated my father.[17]

In his review of weekly magazines for boys, *Gem* and *Magnet* (in *Horizon*, 1940), George Orwell examines the rigid genre conventions that govern these safe, unimaginative and entertaining adventures—for eleven-year-old boys—by male students at the fictional public schools of Greyfriars and St. Jim's. Yet Orwell sounds like he is inadvertently describing this police chief and his somewhat arrested personality:

> The stories [are] of what purports to be public-school life ... [at] Eton and Winchester. All the leading characters are fourth-form boys aged fourteen or fifteen.... These boys continue week after week and year after year, *never growing any older*.... All the principal characters.... Billy Bunter and the rest of them ... [are] *exactly the same age as at present*, having much the same adventures and talking almost exactly the same dialect[18] [my italics].

Old Etonian Orwell rejects, as a matter of course, that anybody over the age of fifteen could possibly take these stories seriously, certainly not as a realistic depiction of life at Eton: "Needless to say, these stories are fantastically unlike life in a real public school.... Sex is completely taboo especially in the form *in which it actually arises* at public schools"[19] (my italics). Whether Macnaghten ever read these boys' weeklies is unknown but, by Orwell's criteria, "Eton Memories" could have been snugly serialized by either *Gem* or *Magnet*. In it Macnaghten describes a fight—no names are supplied—that could be the climax of a rip-roarer at Greyfriars or St. Jim's:

> The only real mill [fight] I can recall to mind was one between a plucky baronet and a boy who rejoiced in the nickname of the "World," while his two great pals were known as the "Flesh" and the "Devil." I remember the names of all three, but have lost sight of them for many years. I have little doubt, however, but that they all turned out well and have done good work in the world, but, as a triumvirate, they were certainly not popular at school. The World was a smart-dresser, tall, strong, good-looking, and, I fear, somewhat of a bully. The baronet was shortish, thick-set, and clumsy to look at.... He was a good boxer, cool as a cucumber.... I believe the World threw a cherry-stone at the baronet, who

resented such action, and flung a strawberry pottle.... The World, incensed, demanded the baronet take a licking, and a fight was arranged.... I am thankful to say that I did not attend the show.... The spectacle was gruesome. The punishment inflicted had been very considerable, and I do not think the World appeared in public for quite a fortnight. The bruising baronet was almost untouched.[20]

Behind this self-portrait of a boy-man trapped in amber we get the occasional glimpse of a potentially more calculating mind, one that had learned early how to navigate through the jungle of office politics. "Old Mac" was called before the headmaster over a complaint by a teacher for being caught coming out of a local public house known as the Tap. Just about everybody, Macnaghten shrugs, visited Tap (which he praises for serving the best "Welsh rarebit" and beer he had ever consumed). What was relevant for the adult Mac is the lesson the head imparted to the boy—don't get caught, Mac![21] As if the lesson had been learned, Macnaghten describes a "sorrowful parting" with a sister who was travelling to live in India (she is not named) and his subsequent purchasing of some "big, black cigars" to help distract him from his melancholy. Instead they made him feel ill ("green faintness") and he stopped. But the windows on his train carriage were shut and so "a nicotian atmosphere pervaded ... which could have been comfortably cut with a blunt pair of scissors." Once back in his dorm he anxiously hoped to fool his tutor and avoid the Block. Though he knew he reeked of smoke, when his spluttering, affronted tutor called his name he pretended to be instantly asleep. That was not quite the end of the human ashtray escapade:

> The next evening tutor came and found me sitting on my bed, clothed, and in my right mind. He would never punish a boy if he could help it, and was always most specially kind to my unworthy self. Thus he addressed me:
> "Last night, when I came into your room, there was a vile smell of smoke; now I cannot bring myself to believe that you had been smoking; in fact, in fact" (and during part of the speech he was, in effect, edging towards the door), "I'll not believe it, I'll not believe it," and, having conquered his own unworthy (?) suspicions, the good man dashed out of the room. It was a lesson to me, though, and I do not think I smoked much afterwards.[22]

The real lesson the boy had learned was that if you keep your mouth shut, concede nothing, enough "front" can rescue a gentleman from a very "sticky wicket."

In 1872 Macnaghten suffered a devastating blow—he graduated (his mother, Isabella, passing away the year before is left unmentioned). His father, predictably, asked his youngest son what he wanted to do with his life, to which he replied, "I think I should like to be an actor."[23] After a strained silence as his father recovered from the shock, young Melville was told that such an aspiration was quite insane, yet the older man would not stand in his son's way if he insisted on going on the stage. Mac seems to have lacked the courage—or at least the contacts—to even take the first tentative step towards a career treading the boards. Instead he accepted a cushy sinecure in a merchant firm thanks to Dad. Though he glosses over this lost year, Mac must have been very bored and frustrated while he tried to figure out what he would really like to do as a career. Despite being a true-crime buff, the notion of applying to Scotland Yard seems not yet to have entered his head. We will also see that the desire to become an actor, to play a role, was also an unfulfilled aspiration that would be fulfilled by other means.

One way for Macnaghten to keep alive the spirit of his carefree Eton days was to frequently revisit the school as an Old Boy. For example, we know from the *Eton College Chronicle* of October 9, 1873 (found by Paul Begg), that Macnaghten was back on the previous September 28 captaining a cricket team of Old Boys and thus satiating two of his adolescent obsessions simultaneously. Yet the day was blighted somewhat by a dramatic and unusual event for the school: a serious crime was committed on the hallowed grounds (perhaps this bold act of theft fulfilled the third of Macnaghten's obsessions). On that day a servant at Eton noticed two men, strangers to him, emerging out of the Lower School passage. Upon investigating he discovered that valuables were missing: a small tankard, some quality clothing, but much more irreplaceably the House Singing Cup. The police quickly launched an enormous dragnet, as if the Crown Jewels had been swiped, even searching trains. Whether Macnaghten joined this search for the thieves is not known, though it is easy to imagine him in the thick of the hunt. The main culprit was soon found, as was widely trumpeted in the press, for example in the *Times* of October 7, 1873:

THE ROBBERIES AT ETON COLLEGE

On Sunday afternoon M. Ostrog was arrested at the Fox and Goose Inn, Burton on Trent. He vehemently protested that he was a Swede, and was simply visiting the breweries. At the police station he tried to escape, but was instantly seized. He then drew a loaded eight chambered revolver, but Mr. Superintendent Oswell seized his hand and prevented him from firing. Yesterday M. Ostrog was conveyed from Burton to Slough for identification by Mr. Superintendent Dunham, of the Slough Constabulary, who holds a warrant for his apprehension.

Michael Ostrog was a tall, slim, dark complexioned Russian, then aged about 37, with some education, who cultivated an exotic image of a lonely exile from Czarist tyranny. This is how he was lushly described in the *Herts and Essex Journal* on February 6, 1864: "Genteel in appearance, affable in speech, and most interesting and engaging in manners, his troubles had cast a semi-martyrdom around him." It is to be doubted that Macnaghten entertained such an indulgent view of a miscreant who had stolen from mere children, had threatened violence against the constabulary and, perhaps most appalling of all, had violated the manners of a class-stratified society by assuming the unearned pose of a gentleman.

Michael Ostrog was a confidence man, and his modus operandi never altered over the course of a mostly unsuccessful and unlucky career as a habitual criminal, both in England and abroad. Often using an assumed name, the articulate Russian would ingratiate himself with some credulous gentlefolk—sometimes posing as a doctor peddling a hard luck story—and the moment their backs were turned would steal some objects of value that he would then pawn. Usually just as quickly he would be caught and either claim to be somebody else, or feign insanity, or even act in a manically violent way. The Russian would dutifully serve his sentence and then, being a classic recidivist, start the sad, self-destructive cycle all over again. Perhaps in some way Ostrog *was* unhinged? *The Graphic* of October 11, 1873, proposed a solution: "We venture to think that the best use to put M. Ostrog to, would be to hang him." Could not Ostrog find some sort of gainful occupation among the snobbish dullards of the English bourgeoisie? The same question about this oddball was more politely asked by the *Buckinghamshire Advertiser* on January 10, 1874:

Ostrog is no ordinary offender, but a man in the prime of life, with a clever head, a good education and polished manners, who would be certain to succeed in almost any honest line of work to which he might devote himself, but who, nevertheless, is an inveterate criminal.... [He] risked his liberty and forfeited a position which he had obtained in respectable society, by pilfering a few books and a silver cup, worth to him about 5 pounds. The case is altogether a psychological puzzle.

Michael Ostrog remains a puzzle to this day; one wonders if he was more content being in prison. It is unclear if Ostrog was born in Warsaw (and therefore was a Polish-Russian), if he was Jewish or of the Orthodox faith, whether he served in the Russian army or navy, or neither—or both. It seems very unlikely that he had any medical training, for surely he would have had a chance of legitimate employment. After being taken into custody over the Eton escapade he feigned insanity by starving himself. When that scam failed, the Russian tried to elicit sympathy by trying to drown himself in a bucket of water. His trial went ahead on January 5, 1874, and, characteristically, the defendant did himself no favors before the judge, Richard Grenville the Duke of Buckingham, by his persistent and irritating interjections. Ostrog tried to impress the court with a technical defense (he had only *received* stolen goods), saying that he was of noble birth–just like you, sire!–and pompously demanded a jury to be at least half composed of foreigners. Ostrog, reportedly to his "chagrin," was sentenced to ten years' penal servitude to be followed by seven years of police supervision.[24] If Macnaghten was interested in 1873–as he certainly would be once ensconced at Scotland Yard—he would have discovered from the press accounts and his Old Boy cronies that Ostrog had first been sentenced for these kinds of shenanigans ten years before. It was a custodial sentence of less than a year, as Ostrog was convicted of stealing an opera glass and case from Charles Levi at Oriel College, Oxford, and also some belongings from George Frederick Price at New College, Oxford—from which the likely Ripper graduated. During this idiosyncratic episode Ostrog used variations of the name Max Grief Goussler. Once free Ostrog upped his rank to that of a prince and he was off again, one petty act of thieving after another until, a decade later, he began his misadventures at Eton, and thus came to Macnaghten's attention.

As we might expect, Old Mac, with his long and accurate memory, did not easily forget this petty, foreign swindler and reprobate who had dared to violate his beloved alma mater (especially as he would do it more than once). Quite unknowingly, Michael Ostrog would play a minor though significant role in Melville Macnaghten's machinations over "Jack the Ripper" in the 1890s and 1900s—but the future police chief had to first survive a lengthy sojourn in the Far East.

II

SENT DOWN

A gentleman of large Indian experience was recommended for the post.... Sir Charles Warren withdrew his recommendation.... Circumstances had come to his knowledge which made it undesirable that the gentleman in question should be appointed.—The Star, 1888

"Bloody Sunday" in Trafalgar Square ... had upset the Londoner's peace of mind, and he had begun to think there was a dragooning spirit abroad.... Police were on the way to becoming the masters, rather than the servants, of the rate-payers.—Sir Melville Macnaghten, 1914

In his provocatively revisionist *Empire: How Britain Made the Modern World,* Niall Fergusson wonders how a few thousand Britons (less than a thousand civil servants backed by less than a hundred thousand soldiers) successfully ruled 250 million Indians—"How did the Victorians do it?"[1] Three generations of Macnaghtens were among those who did it. After several unhappy months at a desk job, Macnaghten surprised his father by suggesting that he might shift gears completely and work as an overseer on the family estates in Bengal. Understandably his father thought this was an even more appalling idea than his son becoming an actor, as he was worried that his gregarious son would be too isolated in the jungle.

Maybe that was the attraction: to leave England and thus break the Etonian addiction, while yet leading a life full of adolescent derring-do (where his nickname became "Young Mac"). Macnaghten's India sojourn lasted twelve years, beginning the month after the Ostrog affair, and is characterized in his memoir, predictably, as having been spent "with very considerable pleasure." Yet beneath the cheerful clichés "Young Mac" concedes that a planter's life was "lonely," he yearned for cricket—which he could only catch occasionally in Calcutta—and he had only meager success as a hunter of pigs, leopards and jackals.[2] In 1878 Macnaghten married a very suitable bride in terms of Victorian codes of respectability, Dora Emily Sanderson, the daughter of a canon of the Church of England, who was also a headmaster of an exclusive boys' school, Lancing College. According to Christabel, it was a very happy union and her mother was quite the knockout:

> My mother had quite a different character: she had a sort of instinctive wisdom and common sense which complemented my father's more showy intelligence, and she was outstandingly beautiful. Osbert Sitwell has recorded in his autobiography that Margot Asquith told him my mother was the most beautiful woman she had ever seen. And

Margot Asquith had known, or anyhow had seen, all the most beautiful women in her generation.[3]

Macnaghten does not write about his private affairs or the history of the Raj, or Indian customs, or the phasing out of the East India Company's once-hegemonic control as a result of the mutiny of 1857, but he does give his attention to an incident in which he was seriously assaulted—a life-threatening incident that would have profound and *positive* repercussions on the rest of his life. This local Hindoo rebellion of 1881, quickly suppressed, led him, eventually, to Scotland Yard in 1889 (where his nickname became "Good Old Mac"). Lord Ripon (1880–1884) was the most popular viceroy among the Indians, to whom he was known as "Ripon the Good." It is easy to see why. A Liberal and a democrat, Lord Ripon pushed for reforms that would enhance self-government and abolish, where possible, all forms of discrimination against Indians within their own country. This brought the viceroy into conflict with more conservative voices, at home and in the Raj, including Macnaghten. This is his unusually dismissive and sarcastic prelude to the insurrection, which he blames on well-meaning do-gooders, and most definitely not on the misguided locals ("excellent fellows"): "During Lord Ripon's vice-royalty breathless benevolence stalked through the land and unsettled the minds of the cultivators of the soil."[4]

"The most beautiful woman"—A portrait (c. 1902) of Dora, née Sanderson, the future Lady Macnaghten (reproduced with the kind permission of her grandson Mr. Christopher McLaren). Margot Asquith paid Dora Macnaghten this singular compliment.

The other targets of blame are certain unscrupulous "agitators" who poisoned relations between landlord and tenant, including distributing an "unsettling" leaflet that threatened the Hindoo "that the two sons of Siva would eat his head." Macnaghten claims to have been a popular and generous landlord and this is no doubt true. What he cannot conceive is that it might have been irrelevant; that beneath the smiles and bows was a seething resentment against Imperial rule. Courageously Macnaghten hurled himself into the thick of the action when he heard that tenants were driving away members of his team who measured their rent—and it nearly got him killed: "Now, when anything of this kind happened, I always made it a rule to make a personal and local investigation, so went straight off to the village; but the cultivators on this occasion acted even as the wicked husbandmen of the parable, and assaulted me so badly that I was senseless on the plain, and many of my servants were also badly beaten." He is typically modest about his brave sortie: "I never realised the danger I was in until afterwards. But to cut a long story short, I was able to return to the village, with adequate police at my back, next morning, and to identify many of the ringleaders."[5]

The ringleaders received heavy sentences after an inquiry into the riot by Ashley Eden, the lieutenant-governor of Bengal. But it was Macnaghten's meeting the inspector-general of Bengal, James Monro, with whom Macnaghten worked in this inquiry and formed an abiding friendship "which has lasted a lifetime," that proved a career-changing event for Mac. Monro, a Scot (1838–1920), had been educated at Edinburgh and Berlin colleges. Rising through the ranks of the colonial service, on merit, Monro believed in authoritarian discipline as fervently as he did the imminent Second Coming of Christ. Men who worked below Monro admired and adored him, whereas those who worked above the ex-Indian autocrat found him to be prickly and difficult. As inspector-general, Monro was renowned for his intelligence, courage, extraordinary memory, and the affection and loyalty he inspired among his staff.[6] He also solved a couple of cases of murder. No wonder Macnaghten and Monro got along: both were men of action fascinated by crime mysteries, both were blessed with retentive memories, and both won the affection and loyalty of their underlings. After his Indian service James Monro would be appointed assistant commissioner (later commissioner) of the Metropolitan Police, and would recall how impressed he had been by Macnaghten's shrewd and fair handling of the Hindoo revolt; that the latter had remained calm, judicious and had only sought justice, not retribution.

On March 2, 1882, Queen Victoria, accompanied by her daughter, Princess Beatrice, had arrived at Windsor in a train and transferred to a carriage. A small crowd was there to wave and cheer the reclusive monarch. Among the crowd were some boys from Eton, including Gordon Chesney Wilson—an Australian—and Leslie M. Roberts. As the royal carriage prepared to clop away from the platform, Wilson was startled to see that the man next to him was pointing a revolver at the queen. As he fired, Wilson instinctively struck at the man's arm with his umbrella. The would-be assassin's shot missed, exploding near the hind-hoofs of one of the royal horses. Wilson jumped on the man, as did Roberts, along with a superintendent and a local photographer. The boys would not let the gunman go until the police arrived. It was the seventh attempt on Her Majesty's life, though this time the motive was not political. The putative assassin was a deranged Scotsman named Roderick Maclean who was offended that a poem he had sent to Victoria had been rebuffed. *The Guardian* reported about the sensational events on March 4, 1882, singling out the heroic Etonians:

> The Queen has not suffered from the attempt made upon her life by the man Maclean, and Her Majesty continues calm and in excellent spirits. ... It may here be mentioned that two Eton scholars, who are described as "brave, stalwart boys," named Wilson and Robinson, who were the means, by hustling the would-be regicide, of saving the life of the Queen, met with a tremendous ovation of applause from their college chums when they returned to Eton last night.

The pair of youthful heroes, flanked by a circle of all 900 of Eton's students, the headmaster and the provost, attended an audience with a grateful Queen Victoria in Windsor's courtyard. One can only imagine the pride Macnaghten must have felt that an Etonian—albeit a colonial—had shown such quick wits and saved, not just anybody, but Her Majesty. In 1883 he published in Calcutta a small book, *Sketchy Memories of Eton* (essentially the first draft of his memoir chapter), which showed that even thousands of miles away he could not quit the habit. In his most private daydreams did Mac wish it had been he who had saved Victoria? Did he envision himself receiving the acclamation of a grateful school and sovereign? When he learned that Monro, whom he had so impressed, had become assistant commissioner in 1884, did Macnaghten first entertain the notion of leaving India for good and joining Scotland Yard? It is hard to overestimate what a moment this must have been for Macnaghten, when he began to imagine himself as a sleuth. To be the man who is first at the crime scene, however grotesque—the more grotesque the better!—who puts together the clues, who solves the mysteries that baffle the plods, who protects the innocent and dispatches the guilty to prison or the gallows, who earns the acclaim of a grateful society—and the head of state. That he saw himself as a street cop, a bobbie, is very unlikely, because that vocation was, for a well-born Victorian gentleman, simply impossible.

Between Sir Robert Peel's push, as home secretary, for some kind of civilian policing force in 1829 to bring order to anarchic, congested streets, and Scotland Yard's hunt for the Ripper in 1888, the image of the bobbie had been transformed. He had gone from a figure of public suspicion and derision—by a populace sensitive to a Continental-style state security—to an accepted fixture of English life. Far removed from the French police state, and their secret police organizations, British policeman wore uniforms as clear signs of identification: a frock tunic, a combed helmet and armbands indicating rank—constable, sergeant, inspector and superintendent.[7] Compared to the American tradition of armed sheriffs, deputies and posses, the British bobbie (originally a term to ridicule Peel that, over time, settled into a positive nickname) was absurdly vulnerable—but this was part of the 19th century social compact that these were police, not soldiers, so they carried only a whistle and a truncheon. Initially, plain-clothed detectives were therefore resented and distrusted because they blended in with the public like spies. In London, jurisdiction was split between the inner city and the rest of the metropolis (shorthanded to the City and the Met). Most police were recruited from the working class, whereas the senior administrative positions were for gentleman solely chosen at the whim of the home secretary. In his memoirs Macnaghten provides a vivid anecdote about this essential difference between police-soldiers as agents of state coercion, such as in France, and English constables as public servants—and claims his charm did the trick better than a phalanx of armed gendarmes, despite needing subtitles:

> But what strikes one more than anything else in going the rounds of Paris, visiting its thieves' dens, etc., is the apparent fear that the French police have of their criminal classes. There was one particular place which the [Fingerprints] Committee visited in 1893 where we were only allowed to go in accompanied by five detective officers, all armed with revolvers. Three of them entered the house with us, two remained in the street with their pistols pointed up at the windows. The inmates certainly were a wild lot, semi-nude and ferocious of aspect. A few francs, however, procured many bottles of red wine, and songs were then sung about the guillotine and the nice workmanship of M. De Paris (the public executioner)—at least so I was told, for not one word of the concert could I comprehend.[8]

Contrasted with such continental ebullience is the grumpy attitude of English baddies, balanced by their inherent respect for the local constabulary. We can assume that the following generic example is based on what Macnaghten experienced:

> Similarly, if you entered one of the worst houses where thieves resort, you would not need the tramp of the armed men to assure safety. One local Criminal Investigation Department

officer would be sufficient, and if, during your visit, he happened to spy a "wanted" man sitting in the corner of a cellar, he would combine business with the pleasure of your company, and ask "Jim" to "come along," for some offence which he would specify, and, in nine cases out of ten, "Jim" would come like a lamb. There is no doubt that behind the Metropolitan Police officer there is a very strong moral force, due perhaps to the fact that, for the most part, the citizens of London are extremely law-abiding and ready at all times to assist the powers that be.[9]

From the perspective of the 21st century it seems archaic and unfair that a "toff" of the Old Boy Network, like Macnaghten, could simply parachute into a vocation for which he had not the slightest training or education, and thus block the promotion of men on the force who had paid their dues. But Victorian England was not a meritocracy, and did not pretend to be one; upper class gentlemen as a matter of course took the leading positions in the state. If anything Macnaghten distinguished himself from much of his privileged class in that he was trying to angle his landing to cheerfully embrace the *hoi polloi*. I believe that he nursed ambitions to win himself an administrative position—partly due to his social rank and insider contacts—but then, through diligence and success, to bend that position to his will; to become a roving sleuth at the head of a team of hand-picked acolytes. To some extent, by joining Scotland Yard, Melville Macnaghten would declass himself. From 1881 to 1888 the British constabulary faced twin insurrectionary challenges: by the fed-up poor and fed-up Irish-Catholic nationalists—who called themselves Fenians (adapting an archaic word for soldiers). The latter launched an audacious bombing campaign, using dynamite, against mainland Britain to try and convince the English to quit their country—where affluent, Irish Protestants were happily loyal to the English state—leading to the creation of the Special Irish Branch (just titled Special Branch by 1888). In the wake of such shocking acts of terror Macnaghten's Bengal admirer, Monro, became the new head of Special Branch in the expectation that his years in India dealing effectively with agitators and secret societies made him the right man to restore public confidence. Monro also became the first administrator with the title "Assistant Commissioner (Crime)" while also wearing the hat of Director of the Special Irish Branch (Section B), and Head of Special Branch (Section D). Monro was answerable only to the home secretary and not to his immediate superior, the commissioner of the Metropolitan Police—a loose bureaucratic arrangement that would lead to an inevitable clash between the top men. Nevertheless Monro's initial appointment was greeted with hope that the man who had done so well in Bengal would now do the same at home.

On February 8, 1886, the mutton-chopped commissioner, Lieutenant Colonel Sir Edmund Henderson—who had helped run a convict settlement in Western Australia and in England allowed police to wear facial hair—was preoccupied with the Irish problem. Henderson therefore fatally underestimated the latent rage of the underclass at home, and consequently a Trafalgar Square demonstration escalated into a major riot. What began as a mass meeting of the unemployed followed by a peaceful march to Hyde Park ended up as a rampage by thousands of vandals and looters from Pall Mall through Piccadilly, Mayfair and into Oxford Street, where the police finally regained the upper hand. Apparently the violence was triggered by some especially stupid "toff" who made some disparaging gesture at the marchers from the window of the ultra-exclusive Carlton

Club—which was promptly shattered by a volley of rocks. Henderson somewhat unjustly took the blame for the whole debacle and resigned. Queen Victoria, as they say, was not amused, writing to her prime minister whom she detested, Gladstone, whose reformist (i.e., socialistic) policies she partly blamed for causing this blot on her reign.

Enter the man on a white horse: Major-General Charles Warren. Despite the monocle and bristling manner, he had been a noted archaeologist, shown compassion and common sense towards the safety of tribal women and children in South Africa and, at considerable cost to his military career, had unsuccessfully run as an Independent Liberal (on a progressive platform that promised mass education and self government for the Irish).[10] This did not prevent Warren's mobilizing police forces like Wellington at Waterloo in order to quash, with measured brutality, the next spontaneous surge by the desperate mob—10,000 strong—to control the streets of London. On the 13th of November 1887, the day that became known as "Bloody Sunday," a battle was fought between, on one side, a raging mob armed with bars, sticks and knives, and on the other thousands of constables, hundreds of mounted constables and Life Guards (plus thousands more constables held in reserve just in case), who blocked the human surge from breaking into the square. Hundreds were injured, but considering the violence of the mêlée there was a remarkable lack of fatalities. Warren's punitive actions earned the hatred of many workers—and their advocates in the tabloid press. This was offset by the support of many of the bourgeoisie, yet the seeds of the commissioner's downfall had been sown as the threat of insurrection faded and Sir Charles (Warren had been hastily knighted after Bloody Sunday)—and the police—were seen, the following year, as pathetically ineffectual at catching a single blood-lusting lunatic who was also trampling on the poor. Macnaghten must have thought that all the action was in London, and he was missing his chance to do his bit for queen and country against the unwashed and the terrorists. Actually he would be there for the worst wave of atrocities in 1893–4, but he never lost his faith in the basic goodness and cohesion of British society. As he wrote in his autobiography, the very idea of anarchism

> is foreign to the nature of the British. Although we are inundated with the scum of other countries, and various parts of London swarm with Nihilists from Russia, Advanced Socialists from Germany, and Communists from France (to say nothing of a large contingent of knifing Neapolitans), yet all these gentry are perfectly well aware that, if they begin throwing bombs about in the London streets, the British workman (honest fellow, though occasional grumbler, that he is!) would be the first person to hoof them out of the country with an uncompromising and hobnailed boot, and that then the gates of their very last city of refuge would be banged, bolted, and barred against them. It is this that has given, and that continues to give, to England a very great immunity from the crimes which so often terrorise the dwellers on the continent [78–79].

Another attraction of joining the police force was that Macnaghten would be with his men all day having jolly adventures. Of course, none of his colleagues would be Etonians, but these hardy workers would all inevitably defer to him as their social superior, and soon discover that he was also their caring mentor ("To one's tutor one owes everything at Eton"), their pal and comrade-in-arms, willing to get his hands just as dirty. What if he rose all the way to become assistant commissioner? Then Macnaghten could escape his desk and become nothing less than Scotland Yard's pre-eminent super-cop, racing through the streets in a special coach (it would be a motor car by the 1900s) with his loyal boys at his side, the public confident their premier sleuth must be heading out to solve the latest mystery. He could already see his future obituary reading something along these lines:

> "MACNAGHTEN OF THE YARD"
> BRITAIN'S GREATEST SLEUTH AND THE MYSTERIES HE SOLVED

Which is exactly how it did read in the *Sunday Post* of May 15, 1921. Upon returning to England, Macnaghten engineered being offered the post of assistant chief constable at the Metropolitan Police Department by his admiring patron James Monro. What was Macnaghten's response? This is the thoroughly sanitized version he provides us in *Days of My Years*:

> Flattering though the proposal was, *I was not in a position to accept it at the moment*, as family work and private interests claimed my whole attention, but, when the offer was again made a year later, I gladly answered it in the affirmative, and the necessary formalities having been gone through, I started my work as a detective officer in Metropolitan Police[11] [my italics].

Behind these bland, sunny lines is a remarkably ugly and traumatic chapter in Macnaghten's life, over which he has drawn a veil, without admitting to his readers that he is doing any such thing. The truth is that he eagerly accepted the offer and then it was cruelly snatched away. Macnaghten suffered the indignity of being "sacked" from Scotland Yard before he had even started. The Old Etonian had been the victim of the turf battle between Monro, as assistant commissioner, and Sir Charles Warren, the commissioner, as the latter did not want the former to have one of his Bengal-Tory cronies making further trouble for him.

A letter to the home secretary, Henry Matthews, has survived, dated March 26, 1888, in which Sir Charles Warren appears to try to sabotage the creation of an assistant chief constable. This position would serve below the chief constable—at 400 pounds per annum, with increments of 25 pounds up to 600 pounds—but he wonders if it would really suit the inexperienced Macnaghten. Warren also threatens that this would-be cop could be "transferred," i.e., demoted, at any time:

> I have to submit to the Secretary of State a copy of a minute by Mr. Monro, Assistant Commissioner, Criminal Investigation Department, recommending Mr. Melville Leslie Macnaghten for the post. I have the fullest confidence in Mr. Monro's judgement; but at the same time have no personal knowledge of Mr. Macnaghten, and I have strongly in view the fact that this gentleman has had no former official, military, or Police experience, and also that although he may be appointed with a special view to duties in the Criminal Investigation Department, he must be (as any Police Official is) liable to transfer to any other duties which the Commissioner may call upon him to perform.

Upon further consideration of this chess move by his perceived rival, Warren pushed to exclude Macnaghten altogether. The reason he gave to Matthews was that the Hindoo uprising disqualified Monro's choice, although the uprising was the very example which the assistant commissioner had used to push for Macnaghten's suitability. Monro had written to Warren of his protégée, "I saw his way of managing men when I was in India and was struck by it, for he had a most turbulent set of natives to deal with, and he dealt with them firmly and justly." Warren countered in writing that Macnaghten "is the one man in India beaten by Hindoos," and he vetoed the appointment. Trying to balance competing interests and rivals, Matthews this time sided with Warren. This was very embarrassing for Monro as he had all but promised the job to Macnaghten. If that was all not galling enough, the would-be sleuth's professional humiliation had spilled into the public arena—though without his being named—in the *Star* of September 5, 1888: "A gentleman of large Indian experience was recommended for the post, with the acquiescence of the Chief Commissioner, and the recommendation was formally made to the Secretary of State. But before the appointment had been actually made Sir Charles Warren withdrew his recommendation, on the ground that circumstances had come to his knowledge which made it undesirable that the gentleman in question should be appointed."

By then the Jack the Ripper murders, terrifying the populace, were in full swing, putting Scotland Yard, Warren, Monro, and Matthews all under enormous public pressure and, to some extent, at odds with each other. Macnaghten, with his fascination since childhood for the gruesome, must have been champing at the bit to hop aboard and, hopefully, help catch the Whitechapel fiend. A fellow would probably be knighted for such a coup, he must have mused. Instead he was being ignominiously marked down as undesirable by a knight of the realm as if he had been expelled from Eton (or "sent down," as such disgrace was called). So painful was this whole period in his life that Macnaghten could not even glance at it in 1914. He simply fibbed, self-servingly claiming he had refused the flattering offer until more advantageous circumstances. In his book there are no toxic feelings expressed by anybody towards anything. It is a very revealing insight into Macnaghten's capacity to practice deception in order to beguile a specific audience.

Only towards the end of Macnaghten's memoir do we find a deflective demolition of the unnamed Warren. During the Ripper murders the commissioner was very much the hands-on chief and thought two bloodhounds—named Barnaby and Burgho—might be the answer to catching the maniac. The commissioner ran around Hyde Park to see if the dogs could pick up his scent, with mixed results. Commendably, Warren was trying new things—anything—to stop a vicious killer. But reliable sniffer-dogs were, like the science of fingerprint identification, still well out of reach in 1888. In the 19th chapter of his memoirs Macnaghten denounces the whole idea of using sleuthing canines as "nonsense"—strong words for "Good Old Mac." From this lover of boxing comes first a crushing left hook, one worthy of the bruiser at Eton who, "Mac" wrote, was nicknamed the "World":

> During the last twenty-five years much nonsense has been talked and more nonsense has been written about the employment of bloodhounds by Metropolitan Police. I cannot call to mind a single case in which they would have been of the slightest use in the detection of crime, even if kennels had been established at the Yard and properly trained hounds had been at once available. At the time of the Whitechapel murders the idea was first mooted.

This was followed by a vicious upper cut into Warren's noble jaw, to do the "Flesh" proud:

> I cannot conceive a more impossible locality in which to expect hounds to work! Or how any sane individual could ever have dreamt of success in this direction. Certain it is, however, that the notion did find some favour with a highly placed police official, and that he himself arranged to be hunted by bloodhounds in Hyde Park.

Finally, Macnaghten dragged in the London riots and their brutal suppression:

> The thing appeared in the papers and just ridicule was incurred. It was incurred, too, at a time when the "man in blue" stood none too high in the public estimation. "Bloody Sunday" in Trafalgar Square and one or two other unfortunate incidents had upset the Londoner's peace of mind, and he had begun to think there was a dragooning spirit abroad in the town, and that police were on the way to becoming the masters, rather than the servants, of the rate-payers.[12]

As for ridicule in the press, Macnaghten knew all too well that humiliation far worse than bending over the Block at Eton when he had been cashiered from the Force. His rise as "Macnaghten of the Yard" had been blocked by a certain "highly placed police official"—and it still rankled twenty-six years later. Dwelling with such vitriol on the failure of the bloodhounds in 1888 gives us a more candid glimpse into his authentic bitterness about Warren's veto than his discreet spin about being "flattered" but having to turn the initial offer down. I believe that this professional setback, though triumphantly reversed within a few months, so deeply affected Macnaghten that behind his affable, uncomplaining front he was left feeling forever alienated and wary of his departmental and political superiors and would—in the case of his Ripper solution—plot his moves on the chess board as secretly and as ruthlessly as they had once been played against him.

In a narrow sense, Warren's antipathy towards Macnaghten would be proved justified as the latter was, at times, a rogue element inside the Force who would, for example, place on file information regarding the Ripper case that he knew would be misleading if read by his police colleagues or anybody at the Home Office—as his first loyalty was to his individual conscience as it had been molded during his joyful school days. That entailed loyalty to one's chums, as we will see in the case of the Ripper's true identity. I doubt "Good Old Mac" paused for a moment when faced with a choice between bureaucratic accuracy or risking the embarrassment of a friend (and his friend's noble family) whose service to the realm was above and beyond the call of duty—but who had the bad luck to be related to the bloody miscreant.

As it turned out, Macnaghten's cherished sleuthing ambitions—to have a job that would daily fulfill his adventurism—would be rescued by the same political infighting that had blocked him; Warren resigned at the end of 1888 and Monro became the commissioner, thus catapulting Mac back into contention as assistant chief constable. Yet there really were some vital "private interests claiming his full attention": Macnaghten's father, with excruciating timing for the family, died on Christmas Eve.

Always there was Eton as a shining beacon to steady "Old Mac" on how to behave and persevere during his harrowing ride through this darkest of dark valleys, by quoting, as he had at school, some doggerel by William Makepeace Thackeray:

> Who misses or who wins the prize;
> Go strive and conquer if you can,
> But if you fall, or if you rise,
> Be each, pray God a gentleman.[13]

III

CUSTARD AND MESS

Mr. Sims maintains that it contains nothing that has not a substratum of sheer fact, although, as he admits, the superstructure of exaggeration is often lofty.—The Era, 1892

… the identity of "Jack the Ripper…." It is consideration for his relatives which has prevented "Dagonet" from making a full disclosure of such evidence as he possesses.— The Gloucester Citizen, 1905

London's population by 1888 was nearly four million, the largest city in the world. Over the course of the 19th century Britain's Industrial Revolution, fuelling colonial predation had transformed this small island state with a powerful, steam-driven navy into a closed trading bloc that dwarfed those of Germany and the United States. Thanks to mass production, a thriving trade, owning India, the invention of the telegraph and building faster railways—including the London Underground—plus a flexible, responsive plutocracy (which for example could phase out slavery)—the English, by 1888, were the richest people on earth. Leisure and disposable income meant the growth of musical hall entertainment and sporting venues for cricket and football, and cycling and tennis were also hugely popular.[1]

Unfortunately not everybody was enjoying the fruits of this industrial boom. At the other end of that same sprawling metropolis was the East End, home to slightly less than a million inhabitants of whom about 80,000 lived in the Whitechapel district. Over half of all children died before the age of five. Thousands of houses were condemned by inspectors as uninhabitable—yet people tried to exist in them, sometimes living a dozen to a room—and many were brothels; one in sixteen women were prostitutes. It was as if the visual transition of *The Wizard of Oz* (1939) had been reversed; people left colorful, cosmopolitan London and took a detour into terrifying, black-and-white grimness. Writers and reformers spoke of "exploring" London's East End; to them it was nothing less than a steep descent into barbarism. The founder of the Salvation Army, Charles Booth, described the location as "a dark continent that is within easy walking distance," populated by "nameless abominations."[2] Reformers such as Andrew Mearns in *The Bitter Cry of Outcast London* established for readers the human degradation just a few suburbs removed from middle class security or Oz-like affluence:

> Here are seven people living in one underground kitchen, and a little dead child lying in the same room. Elsewhere is a poor widow, her three children, and a child who had been

dead thirteen days. Her husband, who was a cabman, had shortly before committed suicide. Here lives a widow and her six children, two of them are ill with scarlet fever, in another, nine brothers, and sisters, from 29 years of age downwards, live, eat and sleep together. Here is a mother who turns her children into the street in the early evening because she lets her room for immoral purposes until long after midnight, when the poor little wretches creep back again if they have not found some miserable shelter elsewhere. Where there are beds they are simply heaps of dirty rags, shavings or straw, but for the most part these miserable beings find rest only upon the filthy boards.[3]

Another factor that would contribute to the Whitechapel murders' creating the potential for civil insurrection was enforced emigration colliding with entrenched anti–Semitism. After the assassination of Czar Alexander II in 1881—in which a single woman of the Jewish faith was peripherally involved—the vengeful state sanctioned pogroms against Jews across Russia. Many thousands of Slavic Hebrews fled to the relative safety of England's democracy and ended up either unemployed or working in the textile industry, their appearance, religion, language and customs looked upon with smoldering resentment and suspicion by the home-grown destitute. Not without good reason did Her Majesty's ministers fear an ethnic explosion, particularly if, God forbid, the Ripper turned out to be Jewish—sure to light the fuse of "the fire this time."[4]

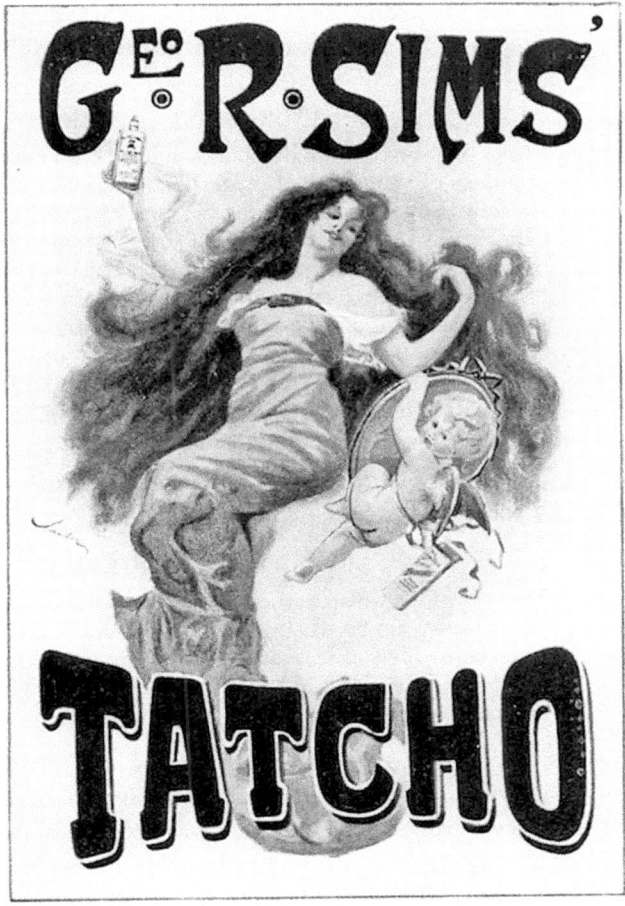

The forgotten populist—A typical commercial advertisement by George R. Sims. Once as popular and socially influential as Charles Dickens in his heyday, he is now completely forgotten, yet "no other journalist has ever occupied quite the same place in the affections ... of the great public," wrote *The Times*, September 6, 1922, in its obituary of the best-selling writer.

Awareness by England's so-called better classes of this other London, before the Ripper struck in 1888, was initially spurred by a literary behemoth. This was George R. Sims, who was just as well known by his Shakespearean pseudonym "Dagonet" (the name of a buffoonish knight at Arthur's Court mentioned in *Henry IV Part II*). He was an eclectic writer-journalist equally at home in the company of high society and its rarefied worlds of palaces, museums and opera houses, as he was in the sleazier music halls, the raucous boxing rings and at the thunderous racetracks. *The London Times* of September 6, 1922, lamented the passing away of this one-man institution:

> G. R. SIMS
> JOURNALIST, DRAMATIST, AND BOHEMIAN
> Mr. G. R. Sims, whose death is announced on another page, will be deeply regretted by hundreds of thousands of readers and playgoers who had never known or seen him. Yet so attractive and original was the personality revealed in his abundant output—for he was a wonderfully hard worker—that no other journalist has ever occupied quite the same place in the affections not only of the great public but also of people of more discriminating taste. Sims was indeed a born journalist, with the essential flair added to shrewd common sense, imagination, wide sympathy, a vivid interest in every side of life, and the most ardent patriotism. But he was more than a journalist. He was a highly successful playwright in farce and melodrama, a zealous social reformer, an expert criminologist, a connoisseur in good eating and drinking, in racing, in dogs, in boxing, and in all sorts of curious and out-of-the-way people and things.[5]

Thirty years before, the *Era* of August 27, 1892, had published a wide-ranging profile and chummy interview with the popular writer under the inviting headline:

> GEORGE R. SIMS AT HOME
> There is probably no author who is so well known to his readers as Mr. George R. Sims. For fifteen years he has been impressing his bright and interesting personality upon them. They know his sturdy, square-built figure when they meet him walking down the Strand or driving Faust Up to Date through the parks. They can point to his house in Clarence-terrace, Regent's Park, as they pass, and never hesitate to address him there.

Born in London on September 2, 1847, the son of a successful businessman and eldest of six children, George Robert Sims married three times (and twice was widowed) but never had any children. He was brought up with a passion for social reform due to having a grandfather who had been a Chartist and a mother who had been president of the Women's Provident League "[who] took an active interest in other institutions dealing with questions affecting the legal and social status of women." Young George was educated at Hanwell Military College—where as a student he wrote his first article complaining of "certain abuses of school management"—and later at elite schools in both Paris and Bonn (from the latter he was reportedly expelled for "boisterous" misbehavior). Rather like Macnaghten, young Sims ended up at a city desk job in his father's mercantile business, and just as energetically plotted his escape:

> I had dreamed of being a circus rider, a barrister, a soldier or a stock-broker. I settled down at the age of nineteen into a city-clerk. Perhaps "settled down" is hardly the word. I was diligent at my calling by fits and starts.... Later on I thought I would write books, and I took to studying character. Being of a Bohemian turn of mind I did not care to dress for dinner daily in order to study "society." I found it more convenient to go into back streets, bar parlous, penny gaffs; to stand outside workhouse doors, to hang about the early markets, and to see life as it is among the masses. These early experiences probably influenced my mind strongly in the direction it has since taken.

He had been writing prose and poetry since he was a boy. With some luck, pluck and useful contacts in the Unity Club—which was patronized by actors, writers and journalists—Sims became a jobbing wordsmith for *Fun* and the *Weekly Dispatch* before he was thirty. Fluent in French and German, he successfully adapted the play *Le Centenair*, followed by another hit with *Crutch and Toothpick*. He achieved literary stardom with his play *The Lights o' London* and his career as a commercial writer on his own terms was established.⁶ Sadly almost all of Sims' voluminous writings for over half a century are completely forgotten, perhaps never to be revived—with the possible exception of his 1879 poem, "In the Workhouse—Christmas Day," a take-no-prisoners assault in the form of a monologue on the inhumane conditions in British workhouse-factories, as codified by the 1834 Poor Law. For several generations of British school children this poem became a standard they had to learn to recite by heart. Here is the first verse, reminiscent of *Oliver Twist*:

> It is Christmas Day in the workhouse,
> And the cold, bare walls are bright
> With garlands of green and holly,
> And the place is a pleasant sight;
> For with clean-washed hands and faces,
> In a long and hungry line
> The paupers sit at the table,
> For this is the hour they dine.

In a lively recent work, *Conan Doyle and the Crimes Club* (Fonthill, 2013), Stephen Wade devotes a chapter to Sims as he was also a member of this Edwardian gentlemen's club (originally named Our Society) that was patronized by the creator of Sherlock Holmes. He confirms the iconic popularity of the writer whom "many at the time thought was, in many ways, a fresh version of Charles Dickens…. Along with bully beef and old folk songs, [Sims] somehow defined what English culture was all about."⁷ George Sims not only defined English culture, he challenged it. Sims' restless curiosity and robust social conscience led him to "explore" the "Horrible London" of the East End and report on what he found in the widely read pages of *The Pictorial World* (1881, complemented by graphic illustrations by Fred Barnard) and re-titled as a book, *How the Poor Live*. Not only did these pieces publicize systemic poverty; they also mobilized others to make their own "explorations," including influential inquiries by Andrew Mearns (*The Bitter Cry of Outcast London*) and General Charles Booth—the founder of the Salvation Army—(*Life and Labour of the People of London*). This resulted in greater activism by churches and charities and some attempts at governmental amelioration by both Tories and Liberals. Apocalyptic warnings by Sims about a potential revolt by a "mighty mob of famished, diseased and filthy helots is getting dangerous, physically, morally, politically dangerous" were prescient, as they anticipated the Trafalgar Riots and Bloody Sunday.⁸ At the same time Sims' vivid, empathetic prose created sympathy for the blighted masses who were either invisible or too cozily written off by the better-off as worthless, lazy, drunken, thieves, murderers and incorrigible "nymphomaniacs." As Sims recalled with justifiable pride in his best-selling memoir of 1917:

> These illustrated articles made something of a sensation. The clergy preached sermons upon them, as they did many years later when on Citizen Sunday the subject chosen for pulpit discourse in a hundred churches was "Cry of the Children." The way in which men and women were herded together in the vilest and most insanitary conditions in the capital of the British Empire touched the public conscience, and for a time "slumming" became fashionable. Eventually I was invited to be witness before the Royal Commission

on the Housing of the Poor, of which the Prince of Wales was the president, and Sir Charles Dilke, I think, the chairman.[9]

If he was as famous as Charles Dickens, George Sims was, however, not a literary artist of the same quality, being essentially a glorified but profitable hack. At one point in his career Sims achieved the rare distinction of having no less than four of his plays performed at West End theatres simultaneously. In the 1892 interview, he biliously decried the critics who rejected him: "Finally there is the new criticism. What a dreary lot of twaddle is written about the stage nowadays! ... Do you remember Dr. Khan's Anatomical Museum, where the model of a beautiful woman was taken to pieces before one's eyes, to the point of causing extreme disgust? That is the New Criticism!" Perhaps Sims should have used the analogy of the Ripper for a New Critic. The Whitechapel murders were a tabloid mother lode he frequently returned to in his journalism between 1888 and 1917. Some loyal readers must have noticed that after 1899 Dagonet changed his tune completely: "Jack the Ripper" went from a mystery that had confounded the constabulary to a tale of how Scotland Yard detectives had been fast closing in on an insane English surgeon as the culprit. (It had apparently been a very close thing; the warrants for this suspect's arrest had been issued but the next time the cops laid eyes on the fiend he was a waterlogged corpse).

One of George Sims' many fictions that so displeased "cultured and distinguished men" was the female detective Dorcas Dene, the protagonist of a series of not particularly compelling mysteries. These short narratives are, nevertheless, a vital primary source in helping us to reconstruct Jack the Ripper's true identity (another short narrative, *The Priest's Secret*, written the same year as the interview, is particularly revelatory—see chapter 11). Though a Leftist (who was asked more than once to run for a seat for the Liberal Party—he repeatedly declined), Sims was never able—or desired—to make the leap to anything remotely resembling revolutionary socialism, as he was less a fire-breathing radical than a precursor to modern Hollywood stars and other photogenic celebrities who lend their fame to promoting awareness of various world ills and commercial products. Sims had no qualms about licensing his name and image to promote products— such as dog food—most famously a hair restorer that was guaranteed to retard baldness (and to make a lady's hair even more luxuriant):

TATCHO

The certain, trusty, genuine, right, honest, hair grower. There is no other. Without Tatcho loss of hair is inevitable, but Mr. Ge. R. Sims has altered all that. If your hair has become scanty or grey get Tatcho today. It will bring back the hair of your youth, make a new being of you, and give you a new grip on life.

Apart from raising public awareness of the evils of poverty, George Sims' greatest legacy to his fellow citizens was mobilizing public outrage over the infamous false conviction of an innocent foreigner, Adolph Beck. The bungled case led the chastened ruling elite to respond by creating the Court of Criminal Appeal, the last judicial chance for the wrongly convicted (see chapter 15). By the early 1890s Sims was a close friend of Melville Macnaghten, who in his 1914 memoir (in which *he* took the lion's share of the credit for clearing Beck) wrote about the former with great affection, complimenting the famous writer on his broad knowledge of crime, his ready wit and his remarkable ability as an extemporaneous public speaker. He nicknamed his friend "Tatcho," perhaps as a friendly joke lampooning Sims' alleged hair restorer.[10] Exactly how close were these two English gents? Apparently close enough for "Good Old Mac" to provide "Tatcho" with reproductions of the Whitechapel fiend's handiwork, as the writer boasted in a long piece he wrote on the Whitechapel case for the September 22, 1907, issue of *Lloyds Weekly* magazine: "I have in my museum some curious documents and gruesome photographs connected with the crimes. Two of them are unprintable. The photograph of the scene in Miller's-court is not one to be looked upon except by those who have in the exercise of their calling to study all phases of human perversion." Unbeknownst to the Edwardian public, George "Tatcho" Sims was also Macnaghten's public mouthpiece on the Ripper, specifically in a regular tabloid column admired by the *Times* of 1922 for Sims' extraordinary regularity:

MUSTARD AND CRESS

As a journalist Sims was most famous for the page called "Mustard and Cress," which he contributed under the pen-name of "Dagonet" to the *Referee* every Sunday, without a break, since the paper was founded in 1877. Last Sunday, the day after his operation, the usual three columns duly appeared and showed no sign of lessened interest and liveliness.

In the 1892 interview, in which Sims says he refused, on principle, to use a stenographer, he also boasted of how nothing could stop his column from being written—reportedly in a terribly illegible hand—and filed on time, every time: "Ever since I commenced to write 'Mustard and Cress' for 'The Referee,' fifteen years ago, I have turned out my three columns each week, without intermission or assistance, in sickness or in health. It has found its way to London from all sorts of curious places where it has been written. Once, 'Mustard and Cress' was compiled in an African desert, with roaring lions around—although, let me add, in this strictly veracious conversation, there was only one lion, and it was caged." The visiting reporter of 1892 was privileged to see Sims' column actually being constructed, with the usual mixture of bombast, topical appeal and populist breadth—reminiscent of today's "shock jock" radio commentators (and with about the same glancing respect for the facts):

*"Tatcho"—The Hair Restorer—*Sims was not above lending his name to commercial products as with this 1897 hair tonic. Sir Melville Macnaghten nicknamed the famous writer after this product. In later years Sims reportedly went bald.

When the writer called on Mr. Sims one recent Friday morning, the concoction of "Mustard and Cress" was in progress. It had been begun in bed during the sleepless hours of the early morning, when it took the form of rough pencil notes. "Mustard and Cress" is primarily *a running comment on current events*, and has never, in its *wildest flights of egotism and fancy*, quite lost that form. ... Mr. Sims maintains that it contains nothing that has not *a substratum of sheer fact*, although, as he admits, *the superstructure of exaggeration is often lofty* [my italics].

Some Ripper books rather lazily describe George Sims simply as a journalist; while technically true, this is misleading. Freed from the drudgery of the mere beat-reporter, Sims was a celebrity who wrote about whatever took his fancy, pleasing a massive readership that could not travel to the same exotic locales or meet the Victorian equivalent of the jet set, as the author boasted in his 1882 interview:

"To return to 'Mustard and Cress,' sir. Have you anything to say in regard to the charge of egotism that is often brought against it?"

"Simply that—it suits my readers, which is surely excuse enough. 'Mustard and Cress' is just an 'open letter'—a free communication from a man of the world to his friends. It brings me an amazing amount of correspondence each post—argumentative, abusive, congratulatory, confidential."

High-brow detractors (the "New Critics") derided the colorful, idiosyncratic column as "Custard and Mess," yet these "Dagonet" pieces provide vital insights into what both the police chief and the best-selling writer really knew about "Jack the Ripper."

Let us jump ahead to 1905.

The agreeably pudding-faced Robert Sagar was a highly regarded policeman, an ex–City of London detective-inspector who had been involved in the 1888–1891 failed investigation to catch "Jack the Ripper," the serial killer of East End prostitutes. But was it a total failure? Had Scotland Yard detectives, in fact, fathomed the identity of the killer but due to circumstances beyond their control been unable to bring him to trial? Upon retiring Sagar was praised in a profile in the *London City Press* of January 7, 1905, as knowing "as much about those crimes, which terrified the metropolis, as any detective in London." Sagar assured the public that the Ripper had indeed been identified, as a deranged, lower-class nonentity: "The police realized, as also did the public that the crimes were those of a madman, and suspicion fell upon a man, who, without a doubt, was the murderer. Identification being impossible, he could not be charged. He was however, placed in a lunatic asylum, and the series of atrocities came to an end." Sagar surmised that the killer was of the Hebrew faith because he had allegedly written some graffiti near one of the murder sites that blamed the Jews (though surely this could be interpreted as an act of *anti*–Semitism by a Gentile killer?). They'd had this lunatic under surveillance and he was, Sagar claimed, definitely the man: some anonymous, lumpenproletarian wretch.

Robert Sagar's revelation was refuted, however, by George R. Sims who, though neither a retired nor active member of the constabulary, via Dagonet's opinion in "Custard and Mess" had enormous influence on the media and the public (due to the exoneration of Adolph Beck if nothing else). Without revealing the exact source of his insider information (everybody knew that Sims knew everybody, and was especially chummy with the assistant commissioner of the Criminal Investigation Department), he assured his legion of readers, again and again, that the murderer was a Gentile, an English gentleman and a reputable surgeon afflicted with a dual personality—remarkably reminiscent of the novella and play *Dr. Jekyll and Mr. Hyde*. Two days after the Sagar revelation, George Sims' hallowed opinion was mentioned by a fellow unnamed journalistic acquaintance in an article in the *Gloucester Citizen* of January 9, 1905. The reporter scratches his head over Sims being so certain that the opinion of a field detective from 1888 is so hopelessly mistaken:

> Inspector Robert Sagar, who is just retiring from the City Police, is entirely at variance with Mr. George R. Sims as to the identity of "Jack the Ripper." I see he has just stated, in an interview, that the City Police fully believed this man to be a butcher who worked in Aldgate, and was partly insane. It is believed that he made his way to Australia and there died.

Not for the last time do we see that reassuring element common to all the police "solutions" to the Ripper case: rest assured, ladies and gentleman, the monster is no more (though as we will see, only Macnaghten's suspect was actually six feet under). There then follows a striking paradox. The reporter outlines the profile of Sims' Ripper while lamenting that the famous writer cannot provide more information, at least not without putting in peril the reputation of the deceased suspect's respectable relations:

> Mr. Sims, from information which came under his notice, has told me on more than one occasion he is convinced that these murders were committed by a medical man who afterwards committed suicide near the Embankment. This man was well-known in London as subject of fits of lunacy, and *he belonged to one of the best families* in town. It is *consideration for his relatives* which has prevented "Dagonet" from making *a full disclosure* of such evidence as he possesses.... The doctor in the Sims' theory was never in the asylum [my italics].

The reporter has that last detail wrong (unless Sims later altered his account). From 1902, Dagonet in "Mustard and Cress" (and under his own name in *Lloyds Weekly* magazine, and in his memoirs) claimed that the "Mad Doctor" *had* been a voluntary patient in an asylum—twice—wherein he was diagnosed as a homicidal lunatic. The rest is correct: a sometimes insane gentleman-physician from a prestigious family who drowned himself off the Thames Embankment (located in the central part of the metropolis). And therein lay the paradox. While claiming he must protect the killer's relatives from shame and scandal, Sims reveals more than enough data for the particular upper-class people who must know of a London-based, affluent family with a medical member who committed suicide in the River Thames *to recognize them*! A self-made, literary star, Sims was nobody's fool, so how do we explain this seeming contradiction? Could it be that there was no contradiction because Sims quietly knew that the data he divulged would *not* help anybody discern the true identity of "Jack the Ripper"?

A few months later, an aged Ripper allegedly confessed in New York City. The self-proclaimed murderer was Charles Y. Hermann, the son of a British army officer and, clearly to the press and his attending physicians, a poor soul suffering from geriatric delusions. The July 14, 1905, edition of the *Grey Argus Report* records George Sims' witheringly sarcastic response:

> An Express representative called on Mr. George R. Sims, whose knowledge of the official investigations into the murders is probably unsurpassed. Sims, "I can only say" he remarked, in reference to the alleged confession, "that if this man is 'Jack the Ripper,' his case is the most marvelous yet presented to students of criminal insanity, and that the age

of miracles has returned to us. It would be most extraordinary if a man could survive for sixteen years a series of murders that were the most horrible, sickening and diabolical in the annals of crime."

In referring to "the age of miracles" Sims means that the Whitechapel crimes were so unspeakably repulsive that they must have cracked open the murderer's mind like a warm boiled egg. Ergo, he could not have gone on living beyond that night, and ergo he was not in New York sixteen years later making a confession. This is quite a sweeping presumption about what psychotic people are and are not capable of, but Sims apparently had official support. A Scotland Yard worthy was also interviewed and backed the writer to the hilt—though his identity was withheld (as this book will show, it can only be the man whom Sims called' "my friend of many years,"[11] Melville Macnaghten): "An official of Scotland Yard said that the identity of the perpetrator was known to the Home Secretary. 'He committed suicide in the River Thames,' he declared, 'after the last murder, and his body was found a month later. There is absolutely no mistake about it. All the facts are set forth in official documents, and are too well supported by evidence to be disbelieved.'"

According to this surely authoritative source, the solution was confirmed in a definitive document of state that succeeding home secretaries could access and where they could read the name of "Jack the Ripper" for themselves. Interestingly, this unidentified official never uses the word "doctor." Not for the first time, George Sims—backed by the unnamed top cop—was most insistent that the real killer had no time to confess anything to anybody.

But what if he had? What would "Jack" have said, and to whom would he have divulged his ghastly crimes? Upon hearing such a confession of horror, would that person not feel duty-bound to go straight to the nearest police station and turn in the monster?

IV

TERROR STRIKES LONDON

No-one who was living in London that autumn will forget the terror created by these murders.—Sir Melville Macnaghten, 1914

JACK THE RIPPER is the hero of the hour. A gruesome wag, a grim practical joker, has succeeded in getting an enormous amount of fun out of a postcard which he sent to the Central News. ... Of course the whole business is a farce.—George R. Sims (Dagonet), *The Referee*, 1888

In a work that had a profound impact on readers (among them George Orwell while a student at Eton), American author Jack London had observed in *The People of the Abyss* (1903) that there was nothing glamorous, let alone enticing, about the human detritus he encountered in the East End. These were prostitutes circling Christ Church in Spitalfields (adjacent to Whitechapel) to avoid being arrested for loitering. He described them as "a welter of rags and filth, of all manner of loathsome skin diseases, open sores, bruises, grossness, indecency, leering monstrosities and bestial faces.... They will sell themselves for thru' pence or tu'pence or a stale loaf of bread."[1]

In 1914 Macnaghten recalled the widespread panic caused by the Ripper murders, and why it was quite "unreasonable" (his tone bordering on the nostalgic):

> No-one who was living in London that autumn will forget the terror created by these murders. Even now I can recall the foggy evenings, and hear again the raucous cries of the newspaper boys: "Another horrible murder, murder, mutilation, Whitechapel." Such was the burden of their ghastly song; and when the double murder of 30th September took place, the exasperation of the public at the non-discovery of the perpetrator knew no bounds, and no servant-maid deemed her life safe if she ventured out to post a letter after ten o'clock at night. And yet this panic was quite unreasonable. The victims, without exception, belonged to the lowest dregs of female humanity, who avoid the police and exercise every ingenuity in order to remain in the darkest corners of the most deserted alleys.[2]

Macnaghten mentions the first murder, quite accurately, but also makes it clear that this first lethal attack against a poor, defenseless "unfortunate"—the polite Victorian euphemism for a prostitute—was a heinous crime by a "rip gang": a gang of marauding thieves:

> The attention of Londoners was first called to the horrors of life (and death) in the East End by the murder of one, Emma Smith, who was found horribly outraged in Osborne Street in the early morning of 3rd April 1888. She died in the London hospital, and there is no doubt that her death was caused by some young hooligans who escaped arrest.[3]

Into the abyss—A grim photograph of poor citizens on a Whitechapel street circa 1888 (Stewart P. Evans).

Emma Smith had to limp alone, mortally wounded and in excruciating pain, back to her hovel and then gain some assistance to go reluctantly to the London Hospital on Whitechapel Road—where she eventually fell into a merciful coma never to regain consciousness.

Macnaghten then describes a second Whitechapel murder of a prostitute that, again, he does not attribute to the Ripper but which did fuel a mounting sense of alarm that a different kind of murderer (or murderers) was at large in London:

> On 7th August the body of Martha Tabram was discovered lying on the stairs of a house in George Yard. Her death was due to a number of wounds in the chest and abdomen, and it was alleged that a bayonet had been the weapon used upon her. The evening before she had been seen in the company of two soldiers and a female friend. Her throat was not cut, and nothing in the shape of mutilation was attempted.[4]

Martha Tabram (a.k.a. Turner) was plump and dark-haired and, though only 39 at the time of her death, was prematurely aged by grinding poverty and marital abuse. By the night of August 6, 1888, Tabram was an alcoholic selling herself on the street to pay the rent. One or more of her clients, presumably inebriated soldiers, struck her with their ceremonial swords, perhaps as a debauched "prank" that got out of control. In the morning Tabram was found by a fellow tenant, dead in a pool of her own blood on the first floor landing of the George Yard Building. Her legs were spread as if she had just finished intercourse. Tabram had been stabbed 39 times, and every one of her internal organs had been punctured—along with the breasts and groin area.

Inspector Edmund Reid of the Met made extensive efforts to get these soldiers identified by eyewitnesses. But a prostitute (nicknamed "Pearly Poll") and a bobbie picked out men (at military barracks at Wellington Barracks in Birdcage Walk) who it turned out had rock-solid alibis. In his memoir Macnaghten seems to have believed that the prostitute *had* spotted the correct men (at an earlier Tower of London parade set up as a police identification line-up) but had refused to do her civic duty, maybe out of fear of reprisals: "I think I am right in saying that the soldiers were detained, but that the available witnesses failed to identify them."[5] These two atrocities four months apart presaged, according to Macnaghten, similar ones by a single maniac who was not motivated by money or addled by booze. Two comparable ripping murders were followed coincidentally by a lone madman using an almost identical *modus operandi*. It begs a question which Macnaghten does not consider—did "Jack" gain inspiration from the murders of Emma Smith and Martha Tabram, and the mass coverage these shocking crimes engendered? This theory of the Ripper as a copycat will be explored in Chapter XVII.

Mary Ann Nichols, nicknamed "Polly," was 42 and a dirt-poor prostitute. She would become the first victim of the Ripper because she lacked four-pence for a bed in a Spitalfields doss house. Polly had been married to a printer's machinist, William Nichols, and though they had five children she slid into a dissolute life. By 1881 the marriage broke up in acrimony. She took her husband to police court to pay maintenance for her and the children, and accused him of abandonment for running off with the midwife who attended the birth of their fifth child. Polly Nichols' biggest downfall was that she had become a quarrelsome alcoholic, and this made her life difficult under any roof; whether it was living with her father for a while in Camberwell or trying to be gainfully employed as a domestic servant at Ingleside, Wandsworth Common. Polly's addiction got the better of her. She stole three pounds from her employers and then disappeared into the East End.[6]

On August 30, 1888, Polly Nichols was thrown out of her squalid abode yet cheerfully boasted that she would soon have the necessary funds because, while she possessed practically nothing but the dirty clothes on her back and a broken piece of mirror, she had just acquired a new hat. "Never mind, I'll soon get my doss money, look what a jolly bonnet I've got now," said Nichols as she departed into the "City of Dreadful Night."[7] Nichols was last seen by a fellow prostitute, drunk and staggering, heading eastward along Whitechapel Road—about an hour before she met her final client. If his intention was to escalate the stir caused by the previous two murders, Polly Nichol's killer succeeded, as can be seen from the resulting media frenzy.

Yet in 1914 Macnaghten is quite terse about the crime, the very first by "Jack the Ripper," to the point of underplaying the extent of Nichols' mutilations, though these were not fully discovered until she was examined at the Whitechapel mortuary (little more than a dingy shed). "The first real 'Whitechapel murder' ... took place on 31st August, when Mary Ann Nichols was found in Bucks Row with her throat cut and her body *slightly mutilated*"[8] (my italics). A Dr. Rees Llewellyn found that the woman's body was still warm at the scene and deduced that she had been murdered probably not more than thirty minutes before. A newspaper of the day supposedly quoted Llewellyn as exclaiming, "She was ripped open just as you see a dead calf at the butcher's." No defensive wounds were found, such as bruises on Nichol's arms, suggesting that the killer had done the deed with enormous speed. Polly had died instantly. Her genitals, furthermore, were seen to have two small stab wounds. At the dapper Coroner Wynne Edwin Baxter's subsequent inquest—he was openly critical of the police for not discovering the more extensive mutilations at the crime scene—Dr. Llewellyn speculated that this strangely disturbed killer "must have had some rough anatomical knowledge, for he had attacked all the vital parts," with the mutilations delaying the murderer by no more, the doctor speculated, than five minutes.[9]

Writing twenty-six years later, Macnaghten is sure about which murders are by the Ripper and which are not, and he excludes the first two prior to Polly Nichols, whereas in 1888 the police, according to the *Times* of September 3, 1888, were scrambling to reverse their assumption that Smith and Tabram had been dispatched by a rip gang or debauched soldiers. If it was the new assassins' intention in his gory debut to take retrospective credit for the earlier murders, he was succeeding: "The police admit their belief that the *three* crimes are the work of one individual" (my italics). As the succeeding homicides grew into a crisis with an unknown killer on the rampage, Chief Inspector Donald Swanson was placed in overall charge of the investigation as the day-to-day operational head of the inquiry. His job was to try to process all the paper work, now rapidly piling up, and find the killer. Macnaghten in 1914 had nothing but praise for this colleague: "Donald Swanson was a very capable officer with a synthetical turn of mind, who subsequently held the post of Superintendent at the Department for seven years. To him was entrusted in 1888 the general supervision of the inquiries made into the Whitechapel murders."[10]

Answering directly to Swanson were a trio of detective inspectors: Frederic Abberline (the highest ranking, as he was an inspector first class), Henry Moore and Walter Andrews. Macnaghten praises the first as knowing "the East End of London as few men have since known it."[11] At this critical juncture, when the genuine "Jack" had killed and ripped open but a single victim, CID was itself effectively decapitated by the long-threatened resignation of James Monro as assistant commissioner (who yet retained a bureaucratic beachhead by still commanding the antiterrorist Section D, which maintained his direct access to the home secretary). He was replaced by Irish-Protestant barrister Dr. Robert Anderson, who though inexperienced was well connected: he was the son of the Crown solicitor for Dublin and the brother of the man in charge of state prosecutions.

Apart from some experience with counter-intelligence against Irish-Catholic terrorists, Anderson had been recently languishing in the Prisons Department.[12] Though honest and dedicated, Anderson was also conceited and indiscreet. His working relationship with Macnaghten, a subordinate in many ways his temperamental opposite, would prove problematic, even adversarial; this may have been because "Mac" did the legwork while his egocentric boss took the credit. Much later the pair of chiefs would be at odds over the exact identity of the Ripper, though ironically both asserted that the man was a deceased maniac (and yet only one of those suspects was actually dead—and it was not Anderson's). At the time Polly Nichols was found murdered, Sir Charles Warren was trying to recover from a bout of poor health on a French beach. Anderson must have thought this was a very good idea, as his own stamina was apparently under intolerable strain, so he took off, with permission, for Switzerland on September 7, 1888. He had been assistant commissioner for all of a week. With excruciatingly unlucky timing, Anderson's departure for his sojourn in the Swiss Alps coincided with the eve of the next horrific murder, which would focus the minds of all Londoners—certainly of tabloid journalists.[13]

A short woman with a prominent nose, Annie Chapman, 47, was a prostitute also known as "Dark Annie" who already suffered from a terminal lung condition. By September 8, 1888, Chapman was a destitute widow, the mother of a handicapped son and a deceased daughter, driven into prostitution by poverty.[14] Macnaghten writes of her terrible end on that date: "This was succeeded nine days afterwards by the murder of Annie Chapman in the backyard of a house in Hanbury Street; the throat was cut in a precisely similar manner, but the mutilations were of a much more savage character."[15] At the inquest into Annie Chapman's death, Dr. Bagster Philips testified that, shockingly, the murderer had absconded with some of the victim's organs, including the womb, and must possess at least some basic anatomical and surgical knowhow.[16]

Now unreasonable terror gripped the city, despite most Londoners being neither middle-aged harlots nor ever setting foot in the East End. With the Annie Chapman murder, George Sims as Dagonet for the first time turned his attention to the Whitechapel murders in his "Mustard and Cress" column for the *Referee* of September 9, 1888. This began a commentary on the crimes that would last practically up until Sims drew his last breath. At first, however, his sensibility as a dramatist trumped his journalistic nose for a big story. For once in his long career Sims was lagging behind popular tastes: "The element of romance is altogether lacking, and they are crimes of the coarsest and most vulgar brutality—not the sort of murders that can be discussed in the drawing-room and the nursery with any amount of pleasure." (With remarkable prescience Sims anticipates Orwell's antipathy to the crimes; they were simply too grotesque to garner the status of a classic crime tale.) He followed this by being rudely dismissive about Scotland Yard's Criminal Investigation Department:

> The police up to the moment of writing are still at sea as to the series of Whitechapel murders—a series with such a strong family likeness as to point conclusively to one assassin or firm of assassins. The detective force is singularly lacking in the smartness and variety of resource which the most ordinary detective displays in the shilling shocker.

Despite a barrage of criticism from all quarters—including Her Majesty—the police of 1888 were investigating a plethora of potential Rippers, running the gamut from the more-than-plausible to the desperate long shot (it is not within the scope of this book to cover them all). These were often men who had "anatomical knowledge" of one sort or another, or were known to be mentally disturbed, or both. Sims/Dagonet gleefully reported on a terrific bit of tabloid tomfoolery: that the murders were being committed by an escaped ape—an obvious lift from an Edgar Allan Poe short story from 1841, *The Murders in the Rue Morgue* (the American author had originated the literary genre of a baffling murder mystery solved by a brilliant detective using cool-headed deduction).[17] More serious were the investigations into a *human* suspect who might have the required "anatomical knowledge."

At 20 Abercorn Place, Maide Vale, lived the widow Laura Tucker Sanders with her six children. At this time, 21 years had passed since the death of her husband, an Indian army surgeon, who had taken his own life with a pistol. Her eldest child, John, age 26, once a shy and retiring medical student, had tragically and steadily deteriorated into a violent and tyrannical madman. John Sanders would spend the rest of his short life in and out of private asylums. Gossip somehow began to circulate that this clinically disturbed young man was the Whitechapel murderer. Inspector Frederic Abberline duly had a subordinate check out this Sanders lead. Donald Swanson later informed the Home Office, "Enquiries were also made to trace three insane medical students who had attended London Hospital. Result, two traced, one gone abroad."[18] Towards the end of October 1888 the home secretary, Henry Matthews, under enormous pressure for a breakthrough, was not satisfied and wanted to know "when the third went abroad and whether any further enquiry has been made about him." Sir Charles Warren responded by quoting a report by Inspector Abberline, which contained a basic investigative error, as the address had been mis-transcribed as Aber*deen* Place. Consequently the erroneous opinion was given by the commissioner that a mother and son named Sanders had gone abroad two years before.[19] The mistake about the address does not inspire confidence, but Sanders appears to be in the clear: he was an inmate of a private asylum in Kent at the time of the murders.[20] As we will see, Macnaghten would use the insane medical student "suspect" for his own propagandist purposes (see Chapter XV).

Another significant Whitechapel suspect in 1888 involved a local man of the East End with a nasty reputation regarding harlots and who, allegedly, had a catchy nickname: "Leather Apron." The origins of this figure, or rumored figure, began appearing in some newspapers after the murder of Polly Nichols. The murder of Annie Chapman increased the sense of urgency on the part of the police to identify this figure. An unemployed shoemaker, John Pizer, a Jewish immigrant—who may have been nicknamed "Leather Apron"—narrowly avoided being torn apart by an enraged mob, as he had been named in *The Star* newspaper. Traced to his family home at 22 Mulberry Street, Pizer opened the door to Sergeant William Thick, who promptly took the terrified man to Leman Street Police Station for further questioning. Placed in a lineup, Pizer was positively identified by Emanuel Violenia. The witness was sure that Pizer was the man he saw arguing with the latest victim and, what is more, saw him threaten her with a knife. Violenia knew him by the nickname "Leather Apron." For a brief moment it must have seemed to the relieved constabulary that the case was solved.[21]

The Jewish residents of the East End held their breaths. Newspapers were torn between reporting frankly on outbreaks of sectarian victimization and veiling it from their readers lest they be responsible for inciting more of the same. For example, the *East London Observer* reported that "the crowds began to assume a very threatening attitude towards the Hebrew population of the district.... No Englishman could have perpetrated such a horrible crime as that of Hanbury Street therefore the crowds proceeded to threaten and abuse the unfortunate Hebrews as they found in the streets." Instead of becoming the feared pogrom against the Jewish population, the whole furor petered out because John Pizer was discharged. The police quickly came to sour on the unreliable, attention-seeking Violenia, but more decisive was the fact that Pizer had an iron-clad alibi. Dagonet in the September 16 issue of the *Referee* had nothing but contempt for the whole John Pizer/"Leather Apron" debacle: "Up to a few days ago the mere mention of Leather Apron's name was sufficient to cause a panic. All England was murmuring his name with bated breath." John Pizer threatened the *Star* with a lawsuit for slander, and the tabloid coughed up for an out-of-court settlement.[22]

By the end of September 1888 the government was under enough pressure from the tabloids—whose circulation increased exponentially with every unsolved murder—

that the Home Office made its displeasure known sufficiently for Dr. Anderson to cut short his holiday.

He agreed, but only in the sense that he would relocate to Paris in order to be able, if required, to rush back to London. With awful timing, the assistant commissioner arrived in the French capital just as the murderer upped the ante by offing two victims in the same night. As Macnaghten wrote, who was in London:

> When public excitement then was at white heat, two murders—unquestionably by the same hand—took place on the night of 30th September. A woman, Elizabeth Stride, was found in Berners Street, with her throat cut, but no attempt at mutilation. In this case there can be little doubt but that the murderer was disturbed at his demoniacal work.[23]

Elizabeth Stride, 45, was tall, though malnourished and missing many of her teeth. Born Elizabeth Gustafsdotter, she was a Swede and a farmer's daughter who was nicknamed by the time of her death "Long Liz." As with Nichols and Chapman, Stride, despite attempts at gainful employment, had drifted into prostitution in both her home and adopted countries. Her new surname came from marrying John Thomas Stride in 1869, but this union was over by about 1877 and she had become a regular streetwalker. Liz Stride probably dissembled when she claimed to people that she had borne her ex-husband nine children and that she was a survivor of the sinking of the pleasure steamer *Princess Alice* (she told people the shipwreck caused her to lose her husband and her front teeth).[24]

Just after midnight on the night of September 30, 1888, a steward of a Russian-Jewish socialist club was driving his pony and barrow into Dutfield's Yard on Berner Street. Suddenly his pony reared back from something blocking the gateway. Stepping down, he discovered that the "bundle" was a woman's body, still warm, lying in a pool of her own blood. She was later identified as Liz Stride. Her throat had been deeply cut, but otherwise she had not been mutilated. In Stride's left hand, she clutched a packet of cachous (a breath freshener) wrapped in tissue paper. Again the murderer seems to have attacked so swiftly that Stride never had time to react, not even to drop her sweets. It is possible that the club steward, Louis Diemschutz, interrupted her killer before he could satiate his desires to hack away at Stride's corpse. He may have been there nearby, hiding and watching in the dark, cursing himself for having chosen a victim in too public a location even at this late hour. Macnaghten saw this, the lack of any savagery—as many did then and do now—as the motive for the enormous risk of quickly hunting for another victim while the first was not even cold and barely ten minutes' walk away:

> The madman started off in search of another victim, whom he found in Catherine Eddowes. This woman's body, very badly mutilated, was found in a dark corner of Mitre Square. When the double murder of 30th September took place, the exasperation of the public at the non-discovery of the perpetrator knew no bounds.[25]

Catherine Eddowes, 46, a native of Wolverhampton and one of 11 children, had teamed up with an unemployed drunk named John Kelly (later he would deny that he had lived off his girlfriend's "immoral earnings"). The pair subsisted on a degrading grind; scrounging for food, drink and lodgings practically on an hourly basis. Poor Eddowes almost avoided being the next victim, as she had been earlier in the evening sleeping off a drunken binge in a jail cell at Bishopsgate. Once able to stagger she was discharged. Police Constable Edward Watkins, a 17-year veteran on his usually repetitious and dreary beat had an encounter with pure horror. Passing through Mitre Square at 1:30 a.m., he saw nothing amiss in the gloom as he swung his bull's-eye lantern. On his very next round no more than 14 minutes later, Watkins was confronted by the body of a woman lying in a pool of blood face-upwards, her face and ears savagely hacked. It was Catherine Eddowes. Pieces of her intestines were displayed both next to her and draped over her right shoulder. Later an ear of the victim dropped off as it was being moved to the mortuary. Mitre Square was ringed with people in their homes, some with open windows, and yet no scream or sounds of struggle had aroused anybody's suspicion. A postmortem examination would reveal that the left kidney had been removed along with a section of the womb.[26]

Catherine Eddowes' lightning-fast murder happened in the entirely separate police jurisdiction of the City of London, headed by its own commissioner, Major Henry Smith. London's other parallel police force was now directly involved, creating yet another diffusion of the lines of authority that would, if not compromise, then certainly complicate the investigation. As the killer fled back into the heart of the East End, having killed two women in less than an hour and eluded all of the patrols by both the constabulary and concerned citizens, he apparently stopped in Goulston Street to dispose of a piece of material torn from Catherine Eddowes—and perhaps to write a cryptic message on a nearby wall in chalk. The writing was found along with the bloody bit of torn garment by Constable Alfred Long, who claimed he was sure neither had been visible at the beginning of his round. The writing was described as being in a neat "schoolboy hand" and, reportedly, had the word "Jews" misspelled as "Jewes" (or possibly as "Juwes")[27]:

> The Jewes are
> The men that
> Will not
> Be Blamed
> For nothing

Arriving at the scene, Sir Charles Warren agreed with the concerns of Superintendent Thomas Arnold: that to maintain public safety the graffiti must be immediately removed, even before it could be photographed. But was the message by the killer, or likely to have been? Considering his perilous circumstances, would he really stop to make a comment on a wall in chalk? Whether the writing was by the killer's or not, the commissioner commendably and responsibly worried about a riled-up mob attacking a defenseless minority group. The press was predictably merciless in their condemnation of the obliteration of a clue that might have led to the killer's identification.

Only in the aftermath of the double murder did the nickname of this serial killer finally appear, never to be forgotten by popular culture: "Jack the Ripper." Appropriately for a case riddled with fiction and hoaxes, it was likely not an invention of the murderer.[28] In his 1914 memoirs Melville Macnaghten explains that the source was a letter originating with the very tabloids that profited from the murders. Macnaghten gives CID—and therefore Dr. Anderson—a backhander from retirement for taking seriously this particular letter:

> On 27th September a letter was received at a well-known News Agency, addressed to the "Boss." It was written in red ink, and purported to give the details of the murders which

had been committed. It was signed, "Jack the Ripper." This document was sent to Scotland Yard, and (in my opinion most unwisely) was reproduced, and copies of same affixed to various police stations, thus giving it an official imprimatur.[29]

Amidst the flood of bogus correspondence why did police regard *this* communication as authentic? Thomas John (Tom) Bulling of the Central News Agency, 5 New Bridge Street, Ludgate Circus, City of London, claimed to have received the communication dated September 25, 1888, and postmarked two days later—and had initially dismissed it as a joke. Here are some relevant excerpts of this chortling, sophomoric effort (who complains at having to use red ink instead of real blood):

> Dear Boss, I keep on hearing the police have caught me, but they won't fix me just yet. ... I am down on whores and I shant [*sic*] quit ripping them till I do get buckled. ... The next job I do I shall clip the lady's ears off and send back to police officers just for jolly...
>
> Yours truly Jack the Ripper...
>
> They say I'm a doctor now ha ha.

The "Boss" in question refers to the head of the Central News Agency. With incredible good fortune, at least for news sales, Tom Bulling forwarded it to the police on the very eve of the double murder.

On October 1, 1888, the same journalist forwarded a postcard, supposedly written by the same hand, and again signed "Jack the Ripper":

> I wasn't codding [*sic*] dear old boss when I gave you the tip, you'll hear about saucy Jacky's work tomorrow double event this time number one squealed a bit couldn't finish straight off. Had not time get ears for police thanks for keeping last letter back till I got to work.

Sure enough, one of Catherine Eddowes' ears had been mutilated and the "double event" promised had taken place, yet the postcard-writer may have been able to gain this information from the early edition of a newspaper. Neither document contained information, or a foreshadowing of actions, that could only have been known to the genuine killer. Sir Melville Macnaghten tells us that from the first he believed it was probably written by a journalist, and that by June of 1890 he had identified the pest: "In this ghastly production I have always thought I could discern the stained forefinger of the journalist indeed, a year later, I had a shrewd suspicion as to the actual author! But whoever did pen the gruesome stuff, it is certain to my mind that it was not the mad miscreant who had committed the murders."[30]

Macnaghten does not offer a name for the likely journalist-hoaxer, but another senior police figure, John George (Jack) Littlechild, head of Special Branch in 1888, did in a private letter to George Sims in 1913. Writing 25 years later, Littlechild claimed that the inventor of the name was none other than the journalist Tom Bulling—aided and abetted by his opportunistic superior, Charles Moore. When serialized in *Lloyds Weekly* magazine, the first chapter from Macnaghten's memoirs to be published was not about his Eton days, or any other murder case—it was his fourth chapter on "Jack the Ripper." In that work Macnaghten laments, "The name 'Jack the Ripper,' however, had got abroad in the land and had 'caught on'; it riveted the attention of the classes as well as the masses."[31] On October 7, 1888, Sims as Dagonet weighed in with a "Mustard and Cress" column and confidently—and accurately—judged it to be a transparent journalistic scam: "JACK THE RIPPER is the hero of the hour. A gruesome wag, a grim practical joker, has succeeded in getting an enormous amount of fun out of a postcard which he sent to the Central News. ... Of course the whole business is a farce. The post-card is an elaborately-prepared hoax." Sims makes the devastating point that most of the public did not even know there was such a thing as a press repository that sold copy to papers:

> The fact that the self-postcard-proclaimed assassin sent his imitation blood-besmeared communication to the Central News people opens up a wide field for theory. How many among you, my dear readers, would have hit upon the idea of "the Central News" as a receptacle for your confidence? You might have sent your joke to the "Telegraph," the "Times," any morning or any evening paper, but I will lay long odds that it would never have occurred to communicate with a Press agency.
>
> Curious, is it not, that this maniac makes his communication to an agency which serves the entire Press? It is an idea which might occur to a Pressman perhaps; and even then it would probably only occur to someone connected with the editorial department of a newspaper, someone who knew what the Central News was, and the place it filled in the business of news supply. This proceeding on Jack's part betrays an inner knowledge of the newspaper world which is certainly surprising. Everything therefore points to the fact that the jokist [sic] is professionally connected with the Press. And if he is telling the truth and not fooling us, then we are brought face to face with the fact that the Whitechapel murders have been committed by a practical journalist—perhaps by a real live editor! Which is absurd, and at that I think I will leave it.

Though the graffiti and the "Boss" correspondence proved to be dead-ends, the double murder did produce a potentially reliable witness who might have seen the murderer himself.

V

FIEND IN FLIGHT?

Dr. Tumblety was arrested some time ago in London on suspicion of being concerned in the perpetration of the Whitechapel murders.... Liberated on bail ... he has sailed for New York.—The Dundee Courier and Argus, 1888

The woman has recovered sufficiently to tell something of the man who wounded her. She says he is about 30 years old, tall, fair and wearing a light moustache. He was well-dressed, spoke with a purely English accent.—The Bridgeport Morning News, 1888

Born in Warsaw of German descent, Joseph Lawende (1847–1925) was a respectable, middle-aged travelling salesman in the cigarette industry, a devoted family man and an Orthodox Jew.[1] On September 30, 1888, at about 1:30 a.m., Lawende was leaving the Imperial Club accompanied by a couple of friends. As they exited, all three men noticed a couple standing and chatting near Church Passage, which led into Mitre Square. Only Lawende, about 15 feet away, got a good look, or as good as was possible in the dimly lit street. He saw that the woman was about five feet tall and that the man was a few inches taller. The woman had her back to him, and Lawende only later identified Eddowes by her clothes: a black jacket and matching bonnet (she was also found to be wearing men's lace-up boots). The woman, said Lawende, had her hand on the man's chest, suggesting a relaxed assignation. Upon being located by the police the eyewitness was treated as their paramount witness; they not only sequestered him but also paid his expenses. CID was trying to keep his description of the suspect out of the newspapers, which were predictably furious—one calling this policy "idiotic."

The Times of October 2, 1888, nonetheless scooped all other papers in publishing Joseph Lawende's description of the man who had allegedly been seen with Eddowes a mere 15 or so minutes before her dead body was found mutilated on the sidewalk by a sickened P.C. Watkins: "of shabby appearance, about 30 years of age and 5 ft. 9 in. in height, of fair complexion, having a small fair moustache, and wearing a red neckerchief and a cap with a peak." At the October 11, 1888, inquest into Eddowes' murder, the City solicitor, Henry Crawford, attending on behalf of the police, requested that the full description of this suspect be limited to no more than his peaked cap. Lawende is recorded to have claimed, "I doubt whether I would know him again."[2] This might have been the case, but it may also have been part of a police stratagem, to which Lawende acquiesced, to give the murderer a false sense of security—in other words this witness *could* recognize the man again. We will see that it is likely that Lawende was indeed used by police to try to identify Ripper suspects in 1891 and as late as 1895. By October 19, 1888, the constabulary relented and published a description of the suspect in the *Police Gazette* (matching almost word for word what Chief Inspector Donald Swanson had recorded for the file):

> At 1:35 a.m., 30th September, with Catherine Eddowes, in Church Passage, leading to Mitre Square, where she was found murdered at 1:45 a.m., same date—A MAN, age 30, height 5 ft. 7 or 8 in., complexion fair, moustache fair, medium build; dress, pepper-and-salt material, reddish neckerchief tied in knot; appearance of a sailor.

On October 21, 1888, Dagonet in "Mustard and Cress" ignored this description, instead reporting on his own foray into Whitechapel after dark. He hoped to write an article called "A Night with Jack the Ripper" and imagined that having "handed him over to justice," he would receive a personal commendation from Her Majesty. Sims and a companion, both dressed as proles, discovered Whitechapel crawling with similar "amateur detectives" obviously on the same quest. The locals, Sims wrote, had absorbed the murders as part of their culture: "The general body of sightseers and pedestrians were making light of the matter. Along the pavement, which for many a mile is hedged with shooting-galleries and various arrangements based upon the six-throws-a-penny principle, plenty of hoarse-voiced ruffians were selling a penny puzzle in which the puzzle is to find Jack the Ripper."

But the fiend seemed to have hunkered down throughout October. As the following month approached, a major festival for the poor—and a potential headache for the police in terms of crowd control—was being prepared for November 9: Lord Mayor's Day. It meant a free meal, so long as the individual qualified as close to death from privation. A multitude would have no trouble meeting this criterion. The celebration would involve closing whole streets for a procession and providing a meat dinner for 2,000 destitute East Enders in the Tower Hamlets Mission-hall. Altogether the number the Lord Mayor would have to entertain, and the police would have to keep orderly and happy, could swell to up to 10,000.[3] On this day when the Victorian elite could congratulate themselves on their Christian charity, the killer would stage his most sickening spectacle, perhaps to spoil the festivities. Until then Sir Charles Warren made the necessary preparations to prevent any unpleasantness by such a large and possibly unruly crowd.

It is ironic that Sir Charles, having previously rejected Macnaghten as unsound, should have committed a gaffe that would bring him into a self-defeating confrontation with his political masters. The commissioner had written a magazine article that made a full-throated attack on the fickleness of the populace and the spinelessness of governments—be they Liberal or Conservative—when it came to supporting the constabulary. Warren unapologetically defended his brutal response to the Bloody Sunday riots of the previous year and was scathing about criticism of the police for simply doing their job, preventing mob insurrection. Home Secretary Henry Matthews reacted coolly to the article by writing to his commissioner to remind him that any contact with the media had to be cleared by the minister's office. Warren professed to be shocked that there even was such a rule (and said that he would never have accepted the position in the first place, had he known). Consequently the commissioner, under strain over a number of issues, offered to resign on November 8, 1888, and, two days later, Henry Matthews accepted.[4] Warren's policing career had begun with the big bang of Bloody Sunday and ended with a whimper two years later, over some obscure essay.

On the day in between, November 9, 1888, Lord Mayor's Day, at about 10:45 a.m., a landlord named John McCarthy who lived at 26 Dorset Street, Spitalfields, sent one of his employees, Thomas Bowyer, to collect some back rent from a tenant who lived at 13 Millers Court in the same street. The tenant was 25-year-old Mary Jane Kelly who, in stark contrast to the previous victims, was young and pretty (though no photograph of her has survived). The apartment at 13 Miller's Court was merely a single room, one that could accommodate a bed and a table next to a fireplace. Kelly was recently separated from her partner, Joseph Barnett, a 30-year-old unemployed fish porter who lived at Bishopsgate. They had fallen out on October 30, 1888, over Kelly's resorting to prostitution because of their impoverished circumstances. He had moved in with his sister as he could not pay his own rent. Mary Jane Kelly's background is very sketchy. She may have been born in Limerick, Ireland, in about 1863, the daughter of an ironworks gauger, and may have had six brothers and one sister. She may also have been married at the age of 16 to a collier who was killed in an explosion. She seems to have come to London in about 1884, to have drifted quickly into prostitution and, perhaps, to have briefly relocated to France with one of her clients. Apparently she did not like life across the Channel, but she did like pronouncing her name as "Marie Jeanette." Bowyer knocked at the door, knowing that this was a tenant who seriously vexed his employer because she was by this time six weeks in arrears. Receiving no reply, the young man ambled around the side and noticed that a window was broken; he was able to push to one side a makeshift curtain. He was greeted with a sight that Macnaghten could only compare with a scene out of Dante's *Inferno*:

> After this double murder the town had rest, forty days, and public excitement, to some extent, calmed down. But worse remained behind! On the morning of 9th November, Mary Jeanette Kelly, a comparatively young woman of some twenty-five years of age, and said to have been possessed of considerable personable attractions, was found murdered in a room in Miller's Court, Dorset Street. This was the last of the series, and it was by far

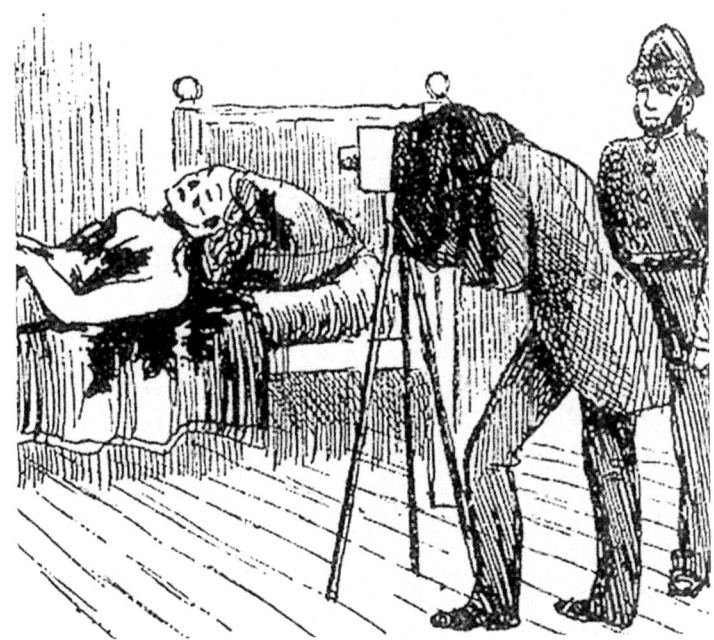

The spoiling of Lord Mayor's day—The real injuries inflicted upon Mary Jane Kelly's remains were far more grotesque than shown by this speculative 1888 illustration (Stewart P. Evans).

the most horrible. The mutilations were of a positively fiendish description, almost indescribable in their savagery, and the doctors who were called in to examine the remains, averred that the operator must have been at least two hours over his hellish work. A fire was burning low in the room, but neither candles nor gas were there. The madman made a bonfire of some old newspapers, and of his victim's clothes, and, by this dim, irreligious light, a scene was enacted which nothing seen by Dante in his visit to the infernal regions could have surpassed.[5]

Mary Kelly lay almost naked on the bed, on her back with her legs spread. Her face and body had been savagely mutilated, and lumps of innards had been deposited next to her on the table. Blood was everywhere. Bowyer reeled back and breathlessly ran to tell his employer. John McCarthy wasted no time informing the police, and detectives hurtled to the scene of the crime as crowds gathered for the festivities. There was a frustrating delay before the police could break down the door to behold the bestial destruction. Two hours were spent waiting for the arrival of the bloodhounds Warren had experimented with, Barnarby and Burgho, only for Abberline to be belatedly informed that the canine sleuths had been returned to their owner a fortnight before.[6] This latest, most appalling murder caused a predictable media explosion, providing a megaphone for a public outcry that reached the Palace and the halls of Westminster. Dr. Thomas Bond was 47 years old and the most esteemed forensic surgeon of his day. After examining Kelly's remains, he rejected the notion that the killer displayed any surgical skill beyond a butcher's:

> The whole of the surface of the abdomen & thighs was removed & the abdominal cavity emptied of its viscera. The breasts were cut off, the arms mutilated by several jagged wounds & the face hacked beyond recognition of the features. The tissues of the neck were severed all round down to the bone. The viscera were found in various parts viz; the uterus & kidneys with one breast under the head, the other breast by the right foot, the liver between the feet, the intestines by the right side & the spleen by the left side of the body. The flaps removed from the abdomen & thighs were on a table. ... The face was gashed in all directions the nose, cheeks, eyebrows & ears being partly removed. The lips were blanched & cut by several oblique incisions running obliquely down to the chin. There were also numerous cuts extending irregularly across all the features. ... Both breasts were removed by more or less circular incisions, the muscles down to the ribs being attached to the breasts ... the Heart absent.

A number of locals claimed to have seen and/or spoken to Mary Kelly in the last hours of her life and were quickly interviewed by police and the press. Some testified at the hurried inquest, this time not run by the attention-seeking Wynne Baxter but instead by Dr. Roderick Macdonald, who, perhaps trying to ingratiate himself with the constabulary, opened and closed the proceedings on the same day, November 12, 1888. That evening a previously unknown witness, George Hutchinson, an unemployed laborer who was acquainted with Kelly, walked into Commercial Street Police Station to make a formal statement to the effect that he had seen Kelly in the hours before she died. He claimed to have seen the young woman in the company of an affluent client. This witness statement was so minutely detailed, it seems too good to be true:

> A man coming in the opposite direction to Kelly tapped her on the shoulder and said something to her. They both burst out laughing. I heard her say all right to him.... They both then came past me and the man hid down his head with his hat over his eyes. I

stooped down and looked him in the face … age about 34 or 35. Height 5ft6 complexion pale, dark eyes and eye lashes, slight moustache, curled up each end, and hair dark, very surley [*sic*] looking dress long dark coat, collar and cuffs trimmed astrakhan … dark felt hat turned down in the middle. Button boots and gaiters with white buttons. Wore a very thick gold chain, white linen collar. Black tie with horseshoe pin. Jewish appearance.

Though Inspector Abberline judged the witness to be truthful and reliable, Hutchinson, having emerged too late to testify at the inquest, was never cross-examined in a public forum and his sighting, though it received gleeful and widespread tabloid coverage, seems to have been quickly discarded (perhaps the police found the relevant client and he was cleared). It has to be said that it reads suspiciously like a scene from a cheap pantomime, one complete with the predictable stock villain: the wealthy, swarthy Jew who propositions a pretty, young Gentile. Even if the story was true in every detail, the real Ripper's *modus operandi* was not to be seen so boldly in the street by witnesses, before killing a victim. On November 18, 1888, Dagonet complained that the multiplicity of witness sightings swirling around the murder of Mary Jane Kelly was due simply to overactive imaginations, as some were sure they had spoken to Kelly *after* the time the coroner judged she had been cut to ribbons.

In the wake of the latest murder there were voices raised, and not just from the opposition benches, calling for Henry Matthews to resign; they claimed that he had lost the confidence of the House and the public and should go. For reasons of practical political necessity, Prime Minister Salisbury had no intention of letting that happen, however much he may have, in private, shaken his head over his home secretary's lack of political smarts. The circumstances of the Warren resignation then spilled out into the public, with the home secretary and the soon-to-be-ex-commissioner disputing, in the Commons and letters to the editor of the *Times,* why it had happened and who exactly was at fault. Such a public brawl between two such high officials could hardly reassure the public that those at the top were any closer to stopping the maniac.

While some tabloids gleefully linked the announcement of Warren's resignation to the latest Whitechapel atrocity, Sims/Dagonet, on November 18, 1888, understood it was actually due to a dispute between the commissioner and the home secretary over "a question of professional etiquette." Sounding almost remorseful, Sims wrote that he would not join in the "chorus of jubilation" over Warren's demise, now paying him the backhanded compliment that "he was too good a soldier to be a good policeman." Warren had, furthermore, quashed the "grave danger which threatened London" (the rampaging mob) with his invaluable "soldierly qualities" (as noted, the rich writer was no revolutionary). By contrast, Sims was scathing about the Tory home secretary: "He enjoys the unenviable distinction of being cordially detested by all political parties, and the supporters of the Government to which he belongs are quite as disgusted with him as are the supporters of the Opposition."

Mary Jane Kelly, a totally obscure figure in life who, had she simply starved to death or slit her own throat would not have received even a brief death notice in any newspaper, received a send-off on November 19, 1888, that bordered on mass hysteria. *The East London Advertiser* five days later described "a scene of turbulent excitement" among a huge crowd noticeably dominated by women "struggled desperately to get to touch the coffin." Within just a few days, another East End prostitute (named Annie Farmer, but more often known as "Dark Sarah"), seemed to have escaped the same fate as Mary Jane Kelly. Some of the circumstances were eerily similar: a client turning on his would-be victim in her squalid abode. But this time he failed to kill the woman and had to flee—and was seen by witnesses. Yet the story was almost as quickly debunked by the police and press as merely conjured up by an attention-seeking harlot, as we see in the headline of the *Evening Star* (Washington, D.C.) of November 22, 1888: "IT WAS NOT 'THE RIPPER.'" ... Yesterday's London Sensation Gotten Up by a Drunken Woman. ... on further investigation by the police, entirely discredited." The prostitute and client had gotten into some kind of drunken fracas, he had fled and she had tried to make a tabloid meal of her misadventure. Yet as can be seen from a comparable article in the *Bridgeport Morning News* of the same day—which took the woman's claims far more seriously, as her assailant allegedly brandished a long knife—the alleged assailant had been seen speedily threading his way through the East End labyrinth. The same newspaper claimed that the English police were convinced that this was the same man that had committed the other murders. Was it because of the suspect's obvious resemblance to Joseph Lawende's description of "Jack-the-Sailor" that perhaps some in CID were not persuaded to write it off as a self-inflicted sideshow? The same article provided this description of the fleeing client:

> The woman has recovered sufficiently to tell something of the man who wounded her. She says he is about 30 years old, tall, fair and wearing a light moustache. He was well-dressed, spoke with a purely English accent, and from his conversation was evidently well acquainted with Whitechapel and the habits of the women there. ... From the information which she has given, the police have gained new confidence and believe now that they can run the murderer down. ... The woman says she is fully able to identify the man, and gave a description to the police. The police are hopeful of soon capturing him.

Spurred by the death of Mary Jane Kelly, the possible near murder of "Dark Sarah," the resignation of the commissioner, the public howls for Matthews' head, and a petition pleading for help from the poor women of the East End (organized by the activist wife of the Reverend Samuel Barnett—see Chapter XVII) a stung Queen Victoria now prodded her government to do something: "The new most ghastly murder shows the absolute necessity for some very decided action. All these courts must be lit, & our detectives improved. They are not what they should be. You promised, when the 1st murders took place to consult with your colleagues about it."[7] Lord Salisbury, her premier, though a die-hard monarchist was no shrinking violet when it came to defending himself and his government against his often prickly sovereign's missives: "This horrid murder was committed in a room. No additional lighting could have prevented it." The dour queen, the "Widow of Windsor," was not without compassion. Her Majesty had also seen prime ministers come and go for half a century and was not so easily put off. Dictating to her private secretary, Henry Ponsonby, Victoria, mourning the loss of Warren, strongly advised Salisbury to resist the tabloid pressure to sack Henry Matthews as well. She also shared her fears "that the Detective department is not so efficient as it might be"—and her own ideas on catching "Jack": assign more detectives, check out men who live alone, search every boat. In the midst of this desultory ending to the "Year of the Terror" there was a startling reference in the *Pall Mall Gazette* of December 31, 1888, that points to Scotland Yard's investigating a major suspect in 1888, and what is more, doing so abroad:

> Inspector Andrews, of Scotland Yard, has arrived in New York from Montreal. It is generally believed that he has received orders from England to commence his search in this city for the Whitechapel murderer. ... The supposed inaction of the Whitechapel murderer for a considerable period and the fact that a man suspected of knowing a good deal about this series of crimes left England for this side of the Atlantic three weeks ago, has, says the "Telegraph" correspondent, produced the impression that Jack the Ripper is in that country.

Coroner Wynne Baxter had referred, with some controversy, to an unidentified American physician whose attempts to buy anatomical specimens may have, inadvertently, inspired some brutish characters to murder harlots in order to sell their organs. This American may have overlapped with another man from the same country who ran a lucrative herbal shop near the East End. It is this second American suspect whom Inspector Walter Andrews was investigating in North America—though in Canada, not the U.S.A.—while escorting a swindler named Roland Gideon Israel Barnett back to his own country. Though British newspapers made only elliptical references to this Irish-American suspect, Scottish readers were much better informed, presumably because of the more draconian libel laws below the border (where even a low-life such as John Pizer could win an out-of-court settlement). This is from the *Dundee Courier and Argus* of December 26, 1888, wherein the suspect is named:

> IS THIS THE WHITECHAPEL MURDERER?
> AN EXTRAORDINARY PERSONAGE
>
> A man calling himself Dr. Tumblety was arrested some time ago in London on suspicion of being concerned in the perpetration of the Whitechapel murders. The police, being unable to procure the necessary evidence against him, in connection therewith, decided to hold him for trial for another offence ... liberated on bail ... it is taken for granted he has sailed for New York. The man is declared by U.S. papers to be well known for his eccentricities.

Though the documentation has not survived it is assumed that Inspector Andrews was unable to find anything incriminating against "Dr. Tumblety" (except perhaps further evidence of his homosexuality, the crime he had actually been charged with in London). We know that this flamboyant figure was a significant CID suspect—at least for a while—due to the 1913 private letter mentioned earlier from the retired head of Special Branch, Jack Littlechild:

> Amongst the suspects, and to my mind a very likely one, was ... an American quack named Tumblety and [who] was at one time a frequent visitor to London and on these occasions constantly brought under the notice of police, there being a large dossier concerning him at Scotland Yard. Although a "Sycopathia Sexualis" [*sic*] subject he was not known as a "Sadist" (which the murderer unquestionably was) but his feelings toward women were remarkable and bitter in the extreme, a fact on record. Tumblety was arrested at the time of the murders in connection with unnatural offences and charged at Marlborough Street, remanded on bail, jumped his bail, and got away to Boulogne.

The wily Tumblety had blown town in yet another potential embarrassment for Scotland Yard, one thankfully ameliorated by the English press giving the story short shrift. By contrast, the American press trumpeted the return of the eccentric prodigal. Yet amidst all the tabloid jocularity about Dr. Tumblety's latest escapade, Scotland Yard was not laughing. They were trying to find out if this man was the Ripper, or not—as seen in the *Brooklyn Citizen* of November 23, 1888, which reported that the new assistant commissioner, Dr. Robert Anderson, was requesting from New York police samples of Tumblety's handwriting (possibly to compare to the letter and postcard that had coined the nickname):

> IS HE THE RIPPER? ... Police Superintendent Campbell received a cable dispatch yesterday *from Mr. Anderson, the deputy chief of the London Police,* asking him to make some inquiries about Francis Tumblety, who is under arrest in England on the charge of indecent assault. ... Tumblety is referred to in the dispatch in the following manner: "He says he is known to you, Chief, as Brooklyn's Beauty." ... Tumblety was arrested in London some weeks ago as the supposed Whitechapel murderer. Since his incarceration in prison *he has boasted of how he had succeeded in baffling the police* [my italics].

It was also claimed—in the American press at least—that the failed attempt on the life of prostitute "Dark Sarah" had reassured some at CID that Tumblety was probably not the killer, as we see in the *Bridgeport Morning News* (Connecticut) of November 22, 1888, the day before: "Coming at a time when people were beginning to think that the Dr. Twombelty [*sic*] now in custody might really prove to be the Whitechapel fiend, this morning's affair has renewed all the old excitement, and the bewildered Londoners are helplessly wringing their hands and wondering if the horrors will never be brought to a stop." Trying to catch a killer with no connection to his victims, chasing a multitude of leads, Scotland Yard arguably resembled Dr. Dolittle's pushmi-pullyu, with a head at each end. As December 1888 turned into January 1889, it seemed the fiend, who maybe had fled abroad, or maybe had been seen fleeing from a victim in London who survived, or maybe had done neither, had hunkered down yet again. The day after the announcement of Monro's appointment as commissioner to succeed Sir Charles Warren—the crucial promotion that would rescue Macnaghten's stillborn policing career—the corpse of an Englishman was pulled from the River Thames. No London paper covered the tragic suicide of one of their own barristers, perhaps because the deceased was originally from Dorset and had, for reasons known only to him, drowned himself at Chiswick several kilometers from the center of the metropolis. One of the first references to this sad end to a promising life is found in the *Thames Valley Times* of January 2, 1889:

> BODY FOUND IN THE THAMES OFF THORNEYCROFT'S
>
> On Monday the body of a gentleman was found by Henry Winslade, waterman, in the Thames, off Thorneycroft's Wharf, and has since been identified by a season ticket and certain papers. Deceased was not a resident of the district, and the body had been in the water nearly a month. Deceased was about forty years of age, and the brother of a gentleman living at Bournemouth. The Coroner was acquainted with the fact that the remains had been removed to the mortuary, and an inquest will be held today.

Either on May 23 or June 1, 1889, Melville Leslie Macnaghten (he owned to both dates in 1913 and 1914, respectively) started work as assistant chief constable at CID, the fourth highest ranking administrator at Scotland Yard. To his lifelong chagrin he had missed the Whitechapel fiend's initial reign of terror, yet he had no sense—at least in 1889 to early 1891—that he was entirely too late; that the hunt for the fiend was over because the killer was either abroad or deceased. The month before Macnaghten started his career on the force as a sleuth, he probably knew from his regular visits to Eton that a distasteful figure from the past might have made an unwelcome return. A bold-asbrass thief had pretended to be from Windsor Castle and approached Eton College's jeweler and watchmaker, a Mr. Betjeman. The stranger claimed he needed to see watches and chains for Prince Teck. Items of an appropriately royal standard were sent for from London and the emissary, now attired in a mortar board as worn by Eton masters, arrived to take possession. The sales assistant, Mr. Rowell, smelled a rat and insisted on accompanying the man to Eton, where the boys, seeing the head gear, raised their own hats in salute. Thinking the students recognized the stranger, Rowell handed over the expensive watches. Swiftly discovering his mistake, the sales assistant scrambled to confront the imposter, but within the moment it took to enter a different room, the bird had flown. The thief hitched a ride to visit a pawnshop in Staines before going on to Richmond and vanishing. The confidence man had left behind the stolen Eton cap in the cab. Good God, was it that Russian swine, Michael Ostrog, befouling Mac's beloved Eton—again?

VI

MAN'S MAN

I knew how it was that this tall, charming-mannered man had managed to win and keep the respect and devotion of all kinds of men in all ranks of service. With fine tact he said just the right things in just the right way.—Fred Wensley, 1931

I suggested a visit to the Prussian Eagle ... where dancing was carried on by German ladies.... We naturally desired to make ourselves popular, and to that end stood "rum shrubs to the ladies all round." ... We were quite a success.—Sir Melville Macnaghten, 1914

In 1898 Frederic Porter Wensley was an inspector at CID. Despite being very effective at catching crooks, his career was stalled. He approached his immediate superior to ask for a promotion and found him less than sympathetic. The detective-inspector bluntly told Wensley, "I'm not going to have you transferred after I've taught you all I know." Not easily put off, Wensley appealed to his superintendent—who absolutely refused to second-guess the decision of the man below *him*. "Well Sir," replied Wensley, "I will appeal to Scotland Yard"—meaning he would try his luck with the head honchos at central office. The superintendent warned Wensley that though he was well within his rights to do so, it was "a daring thing to do." Wensley knew that he was risking career suicide, but he judged that he had an ace up his sleeve, no less than the support of one of the chief constables, Melville Macnaghten of CID.[1]

Ten years before, Fred Wensley had joined the Metropolitan Police. Despite his acute frustrations in the 1890s, he would enjoy one of the most distinguished and acclaimed careers in the history of Scotland Yard. Despite a modest background he would rise to be chief constable—on merit. Back when he started trying to quickly learn the job on the street, he found, along with many, that the Whitechapel murders engendered "an atmosphere of terror." Wensley was among the scores of bobbies transferred into the district to try to catch the killer. The cops did make one advance—nailing bits of rubber to their shoes to provide them with a stealthier approach. Wensley would need them, as he ended up—even as he was commended for his courage at thwarting robbers and cutthroats—working in this poverty-driven locus of crime for nearly a quarter of a century. He finally made it into CID in 1895. Though he was sickened by the "scum," it gave Wensley invaluable experience of London's criminal fraternity, "the finest training ground imaginable for a young detective."[2]

By Easter 1896, Fred Wensley had been apprenticed as a CID detective for the past six months. On this Saturday afternoon he was hungry and about to grab some lunch with a fellow policeman as the pair walked along Commercial Road, Whitechapel. Suddenly news arrived of trouble on Turner Street. Arriving at the scene, the police found that a crowd had gathered outside a house where an elderly Jewish man and a woman had been bloodily murdered. In the confusion, other police ran off to get medical assistance, not realizing—as Wensley and his colleague did—that the killer had shimmied his way into the ceiling and was still lurking there. Both officers scrambled up the same way onto the roof and saw the murderer, who used the alias William Seaman, scuttling away. Wensley moved faster then he ever had in his life to catch up with the miscreant. The latter tried to jump to freedom into the crowd below—and not surprisingly ended up bashed and unconscious. But some of the same gawkers had mistaken Wensley's soot-covered head emerging out of the tiles for another criminal, and an entirely erroneous rumor got around that Seaman had an accomplice who managed to escape.

The protégé—Frederic Porter Wensley had a long and distinguished career at Scotland Yard. He wrote that he owed his rise partly to the patronage of Sir Melville Macnaghten—yet he knew nothing about his mentor's Ripper solution (photograph undated) (Stewart P. Evans).

Soon after this, the chief constable of CID, Melville Macnaghten, unexpectedly strolled into Leman Street police station in order, he said, to personally investigate this rumor of a "second man."[3] One can imagine Wensley's wariness at suddenly being confronted by his superior—was he on top of the facts of the case? Would he be able to articulately and appropriately brief the chief constable? Was his top button done up? How would the chief constable react to being informed that he had wasted his time—that the "accomplice" was the very police officer to whom he was now speaking? Another factor at play here was class. Fred Wensley was from "yeoman stock," a country boy who dreamed of becoming a detective, whereas the police chief towering over him was not only an upper-crust gent—most of them were—but one with a formidable pedigree. The son of one of the last chairmen of the East India Company, a graduate of exclusive Eton, an Indian planter ally of ex-commissioner Monro—he was practically the Victorian establishment personified. His resume did not determine his manner, though, for in that regard Melville Macnaghten was the very antithesis of a stiff and hierarchical boss. Any feelings of trepidation must have rapidly dissolved the moment the chief constable extended his hand and let his twinkling eyes and boyish grin meet the other policeman's. Fred Wensley became the latest recipient of the "Good Old Mac" treatment and he—like so many men—was positively dazzled. The chief constable treated Wensley not as a handy subordinate from whom to extract some pertinent information, only to then turn on his heel as the dismissed minion receded back into the woodwork; instead, the chief acted as if Wensley was a long-lost chum. In his own memoir the retiring chief constable (1924–1929) wistfully recalled this fortuitous encounter, one that would prove so critical to his career: "I knew how it was that this tall, charming-mannered man had managed to win and keep the respect and devotion of all kinds of men in all ranks of service. With fine tact he said just the right things in just the right way to impress a young detective officer, and asked me to accompany him to the house."[4]

The pair had just met and already were embarked on their first adventure, like two schoolboys playing hooky from class. (And this lark did get Wensley into trouble with his immediate superior: "I was rapped over the knuckles by my local inspector ... but I had gained a firm friend.") Even though the case was essentially open-and-shut, the restless Macnaghten wanted to view the scene of the crime—to immerse himself in the house of horror while hearing a blow-by-blow description of this exciting episode. But at the front door Macnaghten and Wensley found them barred by a determined relative of the victim, as he had been told by a detective inspector not to let anybody in, "not even the Commissioner himself." Certainly he was not going to step aside for a mere chief constable. The two policemen would recall this "trivial incident" with a "chuckle" thereafter (*our* enjoyment is spoilt by Wensley's casually anti–Semitic attitude):

> So there was I, with one of the highest officials in the service, held up by a voluble Jew.... My arguments, my explanations were waved aside, and the amused Chief Constable thoroughly enjoyed the little interlude. My persistency won at last, although it was clear that the little Jew still had grave doubts as he stood aside to let us in.[5]

From that moment Wensley found that Macnaghten stayed in touch, offering him encouragement and friendship. Perhaps Macnaghten had eagerly sought out this fellow "man of action," as Wensley had proved himself with his rooftop escapade, because he was exactly the kind of heroic sleuth "Mac" aspired to be. As the retired chief wrote in 1914:

> I have spent many nights in the worst parts of London, but—unless criminal investigations were afoot—the interest was in the officers who accompanied me rather than in the sights which I saw or the scenes through which I passed. To know one's officers and their capabilities is half the battle in detective work. To gain this necessary knowledge one must get to know them personally and locally.[6]

From a less idyllic point of view it can also be seen that Macnaghten was a shrewd judge of men, of subordinates whom he could flatter, cultivate, and promote—and who would be unquestioning in their loyalty to him. In a moving tribute Wensley reminisced about his late mentor:

> Ever after, Sir Melville showed almost a paternal interest in my work. No doubt he gave the same impression to others, for he always had the knack of drawing the best from a man. Even that little intimate touch "Fred" instead of the official "Mr. Wensley" on occasions when we were alone together in after years, when he had become assistant commissioner, was calculated to give a human and inspiring tone to our relationship. He was a very great gentleman, and I owe much to him.[7]

In his memoirs, Macnaghten practically admits to creating his own cadre inside CID in the final chapter, wherein he writes with anguish about having to retire and be separated from his boys: "To give up my work and my officers! In the latter I was parting from men who had done everything for me, and who had never, on any single occasion failed me at a pinch."⁸ Which brings us full circle to Fred Wensley heading off to see Macnaghten, in 1898, in the hope of gaining a sympathetic ear for his professional woes. The gamble paid off handsomely and provides a telling insight into how Macnaghten solved problems that involved competing interests, and yet still came through for his chum: "I laid my case before Sir Melville Macnaghten. He cut the knot in his own way, and I was promoted, the same day, to detective sergeant to remain 'over strength' in the H division. Thus everyone was satisfied."⁹

Wensley was still stuck in this open sewer, and that would mollify his immediate superior, but he had also been promoted. Frederick Wensley's memoir anecdote provides us with an invaluable insight into Melville Macnaghten's *modus operandi* as an administrator at the Met: he fled his desk and paperwork to prowl the mean streets, and craved the company of new best pals with whom he could have adventures (that topped anything in *Gem* or *Magnet*). Furthermore, "Good Old Mac" could be, to some extent, a power unto himself at CID to provide help to the same cronies. In 1890 Macnaghten was promoted to full chief constable after "Dolly" Williamson retired due to persistent ill health. As if to refute the long-departed figure of Sir Charles Warren and his qualms about the choice of Macnaghten, James Monro fulsomely praised his protégé in an internal memorandum before his promotion:

> I always had a high opinion of [Macnaghten's] qualifications and abilities, but he has shown an aptitude for dealing with criminal administration and a power of managing and dealing with men for which I was not prepared; he has been doing Mr. Williamson's work for months, and he done it with remarkable efficiency and success.¹⁰

In an obituary to Macnaghten in the *London Times* of May 13, 1921, it is mentioned that he "was equipped for his duties with a marvelous memory, which his colleagues often tried vainly to catch tripping. He never forgot a face or a name connected with any of his cases, and he knew the characteristics and histories of practically every man in the department, which numbered some 700." As mentioned in the introduction, an anonymous friend sent a tribute to the *Times* about Macnaghten asserting that "all his men admired and respected him, and he infused them with his own spirit of industry and devotion." When Macnaghten retired in September 1913, the assistant commissioner was given an emotional send-off by all of the policemen whom he had cultivated, promoted and befriended. *The West Gippsland Gazette* of September 2, 1913, reports on this farewell ceremony (attendees included Fred Wensley), and it provides another telling glimpse into Mac's "Boys' Own" methods while again celebrating his formidable powers of recall:

> The Chief Constable [Dingham], in handing the cup to Sir Melville, expressed the regret which was felt by all ranks at his retirement.... Mr. Dingham also referred to the marvelous memory of their retiring chief, and pointed out that in dealing with the men under him Sir Melville had always been reluctant to rebuke or reprove any officer unless it was absolutely necessary in the interests of the Force.

The Sunday Post of May 15, 1921, published a tribute by an unnamed fan of the ex-chief who had just passed away. We see again the same sincere affection expressed for the loss of such a likeable man:

Known to the youngest recruits as "Mac"—the best compliment that could be paid to the chief—Sir Melville Macnaghten, who has just passed away in London, was one of the few examples of a departmental chief in the right place. He was no square peg in a round hole. A cultivated man of quiet tastes, the Assistant Commissioner of the Criminal Investigation Department of the Yard made it his motto never to ask a detective to do what he was not prepared to do himself....

KEEN STUDENT OF CRIMINOLOGY

The study of crime was his hobby, & a keen judgment of character enabled him to select the best men for the elucidation of crime to work in conjunction with him. The most famous officers in London speak of him in terms of admiration, "There was a man!," they would say whenever his name was mentioned....

His house in the West End was never closed to the men who worked with him. Any hour of the night, after dinner, you would see a light burning in his study, which meant that perhaps a couple of Inspectors, or even a detective-sergeant, had dropped in to have a pipe with the Commissioner, and tell him how they were faring in their hunt for a famous criminal.

The police chief justifies this after-hours conferring—as if Macnaghten were a kindly sage or tutor counseling new boys—in chapter 13 of *Days of My Years*, particularly if it involves a case proving difficult for the detectives to crack: "In all cases of this kind it is well to encourage the officer in charge by getting him to run round to one's house in the evening. One can then learn, over a cigar, what has been doing and what it is proposed. Even if nothing comes of it, the officer goes away in good heart and cheered for his morrow's work."[11]

In the previous *Sunday Post* piece even Macnaghten's good looks and impressive bearing come in for praise, as does the claim that he personally tried to help criminals ("lags") to go straight: "In appearance the great sleuth was one of the handsomest men at the Yard. Tall and military-looking, he was one of the kindest-hearted police officials I ever knew, and many an old 'lag' had reason to thank him for encouragement and help when he decided to turn from dishonest ways and begin a new life."

According to a couple of newspaper sources (but not the ex–police chief's memoirs), this camaraderie shown by Macnaghten towards his worshipful detectives was formalized into a kind of fraternity—a CID within CID. The November 25, 1910, issue of the *Albury Banner and Wadonga Express* (New South Wales) reproduced an article with a terrific "shilling shocker" title:

SLEUTH-HOUNDS OF SCOTLAND YARD

It reads like something conjured up by Sherlock Holmes' creator, Sir Arthur Conan Doyle, complete with a secret room where the "Council of Seven" covertly meets to smash evil-doers—and the *capo régime* is none other than Melville Macnaghten, by then assistant commissioner:

In the great, rather grim, red-brick building which, like a medieval fortress, dominates the Thames within stone's throw of the Houses of Parliament, there is a large, barely furnished room which holds more secrets than any other in London, with the possible exception of the room of Cabinet mysteries. It is the nerve-centre of [the] English great and complex detective system, which controls the currents radiating all the world over for the discovery of crime; and it is in this secret chamber that the mysterious Council of Seven hold their meetings to unravel the tangled skeins of tragedy.

Somebody was sure having fun. It reads like a bunch of nefarious, reactionary nabobs preparing to launch a coup against a soft-headed Bolshie government. Behind the hype, the group seems to have been a regular clearing house for Macnaghten and his men to bypass bureaucratic logjams; to have the "best detective brains" sift through cases, openly and quickly—specifically cases that had not led to a quick solution or arrest. The council was reportedly formed in the mid–Edwardian years. The members were, allegedly, not permitted to speak about its existence, yet here is an article delineating how it operated and who was in it:

> The head of the Council is, by his office, Sir Melville Macnaghten, Chief of our Criminal Investigation Department—a man who probably knows more about crime than any other in the United Kingdom. Few men look less like a catcher of criminals than Sir Melville, who suggests rather a prosperous and genial stockbroker than a Sherlock Holmes, but, all the same, he is an expert in crime to the tips of his fingers. Apart from his long experience of crime and its professors he is a born detective, if ever there was one. So intuitively clever is he that it is said he can tell, after a few minutes' conversation with a criminal, of what particular branch he is a specialist, and his resources and tenacity are just as wonderful as his instinct for discovering clues.

Amidst all this back-slapping, manly high jinks, Melville Macnaghten appears never to have confided to any of them his true solution to the Jack the Ripper mystery (except probably Chief Inspector Vivian Majendie of the Home Office, as he was himself distantly related to the likeliest suspect and the main reason for Mac's discretion—see Chapter VIII). When it came to the Ripper's identity, "Good Old Mac" refrained from showing his hand with his colleagues—including the not-so-secret "magnificent seven"— about a case with which he was so obsessed. This strict withholding can be seen in Fred Wensley's 1929 memoir. The retired chief constable's musings about the Whitechapel murders proves—by his adding the Frances Coles murder of 1891 to the list of the Ripper's crimes—that he was completely oblivious to a supposedly definitive solution entertained by his beloved chief, one that had the miscreant safely deceased at the end of 1888 after killing only five "unfortunates":

> During my first year of service the Jack the Ripper murders occurred in Whitechapel. Again and again bodies of women, murdered and mutilated, were found in the East End; but every effort to bring the assassin to justice failed. For a while there was an atmosphere of terror in the district. ... Officially, only five (with a possible sixth) murders were attributed to Jack the Ripper. There was, however, at least one other, strikingly similar in method, in which the murderer had a very narrow escape. This occurred something more than two years after the supposed last Ripper murder.[12]

The journalist who wrote the article in the *Van Wert Daily Bulletin* (Ohio) of August 29, 1929, about Fred Wensley—quashing a rumor that the retired Scotland Yard chief was soon to be seconded to the States to solve Chicago's underworld problems—had a far more accurate recall regarding the profile of a gentleman-fiend suspect who had killed himself, one which Sims (and Macnaghten anonymously via Sims) had been relentlessly propagating during the Edwardian years:

> The identity of "Jack" was never disclosed, although Sir Melville MacNaghten, former chief of the CID, said, after his retirement, that the Ripper committed suicide on November 10, *the day following the last of his atrocious crimes*, and that Scotland Yard knew who he was, where and how he died. It was assumed by the public that he was *a man of education*

and position who succumbed to the impulses of a criminal streak and *committed suicide when the police were about to close in on him* [my italics].

If Wensley ever saw those words, he could hardly have believed that this publicity-spin could have originated with the "very great gentleman" he had known and admired, as there was no prime suspect who was about to be arrested as the likeliest "Jack" who killed himself. Yet Macnaghten was indeed the origin not only of the quote above from his own memoir—nominating "on or about" November 10, 1888, as the probable date of the Ripper's demise—but also of Sims' pugnacious reassurance to the public that the police were definitely on the verge of trapping this well-educated maniac (see Chapter XIII). Almost alone, Hargrave L. Adam, the crime writer, saw through Macnaghten's "hail fellow-well met" shtick to the calculating mind behind the grin, as he wrote in 1914: "Sir Melville is somewhat reserved in manner, shrewdly preferring to listen to what you have to say to talking himself. He is most adroit at leading you away from things he does not wish to discuss."[13]

On June 1, 1889, Melville Macnaghten arrived at Scotland Yard to take up his position as assistant chief constable of the Criminal Investigation Department. It is hard to imagine he could resist getting his hands on the Whitechapel-Ripper file. In his memoirs—in which he devotes an entire chapter to the case—Macnaghten brags about a big dive into the files as he opens with a ditty, one from a legion of hoax letter-writers:

> "I'm not a butcher,
> I'm not a Yid,
> Nor yet a foreign Skipper,
> But I'm your own light-hearted friend,
> Yours truly, Jack the Ripper."
> Anonymous
>
> THE Above queer verse was one of the first documents which I perused at Scotland Yard, for at that time the police post-bag bulged large with hundreds of anonymous communications on the subject of the East End tragedies.[14]

From the moment he was sworn in, Macnaghten headed for the East End to try to catch the fiend. Though this proved to be a bust, the assistant chief constable did immerse himself in the poverty, latent violence, and pungent odors of a world far removed from Eton—and still tried to win even these poor souls over with his bonhomie:

> During my first years of police work I was frequently down in the East End o' nights. On one occasion a well-known Member of Parliament begged to be allowed to accompany me. We had (as I knew we should have) rather a dreary and disappointing time of it. One of two lodging-houses had been visited, and nothing is more depressing than that peculiarly abominable and acrid smell which pervades them. I am thankful to think it is absolutely unlike anything else which has ever assailed my nostrils in any quarter of the globe.
>
> To finish up the evening with some miserable pretence at hilarity, I suggested a visit to the Prussian Eagle (I think that was the name of the house of entertainment in Wellclose Square, but it has long ceased to exist), where dancing was carried on by German ladies, and sailors of all nationalities, and where the sight of a drawn knife or two was not infrequent. On entering, we naturally desired to make ourselves popular, and to that end stood "rum shrubs [an alcoholic beverage] to the ladies all round." In consequence we were quite a success, and so the evening ended.[15]

The education of the upper class gent about the ways of the lower orders and criminal classes led "Mac" to muse about a significant difference he observed between French and British prostitutes, as there was an aspect of professionalism regarding the former that quite amused him:

> The English woman, once on the downward path, slides along it with awful rapidity: frequently she takes to drink, loses self-respect, and with it, in many cases, all claim to womanhood. How different are these things in France. Your *cocotte* slips, and goes on slipping, but she does not take to drink, nor does she—to anything like the same extent—lose her self-respect. Many of this class work by day, but continue to amuse themselves by night. They save money, and when Jeanette has found the right Jeannot she marries him, and they live happily ever after!

With droll urbanity, Macnaghten ponders whether the difference between squalor and glamour was due to drinking superior wine: "Is this wholly due to the difference between the national temperaments? Or has the red wine of France a less deleterious effect than the abominable spirities obtainable in too many public-houses in London? As Paul Demetrius used to say in the 'Red Lamp,' 'I wonder!'"[16]

What else would Macnaghten have learned by perusing the Ripper archive back at Scotland Yard? Most of the files have not survived but, based on other contemporaneous sources, we can make a good guess. For example, he would have seen the paradoxical record about the Poplar murder of December 1888. This was the death of Catherine "Rose" Mylett. Aged only 29, her body was found to be still warm as she lay in Clarke's Road on the morning of December 20, 1888. Not only was there no signs of mutilation, but the first bobbies and doctor on the scene assumed she had passed away from natural causes. A subsequent examination revealed a mark around her neck possibly caused by a cord (James Monro thought it was probably a "Jack" murder while Dr. Robert Anderson, though much later, asserted it was not).[17]

I postulate that as soon as he able to access the Scotland Yard file on the Whitechapel murders, Melville Macnaghten read the now-lost report on Dr. Francis Tumblety by Walter Andrews, the inspector who had done a background check on this suspect while visiting Canada a few months before. It would have included the fact that this strange man was a 56-year-old man-mountain who sometimes sported a moustache so large that it would make a walrus envious. Born in Ireland, he was the classic American story of a man who pulled himself up from nothing to become rich and famous, in his case as a crackerjack salesman of lucrative herbal remedies (including a cream to cure acne, popular with the very gender he was supposed to despise, maybe even to enjoy murdering and disfiguring).

Inspector Andrews may have inquired about an article in the *New York World* of December 1, 1888 (alleging Tumblety once possessed a creepy collection of uteri, that he spoke disdainfully of women as "cattle" and, when young, had married a woman who turned out to be a harlot), and perhaps found it to be spurious as the source of the damning tale, a certain "Colonel Dunham," was himself a notorious dissembler (real name: Sanford Conover). With greater certainty we know (and Scotland Yard must have learned) that Dr. Tumblety had a knack for finding himself at the margins of notorious crimes; he had been arrested and cleared of being part of the 1865 plot by Confederate recalcitrants to assassinate President Abraham Lincoln. As mentioned by the *Bucks*

County Gazette of December 13, 1888, this was, astonishingly, not the only presidential assassination with which Tumblety was connected: "Several years later he was an associate in New York of Charles J. Guiteau, who murdered President Garfield." *The Gazette* also claims he was investigated for bio-terrorism: "At the close of the war he was arrested on a charge of complicity with an attempt to introduce yellow fever into New York, and he still claims that the authorities robbed him of several thousand dollars in United States bonds."

In that lost file a clipping may also have been later inserted showing that Tumblety had given a quite bombastic interview to the *New York World* of January 29, 1889 (found by writer-researcher R. J. Palmer), giving "his version of how he came to figure so prominently in the most remarkable series of tragedies recorded in the long list of crimes." In it Tumblety slandered the English police in the most extravagant terms. Yet he provided no alibis for any of the murders and made a potentially incriminating admission by conceding he was quite familiar with the East End; that "in the company of thousands of other people" he went down to explore Whitechapel, where Tumblety claims he found himself being followed by police detectives because he was wearing a slouch hat. This is because, the doctor says, it was believed by the "lower classes" that the murderer wore such head-gear, "and this, together with the fact that I was an American, was enough for the police. It established my guilt beyond any question." Tumblety goes on to provide an implausible motive for the police "harassment"—his wealth, specifically some diamonds in his pocket. According to the doctor it was nothing but an attempted "shakedown." Refusing to hand over his expensive baubles, he landed in prison for a couple of days, though behind the bombast was no doubt a sincerely felt bitterness:

> "When I think of the way I was treated in London, it makes me lose all control of myself. It was shameful, horrible."
> "What do you think of the London police?"
> "I think their conduct in this Whitechapel affair is enough to show what they are. Why, they stuff themselves all day with potpies and beef and drink gallons of stale beer, keeping it up until they go to bed late at night, and then wake up the next morning heavy as lead. Why, all the English police have dyspepsia. They can't help it. Their heads are as thick as the London fogs. You can't drive an idea through their thick skulls with a hammer. I never saw such a stupid set. Look at their treatment of me. There was absolutely not one single scintilla of evidence against me. I had simply been guilty of wearing a slouch hat, and for that I was charged with a series of the most horrible crimes ever recorded."

A little too transparently, Tumblety flatters the corrupt police chief and fellow Irish-American, Thomas Byrnes, who had given press interviews scoffing at the notion that he was harboring the world's most notorious murderer. After some name-dropping, and claims of being a certified life-saver, comes a maudlin pitch, exactly the kind of self-righteous whining typical of guilty men. But of *what* exactly? "I was the victim of circumstances when this horrible charge was first brought, and since then I have been attacked on all sides and no one has had a good word to say for me. It is strange, too, because I don't remember ever to have done any human being harm, and I know of a great many I have helped."

As far as Tumblety's being the Whitechapel murderer, I think that Macnaghten, in June 1889, would have nodded his head in silent agreement with these self-pitying words of the American suspect, that he was a victim of mistaken identity. This is despite what Tumblety had done to swindle customers over the course of his career. For "Mac," here was an eccentric, a poseur, an actor, a lifelong homosexual, a rather distasteful and disreputable oddball addicted to notoriety, not murder, who had found himself caught up in the police net due to the unsophisticated and puritanical suspicions of his superior, Dr. Robert Anderson (and no doubt the head of the Irish branch, Jack Littlechild, too).

In contrast, uniquely among the men at Scotland Yard, whose friendship and companionship he cultivated, Melville Macnaghten had the capacity to look for a Ripper in his own mirror; an English gentleman whose respectable credentials placed him above suspicion, and who was quite beyond earthly justice. It did not come easily to Macnaghten, as he too was a product of a culture that believed, as a matter of science, that it could read criminality in human features—as the case of the falsely convicted British-Indian George Edjalji shows. The young man was sent to prison in 1903 for a series of bizarre mutilations of horses and cattle. Edjalji was also believed by local police to have written a series of abusive letters. Right from the start there were people who believed in the young man's innocence.

Sir Melville was not among them, as he asserted in private correspondence dated 1905.[18] Macnaghten had been struck by Edalji's bizarre correspondence. And the facial features, to "Mac," also told against the Indian: "There is no doubt that the fellow who perpetrated these outrages was *a sexual maniac*, and if physiognomy goes for anything, Mr. Edjalji junior *has the face* of such an individual" (my italics). It took Sherlock Holmes' creator, Sir Arthur Conan Doyle, to admirably turn sleuth, for real, to gain a pardon for the evil-faced but quite innocent man in 1907, which also helped the public push for a Court of Criminal Appeal (Macnaghten would claim to be similarly instrumental in freeing the innocent Adolph Beck—see Chapter XV). The police chief did not claim to know this case in depth, having simply read an article about it in a magazine: "I knew of course something of the case before, and had formed the opinion (possibly quite *an erroneous one* and certainly *founded on inadequate facts*) that the right man had been convicted" (my italics).

Despite the jury's verdict—and that the convicted man looked like a deviant—Macnaghten was not sure he was the guilty party. Whereas his Ripper suspect would have the face of an angel, would never have his day in court, and came from a family with some propensity for mental instability; and yet, in 1913, Sir Melville—at a press conference—would express no caution or hesitation, whatsoever, that this fellow English gentleman was "Jack the Ripper."

VII

THE "LAST" VICTIM

I remember being down in Whitechapel one night in September 1889, in connection with what was known as the Pinchin Street murder.... The code of immorality in the East End is, or was, unwashed in its depths of degradation.—Sir Melville Macnaghten, 1914

Mr. MacNaghten, accompanied by other officials, paid a visit to the spot where the body had been found, and made himself familiar with the surroundings.—*The Sutherland Daily Echo and Shipping Gazette*, 1891

The new assistant chief constable may have also seen another report—now long dust—far more suggestive that "Jack the Ripper" was English, not American. This was an account of the prostitute, Annie Farmer, a.k.a. "Dark Sarah," who was attacked on November 21, 1888, and who "miraculously" survived. In 1888 the press claimed that the police had quickly dismissed this incident as nothing more than a drunken fracas amplified by a Liz Stride–style mythomaniac. Macnaghten, however, may have become aware that CID took a witness to this prostitute's fleeing client so seriously that they were trying to prevent the former's identity from becoming widely known. If so, then from our point of view the only glimpse that remains is in the *Chicago Daily Tribune* of July 23, 1889, in the wake of what was initially considered another Ripper murder that month: "How the Ripper Looks—A Description of the Terror of Whitechapel." The article then identified a hitherto unknown second witness to the alleged attempted knife-murder of prostitute "Dark Sarah" who had apparently been kept under wraps by the police. It was a young man named Frank Ruffell, a driver of a green-grocer's wagon, who was reported to be "level-headed." He claimed to have been ten feet from the door of the lodging house in which the assault had just taken place and saw the fleeing criminal. Only after the young man heard the blood-curdling cry of Annie Farmer, closely followed by her bloody appearance at the door, did he try to give chase; but the man had already vanished into the East End's "rabbit warren." This is Ruffell's description of the assailant who might be the thwarted Ripper, and whom Macnaghten may have read about in a police file now dust:

> [A] man came out and walked rapidly towards me. He was about 30 years old. I could not tell what kind of business he was in. He did not look like a working man, but did not look like a gentleman. He had on a black diagonal suit, his hat was a black round felt, and he had a light mustache cut off square at the sides. It was neither thick nor thin, but about medium. He was about three inches taller than I am, and I am about five feet four. He

had a straight nose of medium size. I did not notice his eyes particularly, but I should think from the colour of his mustache that they were blue. When he came out of the door he was buttoning the top button [of] his coat. It was a cutaway coat. He had no collar on. He put his hands up to his mouth, which was bleeding on the right side. As he passed me he looked at me with a sort of smile and muttered a vile remark. I said nothing. Just after he passed me he began to run.

Macnaghten would have seen—in a presumed report about this closeted eyewitness—that the description broadly matched the one provided by the Polish-German Joseph Lawende. Also from the *Police Gazette* of October 26, 1888, Macnaghten could have seen—if the name had not already popped up on some arm's-length suspect's list—that among those of the criminal underworld who might be "Jack" was none other than that Russian cockroach, Ostrog. And he was missing: "MICHAEL OSTROG, alias BERTRAND ASHLEY, CLAUDE CLAYTON and DR. GRANT.... On 10 March 1888 he was liberated from Surrey Country Lunatic Asylum and failed to report. Warrant issued. Special attention is called to this dangerous man."[1] In chapter 5 of his memoir, "Early Days at the Yard," Macnaghten heaps praise on the chief constable (this was the terminally ill Adolfus "Dolly" Williamson, here left unnamed), whom he now assisted, calling his apprenticeship a "privilege": "[Williamson] had 'risen from the ranks,' and no man ever had a deeper insight into crime.... I have rarely come across anyone in any position of life who had a more 'right judgment in all things.' ... Whatever success attended my labours at the Yard I ascribe to his early teaching."[2] This tutor could not have been more different from the cloistered masters at Eton, and yet he was just as influential on "Mac"—albeit briefly. Sadly, Dolly Williamson was only there at his desk for another three months before retiring, and was deceased six months after that ("worn out with thirty-seven years of anxious work"). He gave advice to Macnaghten that could only have echoed what the young man had been warned by his headmaster when he was sighted coming back from Tap: "'Well my boy, you are coming into a funny place. They'll blame you if you do your duty, and they'll blame you if you don't.' And, indeed, it was not long before I was made to realize that sufferance was the badge of a Metropolitan police officer."[3] Macnaghten boasts that he was always a popular public servant, revealing that he saw his job as being as much about public relations as crime-fighting: "Yet I most gratefully admit that the Press and the public (not always sympathetic with the department over which I had the honor to preside for more than ten years) never unkindly or unfairly criticized my work."[4]

Macnaghten had been at the Yard just a few days when he had a "murder most foul" to investigate—and it involved dismemberment! The boy who once thrilled to Madame Tussaud's gallery of grotesques was now in the thick of real horror and mystery. Near the Thames River at Battersea the left thigh of a woman had washed ashore, while presumably the same person's pelvis had turned up at Horsleydown. As quick as he could get there, "Good Old Mac" was at the river, accompanied by detectives, looking in vain for the victim's "skillfully disarticulated" head. Unlike a couple of other chopped-up cases of the previous year, this woman, "one of the dregs of humanity," was identified; she was a prostitute named Elizabeth Jackson. Unfortunately her killer remained, wrote Macnaghten in the parlance of the era, "undiscovered."

A month later it appeared that "Jack the Ripper" was back, and this time Macnaghten would not be cheated of his chance to catch the fiend. He must have cracked open the champagne!⁵ Alice McKenzie, 39, was a washer-woman, charwoman, a part-time prostitute and a full-time smoker of a pipe (hence known as "Clay Pipe Alice"). She cohabited with a local man named John McCormack. Shortly after midnight of July 16, 1889, a police constable stumbled upon her body on the pavement of Castle Alley. The police at the scene, led by Commissioner James Monro, initially thought the pipe found would identify McKenzie's killer, because it seemed unlikely to belong to the victim. And once again Dr. Robert Anderson had the misfortune to be on leave when "Jack the Ripper" may have struck yet again. Monro took personal charge of the case, as he was sure it was by the same hand: "I need not say that every effort will be made by the police to discover the murderer, who, I am inclined to believe, is identical with the notorious Jack the Ripper of last year." Doctors Bond and Phillips, though, disagreed as to whether this was likely to have been a victim of the Ripper.⁶

The Olean Democrat (New York) of August 8, 1889, had no doubt about the implications of another harlot murder in London's East End, in regards to the dark cloud of suspicion still hanging over the head of one their own, with whom the writer below had an unexpected encounter on public transport:

> I had barely secured a seat in the bridge car when a peculiar looking man entered. He was over six feet in height, his face was square and red, and his gigantic, wiry, black mustache was of such huge proportions and singular cut that it would have attracted attention anywhere. It attracted my attention at any rate and as its owner sat down beside me I immediately decided in my mind that
>
> HE WAS DR. TUMBLETY,
>
> the alleged Whitechapel murderer. I had seen several pictures of that notorious gentleman which were published in "The Herald" about the time he fled from London, and the man sitting beside me closely resembled them.... I asked him his name. "Dr. Francis Tumblety, you may have heard it before," was the quiet reply. I replied somewhat significantly that I had. He said he had been greatly wronged by the press, and gave me a pamphlet containing his picture and a number of notices of a book he had just published. We parted at the Brooklyn end of the bridge. Shortly thereafter, the last Whitechapel murder occurred in London, and as Tumblety was without doubt in Brooklyn at the time, he is evidently unjustly suspected of being "Jack the Ripper."

In the early hours of the morning of September 10, 1889, a dismembered female torso was discovered by a bobbie who had detected the smell of decomposition. Missing the head and legs, the remains of the woman, who was never positively identified, was found under an East End railway arch in Pinchin Street. Most papers could see that the *modus operandi* was significantly different from that of the Whitechapel butcher. Chief Constable Melville Macnaghten still may have surmised—hoped?—that this torso ghastliness was indeed the return of "Jack" and would give him another chance to get his hands around the maniac's neck. His memoir does not mention his reaction to the "Clay Pipe Alice" murder, but it does for the subsequent Pinchin St. Torso mystery, and apart from again revealing his roving-sleuth approach to his desk job it shows his admirable compassion towards the poor:

> I remember being down in Whitechapel one night in September 1889, in connection with what was known as the Pinchin Street murder, and being in a doss house, entered the large common room where the inmates were allowed to do their cooking. The code of

immorality in the East End is, or was, unwashed in its depths of degradation. A woman was content to live with a man so long as he was in work, it being an understood thing that, if he lost his job, she would support him by the only means open to her.

What an incongruous scene this must have been: the toffy-accented, Old Etonian, unaccompanied by other cops, sitting in a dirty hovel with pimps and harlots, and pitying their subsistence on "toasted bloaters" (mackerel or herring lightly smoked and salted) while discreetly censoring their profanity. That they were not married was, from the perspective of his Victorian-Anglican morality, the "depths of degradation"—almost as shocking as making a living from pimping and whoring:

> On this occasion the unemployed man was—toasting bloaters, and, when his lady returned, asked her "if she had had any luck." She replied with an adjective negative, and went on to say in effect that she had thought her lucky star was in the ascendant when she had inveigled a "bloke" down a dark alley, but that suddenly a detective, with indiarubber soles to his shoes, had sprung up from behind a wagon, and the bloke had taken fright and flight. With additional adjectives the lady expressed her determination to go out again after supper, and when her man reminded her of the dangers of the streets if "he" (meaning the murderer) was out and about, the poor woman replied (with no adjectives this time), "Well, let him come—the sooner the better for such as I." A sordid picture, my masters, but what infinite pathos is therein portrayed![7]

"Good Old Mac" shows heart-felt sympathy for these lives that have obviously been ground down by poverty. This anecdote also shows us that Macnaghten could not reassure the prostitute that she need not fear the fiend—as he was deceased—because he did not yet know it. On September 3, 1889, a small story appeared that would evolve into George Sims' most famous "party-piece" about the Ripper, one repeated by no other source (including Macnaghten), that proved he was the murderer's doppelganger. Here is the original version of this tale from the *North Eastern Gazette* of September 23, 1889, and it is worth noting that it is treated as nothing but a fantasy perpetuated by a "crank":

> "JACK THE RIPPER" SEEN BY EVERYONE BUT THE POLICE
>
> The London edition of the "New York Herald" further says:—One of those innumerable *cranks* who have found "Jack the Ripper" called at the "Herald" office yesterday. He has written a complete history of the case, and intends to offer himself as a witness at the inquest on Tuesday next. "I am quite certain I know the man," he said: "I have talked with him many times, and I can show you his photograph"; whereupon he produced one of Dagonet's poems, and pointing to the portrait of George R. Sims said, "That's like the man, sir. My man's face was bronzed, and not quite so deathly pale; but travelling would produce that, sir. That's like the man, sir."

In this first account in the extant record, the witness had apparently spoken with his "Jack" suspect "many times," the implication being recently, in other words after 1888. Regarding his claim of a resemblance to George Sims, the witness did not say this was because the killer had a beard. Instead it was the "contour" of the features, though this alleged "Jack" had a tanned face, unlike the picture of Sims (on the cover of his book, or pamphlet, containing poems by Dagonet). Sims had some fun with this accusation in "Mustard and Cress" in the *Referee* of October 6, 1889. He sent a regular crony/assistant to investigate and provided a humorous gastronomic alibi: that the suspect ate three pork sausages—not to Sims' taste at all. Importantly the witness—who apparently turned out to be a coffee-stall owner—said that he had encountered this stranger after the committing of a single murder, presumably McKenzie's: "His story is very plausible, and there may be something in it, but I can't say that I feel flattered to learn that the notorious lady-killer is as like me ... 'Me think it was Dagonet!' exclaimed the coffee-stall keeper." The witness does not use Sims' name but rather his pseudonym as it had appeared on a copy of his poems: *The Dagonet Ballads*. With perhaps a splinter of genuine discomfort, Sims milked this eccentric bit of business the following week because the "crank" had flashed his picture under the nose of the police: "If my portrait were stuck about London as the exact counterpart of 'Jack the Ripper'—what price me?" By the 1900s this cranky pest would be spectacularly rehabilitated by Sims-Dagonet as a hardy, reliable witness (allegedly one of only two to have seen the genuine "Jack," the other being a beat cop—who it turns out never existed).

On November 4, 1889, the *Pall Mall Gazette* carried a rare interview with Dr. Robert Anderson. It was by an American journalist who had visited the scenes of the crimes. What we see here is what primary sources between 1888 and 1891 confirm—that CID had neither solved the case nor had a prime suspect; as Dr. Anderson said, "After a stranger has gone over it he takes a much more lenient view of our failure to find Jack the Ripper, as they call him, than he did before." There follows a truly black comic moment where the inspector showing the American reporter around barges in on the occupants of the Dorset St. death room:

> We knocked at the door and a woman opened it. She spoke to some-one inside, and then told "Mister Inspector" to come in. It was a bare whitewashed room with a bed in one corner. A man was in the bed, but he sat up and welcomed us good naturedly. The inspector apologized for the intrusion, but the occupant of the bed said it didn't matter, and obligingly traced out with his forefinger the streaks of blood upon the wall at his bedside. When he had done this he turned his face to the wall to go to sleep again, and the inspector ironically wished him pleasant dreams. I rather envied his nerve, and fancied waking up with those dark streaks a few inches from one's face.

As July turned into September, once again Scotland Yard's efforts to find McKenzie's killer—whether it be "Jack" or somebody else—had resulted in disappointing failure. Dagonet in the *Referee* of September 24, 1889, quotes from a Belgian newspaper a bit of drollery that reads like a mouse daring to squeak at a lion irritated by a thorn in its paw:

> "The Independent Belge" waxes facetious at the expense of the British Association. It says that the British are a wonderful people. They have found out the exact date at which the world was created, they have discovered the exact date at which it will come to an end, they have reduced the soul to a given quantity, they have discovered the germ of melancholia, they have found out how to convert Thames mud into butter, they have discovered the cipher used by Pharaoh in his billet-box—but they can't find "Jack the Ripper."

In a terrible blow Macnaghten lost his patron, Commissioner James Monro, who resigned from the Force in 1890 due to constant stonewalling by the Home Office in his attempts to reform the service—uniforms, pensions, overtime—on behalf of the ordinary working policeman (as Sir Charles Warren had tried before him).[8] According to his daughter Christabel Aberconway, her father was a tediously "enthusiastic" Tory, and so he must have despaired at the talk of the bobbies forming a union. Macnaghten was not without some progressive tendencies and tolerance, but they were limited to the mob letting off steam with a "little frothy speech, in our London parks, [which] does very little harm as a rule." He sounds like a Warren-supporter when he writes on p. 79 of his memoir that it is only when the froth may become "flecked with blood that the authorities need adopt repressive measures." Yet after Monro packed his bags for a return to missionary work in India, the government's new policies were revealed to conform to what the now ex-commissioner had demanded. In 1914 Macnaghten effusively praised the man to whom he owed his position yet pointedly refused go over the details as to exactly why this "rock against the storm" had to quit:

> I doubt whether any of the gentlemen who filled this position before or after this time ever gained more completely the affection and confidence of their officers. In him and in his judgment they believed, and knew that he would be a strong rock of defense to them in times of storm and stress. I have no intention of ripping up healed sores, or detailing the reasons which induced Mr. Monro to resign a post for which, alike by nature and by training, he was admirably fitted.[9]

Macnaghten's decision to conceal his Ripper solution—only about eight months away—from the rest of Scotland Yard and the Home Office was partly motivated, I believe, due to reasons of revenge and antipathy; over how he had been previously degraded and now how Monro had been so shabbily treated by political pygmies.

Around the same time as his mentor's downfall in June 1890, Macnaghten finally tracked down the journalist who had faked the letter that created the name "Jack the Ripper." He does not name the reporter but it was accepted by other senior police—including Dr. Anderson—that "Mac" had flushed out the correct faker who had, to some extent, distracted the investigation. The memoir of crime writer R. Thurston Hopkins, published in 1935, backs Macnaghten's claim of having identified the hoaxer. Hopkins discusses the journalist who probably faked the letter—though also without naming him—who had suffered some kind of nervous collapse: "Many old Fleet Streeters had very shrewd suspicions that this irresponsible fellow wrote the famous Jack the Ripper letter and even Sir Melville Macnaghten, chief of the Criminal Investigation Department, had his eye on him."[10] A letter to George Sims by the retired head of Special Branch, Jack Littlechild, in 1913 is the only surviving document, albeit not an official one, that *names* the reporter(s) who invented the name "Jack the Ripper": "With regard to the term 'Jack the Ripper' it was generally believed at the Yard that Tom Bullen [Bulling] of the Central News was the originator, but it is probable Moore, who was his chief, was the inventor. It was a smart piece of journalistic work."

For the first 15 months on the job the chief constable was so committed to learning the ropes ("and getting to know my officers") that he did not take a vacation. After finally resting for most of October 1890, there was a potential double murder though, sadly, nothing to do with the Whitechapel fiend. Fighting the good fight against evildoers was bound to cheer up "Mac" after the unpleasantness over his beloved patron's shafting. A somewhat embittered Macnaghten could at least bury himself in work:

> At 4 a.m., the police bell in my bedroom clanged forth, and I rushed downstairs, knowing full well that something out of the common was on the carpet. I found an officer at the door with a telegram to the effect that a woman had been found murdered in a newly made street at Hampstead, and that, about a mile from where the body lay, a dead baby had been discovered in a perambulator.

Accompanied by a superintendent and a detective-inspector, the chief constable of CID visited the Hampstead mortuary to view the corpses and learned that a local woman, a Mrs. Hogg, was missing. The victim had nearly been decapitated with a knife. As the policemen departed a young woman begged to speak with Macnaghten, and the pair conferred in a nearby alley out of the rain. The girl was the deceased woman's niece and expressed her grave suspicions of a family friend, a Mrs. Pearcey (ironically, the three policemen had just run into this prime suspect as she was an unidentified "friend" who had come with the victim's sister-in-law to identify the body). The trio headed off to interview family members and found the victim's mother-in-law "cheery and chatty." Too much so, as she produced a bottle of port with three glasses. Macnaghten responded with a typically boyish fib:

> Now, when you are not certain as to whom you may be next charging with murder, it is rather embarrassing to have hospitality proffered, and yet a police officer can never afford to be discourteous, and thereby dry up any sources of information which may at any time be forthcoming in the right direction. Therefore the old lady was blandly told that I had made it a rule in India never to drink until the Sun had set, and the Superintendent, with a sigh of relief, remarked that he too was exactly of my way of thinking. And so the bottle remained uncorked and the fine old fruity untasted.

Mrs. Pearcey had been having an affair with the deceased woman's husband and was investigated in her home by CID detectives. Though not an eyewitness, Macnaghten conjured up a macabre scene of the killer calmly tinkling on a piano as the cops found the evidence that would lead to her conviction and execution:

> I have rarely seen a woman of stronger physique than Mrs. Pearcy, and her nerves were as iron-clad as her body. She had, most unconcernedly, conducted the officers to her house, and, while they were searching it from garret to basement, she sat herself down at the piano and strummed away at popular tunes. Upon the officers entering the kitchen, it was very apparent to them that the floor had been recently washed down. But there were tell-tale splotches of blood on the walls and even on the ceiling. Upon a further search being made, a bloodstained poker and knife were found in a cupboard. When the musical hostess was asked for an explanation as to the bloodstains, she chanted a reply, "Killing mice, killing mice, killing mice," and went on with her piano-playing.[11]

Perhaps trying to dilute the horror for his "dear readers," Macnaghten claims the baby was accidentally smothered by Mrs. Pearcey by being placed under the dead body of her mother in the perambulator and pushed off into the night. Mary Eleanor Pearcey (her actual name was Wheeler, she having adopted the surname Pearcey from a man she had never married) was hanged for Phoebe Hogg's murder on December 23, 1890. In 1939 an author named William Stewart would fail to build a case for *Jill* the Ripper, claiming that it was none other than the physically robust Mary Pearcey, mistaken by witnesses on the nights of the murders for a bloodstained midwife.

I speculated earlier that just as the assistant chief constable was diligent about analyzing the voluminous correspondence signed "Jack the Ripper," Macnaghten also did the same with police lists of possible Rippers; these were names of local men who showed mental instability to one degree or another. Macnaghten probably methodically checked the fates and whereabouts of many of these suspects. One of these long-shots was an unemployed, Polish-born hairdresser named Aaron Kosminski, an East Ender of the

VII. The "Last" Victim   81

MRS PIERCEY AT HOLLOWAY JAIL. GLOOMY FORBODINGS!

Jill the Ripper?—One of the most infamous cases in which Sir Melville Macnaghten took a leading investigative role was that of the murders of Phoebe Hogg and her baby in 1890 by her husband's mistress, Mary Pearcey. During and since 1888 a few have wondered—including Sir Arthur Conan Doyle—if the fiend could have been a woman, perhaps disguised as a bloodstained midwife. Sir Melville wrote in 1914, "I have rarely seen a woman of stronger physique than Mrs. Pearcy, and her nerves were as iron-clad as her body" (*Illustrated Police News*, 1890, Stewart P. Evans).

Hebrew faith. On February 7, 1891, aged about 27, Kosminski was admitted to the country asylum Colney Hatch, a public institution. He had been living with relatives within walking distance of all the murders until they had him permanently committed. The trigger may have been that he had threatened a female relative with a knife. A Dr. Edmund King Houchin records that the deranged man had been eating out of gutters, as he refused food: "He is melancholic, practices self-abuse. He is very dirty and will not be washed. He has not attempted any kind of work for years."[12]

Despite menacing his relation, the surviving medical records show that his physicians at Colney Hatch regarded Aaron Kosminski as not a danger to others, let alone a homicidal maniac (this medical opinion from 1894 was confirmed during Kosminski's subsequent incarceration in Leavesden Asylum near Watford). In the surviving Colney Hatch records the reason for the patient's mania was initially listed as "unknown," but at a later point somebody amended this entry, in red ink, to read "self-abuse"—meaning chronic masturbation (and that his attack of mania had been going on for six *years*, not six months).

For Macnaghten to know, as he would record in 1894, that Aaron Kosminski was believed by his doctors to have driven himself insane due to masturbation means that he must have been checking up on this local lunatic *after* he had been incarcerated. I also postulate that "Old Mac" regarded the Victorian-era nostrum that the Sin of Onan caused insanity with some healthy skepticism—maybe he even thought it was scientifically absurd. Alone among police officials, Macnaghten had lived with other boys and young men in close quarters and would have been aware that this "sort of thing" was rife among upper class males and yet left little evidence of long-term harm (otherwise an awful lot of Eton's graduates would have had to transfer virtually straight from school to madhouses).

The same month that the obscure Aaron Kosminski entered institutionalized care for the rest of his life, regional newspapers—with a measure of anxiety—broke what might be a major story concerning the stubbornly "undiscovered" Whitechapel murderer. A London correspondent had picked up some gossip circulating around Whitehall about a member of Parliament who was claiming to have solved the case. The killer was, according to this unnamed politician who represented a "West of England" constituency, a "son of a surgeon" who had killed himself the same night as his last victim.[13] Could there be anything to this scoop, or was it yet another example of the "gift that keeps on giving" for tabloids on a slow news day? Not two days later, on February 13, 1891, this question seemed to be decisively answered in the negative, flushing the weird "West of England" M.P.'s "solution" into the gutter. Another young female had been found in a Whitechapel thoroughfare with her throat cut.

Like Mary Jane Kelly, the victim was young and pretty. Aged 25, Frances Coles was the daughter of a craftsman. Until 1884 she had a respectable job as a bottler in a pharmacy. The work was legitimate but physically painful and poorly paid. Consequently she drifted into prostitution in the East End, and eventually became known on the street as "Carroty Nell."[14] Frances hid her shame from her family, even sometimes attending church with her father. He only learned of her "fall from grace" when he read, along with the rest of London, the coverage of his daughter's demise, as reported, for example, in the *Pall Mall Gazette* of February 13, 1891: "ANOTHER WHITECHAPEL HORROR. / A WOMAN BRUTALLY MURDERED THIS MORNING. / SUPPOSED 'JACK THE RIPPER' CRIME. / DISCOVERY OF AN IMPORTANT CLUE." This was followed by the bizarre speculation: "IS THE MURDERER A WOMAN?" though, as we will see, elements of this theory seems to have emerged from CID.

Frances Coles' body had been found in the early hours of February 13, 1891, by the young and inexperienced Constable Ernest Thompson. The bobbie had heard retreating steps as he approached the woman, but he saw, or believed he saw, signs of life and, as was his duty, stayed with the young woman. For the rest of his brief life (he was killed in the line of duty in 1900) Thompson agonized over not pursuing the killer, as the victim turned to be already deceased.[15]

With the return of the Ripper the police mobilized a veritable army to search houses, streets, ships and the docks, frantic not to let the elusive assassin escape yet again. For Melville Macnaghten, as we see from the *Sutherland Daily Echo and Shipping Gazette* of February 13, 1891, it was a chance to be in the center of the scrimmage and hopefully—at last—catch the fiend: "At an early hour Mr. MacNaghten (Acting Chief Constable) with a large number of the most experienced detectives in the force was soon in the locality, and Mr. MacNaghten, accompanied by other officials, paid a visit to the spot where the body had been found, and made himself familiar with the surroundings."

The *Pall Mall Gazette* had wondered if the fiend might be a "Jill" rather than a "Jack." This was due to finding a second lady's hat in Coles' dress, which could mean a female perpetrator. Far from ludicrous tabloid tripe, this unlikely notion seems to have originated with a senior policeman, none other than Chief Inspector Donald Swanson (who remained in operational charge of the Ripper hunt). *The San Francisco Chronicle* of February 14, 1891, named Swanson as claiming that the discovery of a second lady's hat confirmed this was a Ripper killing: "The theory has long been that he paraded in woman's attire, and *Swanson thinks* he dropped the hat while struggling with his victim" (my italics).

The police hunt yielded a prime suspect who admitted to having bought Frances Coles, his boozy companion of the fateful night, a new hat (presumably mothballing the theory of "Jack" disguised as "Jill"). This man was a ship's fireman, meaning a stoker, tantalizingly fitting—at least in occupation—the best eyewitness description of "Jack" by Joseph Lawende. Aged about 53, James Thomas (Tom) Sadler looked even older, perhaps because of his straggly beard and having led a hard, dissolute life. But he was a sailor, a Gentile, fair of complexion and about five feet six inches in height. Arrested in a public house, Tom Sadler was taken to Leman Street police station. Swanson questioned him extensively about his whereabouts for the previous Ripper murders. At that moment the suspect must have felt that a mountain had fallen on his hung-over head. *The Daily Northwestern Oshkosh* (Wisconsin) of February 16, 1891, describes the excitement, the public relief and the sheer rage of the crowd at the news of sailor Sadler's arrest—that the Whitechapel fiend's reign of terror, now close to three years, was finally terminated:

THIRSTING FOR JACK
Threats of Lynching by the London Mob

SADLER IS IN CUSTODY

THE POLICE ARREST THE SAILOR SUSPECT

The police have in custody a man named Sadler who was a fireman on the steamer which arrived from Turkey and who they have no doubt killed Carroty Nell. An ugly looking knife stained with blood has been traced to Sadler. The station where Sadler was confined was surrounded by an immense crowd of people mostly women. Wild threats of lynching and tearing the prisoner to pieces were uttered by the most excited females. When the man was removed to the court an immense force of police was employed and every precaution was necessary to prevent lynching.

Many newspapers on both sides of the Atlantic enthusiastically covered the further incriminating detail that the accused had sold a knife soon after the murder of Carroty Knell. For example, the *Decauter Morning Review* (Illinois) of February 25, 1891: "DENIED SELLING THE KNIFE. ... A seaman identified Sadler as a man who had come to the Sailors' Home on the morning the crime was committed and sold him a big bladed clasp knife, saying he had cut many a model with the knife." Tom Sadler persistently denied that he had ever sold a knife, yet the witness, Duncan Campbell, picked the suspect out of a lineup. If Sadler were innocent of the Coles murder, the momentum of circumstantial evidence was quickly building. As if things could not get worse for the hapless sailor, his own estranged wife did him no favors by giving interviews to the press that were enormously prejudicial, like this from the *Liverpool Mercury* of February 20,

1891: "I was married on Thursday, but I knew by Sunday I'd made a mistake, and I'd known it ever since." She added that her husband was a violent drunk and knew intimately every gutter of London. The intervention of Mrs. Sadler caused Dagonet in the *Referee* of February 22, 1891, to express his alarm at what he feared was shaping up to be a miscarriage of justice: "Never, surely, was there a more outrageous attempt to prejudice a case *sub judice* than that made by the newspapers which published the statement of Sadler's wife. The statement was really nothing less than the case for the prosecution."

Sims saw the slimy hand of the home secretary behind the whole business, which was almost certainly wrong. Fearing he was being railroaded by a desperate constabulary, the Stoker's Union paid for a lawyer (H. W. Lawless, appointed by the firm of Wilson and Wallace) to mount a decent defense. Very quickly the damning evidence began to wither. The knife in question turned out to be blunt. His claim that the reason he was covered in blood was due to wounds to *his* face and head—because he had been *twice* assaulted by gangs on the night in question, which turned out to be true. The suspect had even informed a couple of bobbies to this effect fifteen minutes before Coles was killed. At the inquiry Wynne Baxter summed up in favor of the accused, and the jury returned a verdict of death by person or persons unknown.[16] On March 2, 1891, Sadler's solicitors were informed by the director of public prosecutions that all charges were being dropped. As the *Trenton Evening News* reported on March 4, 1891, there had also been quite a turnabout in public opinion, reflecting George Sims' dismay that an innocent man had almost been a scapegoat for the gallows:

SADLER GOES FREE.

When Sadler, the alleged murderer of Carrotty Nell, was discharged from jail on the coroner's finding for lack of evidence, the populace who wanted to lynch him when he was arrested assembled in great crowd and made a hero of him, cheering him loudly. Last night Sadler was on one of his accustomed sprees such as got him into trouble. He held quite a reception in an East End place.

The seaman, backed by the same legal muscle, threatened to sue newspapers that had libeled him as a murderer and, as with Pizer, an out-of-court settlement was reached. The real killer of Frances Coles was never identified. As for Tom Sadler being "Jack the Ripper," the dates of his shore leave were not a match, and then there was this crushing *coup de grace* for CID, as reported on February 18, 1891, in the *Daily Telegraph*: "Probably the only trustworthy description of the assassin was that given by a gentleman who, on the night of the Mitre-square murder, noticed in Duke-street, Aldgate, a couple standing under the lamp at the corner of the passage leading to Mitre-square.... The witness has *confronted the witness and failed to identify him*" (my italics). It is a measure of police desperation that they did not even bother with a lineup; it was just a one-on-one "confrontation" between suspect and witness—and it still failed to yield the desired result.[17] "Jack the Ripper's" latest atrocity had proved to be, from the point of view of law enforcement, a spectacular anti-climax to the entire saga: another sensational murder, another harlot victim, a prime suspect under arrest and yet, within a few weeks, Scotland Yard had absolutely nothing to show for it. The queen's men had humiliation all over their faces and could do nothing but concede defeat. They had arrested a low-life who, when freed from custody, ended up being cheered by the would-be lynch mob. Painful as this all must have been for Macnaghten, he alone of the senior police officers correctly recalled the protracted length of the Ripper investigation; far from being a brief "autumn of terror" it lasted multiple seasons (though his memoirs try to have it both ways by blaming the press for all the fuss):

> At the time, then, of my joining the Force on 1st June 1889, *police* and public *were still agog* over the tragedies of the previous autumn, and were quite ready to believe that any fresh murders, not at once elucidated were by the same maniac's hand. Indeed, I remember— two in 1888, *and one in 1891*—which the Press ascribed to the so-called Jack the Ripper, to whom, at one time or another, *some fourteen murders* were attributed—some before, and some after, his veritable reign of terror in 1888[18] [my italics].

At the very moment the case against sailor Sadler collapsed, the chief constable discreetly pursued another line of inquiry—as he would allude to in 1913 and 1914—one that led back to that loose-lipped politician who had confided in his ten best friends that *he* had closed the case. The chief constable was about to fulfill one of his life's greatest desires: to identify the most notorious figure in the annals of crime. But it would also be the start of a very tough knot he would find very difficult to cut if "Good Old Mac" wanted to keep everyone satisfied—as the solution involved, however tangentially, a friend and colleague in law enforcement.

VIII

A Ghost Laid to Rest

The Member of Parliament who recently declared that Jack the Ripper killed himself ... adheres to his opinion.—The York Herald, 1891

The Whitechapel murderer ... put an end to himself.... Certain facts, pointing to this conclusion, were not in possession of the police till some years after I became a detective officer.—Sir Melville Macnaghten, 1914

In mid–1913 Sir Melville Macnaghten reluctantly stepped down as assistant commissioner of the Criminal Investigation Department due to persistent illness (his 1921 death certificate suggests a form of Parkinson's disease). He had been quite a fixture of the Edwardian era, which was now about a year away from being extinguished by World War I. At the standard farewell press conference Macnaghten somewhat startled the assembled reporters by commenting on the "Jack the Ripper" case of over a generation before—a case with which he had never before been associated in the public mind. Without reservation or qualification, Macnaghten claimed that the case had been solved long ago, although the solution could never be tested in a courtroom. The June 4, 1913, issue of the *Washington Post*, as did many papers on both sides of the Atlantic, zeroed in on this unexpected revelation from an insider who would surely know:

FATE OF JACK THE RIPPER

Retiring British Official Says Once Famous Criminal Committed Suicide

The fact that "Jack the Ripper," the man who terrorized the East End of London by the murder of seven women during 1888, committed suicide, is now confirmed by Sir Melville Macnaughten [sic], head of the criminal investigation department of Scotland Yard, who retired on Saturday after 24 years' service.

Sir Melville says: "It is one of the greatest regrets of my life that 'Jack the Ripper' committed suicide six months before I joined the force. *That remarkable man* was one of the most *fascinating* of criminals. Of course, he was a maniac, but *I have a very clear idea as to who he was* and how he committed suicide, but that, with *other secrets*, will never be revealed by me" [my italics].

What were these "other secrets"? Two days later another American newspaper, the *Pittsburgh Press,* carried the same scoop but with added comments by the assistant commissioner. These further admissions strongly implied that, at Scotland Yard at least, the patrician Macnaghten did as he pleased:

Following out his observation regarding the necessity of the ideal detective "keeping his mouth shut," Macnaughton [sic] *carried into retirement with him knowledge of the identity* of perhaps the greatest criminal of the age, Jack the Ripper, who terrorized Whitechapel in 1888 by the fiendish mutilation and murder of seven women.

"He was a maniac, of course, *but not the man whom the world generally suspected*," said Sir Melville. "He committed suicide six months before I entered the department, and it is the one great regret of my career that I wasn't on the Force when it all happened. *My knowledge* of his identity and the circumstances of his suicide *came to me subsequently*. As no good purpose could be served by publicity, I destroyed before I left Scotland Yard every scrap of paper bearing on the case. *No one else will ever know who the criminal was—nor my reasons for keeping silent*" [my italics].

By 1913 the man whom "the world generally suspected" of being the Ripper was the drowned "Mad Doctor" relentlessly propagated by George Sims. And not only the general population; supposedly all of Scotland Yard and successive home secretaries, asserted Sims, had accepted this as the best solution. Having for many years orchestrated this shilling shocker from behind the scenes (to be examined in subsequent chapters), Macnaghten now publicly and flatly rejected it. The "secret" of the Ripper's identity had, he announced, come only to him, and any relevant documentation had now been destroyed by him in some kind of clearing of the decks. Apparently his successors at CID would not have access to this classified solution, which begs a question that none of the reporters thought to ask: were the high officials *during* Macnaghten's tenure also not privy to this hot information? The retiring chief provided no details, whatsoever, about "Jack" except that he took his own life after the Kelly murder (in other newspapers it was reported that he said this happened in November 1888). Why did Macnaghten call him "remarkable" and "fascinating"? Was it simply because the assassin managed to evade capture by the authorities? Is a multiple murderer so remarkable when he was a stranger to his victims in the era before fingerprint and blood-type identification? Moreover, why did this maniac kill himself and how did the secret of his identity become known to "Mac"? Perhaps the police chief's strangely wistful words about the killer reflected his recollecting some other aspect of the latter's true identity that made him, to "Mac" at least, forever fascinating. The crime writer Hargrave L. Adam was frankly appalled by what Macnaghten's 1913 admission revealed regarding the police chief's rather cavalier attitude towards official records. He recalled his disgust in an article for the *Daily Mail* of May 7, 1930 (in which Adam was defending his own book that accused executed murderer and Polish immigrant George Chapman of having been "Jack"):

> Shortly before he retired, Sir Melville Macnaghten publicly declared that he had possessed papers fixing the identity of Jack-the-Ripper but that he had destroyed them! For this he was severely taken to task by the Press, who asked what right he had to do such a thing. He had no right. Obviously if the police possessed evidence of the identity of this great criminal, whom they had failed to catch, it should have been made known and not destroyed. Again, I submit that Sir Melville only thought the papers fixed the identity. They had no more evidential value probably than a mere bare assertion has.

Sir Melville had been deceased for nearly a decade and yet Adam was still peeved at not being able to crack the former's secret, let alone scrounge a glimpse of the bombshell papers before Macnaghten presumably had them burned. Despite his experience as a writer on crime, H. L. Adam is surprisingly naive about politics and public relations and never, arguably, understood to what extent he was being played by "Good Old Mac." After all, how could the police reveal the name of the fiend without denying due process to the deceased? Whereas *we* know what Macnaghten was concealing from Adam and the rest of the journalists. He had, in fact, not destroyed either an official record that named his chief suspect or an unofficial version of the same document that he kept in his private archive. Apart from being deceitful, I think that Macnaghten was signaling that the investigation of this suspect was done by him alone, posthumously and unofficially. Therefore any documentation resulting from it was his property and not the Yard's. It was his to keep or burn. The retiring chief was actually, I think, rhetorically telegraphing a measure of reassurance to the surviving family members of the murderer, that their secret—which had become his possession, too—would exit with his retirement. Nothing to embarrass them would be left behind. If so, we know that Macnaghten was misleading the family (or families) about what remained, as he *had* committed their member's name to the file as a Ripper suspect, although this document was totally unknown until 1966. Putting to one side whether any documents were destroyed, it could be said that the family's secret belief was protected for over half a century. A handful of books rolled out over that time about the murders, but not one came close to discovering the identity of Macnaghten's suspect, their skeptical authors even debunking this solution as nothing but a myth (see Chapter XVI). Thus, perhaps everyone was satisfied for long enough.

We should thank the affronted H. L. Adam for reportedly convincing Macnaghten to write his memoirs, after denying at that 1913 conference that he intended to do any such thing (unless that was another discreet dodge and he was already drafting his book). In those reminiscences of the following year, Sir Melville Macnaghten gave his chapter on the Whitechapel murders an evocatively supernatural title, as if it were a short story by Eton Provost and gothic spellbinder M. R. James:

LAYING THE GHOST OF JACK THE RIPPER

The author means laying *to rest*. From the relative safety of retirement the ex–police chief admitted in that chapter, starting with the very title, something quite revelatory that was ignored in 1914 and by most writers on this subject ever since (Paul Begg is an exception). "Jack" had been a phantom that had haunted Scotland Yard after he had died because authorities were totally unaware that he had self-destructed. The tragic suicide who Macnaghten believed was the Ripper finally came to police attention—or rather his attention—a considerably long time after the barbarism done to Mary Jane Kelly in the early hours of November 9, 1888: "Although, as I shall endeavor to show in this chapter, the Whitechapel murderer, in all probability, put an end to himself *soon after* the Dorset Street affair in November 1888, certain *facts*, pointing to this *conclusion*, were not in possession of the police till *some years after* I became a detective officer"[1] (my italics).

Unfortunately the police chief shares precious few of the specifics of his chosen suspect, at least not in a straightforward manner, and that was his intention: to "draw a veil" over much of his Ripper solution.[2] Consequently his opaque portrait of the likely suspect in "Laying the Ghost of Jack the Ripper" is a candy confection of admissions and omissions, restraint and hyperbole, ambiguous hints and discreet deflections, fact and fiction—as if we attended a Scotland Yard press conference only to be briefed by the Cheshire Cat. This is because Macnaghten and George Sims went to great lengths to keep their secret knowledge of the murderer's particulars versus the public hustle of the "Mad Doctor" carefully compartmentalized from each other. Here in the April 5, 1903, issue of the *Referee* is George Sims' version of Macnaghten's private and posthumous investigation of "some years after," but backdated in "Mustard and Cress" to 1888: "A little more than a month later the body of the man suspected by the chiefs at the Yard, and by *his own friends, who were in communication with the Yard*, was found in the Thames. The body had been in the water about a month" (my italics). Chapter XIII will prove that the anomic "friends" deliberately stand in for the killer's family (while the "Yard" actually refers to just Macnaghten).

In another source, from the Edwardian 1900s, Sims claims that the police already knew the true identity of the fiend *before* conferring with the worried and suspicious pals. If true, who was Macnaghten's source of "private information" that led him to this posthumous suspect—one who could never be questioned, arrested or charged, yet once Macnaghten had gathered "certain facts" inexorably led him to a conclusion that this man was "in all probability" the Whitechapel killer? The likely answer is to be found in a tiny though indispensible primary source so vital it is no exaggeration to characterize it as the Rosetta Stone of the whole subject. Stumbled upon exactly one hundred years and one month later (by veteran Whitechapel researcher Keith Skinner), here is the February 11, 1891, edition of the *Bristol Times and Mirror*:

OUR LONDON LETTER

I give a curious story for what it is worth. There is a West of England member who *in private declares that he has solved* the mystery of "Jack the Ripper." His theory—and he repeats it with so much emphasis that it might almost be called *his doctrine*—is that "Jack the Ripper" committed suicide on the night of his last murder. I can't give details, *for fear of a libel action*; but the story is so circumstantial that a good many people believe it. He states that a man with blood-stained clothes *committed suicide* on the night of the last murder, and he asserts that the man was the *son of a surgeon*, who suffered from homicidal mania. I do not know what the police think of the story, but I believe that before long a clean breast will be made, and that the accusation will be sifted thoroughly[3] [my italics].

The timing of the article, early 1891, dovetails perfectly with what Macnaghten would write in 1914 about the solution not being known until "till some years after," as does the article's implication that the police had never heard of this suspect. It has hardly registered with previous researchers that the ex-chief in his "Laying the Ghost…" chapter almost nonchalantly *extends* the gap between the timing of the Millers Ct. atrocity and the suicide of "Jack" to twenty-four, even seventy-two hours; most definitely not "on the night of the last murder," and furthermore hints—"on or about"—that it might be longer. As we will see, Macnaghten's account of 1914 cleaves closer to the factual timeline of his chief suspect than does the 1891 Ur-source article. This M.P.'s influence, nonetheless, on this subject cannot be overestimated, and yet he quickly faded into the fog, his existence as the likely missing link between the real Ripper and Macnaghten totally unknown until 1991 (and not identified by name until 2008).

The Bristol Times and Mirror is just the tip of what must be a Titanic-busting iceberg. By itself the "son of a surgeon" article raises many tantalizing questions, one of which is why, since the dead cannot be libeled, the reporter is so wary about being sued. His candid caution can only be explained by his trepidation that the *living* would bring a suit of libel, in this case presumably the surgeon father's other heirs, about whom it might be uncharitably thought that they knew of their member's dual identity and yet had done nothing. How would the newspaper defend itself in court? How could they prove that this man was "Jack," let alone that his relations knew and were accessories after the fact, if the police had never even heard of this suspect? They could call the M.P. to testify in their defense about his "doctrine," but what would his certainty be worth, legally speaking?

So menacing was this possibility of a libel action that the *Pall Mall Gazette*, of the same day, altered the tiny article to remove both the reporter's sideways glance at the potential for slander and the identifying detail about the murderer being a doctor's son. This had the effect of making it incomprehensible as to whether it was the son or the father who suffered from "homicidal mania." We see this nervousness repeated the day after the murder of Frances Coles, on February 13, 1891, a crime that, of course, seemed to decisively discredit this politician-turned-Sherlock, in the *Sheffield and Rotherham Independent*: "NOT SO LIKELY NOW." *Lloyds Weekly* newspaper, coming late to the party, ran with the same altered version of the "West of England" M.P. article on February 22, 1891, framed by the dismissive title "REMARKABLE FICTION." Were they being ironic about what they had done to emasculate this potential breakthrough, or were they making the same point as the newspaper above—that the Coles murder had disproven the politician's solution? Whereas back on the day the story broke, the *Edinburgh Evening News* in Scotland, though abbreviating an already brief article, proved to be more forthright and fearless:

> IS "JACK THE RIPPER" DEAD?
>
> A West of England M.P. thinks he has solved the mystery of "Jack-the-Ripper." His theory is that "Jack" committed suicide on the night of the last outrage. He gives a very circumstantial account of a man with blood-stained clothes, who committed suicide on the night of the last murder, and asserts that the man was the son of a surgeon who suffered from homicidal mania.

It is unlikely that Melville Macnaghten was initially aware of this alleged scoop, or would have thought much of it if he had, as the press often ran with far-fetched rumors, tall tales picked up in public houses, and even outright lies they made up about "Jack the Ripper" in order to keep milking this cash cow. Neither the name of the politician nor that of the deceased "suspect" was mentioned, so it was difficult for Scotland Yard to investigate. The senior police administrator with, uniquely, just the right combination of establishment credentials and insider connections to effect such an inquiry was at that moment heading the hunt for the murderer of Frances Coles—initially presumed to be "Jack the Ripper." On February 18, 1891, the very day that it was reported that the (unnamed) Joseph Lawende was failing to identify Ripper suspect Tom Sadler in their "confrontation," the "West of England" M.P., so far still unnamed, resurfaced in the press, this time talking directly to a journalist. This was covered, again only briefly, in regional papers such as the *York Herald* and the *Yorkshire Herald*:

> The member of Parliament, who recently declared that "Jack the Ripper" had killed himself on the evening of the last murder, adheres to his opinion. Even assuming that the man Saddler [*sic*] is able to prove his innocence of the murder of Frances Coles, he maintains that the latest crime cannot be the work of the author of the previous series of atrocities, and this view of the matter is steadily growing among those who do not see that

there is any good reason to suppose that "Jack the Ripper" is dead. So far as Saddler is concerned, there is a strong feeling that the evidence will have to be very much strengthened against him by next Tuesday, if he is to be committed for trial. His manner in the Thames Police-court was consistent with any theory.[4]

Despite another Whitechapel harlot being cut down, whether by Tom Sadler or not, the politician was reportedly immovable about the real "Jack" being a man who took his own life, and did so the same evening as he killed Alice McKenzie in 1889 (or did he mean all the way back to Mary Jane Kelly in 1888?); therefore according to him the Frances Coles murder was definitely not by the same hand. For all the skepticism expressed by Scotland Yard in this second article, the M.P. was anticipating what would become the majority Scotland Yard opinion (including the idea that Kelly was the last victim of "Jack").

As the case against Tom Sadler imploded, it might have been expected that the press would have returned to the "West of England" member, especially as a faction of the police did not believe that Coles' death was a "Jack" murder. Instead the "curious story" went cold, almost as if it had never existed. I believe that at some point during the investigation of the rough sailor, as he paced in his cell and cursed his wife, Macnaghten went off by himself—as he often did—on a quest to track down this loose-lipped politician and nail down this allegation. He probably set off assuming he would quickly discover that this "doctrine" by an investigative amateur was, to be blunt, quite worthless; the product perhaps of family's or neighbor's hysteria—mutating like the malicious gossip that had swirled around the insane medical student John Sanders in 1888. Macnaghten's sensitive political antennae may have been throbbing at the painful thought of this potential embarrassment for the Yard—especially if nothing came of Sadler's arrest—if a Liberal or Tory politician kept shooting off his mouth about a solution that the police had missed, that was really no solution at all. The chief constable of CID would be seeking, under the radar, to expose this "doctrine" as without merit and firmly shut it down; to stop it from being another stick with which the legion of armchair critics could wield against his beloved Force and his boys.

It would hardly have been a taxing inquiry for the Scotland Yard chief. He need only have quietly checked among his long-established friends and acquaintances in the Tory party—then the incumbent government—in the corridors of Whitehall and the exclusive clubs in which the chief constable's appearance would not cause a single eyebrow to rise, as "Good Old Mac" was a fellow member. A few chats with the chaps over cigars and brandy—Macnaghten favored the pipe after what had happened at school—would no doubt quickly have led the senior policeman to a Conservative backbencher who represented the constituency of West Dorset.

The aristocratic Henry Richard Farquharson, as we know from an 1892 primary source (see Chapter XII), was the "West of England" member and, in former years, lived just a few miles from the man who moved to London and became *in all probability* the Ripper. One can imagine "Old Mac's" relief that the "West of England" M.P. was Farquharson because, quite apart from being a fellow upper-crust gentleman, an Anglican, a Conservative, and a Far East plantation owner, the source of this posthumous claim about a surgeon's son being "Jack" was also, thank God, an Old Etonian! Macnaghten nostalgically—if a little cultishly—describes the importance of this mutual antecedent in his memoirs: "There are in this world no friends like old friends, and no old friends quite like old Eton friends."

Four years later Henry Richard Farquharson, aged only 37, died of natural causes while voyaging home from Ceylon. His obituary from the *London Times* on April 22, 1895, mentions nothing about his having solved the Ripper mystery, or about his claiming to have done so. That "curious story" has vanished forever into the ether. But the obituary does mention an unsavory episode that may have somewhat retarded Farquharson's political career: "It will be remembered that after the last general election Mr. C. T. Gatty, his Gladstonian opponent, son of Dr. Gatty, the Vicar of Eccelsfield, brought an action for libel against Mr. Farquharson in regard to certain statements made to his prejudice in the heat of the contest." Farquharson lost the libel case to the tune of 5,000 pounds (later reduced to half that amount on appeal). The M.P. was also a breeder of prize-winning Newfoundland dogs, though local records in Dorset show that a "terrible mistake" by his dog handlers—allowing two sets of dogs to come into a "catastrophic" collision—resulted in 45 of his prized canines having to be destroyed, reportedly nearly along with their keepers: "The two kennel lads were almost killed as well—not by the dogs but by Farquharson who had a remarkably quick temper."⁵

Ripper "Rosetta Stone"—An 1886 sketch of Henry Richard Farquharson, the member of Parliament for West Dorset. Farquharson was a Tory, an Old Etonian, a near neighbor of the Druitt clan, and Sir Melville Macnaghten's initial likely source of "private information" regarding his "curious story" about a surgeon's son, before he conferred with Colonel Vivian Majendie.

In 1892 Henry Farquharson was handily reelected but was plunged into this ugly libel suit by the man he defeated. The hostile press was riveted on Farquharson. Although he lost the case, the truth is somewhat more complicated, and paints a picture of Farquharson as a bit of a political naïf, not necessarily a vicious, bare-knuckle campaigner, however much he brutalized his employees. A tenant on one of the MP's estates informed him that his opponent, Gatty, had been expelled from an exclusive private boys' school, Charterhouse, for "some schoolboy's act of immorality" (*Aberdeen Weekly Journal*, June 17, 1892), and he had used this in the campaign to ruthlessly smear his opponent. In an effective defense in court, Farquharson's lawyers countered that their client was only guilty of indiscreetly telling some of his toff cronies about the allegation. The affronted Liberal had written to his Tory opponent to disavow the story—and the latter had agreeably complied. Far from being embarrassed or trying to bury the slander, it was Gatty who exploited the issue to try to whip up sympathy from voters by distributing handbills with copies of the correspondence. As the *Birmingham Daily Post* of June 20, 1892, reported: "Throughout this contest Mr. Gatty had sought to make political capital out of this personal matter and kept it in the front; while on the other hand, Mr. Farquharson deprecated the subject altogether, and asked the electors to let the election turn on Home Rule."

Even more devastatingly, the headmaster of Charterhouse, Dr. Haig Brown, testified (from documentation) as to why exactly Mr. Gatty left the school: "He was removed by the head master for an offence against purity. Mr. Gatty was then a boy of thirteen. There was a boy at the school then named Lyne, a brother of Mr. Lyne, later known as Father Ignatius, and then Brother Ignatius. Young Gatty had applied to Brother Ignatius, as he was in difficulty, and made a statement to him. Brother Ignatius communicated with witness, who wrote to Gatty's father, and the boy was taken away. He was not expelled." For Gatty it was a spectacular "own goal." According to the headmaster's impeccable records, Gatty had been the victim of the younger brother of a schoolmaster. Rather than subject Charterhouse to scandal, the victimized student was moved on for his own "protection." Though he had not been expelled, the case against Farquharson was faltering. The chief justice, a Liberal grandee, came to the partisan rescue on behalf of Gatty: "The Lord Chief Justice said *everyone knew what went on at public schools*, and any man with a spark of decency would not have referred to it. Yet Mr. Gatty was dragged to the stake for what happened thirty years ago" (my italics). Had he been in court Macnaghten would presumably have cried foul at such revolting slander, for surely the chief justice was not including Eton? Yes, he most certainly was, as Coleridge used Farquharson's own status as an Old Boy against him, heavily implying that where these elite boys' schools were concerned, there was plenty of *that* kind of sordid shenanigans to go around:

> Unfortunately, this was not a solitary case of *what went on at public schools, and Mr. Farquharson must have known it*. ... The Lord Chief Justice said there was a great difference between a boy being taken away by his father and being sent away. There were men justly honoured and trusted whose fathers had taken them away from public schools [my italics].

After this bit of demagoguery from the bench, the crowd predictably applauded as the judge made a show of pretending to be offended: "Stop, stop; this is a court of justice and not a stage play." And so a toff had told another toff a secret about yet another toff that was essentially accurate but had not been verified in its core details.

Another surviving source shows that Henry Farquharson might have believed in deliberately mixing fact and fiction, depending on the situation and context. A neighbor of the M.P., General Pitt-Rivers, was a renowned archaeologist. A Roman coin was found and in an exchange of letters Farquharson tried, on September 5, 1892, to be helpful—and managed to put his proverbial foot in it again: "You ought to write a short magazine article on it, not referring to your discoveries but based on them, a little fiction mixed in, on which to base your tale. A Briton at Rotherly making love to a girl at Woodcuts." Farquharson was not advocating full-blown deceit. He was simply trying to advise Pitt-Rivers how he might drum up publicity for his diggings by writing a piece in a long-standing literary genre: the historical romance. It was promptly rejected with haughty disapproval. A mortified Farquharson tried to make amends with words that arguably apply to his Ripper "doctrine": "History, religious thought, & other serious matters have come to be more popular *when dressed in fiction*"[6] (my italics).

Back in late February 1891 Melville Macnaghten probably met with Henry Farquharson in an exclusive gentleman's club and asked him, on the quiet, about his "strange story." It may have come as a profound shock to Macnaghten when Farquharson said the name "Druitt." The chief constable's close chum and colleague—seconded to the Home Office—Colonel Vivian Majendie had been, since 1871, Her Majesty's counter-terrorist and munitions czar. Much admired for his nerves of steel at disarming Fenian bombs, the colonel had a first cousin named Maria Elizabeth Hill (née DeBoulay) whose daughter, Isabel Majendie Hill, had married a Dorset clergyman named Charles Druitt. This cleric's first cousin was a Montague Druitt, by then deceased. Cousins, once or twice removed at that, are not necessarily close, but the colonel was a certified big shot towards whom every relation would have naturally gravitated. Rendered a widower early in his marital life, with two young children to rear, it is a fair assumption that the ladies of his clan would have helped out their celebrated relation. Consider also that Charles' wife had retained the Majendie name, and that one of Isabel's first cousins was even named after Vivian.[7] Tangible evidence of the colonel's association with members of his extended family is to be found in the *Bath Chronicle* of April 12, 1888. It records Vivian Majendie attending the wedding of Alfred Henry Evans and Isabel Aimee Houssemayne DuBoulay (Isabel Druitt's first cousin). A. H. Evans was an Oxford graduate and later an assistant master at Winchester College. While at university he had played an exhibition match of cricket alongside Montague Druitt (a graduate of both Winchester and Oxford) in May 1880. Even stronger proof of Colonel Majendie's being quite familiar with the Druitt wing of his clan is to be found in the *Hampshire Advertiser* of September 13, 1884:

> The adjourned inquest on the body of the youth Harry Gray, killed by the explosion of a "rocket distress signal," on board a steamer at Bournemouth, was held at the Bijou Hall, Bournemouth on Thursday, before Mr. J. Druitt [Senior] Coroner. Colonel Majendie, Her Majesty's Inspector of Explosives was present.... [Majendie] explained the construction and mechanism of these signals.... In reply to a question of the Coroner, Colonel Majendie said that in the course of his inquiry he thought it necessary that he should take one of the signals from the box on board the steamer and examine it.... [The jury] returned a verdict of "Death from misadventure."

The Druitt mentioned above was a local politician in Dorset and the uncle of Farquharson's "Jack." With his encyclopedia-like, mind did "Mac" also recall the colonel mentioning a few years back at one of their regular dinners a tragedy concerning that side of his family around the time of a marriage: his cousin's son-in-law suffering the loss of *his* own cousin as an inexplicable suicide in the Thames? My God! Was this *the same man*, this "M. J. Druitt"—barrister, teacher and cricketer? With his penchant for public relations, it is hard to imagine that Macnaghten would not have considered the tabloid implications of such a connection; a Ripper who could be linked by the Fleet Street vultures however distantly, irrelevantly and unfairly with law enforcement. Farquharson was likely aware of the familial connection between the Druitts and the Majendie clans, the very reason he had carefully altered some of the data when proselytizing his "doctrine"—just to be on the safe side. In the fictional version of the story as later created by a Sims protégé in 1905, the Druitt figure, Mortemer Slade, has no brothers and sisters—only "cousins" who are horrified at his dual identity (this source, another of the "smoking guns" in favor of the Dorset solution, is thoroughly examined in Chapter XIV).

VIII. A Ghost Laid to Rest

Born in 1836, the son of Major John Routledge Majendie, an Old Etonian (and himself the son of Henry Majendie, the bishop of Chester and Bangor), Vivian Dering Majendie was the scion of a noble family. Educated at Leamington College and the Royal Artillery Academy in Woolwich, he entered the Royal Artillery in 1851. Sir Vivian served with great courage and distinction at Sevastapol in the Crimean War, while during the Indian Mutiny of 1857 he liberated besieged Lucknow. He was also a writer of treatises on ammunition and explosives, and for the popular press. When he died, not from being blown up in the line of duty but quite mundanely of heart failure in April 1898, he was universally praised by the Commonwealth media, including the *Evening Post* (vol. 55, no. 149, June 25, 1898), which wrote that he was in "private life ... exceedingly popular. Of deep religious convictions, his non-professional life was devoted to good works." He was just as fulsomely celebrated in the *Colonist* (vol. 40, no. 9199, June 16, 1898):

> Colonel Sir Vivian Majendie, Inspector of Explosives to the Home Office, who was on a visit to his sister at Oxford, died suddenly on a recent Sunday night.... It fell to his lot during the last quarter of a century to examine and report upon all kinds of bombs, infernal machines, and explosives found by the police in the pursuit of their vocation. In doing so he ran innumerable risks with the utmost coolness and bravery. It is said of him that he carried an india-rubber bag full of nitroglycerine, found in the lodgings of a Fenian, in a four-wheel cab to Woolwich, and that on this occasion he warned the driver not to collide with any other vehicle on the way, else "he might hear no more about it." When the cloak room at Victoria Station had been blown up, he opened a clockwork internal machine which was working at the time, and might have exploded and killed him at any moment. Colonel Majendie was knighted in 1895.

In chapter 7 of Macnaghten's memoir, "Bombs and Their Makers," he describes a couple of atrocities though in a very jovial spirit. For example, he mentions the "crack-brained enthusiast" who blew himself up instead of the London Observatory (and who was the inspiration for Joseph Conrad's *The Secret Agent*): "So violent was the explosion that one of his fingers was found lying under the Observatory wall—so have I seen a bail fly off at cricket in the direction of long leg!" Less tastelessly he recalls a suspicious parcel left under the seat of a London omnibus by its mysterious owner—who spoke with an Irish-American accent. An alert conductor had fearfully carried it to the nearest police station, where it was submerged for hours in water. Macnaghten arrived to discover that the soggy gunk oozing from the suspected bomb was nothing more than harmless figs! In the same chapter, he makes his one and only mention of his friend and fellow crime-fighter who was, we know now, related (by a once-removed cousin's marriage) to Farquharson's suspect:

> At this time the Chief Inspector of Explosives was Sir Vivian Majendie, one of the most delightful personalities I have ever come across, and a very loyal friend. He loved work and he loved play, and all kinds of sport delighted him. No day was too hot for him at Lord's, no night was too long for him at the National Sporting Club. He it was who, supping one Sunday night with a favourite niece, began talking about the Sayers and Heenan fight [a boxing match] when he entered her house at 7:45, and when he left at 10:40 the same subject was still on the anvil of his discussion.[8]

It is odd that a close friend and colleague in defending the realm who was everything Macnaghten worshipped in a manly man—"firm as a rock" against the Indian mutineers;

"cool as an iceberg" in disarming explosives—is fobbed off with such a minuscule and unmemorable cameo. Majendie's cousin's son-in-law, Vicar Charles Druitt, will loom large in this story of various people trying to reveal the essentials about the Ripper's identity, yet keeping the real families involved safely submerged.

IX

SCION OF THE BOURGEOISIE

An excessive indulgence in vice leads ... to a craving for blood. Nero was probably a sexual maniac. ... As you walk in the London streets you may, and do, not infrequently jostle against a potential murderer of the so-called Jack the Ripper type.— Sir Melville Macnaghten, 1914

The first person to speak with authority with whom I discussed the matter was Sir Melville Macnaghten.... He was very confident that the Ripper was the scion of a noble family.—The Daily Mail, 1930

Montague John Druitt, known as "Montie" in the family, was born on August 15, 1857, in Wimborne, Dorset. The great writer Thomas Hardy had lived in Wimborne Minster, turning it into "Warborne" in his works of the 1880s (he may have been known to the Druitts when young). Though it may not have any bearing on the capacity of a murderer to be able to swiftly mutilate his victims and remove a specific organ, Montie Druitt really was the "son of a surgeon." Dr. William Druitt, Sr., had been Wimborne's leading surgeon, a justice of the peace, a member of the Anglican Church Governing Body and a governor of the local grammar school (that had been founded by Henry VII's mother), and a fellow of the Royal College of Surgeons and the London Society of Apothecaries. He was, predictably, a member of the Conservative Party, and he married a local girl, Anne, ten years his junior, who bore him seven children; Montague was the second son. The Druitts were a prosperous Victorian success story, the proof being that they occupied the largest house in the town, complete with

Young Montie—**In this never-before-published photograph of the suspect in a school football uniform, a strong and athletic Montague Druitt, aged 18, reclines against a wall in 1875 (courtesy Warden and Scholars of Winchester College).**

two cottages for servants and stables.¹ Montague grew up a diligent student and a promising athlete. At 13 he won a scholarship to Winchester College (making him a Wykehamist) and for six years he was active in sports, debating and theatre. He won a literary prize and, for what it is worth, a pan for his performance as Sir Toby Belch in *Twelfth Night*—"But of the inadequacy of Druitt as Sir Toby, what are we to say? It can be better imagined than described."² He enjoyed greater success in cricket, as the opening bowler for the First Eleven, and he was a champion at Fives (a game, it is worth noting, that required strength and dexterity in the hands). The records of the school's debating society show that Montie was elected treasurer, and in his final year was elected prefect of chapel, a very prestigious position at Winchester.

The school pictures of Montague show a gawky adolescent growing into a broad-shouldered, handsome, aquiline-faced young man, with hooded eyes and a noble forehead framing a prominent Romanesque nose above the smudge of a square-cut, fair moustache. In other pictures he appears to be of medium build and height. The unchanging feature of his appearance is that he parted his straight hair in the dead center, and presumably did so until the day he killed himself. In 1876, Montague John Druitt was awarded a scholarship to New College, Oxford (becoming an Oxonian), to study for a bachelor of arts degree majoring in the classics. His glaring underachievement at university in managing only a third class degree is the first discordant note we can detect marring Montie Druitt's irresistible rise through the bourgeois elite (though lousy grades did not prevent him being elected steward of the Common Room).³ Perhaps attracted by the sporting opportunities in 1880, Montague Druitt applied to be an assistant master at a public (i.e., a private) boys' school in Blackheath—which in a very modern touch had a swimming pool. The school at 9 Eliot Place was run by George Valentine, born in Bombay to an affluent missionary father. There were about 38 boarders ranging in age from nine to 17, and each boy had his own partitioned section of the large communal bedroom. Though it could boast hardly more students than a single, over-sized classroom, it was a boarding school preparing its clients, reportedly with great efficiency, for the professions and the universities. For a time George Valentine lived at the school with two assistant masters (Druitt and Mark Mann), along with ten domestic staff (including a matron named Mrs. Sims, who was no relation to the famous writer).⁴ Druitt seems to have been in need of a job after the setback of his less-than-stellar degree (perhaps he played too much sport at Oxford).

While being a teacher, presumably of sports and classics, he also trained for the bar. This became, from 1885, his principal vocation and source of revenue, despite still lodging at the school, as his teaching service must have inevitably become minimal (the 1889 press reports of his death headline him as a tragic *barrister*, not schoolmaster). He was also a prominent member of local sporting clubs—very much a young man from the country on the up-and-up in the big city. From 1886 Valentine no longer lived on the premises, and possibly Druitt was in charge during the day, or possibly sometimes as night warden. Locally, Montie was socially active as secretary of the Morden Cricket Club, as well as being honorary secretary of the Blackheath Cricket, Football and Lawn Tennis Club.⁵ Soon after he became a special pleader—a defense lawyer who did not have the status of a barrister yet—and worked cases for the Western Circuit. He had expenses to meet: £500 was borrowed from his father to set up his chambers, while he paid Valentine to lodge at the school. The Law Lists show that Montague Druitt's chambers were in the City at 9 King's Bench Walk, within walking distance of the East End. As a special pleader, Druitt was involved mostly in civil cases, but as we will see his practice began to expand into a case of violent crime too.

Killer or not, he knew tragedy in his own life. On September 27, 1885, Montie's surgeon father died of a coronary, and three years later, in July, on the very eve of the first "Jack" murder of Polly Nichols, his mother developed a serious delusional illness and was placed in Brook asylum in Clapton, London. She would spend the rest of her life in care, dying of natural causes on December 15, 1890 (she died in Manor House Asylum in the same suburb where her Montie's body washed up in the nearby river: Chiswick).[6] Mr. M. J. Druitt was an effective advocate, as can be seen by the coverage of one of his civil cases in the May 23, 1886, issue of *Lloyds Weekly Newspaper*. In the Middlesex sheriff's court, Red Lion square, M. J. Druitt appeared successfully on behalf of Miss Marion Mildon, a lady's maid in the service of a titled family near Selborne, who was suing her deadbeat fiancé, a draper's assistant in a neighboring town. Druitt smoothly won over the courtroom by winning sympathy for his young and attractive client and making a laughing stock of the defendant by having his effusive love letters introduced as evidence. The jury awarded costs to his client. (It helps when the defendant is a no-show and has no legal representation.)

Another, much tougher case was conducted by Druitt at the Central Criminal Court (Old Bailey). He was the single counsel up against a very experienced prosecutor who rarely lost, and as this was September 1888, Druitt—it was later believed—was also terrorizing London in his off-duty hours as a multiple murderer. By day he defended Christopher Power who had "maliciously wounded" a friend, Peter Black, in the latter's home. The circumstances were not in dispute; Power was guilty. The only question was whether Druitt could win a verdict like the poet who tried to shoot Her Majesty— "guilty but insane." If Druitt knew himself to be a cool criminal (except in the climactic moments when he indulged his savage urges), it might have amused him to think that the court—as with the public in general—could be so easily misled by a scary character or a creepy face; that a madman must *appear* to be mad. It was a useful cliché that saved his client's life and, in a quantum leap, advanced his career. Yet Montie could secretly muse that the jurors were being persuaded by a handsome, articulate, educated gentleman, who represented all that was good and true about British civilization, and who secretly enjoyed a hobby that would shock them to their very marrows.

As for a document *by* Montague Druitt, only a couple of completely innocuous letters remain in a West Sussex archive. One is to his uncle, Robert—a surgeon—written on September 16, 1876. Montie, still at New College, Oxford, seems to have helpfully proofed a piece of Latin translation for his uncle's daughter, Katherine (nicknamed Kitty). The letter is addressed to "Dear Uncle Robert" and signed "With affect. Nephew M. J. Druitt": "It is evident that Kitty has a sound knowledge of grammar rules, but does not know that the idioms of the two languages are so different.... I was sorry to hear that you were not so well again and hope you will soon be better. I am afraid Emily and Kitty had a very dull time of it at Wimborne; an attempt of ours to make it less so was met by the assurance of their hostess that she should take care of her own guests herself! I hope you will be able at some time to see me for a day or two in Oxford; I hope very soon to earn something independently." As for his personality, as in what Montie Druitt was actually like to meet, to converse with or to play a game of cricket with, there is nothing except, perhaps, a short story by George Sims published in 1897. He was clearly exploiting the Druitt tragedy, because "The Helsham Mystery," starring his female detective Dorcas Dene, concerns a young aristocrat who has vanished and is believed to have drowned, while his nearest and dearest are frantic with worry (and fear exposure if they go to the cops). Though the titular character of the story is not a murderer, the description of the absented nobleman may echo the tragic barrister: "He was a most lovable and amiable young fellow—highly strung, and sensitive to a degree—romantic undoubtedly, but the soul of honour."

That Lord Helsham is possibly a cameo portrait of Montague Druitt is backed up by this article by an F. W. Memory in the *Daily Mail* of May 3, 1930, in which he mentions once having conferred with the (by then) deceased Macnaghten about the Ripper case: "The first person to speak with authority with which I discussed the matter was Sir Melville Macnaghten.... He was very confident that the Ripper was the *scion of a noble family*" (my italics). Furthermore, the 1905 "Jack the Ripper" serial by Guy Logan, a Sims crony, which fictionalizes the Druitt tale for tabloid readers (to be examined in depth in Chapter XIV), has the Dorset clan relocated from the southwest of England to Yorkshire in the far north and, sure enough, upped to the ranks of the nobility. One more court case shows Druitt's skill and hardly presages a melancholic suicide. On November 29, 1888, the *London Times* covered a civil matter that ended with a not-insignificant victory for the Dorset branch of the Conservative Party. William Druitt and his Bournemouth firm had been retained by the Conservative Party in a dispute over a negated vote, by one of their supporters, in Christchurch, Dorset. It centered on the claim that a Tory could not have his vote counted because he did not pay enough local rates to qualify for the franchise (there were still arcane property and financial qualifications to enjoy the right to vote, until 1928). Having lost his appeal in the local court, Montague Druitt was arguing that the decision was unjust; that his client had met the rate-paying requirements. The very same chief justice, Lord Coleridge, who would later give the hapless Henry Farquharson such a hard time over the Gatty slander, was impressed enough by Mr. M. J. Druitt's nimble advocacy to reverse the decision of a lower court: "Mr. M. J. Druitt appeared for the appellants and argued on their behalf that both were entitled to be registered, not, indeed, for a 'dwellinghouse,' but for a house or 'tenement,' if the value is sufficient." Montie Druitt had worked diligently on this attention-getting case from October 1 until late November 1888. If he was "Jack," he had killed and eviscerated Mary Jane Kelly on the morning of November 9 and, perhaps, had also failed to kill "Dark Sarah" on November 21. On the following Friday this most prestigious of newspapers had mentioned his triumph—and his name—and within a couple of days he had drowned himself in the River Thames. How did Druitt fit in the various lives he seems to have led? For that matter, did Macnaghten make a thorough check of the dates and times to make sure that he was not merely imagining that Montie was "Jack"? Sims would claim that, yes, he did, in the *Referee* of July 13, 1902. After Dagonet muses about the police trying to identify a murder victim in a different case, he compares this faltering investigation to

[a] process of exhaustion which enabled them at last to know the real name and address of Jack the Ripper. In that case they had reduced the only possible Jacks to seven, then by a further exhaustive inquiry to three, and were about to fit these three people's movements in with the dates of the various murders when the one and only genuine Jack saved further trouble by being found drowned in the Thames, into which he had flung himself, a raving lunatic, after the last and most appalling mutilation of the whole series.

The window of opportunity for Druitt to kill the five victims was relatively narrow, but not too narrow for the busy barrister to have had enough time to kill in the East End and then attend his cricket matches—and who among his peers would guess he had ever been, just hours before, anywhere near that cesspit? After murdering Polly Nichols early on the morning of August 31, 1888, Druitt had, for example, thirty hours to next be seen playing a match in Dorset (the train trip was barely three hours). After Chapman was dispatched, the athletic professional had four hours to walk the six miles back to Blackheath and show up ready to bat and bowl at 11:30 a.m. for a match in the same suburb. We are not sure if he appeared in a West Country court on October 1, 1888, after murdering both Stride and Eddowes the morning before but, again, he had a day and a night to get there. We do not know his movements on November 9, 1888, the day Mary Jane Kelly was killed.[7]

Back at that postulated clubby meeting between the aristocratic politician and the upper class police chief, it must have been a vertigo-inducing experience for Macnaghten as Farquharson began to describe a Ripper who could easily have pulled up a chair in their elite club and joined the pair of them for a drink and a smoke. To discover that the "Terror of London" was a tutor of boys and a talented athlete must have caused Macnaghten to feel he was back in fifth form being set up for a prank by "Farquy" and the other Oppidans. Here were two of the chief constable's greatest passions perversely reflected in the murderer onto whom the police chief had projected so much of his hopes—to make a name for himself as a sleuth by catching "Jack the Ripper." A teacher and a cricketer! If "Jack" ended up in Tussaud's, would his waxen facsimile be attired in his cricket whites, a bat in one hand and his father's scalpel in the other? There must have been some consolation that at least he was not an Old Etonian. Whether he took Farquharson's solution seriously or not, the chief constable would have counseled the M.P. to stop talking to the press, as it would be extremely embarrassing for Colonel Vivian Majendie—and for himself at the next election—if the Liberal swill could jest that "Jack the Ripper" had voted for Farquharson. No doubt Farquharson agreed to close ranks to protect the reputation of one of their own, as there was no further contribution by him in the surviving record about the matter.

At this conjectured one-on-one, there were pressing reasons for Macnaghten not to want to believe the M.P.: firstly, it would mean that he had missed catching the fiend, and secondly, it was an institutionally embarrassing resolution for Scotland Yard—they had been fruitlessly chasing a phantom for over two years. What a potential public relations debacle, perfectly capping off the previous ones. Even more acutely painful was that this deranged barrister was distantly related to a Victorian superhero, Colonel Majendie, and such a notorious connection could only soil his name and that of his clan, however unjustly.

How, precisely, did Henry Farquharson learn of the Druitt family's terrible secret about their deceased Montie? Almost certainly because of partisan proximity; the M.P. was a mere nine miles down the road at Tarrant Gunville from Wimborne-Minster, and, more to the point, as a Tory worthy he moved in the same political circles as the Druitts (Montie had an uncle, James Druitt, Sr., who was a local Conservative mayor). It is likely that the secret leaked along the local Tory grapevine. Alternatively, a member of the Druitt clan may have approached Henry Farquharson to take out some kind of "insurance" against exposure by confiding in his sympathetic, local M.P., an aristocrat and an officer of the state—but not a cop, and not obligated to go to the cops. After all, who were they going to arrest? Perhaps the M.P. was convinced by hearing the whole story but wanted to be able to brag about solving the Ripper's identity to some of his fellow nobs. If his cronies could not keep a secret—as *he* certainly could not—Farquharson would do exactly as he had advised the scandalized archaeologist: he would semi-fictionalize the solution just enough to make the real Ripper unrecoverable to the press. It was a momentous step if Henry Farquharson took it, with unforeseen and far-reaching consequences for this subject that endured to the end of the 19th century, through the entirety of the 20th and now into the first decades of the 21st. The M.P. did this simply by truncating the timeline between the final murder and the date of the killer's suicide, creating the remorseful and incriminating self-murder within hours, or less, of the Mary Jane Kelly atrocity: in effect a tormented confession in deed. To obscure the Thames River location of an act of repentant suicide, Farquharson added "blood-stained clothes." Druitt's last suit was actually found soaked with polluted seawater.

These two bits of fiction certainly impressed a good many people who were informed by the M.P. of this melodramatic shilling shocker, yet it concealed the messier, even more disturbing reality that I believe Melville Macnaghten was subsequently told by Farquharson or a family member, or both—that Montie had confessed his monstrous crimes in word to somebody. Rather than allow himself to be sectioned by his family into a madhouse, he drowned himself three weeks after the most gruesome atrocity. Despite all the pressures of class, of religion, of personal disappointment, of professional embarrassment not to agree with the Druitt family's preposterous belief, "Good Old Mac" did—and to his dying day. Like fellow Old Boy Farquharson, Melville Macnaghten eventually found the evidence overwhelming that Montague John Druitt was "Jack the Ripper" (in effect, he became a fellow disciple of Farquharson's "doctrine"). Macnaghten also took on board how Henry Farquharson had deftly mixed fact and fiction, as variations of this self-serving strategy would shield the Druitt tale from anybody (outside the police chief's family) right up until 1959. In his memoirs Macnaghten goes no further than Nixonian "limited hangout" for posterity's sake. Here are the miserly, "Christmas Day in the Workhouse"-sized portions Macnaghten dishes out to us from 1914:

> The man of course was a sexual maniac, but such madness takes Protean forms.... I incline to the belief that the individual who held up London in terror resided with his own people; that he absented himself from home at certain times, and that he committed suicide on or about the 10th of November 1888, after he had knocked out a Commissioner of Police and very nearly settled the hash of one of Her Majesty's principal Secretaries of State.[8]

The unnamed commissioner "knocked out" is his old nemesis Sir Charles Warren, who did not resign over the Ripper case but because of a dispute with the home secretary over an indiscreet letter he published in a newspaper. This is a form of schoolboy revenge by "Old Mac," as he repeats tabloid hyperbole from 1888 that Warren resigned over his inability to defeat the Ripper (nor was the unnamed Henry Matthews in as great a danger of losing his job, as the government might have fallen on the numbers). Tantalizingly, Macnaghten has the timing of the suicide happening *after* the departure of Warren, whose tenure officially ended on November 31, 1888. Montague Druitt killed himself on about December 1, 1888, the very next day.⁹

The contention of this book that Macnaghten also conferred with the Druitts—or at least a Druitt—is both a matter of common sense and completely out of character if the hands-on sleuth did not arrange such an interview (such a meeting may have been organized by Colonel Majendie, and the chief constable met his cousin's son-in-law, the vicar). As already mentioned, such a meeting is described by Sims, although in a veiled way, and is also subtly confirmed in the retired chief's memoir chapter of 1914. This is because the need for a go-between, such as Henry Farquharson or Vivian Majendie, is neutralized by implying, fictitiously and deflectively, that the unnamed Montague resided "with his own people." The average reader would fairly assume that Macnaghten's suspect *lived* with his family, yet the ambiguity of the phrasing does not commit Macnaghten to an absolute lie for broadly speaking Mr. Druitt did live with *his own people*: the students and servants of the Blackheath school.

Nevertheless, in this simplified compression of a much more complicated tale, "Jack," Macnaghten implies, lived with relations. These "people" were therefore not strangers in a lodging house or even close pals. They were family and must have *ipso facto* intimately known of their fellow relation's character, personality, state of mind and of his comings and goings. Any ghastly revelations were strictly a family affair (the same average reader of 1914 would be oblivious to all the "Mac" machinations during the previous decades). "Laying the Ghost…" strongly suggests that the killer's blood, "his own people"—the very last people who would want to believe such an appalling notion about one of their own—were the posthumous accusers against what the author calls this "Simon Pure" (a Victorianism for a Christian who is virtuous only on the surface). They were an unimpeachable source, and Macnaghten, once having spoken with them—or else how could he be so sure?—laid to rest this phantom. However reluctantly and unexpectedly, Macnaghten agreed with their unwanted and wrenching belief. We see this same near-admission in a piece for *Pearson's Weekly* of July 23, 1915, by George Sims, the only time the famous writer ever mentioned, quite accurately, the suburb of Blackheath as the suburban home of the Ripper. Sims pointedly mentions "Jack" with another incontrovertibly solved mystery: the Lambeth murderer of prostitutes, Dr. Thomas Neill Cream (he used poison):

> With Neil [*sic*] Cream murder was a pastime. There was no question of the insanity of revenge upon a certain class of women as there was in the case of the *mad doctor* who lived with *his people at Blackheath*, and who, *during his occasional absences from home* committed the crime which won him worldwide infamy as Jack the Ripper [my italics].

Again, this strongly implies "Jack" had family who have had to face that their loved one was a bloodthirsty maniac, because every time he went out the door—apparently an extremely rare occurrence—it coincided with another East End "unfortunate" being found carved up on the pavement (a plot device shamelessly lifted from a popular novel, *The Lodger*—see Chapter XIV). In that tidbit Sims mentions that Macnaghten included a very long excerpt by "Tatcho" about Dr. Cream in his memoirs, in which the ex-chief opened with this: "The facts of the case were put together some years ago by my old friend Mr. George R. Sims in his succinct and picturesque style, and I feel I cannot do better than reproduce his story almost verbatim. This I do with his kind permission."[10] Yet "Mac" could have easily written this summary himself. By using such a lengthy excerpt I think that Macnaghten wanted to make it clear to the readers of *Days of My Years* that *his* suspect who had committed suicide was the same man as Sims' suicide, but that, by implication, he disagreed with his friend in regards to the *timing* of the act of self-destruction *and* with the level of his functionality in the aftermath of the Kelly murder. "Mac" quotes "Tatcho" "no man in the last stage of furious madness, as the perpetrator of the Dorset Street horror must have been, *could have live*d to embark on a totally different series of atrocities" (my italics). This is at odds with his own chapter's timeline that allows for a compos "Jack" to escape the East End on the morning of November 9 and kill himself the following morning, or the following afternoon, or the following evening, or the following night—or maybe it was later. What it definitely did not allow for was a man unable to do anything but stagger and shriek towards the Thames Embankment and drown himself within the hour. For all his lack of medical training, he confidently diagnosed in 1914 what he thought ailed the barrister: "sexual insanity." Although this sounds like another quaint Victorianism to us, it nonetheless expresses a concept as modern as any current studies of human psychopathology—that killers of strangers can appear completely normal while gaining erotic pleasure from acts of ultra-violence, often misogynistic in nature. The ex-chief chooses a wonderfully evocative word to describe Druitt—"Protean"; derived from the Proteus, a shape-shifting creature of Greek mythology. This was a particularly dangerous type of criminal maniac, as he is able to convincingly assume different roles and different faces with ease.

Melville Macnaghten had absorbed well an important lesson provided by the late Montie Druitt that reverberates well into the 21st century. How often have we turned on the television to see a "nice young man" in police custody, his dumbfounded relations, neighbors and work colleagues expressing utter disbelief, while the police—sometimes bizarrely attired like astronauts—are carrying out large barrels from his modest abode filled with decaying human remains? How about the contradictions thrown up by a Ted Bundy? The handsome law student viciously murdered dozens of women, yet he also saved a handful of anguished souls by working the phones for a lifeline service. John Wayne Gacy entertained children in hospitals as Pogo the Clown. Meanwhile the remains of dozens of young men rotted in the crawlspace under his home. Along the same lines Macnaghten writes: "Sexual murders are the most difficult of all for police to bring home to the perpetrators, for 'motives' there are none; only a lust for blood and in many cases a hatred of woman as woman."[11]

In chapter 10 of his memoirs, "Motiveless Murders," Macnaghten returned to this particular form of mania and provided a more detailed definition: "As I have said before, when writing of the Whitechapel murders, such madness takes Protean forms. Very few people, except barristers, doctors, and police officers, realize that such a thing as sexual mania exists, and, in a murder case similar to the two mentioned above, it is a most difficult task for prosecuting counsel to make a jury fully understand that it supplies and accounts for the complete absence of any other motive for the crime." Macnaghten offers a chilling warning to his readers: that among the dull plebs you pass in the street might be drooling maniacs:

> Students of history, however, are aware that an excessive indulgence in vice leads, in certain cases, to a craving for blood. Nero was probably a sexual maniac. Many Eastern potentates in all ages, who loved to see slaves slaughtered or wild beasts tearing each other to pieces, have been similarly affected. The disease is not as rare as many people imagine. As you walk in the London streets you may, and do, not infrequently jostle against a potential murderer of the so-called Jack the Ripper type. The subject is not a pleasant one, but to those who study the depths of human nature it is intensely interesting.[12]

The accounts by both Macnaghten and Sims beg a question: since they did not really live with him, how exactly did his family know that their Montie was a serial killer? Was it simply because he took his own life three weeks after the murder of Mary Jane Kelly? Or was it because Montie had told them he was in a dark place with no available exit? But if so, why did they not go straight to the police or at least have him forcibly committed to an asylum? Fourteen years after the 1888 murders, Sims revealed to his Edwardian readership that the reason the "friends" had such grave suspicions about the "doctor" was because the latter had been a voluntary patient in a private asylum—wherein he had been diagnosed as a potential homicidal lunatic. This is Dagonet from "Mustard and Cress" of February 16, 1902: "The homicidal maniac who shocked the world as Jack the Ripper had been once—I am not sure that it was not twice—in a lunatic asylum." In Sims' politely disguised version the Ripper, rather implausibly, confessed his maniacal desires to savage harlots a year before the crimes to other doctors—perhaps twice. Why did they recklessly let this ticking human bomb out to prowl the streets?

Since Montie had never been in a mental institution, this may reveal that William and/or Charles Druitt and other family members were determined, if he was found alive, to have him committed for the first time. Yet in his memoir Macnaghten (for reasons explained in Chapter XV) pointedly rejected the notion that the unnamed Druitt had ever been detained in an asylum (let alone twice). Instead he took a crowbar to Henry Farquharson's timeline—slavishly repeated by Sims—in order to wrench apart the date of Kelly's murder and of Druitt's suicide to provide some daylight between them; a gap of at least two days and a night (and perhaps another night), which means that Druitt was functioning well enough to flee the crime scene and alert other people about his inner distress. There is enough of a gap for Montie Druitt to share with somebody his torment, presumably "his own people." They were naturally shattered about his other identity as "Jack the Ripper"; were horrified to find him "absented" and then deceased by his own hand. But who exactly was that somebody in the family to whom he may have confessed? Why did they then not act immediately? Did they feel they were somehow constrained?

X

WELL-DRESSED CORPSE

The terrible series of crimes committed by "Jack the Ripper" were then being perpetrated, and many people believed that he lived in Blackheath.—Vice Admiral H. L. Fleet, 1922

Druitt was the last person to be suspected unless there was evidence.... The very "innocence" of such a man suggested he must have been guilty to be suspected in the first place.—Dan Farson, 1972

"Jack the Ripper" was almost only one degree of separation from Her Majesty, Queen Victoria. Had he not fatally imploded in early December 1888, Montague would have met Victoria's grandson and heir, bar one, Prince Albert Victor, the Duke of Clarence, at what must have been the social event of the Dorset season, as reported in the *Southern Guardian* of December 22, 1888: "On Monday afternoon last quite a flutter of excitement was caused in Wimborne by the sudden announcement that Prince Albert Victor was coming down by the 5.20 express train from London on a visit to Lord and Lady Wimborne at Canford." Among the celebrity guests was the American expatriate and beauty, Lady Randolph Churchill, formerly Jennie Jerome, the mother of the future Tory prime minister, Winston, who would be, though, a *Liberal* home secretary for some of the years Macnaghten was assistant commissioner. Also in attendance was Lord Shaftesbury, the son of the peer who had defined a particular deranged state of mind and body as "epileptic mania."

The Guardian dutifully recorded the extensive body-count of animals and birds that gave their lives so that the duke might keep his boredom at bay, before beginning the cycle of eating, shooting and dancing all over again: "The totals (not allowing for the pickings up of Thursday) for the three days were: 2395 pheasants, 52 partridges, 49 hares, 83 rabbits, 18 woodcock, 4 snipe and 89 wild duck." The newspaper also provides an alphabetic list of who was invited from the region, which is not necessarily the same as who actually attended. For example, listed for "D" was "Druitt, Mrs. and Miss and Mr. Montagu [*sic*], Wimborne," while in "F" was "Farquharson, Mr. And Mrs. Henry, Tarrant Gunville, Blandford." The "Mrs." was Montie's mother, incarcerated in an asylum, the "Miss" was presumably one of his sisters and "Montagu" was at that time a piece of river jetsam. The Duke of Clarence—known as Eddie within the family—would never make it to the throne. He died on January 14, 1892, a victim of the influenza pandemic then sweeping Europe. In a typical bit of regal pragmatism his betrothed, Princess May of

Teck, married Eddie's younger brother instead—very happily by all accounts—and he became the future George V on the death of his father, Edward VII.

From various sources it is believed that the Duke of Clarence was, to some undefined extent, mentally challenged. Becoming king may have placed too great a strain on his narrow shoulders (supporting a long neck topped by a vacant face) and might have undone the institution of the British constitutional monarchy. As it was, fate removed this potential dilemma (and replaced it with the abdication crisis of George's eldest son, Edward VIII, who, though possessed of all his faculties, totally lacked any sense of responsibility towards anything or anyone beyond his own pleasures, flavored by a dilettante's attraction to fascism). Incredibly, Clarence became a Jack the Ripper suspect in November 1970, and though the theory was quickly disproved—court circulars proved that Clarence was in Scotland on the night of the double murder—the notion of a royal connection to the Whitechapel crimes remains forever embedded in the crevices of pop culture. An utterly unreliable source (aged 85 and soon to expire of natural causes) of this nonsense, one Dr. Thomas Stowell, seems to have been inspired by the comments made by none other than Sir Melville Macnaghten. It had been reported in a 1930 newspaper article that "Mac" had told the reporter the fiend was the "scion of a noble family," and consequently this eccentric attention-seeker apparently went the whole hog and picked the Royal Family.[1]

On the other hand, Prince Albert Victor may have been involved in a scandal that would have had serious ramifications for the entire establishment if it had spun out of control. This was the Cleveland Street Scandal of 1889 (though it dragged on for a few years) involving certain aristocrats who were found to be paying working class boys who worked as city messengers for sex. The Tory government was very sluggish about pushing for prosecutions, and the relevant toffs were tipped off so that they could flee to the south of France. Rumors at the time, never confirmed, whispered that Clarence was also a client and that the corrupt and depraved elite were scrambling to shield their own future king. American muckrakers were, as expected, not so shy: "Victor [sic] seems to inherit his father's vices without retaining many of his virtues, and his connection with the Cleveland Street scandal is only another indication of the debauchery which too conspicuously unctures [sic] European royalty."[2]

What does Macnaghten have to say about this notorious scandal in his memoirs of 1914, a scandal by his elite stratum of society, involving "vices" with which he may have been very familiar from Eton, at least by others? Nothing; apparently it never happened. Yet it broke in the press the month after he joined the Force, and one of its leading detectives was none other than Frederic Abberline (presumably to even mention this affair twenty-five years later would be inappropriate for a gentleman). In order for Melville Macnaghten to learn more about the late Mr. Druitt, in 1891, he did not need to check out the 1889 newspaper reports of his death if he had a member of the Druitt family right in front of him (perhaps more than one). Yet he seems to have absorbed a few of these articles' mistaken details, as they were later exploited for his own propaganda purposes (via Sims). The police chief must have had an extraordinary memory, if he did not rely on an M. J. Druitt scrapbook. For example, the *County of Middlesex Independent* of January 2, 1889, gave the first report of the body being found bobbing up near the torpedo works at Chiswick:

FOUND IN THE RIVER.

The body of a well-dressed man was discovered on Monday in the river off Thorneycroft's torpedo works, by a waterman named Winslow [*sic*]. The police were communicated with and the deceased was conveyed to the mortuary. The body, which is that of a man *about 40 years of age*, has been in the water about a month. From certain papers found on the body *friends at Bournemouth* have been telegraphed to. An inquest will be held today (Wednesday) [my italics].

In the writings of Major Griffiths and George Sims, from 1898, Macnaghten would have the publicly unnamed Druitt described as a middle-aged man who had close friends. At the very least, these chums stood in for the older brother who was living and working in Bournemouth. Did these errors in the *County of Middlesex Independent* give Macnaghten the idea for how to veil the suspect's family? Other newspaper reports on Druitt's suicide and burial in Wimborne, Dorset, such as the *Southern Guardian* of January 5, 1889, could only shake their heads at the death's complete inexplicability (the Reverend Charles Druitt attended his cousin's funeral):

SAD DEATH OF A LOCAL BARRISTER.

"The Echo" of Thursday night says:—"An inquiry was on Wednesday held by Dr. Diplock, at Chiswick, respecting the death of Montague John Druitt, 31 years of age, who was found drowned in the Thames. The deceased was identified by his brother, Mr. William Harvey Druitt, a solicitor residing at Bournemouth, who stated that the deceased was a barrister-at-law, but had lately been an assistant at a school at Blackheath. The deceased had left a letter, addressed to Mr. Valentine, of the school, in which he alluded to suicide. Evidence having been given as to discovering deceased in the Thames—upon his body were found a cheque for £60 and £16 in gold—the Jury returned a verdict of "Suicide whilst of unsound mind."

The deceased gentleman was well known and much respected in this neighbourhood. He was a barrister of bright talent, he had a promising future before him, and his untimely end is deeply deplored.

Montie as prefect—**A never-before-published picture of Montague Druitt in 1876 as a school prefect, the only known full-length shot of the future Ripper suspect, and also the only one that clearly shows his profile (courtesy Warden and Scholars of Winchester College).**

The funeral took place in Wimborne cemetery on Thursday afternoon, and the body was followed to the grave by the deceased's relatives and a few friends, including Mr. W. H. Druitt, Mr. Arthur Druitt, the Rev. C. H. Druitt, Mr. J. Druitt, sen., Mr. J. Druitt, jun., Mr. J. T. Homer, and Mr. Wyke-Smith. The funeral service was read by the vicar of die Minster, Wimborne, the Rev. F. J. Huyshe, assisted by the Rev. Plater.

Curiously, Montie is described as having "lately" been an assistant master; actually he had worked at the Blackheath School since at least 1881. Druitt's body reportedly had no papers found on it, yet the police were able to quickly alert older brother William Druitt in Bournemouth. How? The likeliest explanation is that the substantial checks found on the rotting corpse were payment from William's firm of solicitors for the younger sibling's excellent work in the recent successful case on behalf of a disenfranchised Conservative voter. The funeral was very sparsely attended; none of Montie's sisters attended (though it was the convention of middle and upper class ladies not to attend); nor did anybody from his Blackheath life. We see in the surviving diary entries of his cousin Matilda Jane Druitt a glimpse of the wider family's ambivalence, or stoicism (or indifference) towards Montague's death:

Wednesday 2 Jan. Heard of Montie Druitt's death. Mrs. Maberly and Oswald called. Another rehearsal at school.
Thursday 3 Jan. Herbert and I went to Mr. Argyle's funeral. James went to Wimborne with Jim to attend Montie's funeral. Scenes from Pilgrim's Progress acted by Maud and others at School.[3]

Another question raised by these accounts is who exactly was it that received a suicide note—William, or George Valentine the headmaster? *The Guardian* has the latter, while a Chiswick paper has it addressed to the former. For that matter how does one merely *allude* to suicide? The *Dorset Chronicle* of January 10, 1889, has two notes being found (and only one is allegedly addressed—to the headmaster), and that seems unnecessarily redundant by a man about to kill himself:

The deceased had left a letter, addressed to Mr. Valentine, of the school, in which he alluded to suicide. A paper had also been found upon which the deceased had written, "Since Friday, I have felt as if I was going to be like mother," who had for some months been mentally afflicted. ... Deceased was a prominent member of the Kingston Park Cricket Club, and as such was well known in the county.

The newspaper which covered the inquiry into Druitt's death in the greatest detail—though still in too meager and unnecessarily ambiguous fashion—was the *Acton, Chiswick and Turnham Green Gazette*, also on January 5, 1889. It was perhaps filed in haste, as it does not even mention the deceased's name. Yet we see shards of glitter that point to the Mother Lode just out of reach:

FOUND DROWNED.—Shortly after mid-day on Monday, a waterman named Winslade, of Chiswick, found the body of a man, well-dressed, floating in the Thames off Thorneycroft's. He at once informed a constable, and without delay the body was conveyed on the ambulance to the mortuary.—On Wednesday afternoon, Dr. Diplock, coroner, held the inquest at the Lamb Tap, when the following evidence was adduced: William H. Druitt said he lived at Bournemouth, and that he was a solicitor. The deceased was his brother, who was 31 last birthday. He was a barrister-at-law, and an assistant master in a school at Blackheath. He had stayed with witness at Bournemouth for a night towards the end of October.

William Harvey Druitt was older than Montague by one year, the putative head of the family after the death of their father in 1885. He was a partner in a successful firm of solicitors (which included his cousin James Druitt, Jr.) in the thriving seaside community of Bournemouth.[4] Did the Druitt brothers really not confer during November over this important civil appeal to the High Court? And why did George Valentine not testify? Did he not also receive a suicide note? No second note is mentioned here, or alluded to either. In the same article is a confusingly written account of how William learned of his brother's disappearance and what actions he took to find him:

> Witness heard from a friend on the 11th of December that deceased had not been heard of at his chambers for more than a week. Witness then went to London to make inquiries, and at Blackheath he found that deceased had got into serious trouble at the school, and had been dismissed. That was on the 30th of December. Witness had deceased's things searched where he resided, and found a paper addressed to him (produced).—The Coroner read the letter, which was to this effect: "Since Friday I felt I was going to be like mother, and the best thing was for me to die."

It is very unclear from this source exactly what happened on December 30, 1888. Does the reporter mean that upon that date Druitt was sacked, or was it when his brother arrived and learned that his brother's part-time job had been terminated? Surely it did not take William nineteen days to make it to the Blackheath school. Or did the reporter mishear December *thirteenth*, a more logical date for when the brother, having been informed on the eleventh, was able to leave his work in Bournemouth and commence his search for Montie in London? At the inquest the brother testified that he had been tipped off by an unidentified "friend"—that all-purpose anomic designation again—about Montie's going missing. The brother implied that it was somebody with whom his younger sibling worked in the city. Why would Montague not have been allowed to "resign" from the school if he had been sacked to his face? And if sacked in person, why would his ex-employer let him leave his belongings at the school, or for that matter keep them when he vanished? A likely answer is provided by a single, quite neglected primary source: the minutes of the Blackheath Cricket, Football and Lawn Tennis Company of December 21, 1888, which is ten days *after* William was, allegedly, first informed by a friend and ten days *before* Druitt's body resurfaced: "The Honorary Secretary and Treasurer, Mr. M. J. Druitt, *having gone abroad*, it was resolved that he be and he is hereby removed from the post of Honorary Secretary and Treasurer"[5] (my italics).

Did Montie leave word at his various places of work and play that he had to go abroad on some urgent, private matter? Consider that if William Druitt had come immediately to London, he would have presumably found Montie's note (or notes) that alluded to harming himself. If that had happened, surely his Sporting Club would not have fired a man later that month who was believed to be in a state of extreme mental distress, missing and presumed deceased (George Valentine's brother—another William—was sitting on that sporting club's board and would have been duly informed). Logic dictates that Montie Druitt was fired, not allowed to resign, from the school for the same reason he was let go by his club—he was unaccountably absent, having left word he was suddenly going abroad. Initially there was no alarm from family or colleagues, only perplexity. As the weeks passed the missing man, having not contacted anybody, was inevitably fired from various organizations. The date of December 30, 1888, may therefore correctly refer to the date of Montie's dismissal from the school due to still being A.W.O.L. or refer to the brother's late arrival due to thinking, up till then, that his sibling was, say, hunkered down in Paris. Why was William Druitt searching in London for his brother, if the latter had left a message about "having gone abroad"? Was it because William was worried at not having heard from Montie over Christmas, or had he learned—or been told—something so alarming it forced his frantic scramble to investigate where his brother had lodged?

Chapter XIV will examine in detail a George Sims crony, Guy Logan, and his book *The True History of Jack the Ripper* (Amberley, 2013) originally serialized in the *Illustrated Police News* in 1905. Simultaneously unreadable and yet indispensable, it is openly a mixture of fact and fiction inspired by the Druitt solution to the Ripper case. Montague Druitt becomes "Mortemer Slade," a middle-aged doctor who has never had a patient. Towards the end of the turgidly written tale, as the net closes around the fiend, Mortemer Slade considers that he will probably escape the hangman because he is quite insane—but he rejects this fate: "I'd never go back to a madhouse," he thought bitterly. "It's a living hell to a man with brains, and desires, and promptings like mine. No, I'll kill myself first."[6] And there is this bit of fiction about Mortemer Slade that is arguably pertinent regarding why the real Montague Druitt was fired from the school (as he was from his sporting club): "Later in the morning, having snatched a hasty meal at a cheap eating house, he went to his lodging and removed his few belongings in a carpet bag, informing his landlady that *business called him abroad*"[7] (my italics).

Whatever the exact circumstances of Montague Druitt's dismissal—*if* he was dismissed, as we are relying on the compromised brother's testimony—no other newspaper bothered to mention it, and therefore his termination was not linked to his suicide (not even by the one newspaper that does include this detail). Finally, consider that if Druitt was a morose suicide because of vocational setbacks, then Macnaghten would have found that out for himself in 1891 and happily cleared a fellow gentleman. To return to that Chiswick newspaper's 1889 flawed account, William Druitt appears to wander into perjured testimony calculated to mislead the inquiry into his brother's death. For example, he said that he and their insane mother were the only living members of the family:

> Witness, continuing, said deceased had never made any attempt on his life before. His mother became insane in July last. *He had no other relative.*—Henry Winslade was the next witness. He said he lived at No. 4, Shore-street, Paxton-road, and that he was a waterman. About one o'clock on Monday he was on the river in a boat, when he saw the body floating. The tide was at half flood, running up. He brought the body ashore, and gave information to the police. P.C. George Moulson, 216T, said he had searched the body, which was fully dressed excepting the hat and collar. He found four large stones in each pocket in the top coat; £2 10s. in gold, 7s. in silver, 2d. in bronze, two cheques on the London and Provincial Bank (one for £50 and the other for £16), *a first-class season pass from Blackheath to London* (Southwestern Railway), *a second half return Hammersmith to Charring Cross (dated 1st December)*, a silver watch, gold chain with a spade guinea attached, a pair of kid gloves, and a white handkerchief. *There were no papers or letters of any kind.* There were no marks of injury on the body, but it was rather decomposed.—A verdict of suicide whilst in an unsound state of mind was returned [my italics].

Was there a family member whose sworn testimony William so feared that he would rather not admit, even under oath, to their existence? Was this a clumsy attempt to shield the connection to Colonel Majendie of the Home Office? Consider also that by saying that there were no other relations, the older brother had no choice but to claim that he was informed by a "friend" (and once more we see that persistent and edgy oscillation between blood-relations and platonic pals). Though the note was hardly definitive, it did the trick of providing the coroner, Dr. Diplock, with a *deus ex machina* that allowed him to swiftly wrap up the tragedy as a respectable family blighted with inherited mental instability. Did William Druitt write the note himself because Montie's plan to appear to have vanished abroad came undone when the rocks fell out of his pockets, and his corpse floated into view? Such a blatant lie would have been a dangerous and illegal act for William, a respectable solicitor, to have committed.

On the other hand, nobody attended the inquiry who could contradict William or dispute that it was Montie's handwriting. Also Montie's grave says he died on December 4, 1888, and the probate of his will says December 3. Going by the season rail ticket's return date, it is more likely to have been December 1—a Saturday. If you were composing a suicide note would you write "Since Friday…" rather than "Since yesterday…"? You might if you were the brother cobbling together such a note, in haste, and thought that Montie had drowned himself on the following Monday. It seems very odd that George Valentine as Montie's employer of nearly a decade did not attend the funeral. But then nobody from his London life attended. Could it be that George Valentine, the cricket club members and his colleagues at the legal chambers in London were not informed by William Druitt that his brother was deceased, at least not until after he was safely six feet under? Did William exploit what was being covered as a regional tragedy in order to get Montie swiftly certified as temporarily mad and then buried in his home town? Did he only then inform the school? Since an account of the inquest did not appear in any London newspapers, was George Valentine even aware he was supposed to have found some kind of suicide note? Here are the pertinent, terse minutes from the next meeting of the board of the Blackheath Cricket Club in which they try to sugar the bitter pill of having sacked a dead man: "It was resolved that the Directors had heard with much regret of the death of Mr. M. J. Druitt who had zealously fulfilled the duties of Honorary Secretary and Treasurer for three years."[8]

What may have actually happened is that mad Montie left a *genuine* note of contrition among his belongings that was found by the brother, one that outlined in bloodcurdling detail his extracurricular hobby (perhaps found by the headmaster, the "friend" who hastily contacted William Druitt). The shocked pair may have secretly agreed not to reveal the truth, as the school would have inevitably closed due to the negative publicity, and the news would have been potential trouble for the Druitt and Majendie clans. In late 2014 writer-researcher Paul Begg discovered an obscure yet pertinent reference to a Druitt connection to the Ripper saga in, of all things, the memoirs of a British vice admiral. In *My Life and a Few Yarns* (George Allen and Unwin, 1922), career naval officer H. L. Fleet mentioned the following bombshell in passing:

> On January 1st, 1895, my promotion to Captain was gazetted; another spell of half-pay! At Blackheath we found a lot of old friends, and one of my old C-in-C's Sir Walter Hunt-Grubbe, as Admiral at the college. The Heath itself had a bad reputation after dark. When we lived there formerly it was considered dangerous, for the terrible series of crimes committed by "Jack the Ripper" were then being perpetrated, and *many people*

believed that he lived in Blackheath. His victims were invariably women of the unfortunate class, and it was evident that he was a homicidal maniac with *a grudge against such people.* He was never caught, although it was sometimes stated that *he had been and was confined in Broadmoor* [my italics].

The admiral either never knew or recalled nothing about the drowned "Mad Doctor," the wall of fiction that had been built to shield Montague Druitt's true identity. Instead he had heard that the murderer lived on in a mental institution. As we will see in later chapters, this false trail has Mac's fingerprints all over it too. I think that this source from 1922 is evidence either that the truth leaked after Druitt's death and therefore the cover-up involved the school too, or that the chief constable's investigation of 1891 included a trip to Blackheath (or perhaps a naval man was informed by an ex-army officer). This unfortunately led to cognition by a few in that suburb that they were the Whitechapel fiend's neighbors, causing Macnaghten to spread a fictional overlay, i.e., that "Jack" was safely rotting in Broadmoor, the state institution for the criminally insane, deflecting attention away from a barrister's suicide (it is the usual "Mac" shuffle; a bit of data that is accurate followed by some that is not). Perhaps the 1894 tabloid-driven story about a sectioned madman supposedly being the best "Jack" suspect (see Chapter XII) had merged in the admiral's memory with the suburban rumors. In the final analysis it stretches credulity that a British captain could know that the Ripper once lived in Blackheath, and for the "man of action" not to know—and that once the police chief did know, he then did not make a thorough if private investigation of the dead killer's haunts. Ultimately if Henry Farquharson, Melville Macnaghten and George Sims were correct in their posthumous assessment, then William Druitt fundamentally misled the inquiry even if the suicide notes were authentic, and even if it was the incompetent reporter who misunderstood his testimony (that what the solicitor actually said was that he was the only living relative *in attendance.*) This is because he was withholding his belief that his deceased brother was "Jack the Ripper."

Four years later Macnaghten would record this note for a Scotland Yard file (to be examined in greater depth in the next chapter), one he most certainly did not throw on any bonfire at his retirement: "Mr. M. J. Druitt.... He was sexually insane and from private information I have little doubt but that his own family believed him to have been the murderer." The source of "private information" was almost certainly Colonel Vivian Majendie or Henry Richard Farquharson; at the time of writing the latter was still the Tory member for West Dorset (though seeking a new seat that would have covered the East End, had he lived). U.K. television reporter/writer Daniel Farson was the first to investigate Montague Druitt in the modern era. When he came to write his own book about the case, in 1972, Farson grasped the nub of the implication of family suspicion against one of their own:

> We may suppose that William, who represented the family, believed that his brother committed the murders. But, again, why? The suicide in the Thames is no evidence in itself. Yet at the very point where the evidence might seem weakest, I can see its strength. William must have suspected Montague because he had proof. Furthermore, this proof must have been conclusive.... Druitt was the last person to be suspected unless there was evidence.... The very "innocence" of such a man suggested he must have been guilty to be suspected in the first place.[9]

But why did the family "believe," and why did they still after subsequent Jack murders had seemingly exonerated Montie? Why did their local M.P. posthumously adopt it as his "doctrine"? Subsequently, why did a police chief "some years after" with a bias towards the innate goodness of gents of his own class also "believe"? These were all pillars of the establishment trashing one of their own. There is a clue as to the elusive evidence against Montague Druitt in the article by Sims from the September 22, 1907, edition of *Lloyds Weekly,* and again we glimpse Macnaghten's postulated private 1891 meeting with family members—backdated and fictionalized: "The doctor had been an inmate of a lunatic asylum for some time, and had been liberated and regained his complete freedom. After the maniacal murder in Miller's-court the doctor disappeared from the place in which he had been living, and his *disappearance caused inquiries to be made concerning him by his friends* who had, there is reason to believe, their own suspicions about him, and *these inquiries were made through the proper authorities*" (my italics).

Every aspect of Druitt's particulars in Sims' accounts of the 1900s are altered and/or exaggerated: Montague Druitt, the "son of a surgeon," becomes one himself; his body is found with a season rail pass and a sociable barrister becomes a recluse who aimlessly travels on public transport; a couple of soggy checks for a lot of money, and he is later turned into a member of the super-rich; he may have been dismissed from the lesser of his two vocations for a few days, and this becomes a "Mad Doctor" completely unemployed for years. But what element of the truth are Macnaghten and Sims altering when they have the Ripper as a former inmate of a lunatic asylum? Is it just a tasteless lift of the mother's illness? As far as we know from available records, Montague Druitt had never been in institutionalized care, let alone diagnosed as a dangerous lunatic.

If we peel back this layer of the disguise, of the doctor who was himself a patient in a madhouse, we are left with arguably this kernel: the murderer was the ultimate source of his own culpability because it came from his own lips. The "friends" inform the "proper authorities" of their horrible suspicions because the "doctor" had *said* he felt compelled to tear East End harlots to pieces, hence his diagnosis as a homicidal maniac. Did Montie tell his brother that he had such dark desires before he started acting them out? Surely that is ludicrous, as the barrister would have been carted off to a madhouse post haste. Perhaps what is being hidden here is that the murderer actually confessed *after* the five murders to somebody whom Druitt knew would be very reluctant to simply go straight to the nearest police station (again, that does not seem likely to have been a sibling who was also a solicitor).

The likely person would have been some kind of confessor who might reveal what he knew to the family only after Montague vanished, who had taken a sacred vow and could not go to the police, not without breaking the seal of the confessional. Once Montague disappeared, this person with the terrible knowledge felt pressured by the atmosphere of crisis to at least reveal the truth to the older brother—in other words, the confessor-figure was a man of the cloth.

XI

THE PRIEST'S SECRET

A hundred times have I felt that the burden he had imposed upon me was greater than I could bear—that I must go out into the world and cry it aloud. I have felt that I was sharing his guilt—that I was aiding him to deceive and defraud the world.—George R. Sims, *The Priest's Secret*, 1892

The murderer died ... very shortly after committing the last murder. The Vicar obtained his information from a brother clergyman, to whom a confession was made—by whom the Vicar would not give even the most guarded hint.—*The Western Mail*, 1899

In 1899, seven months after Sir Vivian Majendie dropped dead at his sister's, and merely weeks after Major Arthur Griffiths' book on the history of policing and crime first revealed to the public that the Ripper might have been a middle-aged medico who drowned himself in the River Thames, the *Western Mail*—repeating a story from the *Daily Mail*—published a sensational scoop. Well, a sort of scoop, as the article was devoted to mostly whining about a hot story that the paper frustratingly judged it could not publish. An Anglican vicar had sent them an account of the Whitechapel murders in which he asserted that "Jack" had confessed to "a brother clergyman" in 1888.

The frustrating conundrum for the newspaper was that the cleric openly admitted that his piece was—just like the stories by Henry Farquharson, Melville Macnaghten and George Sims—a mixture of fact and fiction, in order to reveal the truth and yet protect people too. The newspaper was still impressed, because the vicar's tale seemed to concur with *some* of the data that had just been published by Major Arthur Griffiths: a Ripper who died in late 1888 and whose last victim was Mary Jane Kelly in 1888 (not Frances Coles in 1891). Here is the *Western Mail* from January 19, 1899 (first published on an online forum, *Casebook: Jack the Ripper*, by the late Chris Scott):

DID "JACK THE RIPPER" MAKE A CONFESSION?

We have received (says the "Daily Mail") from a clergyman of the Church of England, now a North Country Vicar, an interesting communication with reference to the great criminal mystery of our times—that enshrouding the perpetration of the series of crimes which have come to be known as the "Jack the Ripper" murders.... Our correspondent the Vicar now writes: "I received information in professional confidence, *with directions* to publish the facts after ten years, *and then with such alterations as might defeat identification.* The murderer was a man of good position and otherwise unblemished character, who suffered from *epileptic mania*, and is long since deceased" [my italics].

The vicar had sent his account to the press on the tenth anniversary to the month of the date that M. J. Druitt was buried in Wimborne-minster, Dorset. Being a barrister (and a school master) was definitely a "good position," not a great one, not like Montague's father and uncle and cousin, who were surgeons. That he was a man of "otherwise unblemished character" matches the 1889 newspaper articles: "a barrister of bright talent ... well known and much respected." Much more startling is that the vicar claims that his own name identifies the killer (or is this also a bit of deflective fiction?): "I must ask you not to give my name, as it might lead to identification," meaning the identification of the perpetrator of the crimes. Sadly, for us, the newspaper would not publish the cleric's essay in full, but they do provide invaluable glimpses of it—for example that the name Whitechapel is strangely (and pointlessly) fictionalized: "The Vicar enclosed a narrative, which he called 'The *Whitechurch* Murders—Solution of a London Mystery.' This he described as *substantial truth under fictitious form.* 'Proof for obvious reasons impossible—under seal of confession,' he added in reply to an inquiry from us" (my italics).

Understandably, the *Mail* wanted the whole story and sent a reporter to confront the author to wheedle out of the vicar what was fact and what was fiction, but he remained a sphinx. This clergyman, with his paradoxical candid deceit, must have been taking enormous risks with his career in the church, especially if the tabloid decided to go ahead and publish the tiresome vicar's name (only the threat of England's draconian libel laws, as we have seen before, may have held them back—or was it his connection, by marriage, to a deceased knight of the realm?):

> But the Vicar was not to be persuaded, and all that our reporter could learn was that the rev. gentleman appears to *know with certainty* the identity of the most terrible figure in the criminal annals of our times, and that the Vicar does not intend to let anyone else into the secret. The murderer died, the Vicar states, *very shortly after committing the last murder.* The Vicar obtained his information from a brother clergyman, to whom a confession was made—by whom the Vicar would not give even the most guarded hint [my italics].

The element of certainty that we see in sources about or by Farquharson and Macnaghten is here on display too with the vicar. But did he receive the information from a "brother clergyman" or is that fiction too? Did *he* hear the confession, and is that why he is so certain? Was the Ripper a member of his family, so that *his* surname would give away the killer's identity? What little we can glean from his essay is that his tale matches Montague Druitt in a fundamental way. Unlike the Ripper of Farquharson and Sims who kills himself immediately after Kelly, this "Jack" has enough time following the final atrocity to locate a priest, make a confession, and then conveniently expire (the vicar does not say how he died, nor does he rule out suicide). In fact, all of these bits of basic data match Montague Druitt: a respectable, Anglican gentleman with a good job and reputation, who died "shortly after" the Miller's Court atrocity. How then is the Vicar's Ripper, if it is Druitt, being fictionalized at all—apart from the rather pointless alteration of Whitechapel to "Whitechurch"? Does the vicar mean that the fictional element is only the title "under" which dangles some but not all of the truth? The reporter's mission was by no means a total waste of time. He managed to nag the cleric enough to reveal two extra bits of information—one of which could be true of Druitt and another that could not be: "The only other item which a lengthy chat with the Vicar could elicit was that the murderer was a man who at one time was *engaged in rescue work* among the depraved woman of the East End—eventually his victims; and that the assassin was *at one time a surgeon*" (my italics).

Montague John Druitt was never a surgeon, but then neither was the "Mad Doctor" of Major Griffiths' big book, and we know that behind the latter figure *is* the drowned barrister. Also why would a man stop being a surgeon, which is a far more prestigious vocation than any "good position"? As we will see in the next chapter, Druitt was hidden by Macnaghten as the drowned surgeon when disseminated by Griffiths and Sims. The vicar's semi-fictionalized "at one time a surgeon" is surely also Druitt, the difference being that he has blatantly disguised him. The phrase "substantial truth in fictitious form" is a brilliant encapsulation of precisely what Farquharson, Macnaghten and Sims had done and would do with M. J. Druitt (and his family, both Druitt and Majendie)—that is, cloak the truth in untraceable fiction. It is a sort of more polite version of Sims' "superstructure of exaggeration" to justify his less-than-absolutely-factual "Mustard and Cress" prognostications. Ironically, the *Daily Mail* did not realize that in comparing the vicar's dubious account with the major's super-respectable tome, with its unimpeachable links to officialdom, it was, in fact, comparing two semi-fictionalized suspects—who were almost certainly the same man. The pedestrian explanation, that it is all simply a coincidence, frankly strains credulity. If this is not a coincidence, then we know why Montie Druitt was believed to be the murderer—he had confessed his crimes not to physicians (as Sims would veil this element within three years) but to a priest. And what he said must have, later, checked out and not been just the ramblings of a mind that had become as mad as a March Hare. As to that diagnosis of insanity, the members of the families—the ones who knew the secret—seem to have settled on some kind of "epileptic" mental illness as their explanation for the horror that consumed their young and promising relative.

But what does "epileptic mania" mean? It looks to modern eyes to be both absurd and medieval. Here is a definition of so-called "Epileptic mania" from the "Report of the Metropolitan Commissioners in Lunacy to the Lord Chancellor," from 1844, by the Earl of Shaftesbury; it was an attempt at a comprehensive overview of mental illness and institutional care in England and Wales (reportedly there were 6,682 "idiots" in the former but only 811 in the latter):

> Some persons subject to severe paroxysms of epilepsy without suffering obliteration of their intellectual faculties, and even without obvious disorder of the mind during the intervals of their paroxysms, are nevertheless subject to occasional fits of a maniacal character.... Many instances are upon record of such persons, at a time when their disorder had been in abeyance, or even supposed to have ceased altogether, having been seized with a sudden impulse, to commit homicide, infanticide, suicide, or to set fire to houses.

In 1907 George Sims would describe the "Mad Doctor" as "furious," "shrieking" and "raving" after the Kelly murder and being driven to immediately commit suicide. We see exactly the same symptoms referred to in Shaftesbury's Lunacy Report: including "*raving* delirium. The patient ... is seized with *a sudden fury*, during which he sings, roars, *shrieks*, or resembles a man in *a violent fit* of intoxication"[1] (my italics). Although this is an excruciatingly redundant Victorian notion of a particular type of mental illness being confused with a physiological disorder, no wonder the family embraced it; poor Montie had been afflicted with an illness over which he had no control. With epileptic mania sufferers were thought to remain high functioning, in terms of being able to carry out acts of extreme violence, while not necessarily being aware of their own mayhem. A Dr. Otto Juettner had proposed a similar theory as reported in the *Cincinnati Enquirer* back on July 23, 1889: "Is the Famous Whitechapel Murderer an Epileptic?" The doctor's theory was that "Jack" suffered from "insanita epileptica" and that sometimes the victim of such a mental disorder was "unconscious of everything that transpired in the interim." The chatty alienist was startlingly prescient as he used a word that was the same one later expressed by Macnaghten: "In the recurrence of this malady, hate and revenge predominate, and he *gluts* these passions to the utmost limit. Returning sanity makes him forget everything that has occurred and this fact is proved by the lapse of time which intervenes between each crime" (my italics). In his memoir Macnaghten, in his strictly limited portrait of the unnamed Druitt, seemingly provides an allusion to epileptic mania, writing: "Not infrequently the maniac possesses *a diseased body*, and this was *probably so* in the case of the Whitechapel murderer" (my italics).

As for the identity of the priest to whom Montie may have confessed, textual evidence points towards this man being a family member. The two leading candidates are the Reverend William Hough, Montie's London-based brother-in-law, and his first cousin Charles Druitt, whose parish was in Dorset. Another possibility is that *both* ministers were involved; the Reverend Hough heard the confession and Vicar Charles tried to publish a veiled version of it a decade later—or perhaps neither was in on the terrible secret. William Woodcock Hough, another son of an eminent surgeon, was a Cambridge man like Henry Farquharson, and in 1886 he married Georgiana Elizabeth Druitt, Montie's oldest sister. In a tragic coincidence she may also have taken her own life, though when elderly. By the end of her life Georgiana Hough may have suffered from dementia, or was exhausted from physical suffering, or fell from a high window by accident—as her death was publicly reported in the *Times* of June 7, 1933: "The accident happened in the early hours of yesterday, and the Bishop did not know of his wife's death until he awakened at his usual hour. Mrs. Hough, who was a Miss Druitt, had been in ill health for some time." William Hough

The clerical brother-in-law—**The Reverend William Hough, shown here in 1920, was married to Montague's older sister, Georgiana. His rise in the Anglican Church to eventually become the second bishop of Woolwich would have been inconceivable had it become known that he was related to an infamous serial killer (© National Portrait Gallery, London).**

was a churchman who did not just preach the social gospel, he tried to live it by working for over a decade among the poor on London's Old Kent Road. The athletic reverend (an accomplished runner) and his wife, Montie's sister, lived just a few miles away from the young barrister in the 1880s, including at the time of the murders (at 32 New Cross Road, about two and a half miles from 9 Eliot Place, Blackheath). He rose to become a much admired bishop and died in 1934.

Imagine if Bishop Hough's obit had also mentioned that his brother-in-law was discovered by CID to have been the infamous maniac known as "Jack the Ripper"? But then if that had happened, around 1891, William Hough would never have become a bishop in 1918. If it had become known that he had received the confession of the fiend—who still managed to thwart earthly justice—then it is very unlikely Hough could have remained the head of the Corpus Christi College mission either. Tragedy would have compounded tragedy as the poor were not helped by this cleric's zeal, wisdom and energy. Were the Houghs privately relieved at learning of Melville Macnaghten's 1913 retirement comments about destroying all the relevant documentation concerning the Ripper's true identity? William and Georgiana Hough are not listed as attending Montie's funeral in January 1889. That is, of course, suggestive in two opposite directions: that they were not close enough to drop everything to attend (no other sisters attended), or that one, or both, were in such a state of apoplexy over their relative being the Ripper that they could not bear to go (Georgiana may have been as close as a surrogate mother to Montie, the oldest daughter caring for her younger siblings in place of an often infirm or absent mother). Another possibility is that, since Georgiana was pregnant, she may not have been in a state to travel nor would her attendance at such a sad occasion be advisable for a woman with child, and William may have stayed behind to look after his distraught wife.

The Houghs may not have been the only family members comforted by Macnaghten's claim that the secret of the Ripper's identity would travel with him into retirement. Montie had two younger brothers whose lives would have been severely blighted, if not smashed, by the "curious story" that came perilously close to being exposed by M.P. Farquharson. Younger brother Arthur Druitt, born 1863, was another Oxonian who married a surgeon's daughter in Edinburgh. Edward Druitt, born 1859, married a Catholic lady, Christiana Mary Filumena Weld, in Wimborne, who was the daughter of a big shot in South Pacific colonial administration, Sir Frederick Weld. They married on February 19, 1889, just a month and a half after Montie's funeral. They received a telegram from the pope blessing their marriage: If Edward knew the family's secret belief then he must have pondered that His Holiness, Pope Leo XIII, blessed the union of a Catholic aristocrat and Jack the Ripper's brother.[2] Had this been known it is hard to imagine the marriage going ahead at all. The newly wedded couple moved to the state of Queensland on the Australian continent for a number of years (the former British colonies did not federate as a nation until 1901). Edward had a distinguished military career and died in 1922, the same year as Sims. Unlike Arthur, Edward Druitt is not listed as having attended the funeral of his older brother, perhaps because of a family or sectarian split over his marrying into the bosom of Rome. Perhaps there was another reason.

A more circumstantially compelling case can be made for the Reverend Charles

Druitt as the clergyman who, if he did not also hear the confession, publicly revealed it a decade later. He is also the clergyman who was the son-in-law of Sir Vivian Majendie's cousin's daughter. If so, it may have been his connection to the recently deceased Sir Vivian that intimidated a Conservative newspaper to play along, up to a point, with his insistence on being unnamed—even disguised as a Northerner. Born in 1848 and dying in 1900, Charles was also an Oxonian (Exeter College) and became the vicar of East and West Harnham at the time of the Whitechapel murders. He married Isabel Majendie Hill, a vicar's daughter, in Wiltshire on September 15, 1888—just after the murder of Annie Chapman. Montague did not attend that wedding, though his sister Georgiana and her husband the Rev. William Hough did—as the long list of wedding presents received by the newlyweds includes a gift of a library table from the Rev. W. W. and Mrs. Hough and several other guests. Being on his honeymoon from mid–September 1888, the vicar could have, in theory, been back in London within two months—and could have met up with Montie. Charles became a Dorset vicar in 1891 and remained in that position until his death. He was nicknamed "the Pope" by his family. This

A papal blessing—Edward Druitt, younger brother of Montague, had a distinguished military career. His 1889 marriage to a Catholic aristocrat received congratulations from His Holiness Pope Leo XIII. It is hard to imagine these respectable nuptials proceeding—and being sanctified by the Vicar of Christ on earth—if it had been known that Edward was the sibling of "Jack the Ripper."

was possibly a dig at his exhibiting high-handed pomposity or an inflated sense of his own moral authority—perhaps just the kind of autocratic personality that might have unilaterally decided to disseminate the truth about his late cousin.[3] The Ripper allegation against the late Montie Druitt (although unnamed) first emerged out of Dorset. Charles was a vicar in 1899, and the mysterious clergyman of that year warns a *Daily Mail* journalist not to publish *his own name* as he claims it would reveal that of the murderer.

The redundantly fictionalized title of the Vicar's article, "The Whitechurch Murders," is nearly identical to the name of Charles' vicarage: "Whitchurch Canonicorum." In fact the name "Whitchurch" was interchangeable with "Whitechurch," as can be seen by this article from the *Tablet* of July 21, 1900: "The Shrine of St. Candida. Whitechurch Canonicorum, Dorset." This was the title of an article sent to this publication by one Father Ethelbert Home, of Downside Abbey, originally published in the *Somerset and Dorset*. The article, however, was written by none other than the Reverend Charles Druitt. The 1899 cagey clergyman who wrote to the *Daily Mail* is supposedly from the north of England, while Charles lived and worked in Dorset in the southwest. This may still not torpedo his candidacy as the "North Country Vicar," as it might be explained as being part of the fictional protection demanded by the clergyman (and not entirely untrue, as Charles had previously ministered in Yorkshire). In the 1905 Guy Logan serial

The True History of Jack the Ripper—an openly semi-fictional serial about the (unnamed) Montague Druitt—the murderer (and his "cousins") are relocated to Yorkshire in the North to hide everybody's identity.[4]

The West Sussex Records have an article on file published by a regional paper, from about the middle of 1890, with a regular feature titled "District Intelligence." The heading is "Welcoming Back the Vicar," followed by this: "Mr. Druitt had had a great many trials since he came to Harnham. Having come there with an earnest desire to do everything he possibly could for the parishes, he had had to continually contend with the troubles of ill-health." Was Charles Druitt just a country cleric simply suffering unlucky health, or was he, "the Pope," under a severe strain because of what he secretly knew about his deceased cousin? Did his inner conflict resolve itself by confiding what he knew to his M.P. within a few months? When illness overtook him again in 1899 did he decide to communicate the truth about Montie, though in veiled form? Montie's older brother, solicitor William Harvey Druitt, shared his Bournemouth practice with his cousin James Druitt Junior. The latter's father, James Druitt Senior, was also a solicitor and, in 1888, was the Tory mayor of Christchurch, Dorset. In November 1888 he began a memoir of his schooldays and about life in the local area, but then, for reasons unknown, he abruptly abandoned the manuscript. He only resumed it six years later and makes no mention whatsoever of Montague or that wing of the family. Instead he blandly laments, "Now, alas, no representative of the family is to be found" at Wimborne.[5] Both James Druitts, senior and junior, attended Montie's funeral. It is hard to imagine that if Macnaghten met with the older brother he did not also meet with the priest, especially if the latter was the source of the leak in Dorset and had perhaps also spoken about the matter with Farquharson.

Another reason for the chief constable to have a discreet chat with the Reverend Charles was that he was related to his close pal, Colonel Majendie. It is this postulated encounter that may have put Macnaghten on notice of potential trouble down the road for the born-to-rule Tories: the cleric informed the chief constable that he had decided to publish the story, either because he'd made a solemn vow to the murderer to do so or because he believed the truth about Montie should eventually come out. From 1891 Macnaghten may have known that some version of the Dorset solution was scheduled to be given a public airing during his watch as chief constable of CID Montague Druitt left a considerable estate—of cash, not property, worth 2,600 pounds—and this may have been in some jeopardy if the whole story had come out. It did not, and the older brother duly collected the dough.

We also know that the truth about Montie would have precipitated not only the ruination of his family, the tarnishing of the Majendie clan, but also the likely closure of the Blackheath School—and Macnaghten may have wished to protect the school, since he had adored his school days at Eton. I think that Macnaghten may have succeeded in convincing the Anglican minister, if he met with him too, to reveal the truth about the drowned barrister's confession but with two provisos: not to do it until ten years had passed since Montie was buried, and to intermingle the truth with lies. In other words, to imitate fellow Old Boy Farquharson's example of mixing fact and fiction so that the family—and Scotland Yard's reputation—would be safe. If the reverend protested that he could not publish what he knew to be deceitful, Macnaghten, with impeccable schoolboy logic, could have retorted that it would not be a lie if he *admitted he was not telling the truth*. Incredibly, if this came from Macnaghten, he was successful.[6]

I see Melville Macnaghten on a train heading back to London from Dorset in early 1891, puffing on his pipe and feeling quietly elated. He had laid to rest this ghost, and though he was too late—curse you, Sir Charles Warren and your bloody bloodhounds!—at least had the satisfaction of knowing the true identity of "Jack the Ripper." On the other hand, he may have equally felt the same "green faintness" as he had when he tried to smoke cigars as a schoolboy. The killer's identity put in some jeopardy, hard to quantify, the family of a close friend: the Majendies. Should not the highest authorities be informed of what he had learned? It was at this moment that certain powerful elements intersected—his dismissal by Warren before he started at the Met, the squeezing out of his mentor, Monro, his natural compassion towards a "good family" in distress, his need to protect a very distinguished friend, and, perhaps most dominantly, Macnaghten's Old Etonian sense of himself as forever apart from his police colleagues. These factors aligned and he decided, at some risk to his career, not to confide in any of them what he had learned about "Jack the Ripper." Arguably his loyalty to the heroic colonel, whom he would pass over so briskly in his memoir, trumped any other obligations perhaps with barely a second thought. The maniac was, after all, no longer a threat—except to the reputations of both the Druitts and the Majendies. The bottom line for "Mac" was that he did not trust his colleagues to be discreet, especially his tiresome boss, Dr. Robert Anderson.

Apart from perhaps the colonel at the Home Office, who may have already known, did "Mac" inform anybody? I think he told George Sims, who was, after all, also a close friend of Colonel Majendie, and briefed the writer perhaps as early as late February 1891. The chief constable was likely shown photos of the alleged killer as an adult (none of these have come down to us, though the high-school stills show that Montie broadly resembles Lawende's young "sailor," as well as the failed assassin with the aquiline nose and fair moustache athletically fleeing from Annie Farmer, "Dark Sarah"). It is a pictorial likeness of Montague John Druitt that may fix for us the timing of when Macnaghten had made up his mind that the drowned barrister was the Whitechapel assassin.

In the March 1, 1891, issue of the *Referee*, Sims/Dagonet in his regular "Mustard and Cress" column returned to the Ripper story and for the first time took seriously that notion that the 1889 crackpot coffee-stall owner's sighting of "Jack"—who allegedly bore a striking resemblance to the author—was authentic. This is quite a turnaround—and amusingly ironic—compared to what the same author had predicted on November 18, 1888, in the *Referee,* that the murderer must be physically grotesque: "The man's face would betray him to an expert. The features in most of these bloodthirsty maniacs are peculiar—especially the mouth, the chin and the eyes." Not anymore, according to the same source. After worrying that the police were pursuing him as the fiend due to watching somebody who makes frequent trips to the Continent, Dagonet introduced a version of the 1889 coffee-stall witness story that differed markedly from its first appearance, and from the way Sims first jokingly related it. He now provides additional details that anchor it in time to the morning of the double murder of Liz Stride and Catherine Eddowes; in 1889 he had written that it was in the aftermath of a single homicide, by implication that of Alice McKenzie. Tellingly, the original cover portrait was from a book of "Dagonet poems." In March 1891 this became a much earlier picture of Sims on his first book (a collection of short prose pieces, not poems):

> An hour or two after the double murder had been committed on the night of September 30, 1888, a man of strange and wild appearance stopped at a coffee-stall. The coffee-stall keeper (knowing nothing then of the night's tragedy) began to talk about the Whitechapel murder. "I dare say we shall soon hear of another," he said. "Very likely," replied the wild-looking stranger; "perhaps you may hear of two to-morrow morning." He finished his coffee, and as he put the cup down the stall-keeper noticed that his cuffs were blood-stained.
>
> The next morning—or rather, later on that morning—the news of the double murder in Whitechapel fell upon the startled ears of the coffee-stall keeper. "Good Lord!" he exclaimed; "why, that chap last night knew it. He must have been Jack himself!" Walking along he came to a bookseller's and newsagent's. He looked at the placards, and then his eye suddenly rested on a book in the newsagent's window. Outside that book was a portrait. "Christopher Columbus!" exclaimed the coffee-stall keeper; "why that's the very image of him!"
>
> The book was "The Social Kaleidoscope." The astonished stall-keeper bought it, and, later on, when telling his adventures to the police, he produced the book and showed the portrait. ... I investigated the facts. The coffee-stall keeper, who was interviewed, was perfectly candid and straightforward, and at once explained that he didn't for a moment mean to say that I was his blood-stained customer on the night of the murders. All he meant was that his customer's features were very like mine.

The original recounting of this story was treated by Sims as nothing more than an amusing trifle. In a complete about-face, he now argued it was quite plausible as the stranger knew there had been two victims, the stranger was bloody and wild-looking, and the coffee-stall man acted like a commendably responsible citizen by immediately trying to alert the authorities. But to make this credible, Sims had to significantly revise the original—when he had been rudely disparaged as nothing more than a crank. In the original article the witness claimed to have spoken to the fiend "many times," and that the Ripper's face was "bronzed"—not wild-looking—and that its "contour" was very similar to that of George Sims. Either Sims had got ahold of a more accurate version of the story than was first published, or he had rewritten it to make it more credible based on what Macnaghten had recently confided in him.

What is most important to us is that Sims now wrote that the murderer looked very like Sims did on the cover of his 1879 book, his first about the "Social Question." The picture shows a younger and noticeably thinner Sims with his hair not parted in his usual off-center style, but rather right down the middle. In only this picture could Sims be said to resemble Montague John Druitt (although the original account by the "crank" contains details that fit Druitt too: "bronzed" from his cricket matches and resembling Sims in the "contour" of his aquiline cheeks, low forehead and hooded eyes, not because he had a beard—a feature the 1889 article does not mention). Confirmation that the 1879 picture of Sims was *atypical* of the writer is to be found in a recently discovered interview he gave for the *Daily Express* on August 1, 1904:

> The strange case of Adolph Beck, twice convicted erroneously for the crimes of his "double," has induced Mr. George R. Sims to relate in yesterday's "Referee" an extraordinary story of his own likeness to "the demented doctor who committed the terrible Jack the Ripper outrages."

A curious reporter for the *Express* interviews Sims, who essentially repeats what he wrote on March 1, 1891—except that he makes the following observation:

> Mr. Sims said he believed the coffee-stall keeper came across his portrait on the cover of the first edition of "The Social Kaleidoscope," in a shop in a side-street in Southwark. "It was *a terrible portrait*—taken when *I was very ill*. My face was *drawn and haggard*, and surprisingly like the Ripper.... Mr. Sims said that he had *not the slightest doubt* in his mind as to who the "Ripper" really was. "Nor have the police," he continued, "In the archives of *the Home Office* are the name and history of the wretched man. He was a *mad physician* belonging to a *highly respected family*. He committed the crimes after having been in *a lunatic asylum as a homicidal maniac*" [my italics].

Every fictitious element created by "Mac" and "Tatcho" is in place here: "Jack" was an asylum veteran, a "demented" doctor, from a "highly respected family" (arguably a fictional composite of the Druitts and the Majendies), the police are all in agreement about his guilt, and he was the subject of a definitive Home Office report. If we step back we see that by the beginning of the Frances Coles murder inquiry, Sims was scathing about the police and had written, for a couple of years, that "Jack" had never been identified—and would probably only be stopped by old age. After the Sadler embarrassment, Sims suddenly conceded that there was one witness who probably did see "Jack" and that the police therefore had a picture of what the fiend looked like. It is pertinent to mention here that while no picture of Montague as an adult has survived, we do have one of his younger brothers, Edward, from 1888, looking very dashing in his military uniform. With his hooded eyes, neat moustache and aquiline face, he too resembles that 1879 picture of Sims (except that his hair is parted from his left side). As for the reference to a Home Office report, we will see how there were actually *two* such reports by Macnaghten, neither of which made it to that department of state.

And there is the following source, yet another smoking gun. It is a short story by Sims called "The Priest's Secret," published in many newspapers including the *Sussex Agricultural Express* of December 23, 1892. It is arguably textual evidence that the famous writer had been briefed by his friend Macnaghten about the Dorset solution to the Ripper case that concerned their mutual chum, Colonel Majendie—a solution that hinged on a confession to a clergyman.

In Sims' brief tale a wealthy, kindly, modest English gentleman, John Arcwright, is dying in the upstairs of his palatial estate (which seems to be located in Yorkshire). He is attended by his beloved second wife, his personal physician, Hansen, and a young clergyman and curate, the Reverend John Wannop, whom Arcwright has practically treated *as his son*. Though the medical term is not used, the patient displays all the symptoms of "epileptic mania." The local doctor, for example, cannot understand why Arcwright is not being attended to by professional nursing staff because "a man in that condition is likely to do himself or others an injury at any time." The reason for the seclusion is that both Dr. Hansen and the Reverend Wannop know their patron's "ghastly secret."

They cannot risk strangers' overhearing a delirious Arcwright confessing it (his wife already has, but the pair can bluff it out; that her saintly husband has been rendered delusional by his final fever). The secret is revealed at the end. John Arcwright murdered his first wife and child and nearly—but not quite—killed himself in a furious rage, about which he has almost no memory. Aged 30 at the time, he had ended up in a state of destitution, starving along with his young wife and sickly child in the wilds of California. This wasteland of famine and misery is, of course, reminiscent of the East End: "Some of the men and women, rough creatures, hardened to fate by a ceaseless struggle for existence, helped them a little; but times were bad all round and it soon became a case of each for himself and his own."

There are noticeably a number of excuses employed here by Sims to get a fellow gent, about to kill his family, off the hook. As if suffering from famine as grim as any Whitechapel harlot were not enough, the trio are isolated from civilized help while menaced by a marauding gang of cutthroats pillaging the countryside (echoing the East End "rip gang" who killed Emma Smith). Waking with a "strange pain in his head," Arcwright believed he was about to die and thus felt compelled to take a long knife and kill his wife and son as they slept, before a far worse fate befell them due to deprivation—"there is nothing but misery and starvation before them"; again shades of Whitechapel lives blasted by poverty. As he put the blade to his own neck, the cold steel made him come to. He collapsed, later barely recalling his bloody acts. He was soon rescued by other pioneers, who assume his loved ones were massacred by the gang. From that moment, John Arcwright's luck ironically changed for the better and, years later, he returned to England a fabulously wealthy philanthropist.

Let us pause and reflect on the implications of this otherwise disposable melodrama. An English gentleman above suspicion has a dual life as a knife-wielding fiend—when gripped by his uncontrollable mania—and commits multiple homicides (and nearly instant suicide) in an abyss, while people close to him know the real story and want his nearest and dearest protected from the shattering and secret truth. Sound familiar? In an earlier scene, Doctor Hansen and the Byronic figure of the Reverend Wannop have an anguished discussion that sounds eerily like what might have been said between William and Charles Druitt after Montie confessed and vanished:

> "Do you know, Hanson, that when I first became the possessor of the secret of John Arcwright's life I thought it would have killed me."
> "Killed you, why?"
> "You don't understand what it has been to me. I loved this man, I revered him.... I felt to him as a son to a loving father"

The next line of dialogue by the tormented reverend reads as if Sims is taunting the "North Country Vicar" (as he would be known in seven years) before providing him with moral reassurance:

> "You agree with me that it is absolutely necessary to keep silence on the subject. You consider that I have done right in holding my peace all these years."
> "Most certainly, I can quite understand that as a clergyman, you may at first have had some scruples as to your duty, but looking at all the circumstances I think you are fully justified."

The cleric explains to the physician that his benefactor on the eve of his second marriage had some fever, while visiting Rome, and confessed to some of the terrible truth before revealing the rest the following night in a guilt-ridden but lucid state: "He said that all his life he wanted somebody to confide his secret to—someone who would understand him and sympathize with him." But now the priest is overwhelmed by his own sense of guilt at not going to the relevant authorities regarding a confession to double murder:

> "I suffered more afterwards. I suffer more now. I loved this man, my benefactor, my almost father, then, and love him more now; yet not once, but a hundred times have I felt that the burden he had imposed upon me was greater than I could bear—that I must go out into the world and cry it aloud. I have felt that I was sharing his guilt—that I was aiding him to deceive and defraud the world in which he was honoured and respected."

Nevertheless the priest maintains the "sacred trust" after the dying Arkwright begs him not to posthumously expose his dark deeds, as he was the "victim of a moment of madness" and it was up to God to pass ultimate judgment. Was Sims also trying to convince the Rev. Charles Druitt not to spill the beans in half a dozen years? He says: "Buried in their hearts forever is the secret they will carry to their graves. They alone will ever know that the good man, over whose grave their stands a marble memorial on which are recorded his honourable life and his Christian virtues, was a murderer." (Chapter XIV explores further examples of the Druitt tragedy influencing various short works of George Sims.)

On p. 36 of her 1966 memoir, Lady Christabel Aberconway may also have provided a glimpse into the *kind* of meeting that Macnaghten may have had with the priest who heard Druitt's confession. As a little girl she found herself secretly hidden under a vicar's table as he began to earnestly confide in her father what he knew about an alleged murder, and Macnaghten was apparently *not* persuaded:

> I heard my father lighting his pipe; then [the Vicar] lit his. I was too shy to say anything and remained under the stuffy table-cloth crouching as still as a frightened bird. ... [The Vicar said,] "I knew the curate who was there at the time so I got to know all about it. The man had taken the little house by the churchyard for that very purpose. He killed the man and a few days later, when he saw a grave that had been newly dug in the churchyard, just before dawn he went out and dug still lower in that grave and put his victim there.... If the coffin hadn't been moved into a family mausoleum, the crime would never have come to light."
> I heard my father making appreciative and puffing noises through his pipe and then he and the Vicar strolled away. ... That half-heard story haunted me. When, long after I was grown-up, I asked my father about this incident, *he pretended that he didn't remember anything about it*: but somehow I still believe that he did. I have a feeling that perhaps *he himself didn't quite believe* in the story [my italics].

Returning from his postulated private meeting with the Druitts, or a Druitt, such as the Reverend Charles—perhaps accompanied by Colonel Majendie, who introduced them—Chief Constable Melville Macnaghten in February–March 1891 committed nothing to paper regarding his belief that Montague Druitt was "Jack the Ripper." The case was "in all probability" solved, but you cannot arrest the dead. The Frances Coles shambles, involving a blood-stained prime suspect with no alibi for the exact moment of the crime, yet released to public acclaim, was thankfully petering out—as was the strange tale of the loose-lipped politician. Three days after Sims-Dagonet abruptly reversed himself about being the double of the Ripper, and a day after all charges against Tom Sadler were dropped, the *Nottingham Evening Post* returned to the unnamed Henry Farquharson, urging him to divulge what he knew:

The discharge of Sadler to-day ought really to force the *West Country Member*, who believes that he can point to the author of the Whitechapel murders, *to put his evidence before the police authorities*. The man he suspects is dead, but as the police authorities believe the last murder to be the work of Jack the Ripper it would be of immense advantage *in tracking the real murderer* to have all the facts before them [my italics].

Judging by George Sims' abrupt about-face of four days previous, about resembling "Jack," the M.P.'s "putting his evidence before the police authorities"—or rather a single policeman—had likely already happened. Subsequently Melville Macnaghten chose to lie low regarding the Dorset solution, as he knew he had about seven years before he would have to deal with a priest's secret becoming public knowledge. Unforeseen events in early 1894, however, would prematurely force the chief constable's hand.

XII

CHIEF OF SPIN

Mr. Farquharson, M.P. for West Dorset, believed that the author of the outrages destroyed himself. ... This theory is naturally exploded.—The Western Mail, 1892

Many homicidal maniacs were suspected, but no shadow of proof could be thrown on any one.—Sir Melville Macnaghten, 1894

You have to feel a measure of pity for the two stooges who decided on May 3, 1893, to burglarize the mansion at 32 Warwick Square in the exclusive London suburb of Pimlico after a careless servant had forgotten to fasten the lock on the window of the smoking room that faced the street. The crucial intelligence the pair of hapless crooks had not bothered to ascertain was that it was the domicile of no less than the chief constable of CID. In his 1914 account of confronting a burglar in his own home, Sir Melville Macnaghten atypically mentions one of his own children and even his wife, Dora. A son, we learn, was chronically absented from Eton—to the father no doubt a near-tragedy—but his being ill proved fortuitous because since he was sleeping fitfully in his bedroom near the smoking-room, his mother went down to check on him and disturbed an intruder. Awakened by her cries, her husband leapt from his bed and hurried to confront the trespasser, though Macnaghten admits that he feared for the vulnerability of a certain part of his anatomy: "I rushed into the smoking-room, and saw a short, thick-set man dodging round the eight-foot-long billiard-table. I soon caught and collared him (mercifully without having my toes trodden on)."[1]

According to court records Macnaghten testified, "I am Chief Constable of the Metropolitan Police.... The prisoner Driscoll ... said, 'It is only me sir. I have broken in. I am hard up'—I arrested him and handed him over to a constable." This unusual episode also shows that "Mac" was not necessarily a sleuth who jumped to conclusions based on merely circumstantial evidence; he denies, unequivocally, that it was an inside job by one of his own servants despite the unlocked window and the key to the safe having been left in plain view: "These were corroborative coincidences and nothing more." There were no "corroborative coincidences" regarding Montague Druitt's being "Jack the Ripper," yet Macnaghten posthumously accepted *his* guilt. (Macnaghten would also go down in history as the only assistant commissioner of CID who had arrested a burglar in his own home.) But at the time of this bizarre incident, "Mac" was by no means certain he could achieve that promotion, what with tension between himself and his immediate superior, Dr. Robert Anderson, along with harboring the secret knowledge that the Dorset solution to the Ripper mystery was going to be released in a few years—if it did not leak sooner. If that happened how would the chief constable respond; how would the Old Etonian keep everyone satisfied while preventing his mate, Colonel Vivian Majendie and his family from suffering due to a familial association with the late Mr. Montague Druitt?

In May 1889 Michael Ostrog managed to convince a credulous doctor to rescue him from the workhouse by having the schemer transferred to the relatively cushier surroundings of Banstead Asylum in Surrey. Keeping a close eye on this reprobate, Macnaghten wrote the following to the medical superintendent: "I shall feel obliged if you will cause immediate information to be sent to this office in the event of his discharge as the magistrate adjourned the case 'sine die,' in order that he might be again brought up and dealt with for failing to report himself if it is *found that he is feigning insanity*"[2] (my italics). Between late 1890 and early 1891 while out walking the streets of Kennington (plus Brixton, Clapham and Stockwell—but not Whitechapel), half a dozen plumpish, young females were non-fatally stabbed in the buttocks by a male assailant (this bizarre crime even had a name: jobbing). A young man, John Edwin Colocott, who was perhaps somewhat mentally impaired, was arrested as the jobber. In March 1891 his sentencing was dramatically postponed as another deranged young man, Thomas Hayne Cutbush, 26 years old, was arrested as the genuine culprit. To the consternation of his family there was no trial, as Cutbush was swiftly declared insane and committed into the asylum system.[3] Three years later, the strange jobbing episode was to intersect with that of the Ripper in a quite unexpected way.

In 1966, Christabel Aberconway recalled her earliest memory; that of the "bulky form" of Oscar Wilde bending over her pram, much to the disapproval of her nanny ("That dreadful Mr. Wilde stopped me again today and talked to Baby—and she smiled at him!") The playwright's only novel, *The Portrait of Dorian Gray* (Ward, Lock, 1891), has some parallels with Montague Druitt—a perpetually handsome young man leading a debauched, even homicidal life behind a respectable charade—but the titular character is clearly meant to be bisexual (and is totally indolent). When a little older, Christabel wanted to know why this beloved family friend had been sent to prison. Her mother, embarrassed, replied it was for committing perjury, which while not untrue was nothing like the whole truth either. One evening

Guilty of ... forgery?—**The writer and wit Oscar Wilde in 1888. He was a neighbor and friend of the Macnaghtens. Even after his disgrace Sir Melville, who was likely progressively minded about homosexuality, at least in private, still called him a "genius" in front of his daughter.**

Christabel ambushed her father as he came through the door from work at 6:30 p.m. and made the same query. Without missing a beat her father replied: "He was a genius ... but, well, it was for forgery, but we don't speak of it."[4] Oscar Wilde had been proven in court to have paid for sexual favors from a veritable Fagin's gang of street roughs, the exposure of his "deviant" sexuality had led to the tightening of the anti-homosexual laws, and his plays had been banned, yet Christabel Aberconway reveals that her father still considered Wilde a genius. Without skipping a beat he fibbed (though his daughter was not convinced) and turned Wilde into, of all things, a forger. With its Wildean echo of something being not what it appears, a conviction for forgery also had the effect of deflating society's hysterical and hypocritical demonization of the great writer as nothing more than a depraved beast.) From the safety of anonymity I believe that a comparable *ju jitsu* maneuver was implemented by Macnaghten the year after he found Druitt to publicly debunk the Ripper scoop of Henry Farquharson. I think the chief constable chose a newspaper, the *Western Mail* (Cardiff), owned by a Tory backbencher, on whom he could presumably rely to be both circumspect and credulous. In the issue of February 26, 1892, an unidentified Scotland Yard detective talked to the owner, who was also the writer, James McKenzie Maclean, the Conservative member for Oldham: "Tracking 'Jack the Ripper.' Remarkable Statement by a Scotland Yard Detective. The Chain of Evidence All but Complete." The unnamed sleuth assured MacLean that Scotland Yard knew the true identity of the real culprit and had had him under thorough surveillance—"watched and shadowed night and day, awake and asleep"—since he murdered Frances Coles on February 13, 1891. He had not been arrested because there was apparently one last link in the chain of evidence just out of reach. But the Ripper knew he was being watched "and it is, no doubt, from this cause, and this alone, that the Whitechapel murders have ceased."

There is no evidence in available records that Scotland Yard was squandering such enormous resources to keep watch on any prime Ripper suspect in late 1891 and early 1892. Then comes what I argue is the real purpose of the interview—to shut down Tory politician Henry Farquharson's "curious story" of the previous year. The M.P. is named, which may not have been Macnaghten's choice but perhaps could not be avoided, at least not without tipping his hand if he made a fuss:

> Mr. Farquharson, M.P. for West Dorset, was credited, I believe, some time since with having evolved *a remarkable theory of his own* in the matter. He believed that the author of the outrages destroyed himself. But if the police have been on the right track *this theory is naturally exploded* [my italics].

The unidentified police detective breezily claims that even if the murderer is never arrested, they have stopped him in his tracks—and that will apparently do. Another possibility is that the unidentified policeman was not Macnaghten and this policeman was *sincerely* claiming they were watching somebody they strongly suspected, and the M.P.'s theory was *ipso facto* mistaken. Since the assistant chief constable admitted (in his memoirs) that by then he *had* adopted Henry Farquharson's "theory," this is further evidence that he confided in nobody at Scotland Yard that they were chasing a ghost. Nonetheless, I think it more likely to be an unidentified "Mac." That the chief constable had probably "gone rogue" on the Ripper from 1891, in order to protect the good name of Colonel

XII. Chief of Spin

Majendie if nothing else, can be seen by an interview his immediate superior, Dr. Robert Anderson, gave to *Cassell's Saturday Journal* on June 11, 1892. Macnaghten has clearly neglected to brief his reclusive, pious boss that the case is, according to his own No. 2 at CID, solved, as Anderson laments: "I sometimes think myself an unfortunate man.... On the morning of the day I took up my position here the first Whitechapel murder occurred." Anderson shows the reporter some of the gruesome pictures of the Ripper's victims to elicit more sympathy: "There is my answer to people who come with fads and theories about these murders. It is impossible to believe they were acts of a sane man, they were those of a maniac reveling in blood."

In 1893 Macnaghten was part of an official inquiry into the emerging science of fingerprint identification. This provided the chief constable with an opportunity to ingratiate himself with the new Liberal home secretary, H. H. Asquith (whose wife Margot would be so gushing about Dora Macnaghten's physical charms), along with Major Arthur Griffiths, the prisons inspector and crime writer, both of whom would play critical roles in the chief constable's maneuverings over the Ripper's identity. The committee made inquiries into French developments in this field by M. Alphonse Bertillon, the criminologist and "pioneer of identification by anthropometrical methods," whom the cosmopolitan Macnaghten had already met on many previous trips to France.[5]

The trio reported their findings on February 12, 1894, and the very next day a Liberal newspaper, the *Sun,* published a much ballyhooed scoop—nothing less than the alleged true identity of "Jack the Ripper." Without naming the suspect, the *Sun* went hard and loud for the 1891 jobber, Thomas Cutbush, by then languishing mutely in Broadmoor, a home for the criminally insane. The newspaper further claimed that a police detective (the unnamed William Race) was spilling the beans about how Scotland Yard's chiefs knew this man was the fiend but had concealed the truth from the public. The following day the same paper claimed the moral high ground by openly conceding that they could not tell the full story without ruining the maniac's family, "some of them in positions which would make them a target for the natural curiosity—for the unreasoning reprobation which would pursue any person even remotely connected with so hideous a monstrosity, and we must abstain, therefore, from giving his name in the interest of these unfortunate, innocent, and respectable connections." This must have been a very uncomfortable moment for Macnaghten reading this story—it was wrong but *right*. There was indeed concealment at the top about a prime suspect who was beyond charging, and acute anxiety over the suspect's respectable relations, but it involved a single police chief, and the likely "Jack" was deceased.

At this moment there might have been irresistible pressure for an official inquiry into Scotland Yard's Ripper investigation, one that would exonerate Cutbush and Scotland Yard but also would have the unfortunate effect of dislodging the Dorset solution (for example, the vicar might move ahead of the tenth anniversary schedule); and this would inevitably expose Colonel Majendie's unfortunate connection to the killer. In the final installment of February 19, 1894, the *Sun* interviewed a politician towards whom an establishment figure such as Macnaghten, even one with non-Tory friends such as Wilde and Sims, could only feel deep antipathy: Henry Labouchere. The wealthy son of a banker, nephew of a baron, the owner and editor of *Truth*, he was sad proof, for Macnaghten, that being an Old Etonian was no guarantee a man would grow up to be a gentleman. A radical irritant of the establishment, Labouchere was hated almost as much by Gladstone and members of his own party as by his political enemies on the right (Queen Victoria, whom he had insulted, vetoed his becoming a minister, the last time a British sovereign exercised such a prerogative). Though an economic progressive, Labouchere was a militant anti-homosexual, principally as another way of embarrassing and undermining the ruling elite. It was an anti-gay law named after him that ensnared Oscar Wilde (though the writer received two years' hard labor, the Liberal firebrand thought he got off lightly). It must have spoiled Macnaghten's boiled eggs and toast to read at breakfast the following explosive comment about the Whitechapel investigation by this class traitor: "Yes; if I were Mr. Asquith I should elect a clever officer to look into the matter."

In response I think Macnaghten managed to convince fellow Majendie pal George Sims to lampoon the Cutbush non-scoop, and the latter did this by returning to the Whitechapel murders for the first time since 1891 (much more would be done by the famous writer from 1899). Dagonet in "Mustard and Cress" in the *Referee* of February 21, 1894, has the home secretary, Asquith, facetiously replying to a question in the Commons about the Ripper: "I really think it inadvisable to take any proceedings in the matter. You see, it would revive all the horrible stories, and, who knows, it might prove an incentive to fresh crimes of a similar character. Gentleman of the press present will, I trust, kindly refrain from reporting either the question or the answer in the case." For the first time, I think, Macnaghten weighed up committing to the official record the truth about the fiend's identity. It would be highly unlikely that any Tory would question the home secretary over this matter of the lunatic in Broadmoor, as it would inevitably draw attention to a failure of the previous Conservative administration (and conceivably revive talk of Henry Farquharson's "doctrine"). There could be, however, a thorny question raised in the Commons by one of the radicals from the government's backbench (such as Labouchere). If Asquith stood up to deny that Thomas Cutbush was "Jack the Ripper" and some in the press recalled and revived the "son of a surgeon" tale—this time, maybe, with the backing of a clergyman—then Scotland Yard's flank would be vulnerable.

And not just the Yard's posterior would be lined up for a caning over the Block. An inquiry might establish that Macnaghten knew about this prime suspect, albeit a deceased one, and had withheld this information from CID for several years. Druitt was from a Tory family, Farquharson was a Tory M.P., Colonel Majendie was the Tory establishment personified and Macnaghten was a Tory through and through. T. P. O'Connor, the Liberal politician and editor of the *Sun,* could have made great hay with a "Jack the Tory" scandal, one that would have forced Scotland Yard to concede that they have never heard of the man until "some years after." Or would it be insinuated that Mr. Druitt had been tipped off as the net closed, to avoid tarnishing the good name of the Home Office's munitions czar? "Good Old Mac" would be the obvious scapegoat and sacked from the Force—again!

Two days after Sims tried to make light of the scoop, the chief constable quietly opened a second front by writing an internal report that might be asked for by Dr. Robert Anderson, acting at the request of Commissioner Sir Edward Bradford, who would be responding to an urgent query by Home Secretary H. H. Asquith. Even if it was not asked for, the fact of just having Druitt's name in the archive—though unknown

XII. Chief of Spin

to anybody else—could provide some kind of insurance for CID (and "Mac") if the story ever suddenly emerged out of Dorset prior to the 10th anniversary of Montague's funeral. Could Macnaghten both reveal the secret of Montague Druitt and yet also bury him deep within the dusty folds of bureaucratese? How about trying to hustle the notion that Druitt was a police suspect *before* he killed himself, laying a false trail that led away from both Farquharson and Majendie in 1891? But that begged the question of why Druitt was not arrested in 1888. Macnaghten seems to have decided to mislead by appearing to be forthright about conceding a lack of hard evidence against this English gentleman from a good family—obscuring the humiliating truth that the problem was not a lack of evidence, hard or soft, but rather the lack of a pulse.

Dated February 23, 1894, labeled "Confidential" and addressed to nobody, this much-misunderstood document is riddled with institutionally self-serving distortions. The most brazen of these is to claim that Thomas Cutbush was the nephew—practically the *de facto* son—of a retired superintendent, Charles Cutbush, presumably in an attempt to win sympathy from William Gladstone's Liberal government and to implicitly provide a vindictive motive for Inspector William Race's press revelations—in other words, that it was all some kind of petty, vicious sour-grapes payback (a deception that nonetheless substituted for the truth—the real killer *was* distantly related to a Home Office worthy). The most critical bit of slight-of-hand by "Mac" was to create an overdose-of-horror litmus test. Supposedly whichever suspect passed this test must be the likeliest "Jack," a case of deliberately putting the cart before the horse:

> It will be noted that the fury of the mutilations increased in each case, and, seemingly, the appetite only became sharpened by indulgence. It seems, then, highly improbable that the murderer would have suddenly stopped in November '88, and been content to recommence operations by merely prodding a girl behind some 2 years and 4 months afterwards. A much more *rational theory* is that the murderer's brain gave way altogether after his awful glut in Miller's Court, and that he *immediately* committed suicide, or, as a possible alternative, was found to be so hopelessly mad *by his relations*, that he was by them confined in some asylum [my italics].

Such a contrived definition neatly exonerated Thomas Cutbush, who was out and about for years after the Mary Jane Kelly murder, for whoever was the real Ripper supposedly could not speak, or think, or act rationally when he emerged from that little corner of Hades called Miller's Court. To make this plausible, "Mac" would imply that Druitt *vanished* after killing Kelly, whereabouts unknown, ergo he must have been delirious, wandering, eventually to extinguish his body in the river as his mind was already mush. This is how he sought in this document to downplay the man he believed was the Ripper:

> A Mr. M. J. Druitt, *said to be a doctor* & of good family—who disappeared at the time of the Miller's Court murder, & whose body (which was *said to have been* upwards of *a month* in the water) was found in the Thames on 31st December—or about 7 weeks after that murder [my italics].

There is no mention of Dorset, Blackheath, Chiswick (nor of course Henry Farquharson, the Reverend Charles Druitt or Colonel Majendie). And what a peculiarly off-key and implausible phrase is "said to be a doctor," for how could the police not have established what this Mr. Druitt did for a living? It is like writing "rumored to be a lawyer" or "he might have been a priest." A person's vocation, when it is one of the Victorian professions, cannot be a matter of speculation unless he comes from a less than respectable background—and it is explicitly stated that Druitt comes from a "good family." If it came out that this suspect was distantly related to the Majendies, Macnaghten could reply, however unconvincingly, that he, a close friend, had no idea of such a link—CID did not even know if he was a surgeon or not!

I think that Macnaghten wanted H. H. Asquith to reply in the Commons that Druitt *was* a doctor, no ifs or buts, because "barrister," combined with the detail about being fished from the Thames on the last day of 1888, would be sufficient to expose the Druitts and the Majendies among their unforgiving peers. But "Mac" was also loathe to officially align himself with such a ludicrous error and so he made it contingent; made this suspect's vocation only hearsay—told to him by somebody else—in the hope, I presume, that if he was called on the "inaccuracy" he could claim that Montie was mixed up with the suspect's father: a deceased surgeon. He also strains to obscure those three weeks when the Protean Druitt was outwardly functioning better than ever; at the school, at the cricket, winning in the courtroom and travelling on public transport. We can see that he knows full well that a month is the true length of time that the body was submerged and yet strains to close the gap—"disappeared at the time [of the murder] ... *said to* have been upwards *of a month* in the water" (my italics; once more Macnaghten preemptively blames an anonymous underling if this timeline should prove to be faulty).

In the Commons, Minister Asquith, if it came to it, could say that one of the much better suspects than the jobbing madman in Broadmoor was an English physician who killed himself on November 9, 1888. It would have to suffice in obscuring Montie and his relations while it was incumbent upon Macnaghten to prepare fallback plans for a debate in the Commons, if it did cause the Druitt solution to once more spill out of Dorset. This time the "son of a surgeon" tale could take on a life of its own; it would be beyond the control of "Good Old Mac" to balance competing pressures and hence become a tabloid sensation. Thus he was scrambling to get it on an official record that the police *were* aware of this man's potential culpability, and that it had nothing to do with the mere timing of his suicide—which in fact did not fit the "awful glut" phony test anyhow—but rather came from the cognition of family members. With contrasting clarity Macnaghten finished his section on the might-not-be-a-doctor with this: "[Druitt] was sexually insane and *from private information* I have little doubt but that his own family *believed* him to have been the murderer" (my italics).

The chief constable had ticked all the boxes—however awkwardly. On the one hand, the evidence was so thin that the police could not be bothered confirming if the suspect was a physician or not, but on the other hand, were quite certain that this Mr. M. J. Druitt gained erotic pleasure from ultra-violence. Why? The man's own family apparently believed. The reasoning presented here is disingenuously circular: they believed he was "Jack the Ripper" because he was "sexually insane." Turn it around and it has the same meaning: they "believed" that he was "sexually insane" because he was "Jack the Ripper." Or, to hammer flat this stubborn, semantic loop, the Druitt family believed that their member was "Jack the Ripper" because he was "Jack the Ripper." As for the unidentified source of the "private information," this was either a glancing reference to Henry Farquharson or Colonel Majendie, or both, and the vague reference allowed the chief constable to create a little distance from putting on file that he had conferred directly with family members (as Sims would later mention, albeit in veiled form in 1902). The low-born wannabe-toff H. H. Asquith could be trusted to act like a gentleman. Others in his party, however, would probably act in an unscrupulous partisan manner towards Farquharson (by then already damaged goods for libeling his Liberal opponent, Gatty), and so the original source on the Druitt secret remained anonymous in an internal document of state (and remained unknown, in name, until almost a decade into the 21st century).

Another deceitful deflection in Macnaghten's report of February 23, 1894, was to make it seem that there were a couple of other suspects who also, broadly speaking, qualified for the "awful glut" test. He threw in a pair of misfits who were also mentally incapable of functioning outside institutionalized care—or so Macnaghten would allege: "No one ever saw the Whitechapel murderer; many homicidal maniacs were suspected, but no shadow of proof could be thrown on any one. I may mention the cases of 3 men, *any one of whom* would have been more likely than Cutbush to have committed this series of murders" (my italics). Why not just leave it at Druitt as the alternative to Cutbush? Because that would give the game away that the drowned man was really the only possible "Jack." If so, what had CID done about him? Surely a family's belief was, at the very least, proof's shadow? The art of obscuring M. J. Druitt was for "Mac" to make him one of a bunch of mad suspects (if you have only two it looks indecisive, whereas three makes for a list). Who were these other window-dressing suspects going to be? The "awful glut" threshold ruled out the fleeing Dr. Tumblety and the low-life Pizer (and his inconveniently iron-clad alibi) and probably ruled out the "missing" medical student John Sanders. Tom Sadler's movements at home and abroad did not match the 1888 murders, only that of Alice "Clay Pipe" MacKenzie and of course his drinking companion, Frances "Carroty Nell" Coles. It seems Macnaghten decided it would have to be men who were on the original lists as possible "Jacks" but who never amounted to anything: local dregs, lunatics, foreigners, dodgy doctors, victims of gossip and prejudice. Manacled to Druitt, they would become a trio, yet sufficiently altered so that they and/or their own people did not recognize them if their basic identities had been broadcast by the home secretary.

Accessing his memory banks (or the Yard's files), Macnaghten at some point hit upon Aaron Kosminski, the unemployed Jewish hairdresser from a respectable Russian-Polish family, only 24 at the time of the murders and, since February 1891, permanently institutionalized as hopelessly insane. Of course Kosminski was a spectacular flop, measured against the "awful glut" criterion, just like Cutbush; but this could be easily fixed by backdating this minor suspect's having been sectioned closer to the time of Mary Jane Kelly's murder—but not too close, so as to leave a clear run for "Dr." Druitt. The real figure behind Macnaghten's "Kosminski"—no other name is given in the Report—was not stumbled upon until 1987, and even then by accident, and ironically was rejected by his discoverer, journeyman academic Martin Fido, as not being the true Polish-Jew prime suspect partly because he entered the asylum system too late. This is how Macnaghten recasts the Polish madman's biography:

> Kosminski—a Polish Jew—& resident in Whitechapel. This man became insane owing to many years *indulgence in solitary vices*. He had a great hatred of women, specially [*sic*] of

the prostitute class, & had *strong homicidal tendencies*: he was removed to a lunatic asylum about *March 1889*. There were *many circumstances* connected with this man which made him a strong "suspect" [my italics].

Who would be the second camouflage suspect? It would need to be a minor suspect from 1888 who had no known alibi for the murders and who had ended up, at some point, in an asylum. We will never know how long it took for the Old Etonian to settle, no doubt gleefully, on Michael Ostrog for a delicious bit of private revenge. The previous June, the Russian had been arrested for thieving in Canterbury. Instead of being justly tried for robbing Eton in 1889 he managed to convince his naïve captors that he was insane, and as they prepared to deport him to France he made good his escape at Dover. Subsequently in November of 1893 somebody went to "Mac's" alma mater and stole two books and a silver cup. The Russian faker was out there somewhere probably planning yet another sortie against Macnaghten's school, soiling the very ground where he had spent his happiest years. That bloody pest pretended to be a physician and insane—well, now he could be both in this official document (Ostrog was no more a real medical man than Druitt), while being unjustly elevated to the status of a natural-born killer:

> Michael Ostrog, a Russian *doctor*, and a convict, who was subsequently detained in a lunatic asylum as *a homicidal maniac*. This man's antecedents were of *the worst possible type*, and his whereabouts at the time of the murders could never be ascertained [my italics].

That the Macnaghten report was primarily created to avoid admitting that the deceased Druitt was unknown to Scotland Yard for years is shown not only by his memoir's "Laying the Ghost..." chapter, but in a mere aside about another case in the same book: "No light was vouchsafed to us, and after two or three weeks it seemed as if the Muswell Hill murder was going to climb on the shelf of undiscovered crimes alongside Jack the Ripper and the Café Royal case of eighteen months before."[6] As it turned out, the tabloid scoop over Thomas Cutbush (he was never named in the press) quickly petered out. No questions were asked in the House of Commons about it at all. (Labouchere was reportedly unimpressed by the "evidence" put forward by the *Sun*.) Macnaghten quietly mothballed his report in the Scotland Yard files. If a briefing document had been requested, we can never know whether the chief constable would have sent *this* version. What we do know from the limited sources available to us is that this aborted propaganda offensive was relaunched—and rewritten—in 1898, after Colonel Majendie had passed away and on the eve of the vicar's intervention. In fact, it was projected with tremendous success due to the credibility and fame of Dagonet.

Later in 1894 came a shock that must have caused "green faintness" once more for the chief constable. One of the allegedly significant suspects in his report, the Russian "doctor," turned out to have an unimpeachable alibi not only for one of his Eton robberies but also for the Whitechapel murders. The luckless Michael Ostrog was convicted and sentenced to five years (he had tried to impress the jury that he had invented a lifebelt that would help the wearer swim around the world!), but Macnaghten barely had three months to relish the imprisonment of the irrepressible confidence man when the following missive may have arrived in his in-tray, or at least its shocking contents were communicated to the chief constable. Written by a civil servant on October 9, 1894, it said, "Ostrog has established the fact that in 1889, when the offence was committed, he was in prison in France." In a final insult to natural justice, at least to "Mac," Ostrog was to be handed 10 pounds' compensation on release.[7] A cooler head might have considered that, all in all, it had been a lucky escape. For if *that* report had been sent, what with it claiming that a man snugly locked up in a French cell was more likely to be the Ripper than a demonstrably insane, permanently sectioned stabber—or jobber—of young women, then "Mac's" head might have been measured for the chopping block. Yet as we will see, "Mac" could not let go of the loathsome Russian.

The following year produced an even more acute crisis for Macnaghten, one that, again, might have exposed the Dorset solution—and his famous friend's links to it. It was nothing less than a Ripper suspect, William Grant (also known as Grainger), who was Irish, aged about 30 in 1888 and another Gentile sailor caught in the act of stabbing a Whitechapel prostitute who, like "Dark Sarah," survived. Reflecting the elated response of many newspapers across the globe to this fantastic, if belated, denouement to the mystery, here is the *Port Philip Herald* (Australia) of February 12, 1895: "Jack the Ripper Caught Red Handed. A Notorious Assassin Seized by the Police While Mutilating a Woman.... Gives the Name Grant. A Ship's Fireman. The Police Confident." The paper claimed, "The London police are of opinion that at last they have got safely under lock and key the long sought assassin known as Jack the Ripper." It seemed to be the Tom Sadler saga all over again, except with everything going right this time: the suspect was caught "red-handed," the victim survived to testify and a key eyewitness (presumably Joseph Lawende, fetched again from obscurity), at least according to the *Pall Mall Gazette* of May 7, 1895, positively identifying the prime suspect: "There is one person whom the police believe to have actually seen the Whitechapel murderer with a woman.... That person is stated *to have identified Grainger* as the man he then saw" (my italics). Fifteen years later Grant's sometime lawyer, George Kebbell, told the press that he was in no doubt that his former client—whom he strangely believed was deceased by 1910—was "Jack": "After he was arrested there were no more Whitechapel murders.... It was thoroughly recognized at the time that the police had got the man at last." Yet William Grant/Grainger as "Jack the Ripper" came to nothing. Nor did it make any impact on the popular memory of the case. In my opinion this is because at the very moment Grant was identified, Macnaghten took the bull by the horns and decided to mislead Dr. Anderson in order to distract him from pursuing this vile and violent sailor (yet innocent of being "Jack"), and he did this by revealing that the best suspect was long deceased. Except it was not Druitt, but instead Aaron Kosminski, the Polish self-abuser *who was alive* (but who was about as far removed from the Majendies as "Mac" could spin it, and this was the year that the colonel was *knighted*). Macnaghten's boss received a scathing assessment in the *Police Review* of 1901 (after Dr. Anderson, a stuffy, Victorian holdover, had been purged following the accession of Edward VII):

> [Anderson's] temperament, so admirably adapted to his social and religious proclivities, was not such as best fits one for the work of the CID. A Biblical scholar of repute, and a literary recluse, such as he is, would hardly be the man to take an active part in fighting the criminal classes of London. Discreet, silent, and reserved though he was, according to Major Griffiths' estimate, he lacked one inestimable quality to success as the director of the detective staff of the most important Police Force in the world, and that was just the requisite kind of knowledge of the world and men. An acknowledged authority on our

penal system, it was, perhaps, hardly a looked-for choice on the part of Mr. Home Secretary Matthews when Dr. Anderson was transferred from the Prisons Department to handle the reins at Scotland Yard.

This one "inestimable quality" that Anderson conspicuously lacked is exactly the one that his no. 2 had in abundance—a man's man. And not just because it is inconceivable that the prudish Dr. Anderson could ever have been regularly prowling around the East End, let alone buying "rum shrubs" for German dancing girls (see Chapter VII) or attending boxing matches with Colonel Majendie. There was a gentlemanly cold war between these two police administrators, so opposite as they were in temperament, background, interests and attitudes, because neither mentions the other in their respective memoirs, and yet they had worked together, cheek by jowl, for twelve years (the one allusion to an unnamed Macnaghten by Anderson in his book of 1910 slanders him as having nerves of jelly, a low blow dealt with in Chapter XV).

I theorize that the moment Joseph Lawende affirmed to Grant, Macnaghten immediately informed Dr. Anderson of the extraordinary positive identification by the Jewish witness and, predictably, his chief was delighted (so much so that the incident was permanently lodged in his memory, and when those synapses later crumbled his ego reassembled the fragments into a Jewish witness affirming his *Jewish* suspect) but that, with the passage of time, it would be, disappointingly, next to useless in a court of law. Before Anderson could pursue Grant further as the Whitechapel assassin, his chief constable had found a much better bet to be "Jack" from a list of 1888 possibilities (Macnaghten could take no credit, as this suspect was supposedly committed to an asylum three months *before* he even joined the Force). "Mac" further compelled Anderson's attention by informing his boss that the Polish suspect had been a chronic self-abuser. This was catnip to such a prudishly repressed Victorian Protestant fundamentalist. It was followed, I believe, by a huge fib by Macnaghten: this "Kosminski" had expired soon after incarceration (presumably from mental *and physical* exhaustion).

Though he never publicly commented on this R.I.P. aspect of his "Jack," three sources show us that Dr. Anderson likely believed that "Kosminski" was indeed long deceased. His worshipful subordinate, Donald Swanson, scribbled some wildly inaccurate annotations in a copy of his retired chief's 1910 memoirs. Among several errors is the howler that "Kosminski" had "died shortly afterwards"[8]; i.e., soon after being committed (and after supposedly being identified by a Jewish witness who refused to testify). In the same *Pall Mall Gazette* 1895 issue that reported a witness had positively identified Grant, there is this about Donald Swanson: "The theory entitled to most respect…. Mr. Swanson believed the crimes to have been the work of *a man who is now dead*" (my italics). Also Anderson's son wrote a biography of his parents recording, "Sir Robert states as a fact that the man was an alien from Eastern Europe, and *believed that he died in an asylum*"[9] (my italics—Anderson in fact *predeceased* Kosminski by a few months).

In 1910 a hapless Sir Robert Anderson would be engulfed by the outrage of English Jews at his memoir's boast that the fiend was definitely a Hebrew who had been harbored by "low-class" members of the brethren. The mortified old man tried to salve this hurt and to counter accusations of gross anti–Semitism by writing an explanatory letter to the *Jewish Chronicle* (published on March 11, 1910). Regarding evidence, all he provides is a pious old man's horror towards the human body: "If I were to describe *the condition of the maniac* who committed these murders, and the *course of loathsome immorality* which reduced him to that condition, it would be manifest that in his case every question of nationality and creed is lost in a ghastly study of human nature sunk to *the lowest depths of degradation*" (my italics). Tossed off as a mere footnote in his memoir is the alleged positive identification by a Jewish witness, and here Anderson makes a telling slip, at least in the initial magazine-excerpted version: "I will only add that when the individual whom we suspected *was caged in an asylum*, the only person who had ever had a good view of the murderer at once identified him; but when he learned that the suspect was a fellow-Jew he declined to swear to him" (my italics). A suspect who was *already* permanently institutionalized—i.e., mentally beyond ever being charged with any crime—is extremely unlikely to have been thrust into any kind of police lineup, let alone a judiciously dodgy one-on-one confrontation. By contrast the book version of the same memoir emphasized the sexual horror: "a loathsome creature whose *utterly unmentionable vices* reduced him to a lower level than that of the brute"[10] (my italics).

Put all those bits together and we can provisionally conclude that Dr. Robert Anderson and Donald Swanson believed from 1895—virtually the moment the Ripper allegations were shelved against William Grant—that "Kosminski" was the better suspect, and that the Polish lunatic had passed away shortly after being incarcerated in an asylum. It has never been noticed before by previous writers that Macnaghten, both in what he wrote in the revised version of his report and through his proxy Sims (in 1907—see Chapter XIII), clearly knew that Aaron Kosminski was very much alive. I think Melville Macnaghten managed to head off a legal rush to judgment over William Grant, who at least on paper was the greatest living Ripper suspect Scotland Yard ever had, by beguiling both Anderson and, by extension Swanson, whom "Mac" nevertheless respected, with the safely deceased *imbecile*—who *he* knew was really alive. In effect, Macnaghten had disguised Montie Druitt for his colleagues; a sexually deviant suspect, believed by his own family to be the miscreant and who was six feet under. As ever this deflection, or overlay of Druitt's fate onto another quite different suspect, protected Chief Inspector Vivian Majendie from any tabloid tsunami swamping him and his family in the case of somebody's boastful leak from Scotland Yard.

Very soon after the Grant letdown and the elevation of the Polish-Jewish suspect, Dr. Anderson did indiscreetly brag about solving the case to Major Arthur Griffiths (the latter writing under his pseudonym, Alfred Aylmer) for the January–June 1895 edition of *Windsor's Magazine* (without, at this date, any mention of a slam-dunk witness). This is the first time that the locked-up suspect, though abbreviated, entered the public record: "Much dissatisfaction was vented upon Mr. Anderson at the utterly abortive efforts to discover the perpetrator of the Whitechapel murders. He has himself a perfectly plausible theory that Jack the Ripper was a homicidal maniac, *temporarily at large*, whose hideous career was *cut short* by committal to an asylum" (my italics). Anderson had taken the bait—hook, line and sinker. From just this thumbnail summary by the assistant commissioner, we have a suspect who does not at all match the real Aaron Kosminski's timeline. Instead he matches "Kosminski"; the fictional variant created by Macnaghten who existed only in Scotland Yard's archive. Judging by the way Griffiths later wrote on this subject, Anderson's solution was not especially revelatory or impressive. This was presumably because over several years the prisons inspector (and true-crime writer) had conferred with Dr. Anderson, and yet this "caged lunatic" solution had never been mentioned before.

In his essay "Unsolved Mysteries of Crime" in *Cassell's Family Magazine* (April 1896), Major Arthur Griffiths (this time under his own name) mused over Scotland Yard's total inability to catch the Whitechapel fiend, dismissing, among various speculative theories, the notion that he could have been "a real case of Dr. Jekyll and Mr. Hyde. ... No doubt this was a plausible theory, but theory it was, and nothing more. It was never, even inferentially, supported by fact." And not two years later the same Major Griffiths would be suddenly informing readers that there were *three* prime police suspects in 1888 and that the strongest was an English medical man with *a dual identity* who may have committed "the murders under such uncontrollable impulse, and his prompt disappearance [was effected] by returning to his other irreproachable identity."

XIII

Hidden in Hyde

They drew near ... and beheld the face of Edward Hyde.... Life was quite gone.... Utterson knew that he was looking on the body of a self-destroyer.—Robert Louis Stevenson, 1886

The body of the doctor was found in the Thames.... Immediately after committing this murderous deed the author of it committed suicide ... a shrieking, raving fiend.—George R. Sims, 1907

In late 1885 Robert Louis Stevenson awoke from a nightmare. The best-selling author of the children's adventure serial *Treasure Island* (1883) had conjured up a vision of a good man who split off the evil side of his personality into an entirely separate entity. Being from a Scottish background, the author's inspiration was partly the 18th century figure of Deacon William Brodie—respectable pillar of Edinburgh society during the day and a master criminal, burglar and thief by night. Whether Stevenson then wrote most of the novella in one session, burnt it in disgust, then rewrote it all over again is a matter of debate among scholars. We do know the young, brooding author wrote the final draft quickly, and that when it was published by Longman and Green in January the following year, *Strange Case of Dr. Jekyll and Mr. Hyde* caused a sensation.[1] Almost instantly the names became part of the everyday language to describe human duality, and they remain so to this day. Due to being plagued from childhood by weak lungs Stevenson had relocated to the southwest, to the sea air of Bournemouth. By sheer coincidence this classic work of gothic horror/science fiction was composed near the original home of Montague John Druitt, who would, like Deacon Brodie, be considered—at least posthumously—a "remarkable" man in whom starkly contrasting sides fought for supremacy (although, unlike Brodie, the Ripper was never caught and hanged). A little over a decade after his self-murder, Montie Druitt would be intertwined with elements of Stevenson's masterful novella lifted from it by a much more popular writer, George Sims, whose own thoroughly mediocre plays and novels are today as much dust as the bones of their author. (Always in fragile health, Stevenson died in 1894, but his works will never be forgotten.)

The extraordinary twist ending of *Jekyll and Hyde* is that Henry Jekyll, tall, middle-aged, distinguished, and his sinister crony, the younger, shorter, plainer Mr. Edward Hyde, are *the same man*—due to a sci-fi potion concocted by the titular scientist. This must have struck those first readers in 1886 like a thunderclap, but once known it could never be unknown (like the insane Norman Bates impersonating his own mother in Alfred Hitchcock's *Psycho*). From the very first Victorian stage version it was assumed that the audience was aware of Stevenson's *denouement* and it was pointless pretending otherwise. The scientist Jekyll was moved to the center of the narrative, where we watch his descent into vice and mayhem as he repeatedly transforms himself with painful contortions into Hyde (who is now *physically* deformed too). The novella is almost entirely lacking in female characters (Jekyll is an aging bachelor and so are his friends), and this Calvinist lack of sexual interest was rectified by creating for the movies a "good" upper class girl to whom a *younger* Jekyll is engaged along with a contrasting "bad" girl, usually the cliché of the harlot-with-a-heart-of-gold, whom Hyde first debases before murdering. The actual protagonist of the novella is Dr. Jekyll's friend Mr. Gabriel John Utterson, a lawyer who becomes concerned that the shy scientist is being blackmailed by a loathsome low-life crony named Mr. Edward Hyde. To Utterson's mounting alarm, this rude and violent figure has unfettered access to gentleman Jekyll's lab and checkbook—and has been named sole beneficiary in the scientist's will! Confronting his friend, the doctor denies, unconvincingly, that Hyde has anything over him. A year later Hyde is seen by a horrified maid bashing to death Sir Danvers Carew, a member of parliament and a client of Utterson's. The crime takes place at night in the street and seems to have been a completely impulsive act of homicide. The weapon was a walking-stick (one given to Dr. Jekyll by Utterson) found by Scotland Yard detectives at Hyde's dingy digs in Soho. A manhunt fails to find the fugitive. A chastened Jekyll assures his friends that he has ended this strange relationship and produces a letter of apology from the wanted man (but the handwriting resembles the doctor's). After being more sociable for a while, Jekyll abruptly retreats to once more being a recluse. This is around the same time a mutual chum, Haste Lanyon, dies of nervous shock, having left a letter of explanation with Utterson—but

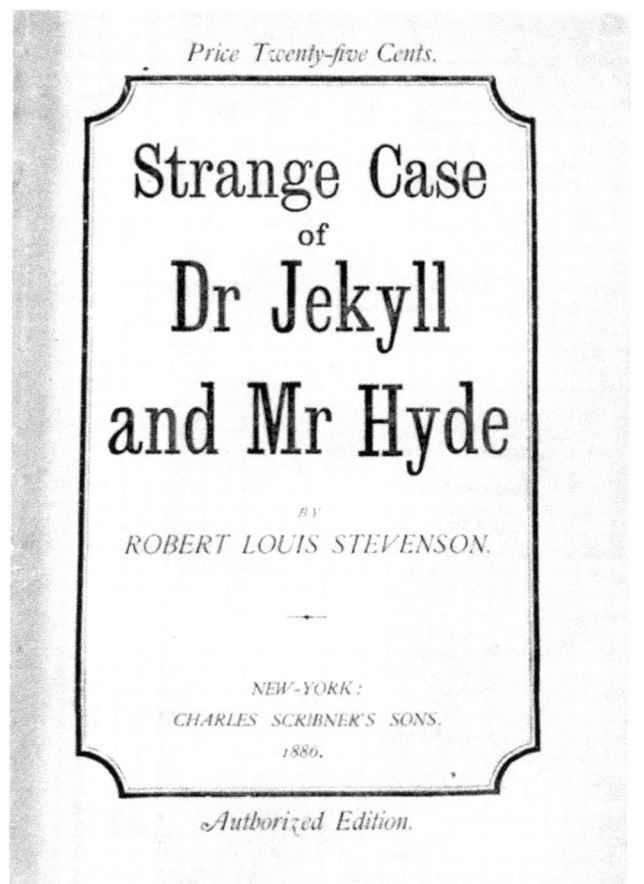

The perfect cover—**The original cover of Robert Louis Stevenson's classic 1886 macabre novella about human duality. Eventually the mad scientist would become the fictional wrappings in which Melville Macnaghten and George Sims would embalm the late Montague Druitt.**

only to be opened after *Jekyll's* death or disappearance. The worried lawyer visits Dr. Jekyll and finds the master's servants in a state of terror, as they believe that somebody else is in the locked lab with their master. A fed-up Utterson bangs on the door and demands to see their master. Hearing a voice that is not the good doctor's, Utterson and the butler, Poole, swing an axe to break into the lab. They think they are about to rescue an imprisoned Jekyll *from* Hyde. But they only find the wanted fiend in his death throes:

> Right in the midst there lay the body of a man sorely contorted and still twitching. They drew near on tiptoe, turned it on his back, and beheld the face of Edward Hyde. He was dressed in clothes too large for him, clothes of the doctor's bigness; the cords of his face still moved with a semblance of life, but life was quite gone; and by the crushed phial in the hand and the strong smell of kernels that hung upon the air, Utterson knew that he was looking on the body of a self-destroyer.[2]

Despite an extensive search, no evidence can be found of the whereabouts of Henry Jekyll. The mystery is solved by two documents found and read by Utterson: Lanyon's letter, which is his mind-shattering account of watching Hyde transform back into Jekyll, and the late doctor's own posthumous testimony in which he explains how his super-advanced research into how chemicals can affect the human mind destroyed his life because, after Carew's murder, he had begun to transform into Hyde *without* taking the potion. He need only fall asleep and awaken as the other. In effect he has become Hyde, and he takes the potion to transform with increasing brevity into Jekyll. Stevenson's final chapter, "Henry Jekyll's Full Statement of the Case," is worthy of Joseph Conrad: a literary *tour de force* of a civilized man's slippery descent into barbarism that forms the essential template for all future adaptations; i.e., the entire story told from the scientist's point of view. Jekyll explains that he was never wholly good and was, like all upright Victorian gentlemen, enduring the tension of his respectable outer life while struggling with an inner life plagued by sinful desires. Those evil thoughts measured, Jekyll writes, only one-tenth compared to his innate goodness, but that was quite enough to render him a moral cripple. Henry Jekyll already led a double life and sought through science (specifically a certain kind of salt) to achieve a spiritual purity by freeing himself from the dark side of his character (which, being only 10 percent Hyde was, as a consequence, much smaller in stature).

Long before Macnaghten and Sims would appropriate the armature of Stevenson's novella to hide Montie Druitt—and by doing so hide their by-then deceased friend Sir Vivian Majendie's familial connection to the suspect—a hit stage version was playing at the same time that the Whitechapel assassin was terrorizing Londoners (though the play did not close because of the murders). The German-born American actor/manager, Richard Mansfield, was enjoying success at the Lyceum theatre essaying the dual role.[3] In New York, the adaptation (by Thomas Russell Sullivan in early 1887) received only a lukewarm reception from critics, but it was "boffo" at the box office. Debuting in London on August 4, 1888 (having been delayed a month due to wrestling in the courts against rival productions that lacked the required copyright), *The Strange Case of Dr. Jekyll and Mr. Hyde* was reviewed with mixed feelings by the *Times*, bemoaning that the more subtle original has been transformed into something much cruder and melodramatic— reminiscent of the difference between the refined Jekyll and the abominable Hyde. Then came the Polly Nichols murder on August 31, 1888—believed by many to be the third murder by the same maniac's hand—and even though neither in the novella nor in this theatrical version is Mr. Hyde homicidal towards females, such a connection was nonetheless made, at least by the opportunistic tabloids. *The Star* of September 11, 1888, published a letter by an "eccentric" that would be nothing short of prescient about the murderer being a gentleman/sportsman: "The murderer is a Mr. Hyde, who seeks in the repose and comparative respectability of Dr. Jekyll security from the crimes he commits in his baser shape ... a statesman engaged in *the harmless pursuit of golf* at North Berwick" (my italics). With his love of the macabre and the theatre, Macnaghten must have adored both the page and stage versions of *Jekyll and Hyde* and read in the press about police speculation that the murderer was such a creature. As "Mac" cooled his heels at home waiting to be brought back in from the cold, I think he slotted away these references to Stevenson's tale in his voluminous memory. By the time 1898 rolled around, he probably knew that he had mere months to come up with some kind of propagandist deflection to draw attention away from the Church of England vicar who was going to release the truth—thankfully itself clothed in deflective fiction—that would potentially lead to the exposure of his by-then deceased friend. The chief constable decided to have Sims primed and ready like a ruthless sniper the moment the vicar put his head above the parapet, but he also decided to, somehow, publish *ahead* of the cleric's scoop to blunt its impact. Enter Arthur Griffiths and his massive tome on the history of Scotland Yard—a major to cover for a colonel.

The original "spider-man"—The "Great Profile," John Barrymore, starring in Hollywood's first monster-movie blockbuster: the silent classic *Dr. Jekyll and Mr. Hyde* (Paramount, 1920) directed by John S. Robertson and adapted by Clara Beranger. The actor eschewed the usual simian features in favor of playing the role as a pointy-headed, snaggle-toothed *arachnid* (even Hyde's fingers are elongated by an extra knuckle). Since it was released a year before Sir Melville's death, it is unlikely he saw the movie, as he was in the last stages of a terminal illness.

In reviewing his 1894 report, Macnaghten decided it needed some serious sprucing up to make it convince the hardnosed jailer. Copied and preserved by Christabel, the Lady Aberconway, this facsimile's existence was not revealed to the public until 1959, and the salient sections were not published until 1965 (the entire document was not available to any but a few researchers until as late as 2012). Nicknamed the "Aberconway Version" or the "Aberconway Papers" by writers on this subject, it is a much maligned and misunderstood document.[4] In many of today's books about the Whitechapel murders it barely rates a mention, being passed over in favor of its non-identical twin that its author had filed in Scotland Yard's archive. Yet the latter document, though official, had zero impact on the primary sources, whereas the contents of the rewrite were disseminated to the late Victorian public, initially by Major Griffiths. In the Edwardian era, George Sims, with a straight face, would characterize this publicity-driven semi-con as a definitive document of state that proved the culpability of the "Mad Doctor."

As Macnaghten revised the document—which is tellingly undated—he downplayed the police detective, William Race, even though he was the cause of all the "jobber" trouble (but that was in 1894, passé a few years later). Much more vital was that Macnaghten decided to impress upon Griffiths that this likely solution was his own: "A much more rational and workable theory, *to my way of thinking*, is that the 'rippers' [*sic*] brain gave way altogether after his awful glut in Miller's Court." Having buried eyewitness Joseph Lawende in the first version, Macnaghten decided that there would still have to be a potential chief witness for the major. Slyly, Macnaghten appropriated the most famous detail about the Frances Coles murder of 1891: that of a young, beat cop, P.C. Ernest Thompson, who was haunted for the rest of his tragically brief life by the notion that he should have run down the fiend. Now a Gentile sees a Jewish man near a crime scene. Because Macnaghten turned the ethnicity of witness and suspect inside-out, Lawende further receded into the woodwork, along with his sighting of a young man who strongly resembled Druitt. The author further tried to cut the knot in his own contradictory way by revealing that his investigation had, for all practical purposes, cleared two men while condemning a third: "Personally, & after much careful & deliberate consideration, I am inclined to exonerate the last 2. but *I have* always held strong opinions regarding no 1., *and the more I think the matter over*, the stronger do these opinions become. The truth, however, will never be known, and did indeed, at one time lie at the bottom of the Thames, if *my conjections* [*sic*] be correct" (my italics).

The critical section on Druitt is markedly reconceived. For example, the line "said to be a doctor" was a non-starter. It would lead Griffiths to reject the policeman's certainty if he showed he did not even know what his favored suspect did for a living. He also implies that "Dr." Druitt, his age upped by exactly a decade, lived with his family at Blackheath. Why then did they not promptly inform the authorities of their suspicions? Macnaghten had to imply that the relations were unreliable and, for that matter, not all that certain. To get the suspect to within striking distance of the East End, Macnaghten throws in the season rail pass (this bit of accurate data alone shows that Macnaghten knew the smallest details about Montie, for how could he know this and yet think his man was a middle-aged medico?):

> No 1. Mr. M. J. Druitt, *a doctor of about 41 years* of age & of *fairly* good family, who disappeared at the time of Miller's Court murder, and whose body was found floating in the Thames on 31st Dec: i.e., 7 weeks after the said murder. The body was said to have been in the water for a month, or more—on it was found *a season ticket between Blackheath and London*. From private information I have little doubt but that his own family *suspected* this man of being the Whitechapel murderer; it was *alleged* that he was sexually insane [my italics].

Between the two versions of the report—regardless of the order in which they were composed—Macnaghten and the Druitt family have swapped places. In the filed version the chief constable is not certain of Druitt's guilt at all (only, paradoxically, that he was a sexual maniac) whereas the family "believed," though of the named suspects the might-not-be-a-doctor best fits the "awful glut" litmus test. By contrast, in the revised version for public consumption it is Macnaghten who is the believer—"after much careful and deliberate consideration"—while the Ripper's now only "fairly" good family merely suspected. And the sidekick suspects in this version? They get to be "sexed-up" to make them more credible—and scary—while practically exonerated too: Kosminski had "a great hatred of women, with strong homicidal tendencies. He was (and *I believe still is*) detained in a lunatic asylum, about March 1889" (my italics). He may have been seen near a victim by a beat cop: "This man in appearance strongly resembled the individual seen by the City P.C. near Mitre Square." And here is what "Mac" does, no doubt with glee, to Ostrog, whom he knew perfectly well by late 1894 could not have been "Jack the Ripper." Way back in the *Birmingham Daily Post* of October 2, 1873, Macnaghten may have read the following about the Russian under the enticing heading, "The Robbery at Eton—a Criminal Romance": "Ostrog, while in London ... courted and won the affections of a most accomplished young lady." The Russian seems to have had the gift of charming the fairer sex. Macnaghten skewers this aspect of his m.o., as a practiced con artist, into something much more sinister and deplorable: "This man was said to have been *habitually cruel to women*, & for a long time was known to have *carried surgical knives & other instruments*" (my italics). It was arguably a petty revenge to take on the Russian, one that has quite misled other writers on this subject.[5] As for the rest, Macnaghten seems to have been anxious for Major Griffiths to be reassured that there were no loose ends. Where he had speculated in the 1894 version that Tom Sadler might have killed Alice MacKenzie and Frances Coles, now it is an underlined certainty regarding the second crime: "I have no doubt whatever in my own mind as to [Sadler's] having murdered Frances Coles" (this bit worked a treat with Major Griffiths, who dropped any specific mention of the embarrassing anticlimax of 1891). For the first time since 1892 the unnamed Montague Druitt was about to return to public consciousness as the Ripper—minus M.P. Farquharson, the Dorset location, and being a surgeon's son—having morphed into Dr. Henry Jekyll and Mr. Edward Hyde, for real. In his book, *Mysteries of Police and Crime*, Major Arthur Griffiths did utilize this supposed copy of the "Home Office Report," yet sparingly and with a definite undertone of caution—even skepticism. Why? Did he think that the data might be exaggerated to improve the image of Scotland Yard? Did he fear that "Good Old Mac" might be using him? Griffiths soberly writes, "The police, after the last murder, had brought their investigations to the point of strongly suspecting several persons, all of them known to be homicidal lunatics, and against three of these they held very plausible and reasonable grounds of suspicion." No doubt unknowingly, the major was repeating the fib that all three were suspects in 1888. This was only true of Aaron Kosminski and Michael Ostrog, and one was minor while the other had been subsequently cleared, but Griffiths records that "concerning two of them the case was weak, although it was based on certain colourable facts. One was a Polish Jew, a known lunatic, who was at large in the district of Whitechapel at the time of the murders, and who, having afterwards developed homicidal tendencies, was confined to an asylum." Griffiths had swallowed the backdating of the Thompson sighting helping to buttress the unnamed Kosminski as a potentially major suspect in 1888: "This man was said to resemble the murderer by the one person who got a glimpse of him—the police-constable in Mitre Court." As expected, the unnamed Ostrog was slandered as a knife-carrying medico whose whereabouts were unknown.

"A Dr. Jekyll and Mr. Hyde in real life"—**Sporting the smudge of a small, fair moustache, Montie Druitt clowns for the camera, aged 19 in 1876 (courtesy Warden and Scholars of Winchester College).**

Now it came to dealing with Montague Druitt. There had been an important innovation since Griffiths had seen the memorandum. Perhaps it was "Mac's" idea, or the major's, or his nervous publisher's, but whoever came up with it—likely Macnaghten, based on the initial mistake in the very first 1889 report about the recovery of the body— the "fairly good" Druitts had been disguised as anonymous chums: "The third person was of the same type, but the suspicion in his case was stronger, and there was every reason to believe that *his own friends* entertained grave doubts about him. He was also a doctor in the prime of life, was believed to be insane or on the borderland of insanity" (my italics). Montague Druitt had become Henry Jekyll and Edward Hyde: a middle-aged medico with concerned friends while constabulary play catch-up to the homicidal half of his dual identity. Hiding the family was a masterstroke (did Griffiths not wonder why, since the relations were being hidden, their culpable member was being left so exposed?), but the lines that followed, I think, would have disappointed Macnaghten as they disturbed the carefully orchestrated Stevensonian overlay he was trying to effect via his literary proxy (who maybe resisted the pull of the puppeteer's strings): "and he *disappeared immediately after* the last murder, that in Miller's Court, on the 9th November 1888. On the last day of that year, *seven weeks later*, his body was found floating in the Thames, and was said to have been *in the water a month*. The theory in this case was that after his last exploit, which was the most fiendish of all, his brain entirely gave way, and he became furiously insane and committed suicide" (my italics).[6] Griffiths had refused to repeat the nod-and-a-wink dodge that the doctor had likely killed himself in early November 1888. Instead he pointedly—and correctly—dated it as happening in early *December* 1888. For three weeks the doctor "in the prime of life" apparently wandered around in some kind of wretched fugue state. Amazingly he was unnoticed by anybody until three weeks later he headed for his rendezvous with the river. This timeline came perilously close to that of the real Montague Druitt, should it have been read by people who knew the Druitts or by graduates of the Valentine school. It would not do, but not to worry. George Sims would very soon ride to the rescue and bring into clearer focus the Ripper's uncanny resemblance to *Dr. Jekyll and Mr. Hyde*. It is a further measure of Major Griffiths' mixed feelings about this scoop—about how the police supposedly nearly caught "Jack"—that not only did he sideline Macnaghten's "Home Office Report" into the introduction, he also insisted on cautioning his readers that the Whitechapel murders were "a mystery which still remains unsolved."[7]

The unconvinced—perhaps even affronted—major was declaring his independence from "Good Old Mac" and the latter's doctrine that there were only five victims by "Jack" and that the case was virtually solved. Nevertheless I think that Macnaghten believed that he had achieved his overall objective of painting this real-life Jekyll and Hyde onto the public canvas. This is certainly what contemporaneous reviewers zoomed towards like moths to flame. Here is a review of Major Griffiths' book in the *St. James's Gazette* of December 16, 1898 (the former policeman and author Stewart P. Evans found this article in a scrapbook that had once belonged to none other than George Sims): "There is, however, one passage, relating to the Whitechapel murders of a decade ago, *which is so striking that no reviewer can fail to draw attention to it*" (my italics). In the *Manchester Times* of February 10, 1899, the scoop received big play but with a decided sting in the tail. Once more Griffiths' crucial paragraph is repeated, almost word for word. From the chief constable's point of view, however, there then came a moment like the one when Dorothy, thanks to Toto's investigation, pulls back the curtain to reveal that the supposedly omnipotent Wizard of Oz is just an old humbugger frantically yanking levers and pushing buttons: "Of course the mystery *is still unsolved*, and failing *authority* for this statement, we are left to adopt any of the thousand and one plausible hypotheses *to explain away police failure*" (my italics). The reason for the open scoffing is because another famous novelist/journalist—this time a right-wing fantasist, William Le Queux—accurately recalled as a journalist the 1888 to 1891 police investigation and the fact that there was never even a hint of a "Mad Doctor" suspect (except for Dr. Tumblety, but he was an American and had not killed himself). Le Queux writes that several of the detectives were his friends and they never enlightened him about this suspect. He correctly judges it to be a face-saving myth: "It was only long after the final crime that the theory above given was started in order to satisfy the public, and to account for the failure to make an arrest." Chapter XVI will examine William Le Queux and his extraordinary solution to the Ripper riddle (involving Rasputin, no less). For now we see that he was, in 1899, quite correct about there being no such police suspect at the time of the murders. Nonetheless Major Griffiths' Ripper footprint was everywhere in the 1900s. To take but one example from many, here is the great English writer Ford Madox Ford mentioning the solution in his *London Town—Past & Present* (Cassell, 1909): "a doctor who was known to be on the borderland of insanity ... whose body, seven weeks later, was found floating in the Thames, having been in the water it was estimated about a month."

Back in late 1898 and early 1899, Macnaghten was playing a spoiler role too, against the vicar and his "substantial truth under fictitious form," which debuted, on schedule, ten years after the Druitt family put Montie into the ground in a Wimborne cemetery. (What the chief constable might not have anticipated was that the cleric could not get his piece published due to his "honest lying.") As examined previously, the unnamed vicar had described the fiend as having the time and lucidity to make a confession to an Anglican clergyman in the wake of the Kelly murder before passing away. Somewhat missed by many reviewers of the time regarding Griffiths' scoop and the vicar's tale was that Macnaghten was attempting to pull a fast one about the Ripper case having ended quickly with Mary Jane Kelly; that her murder being the ghastly finale was realized by law enforcement in 1888. Almost alone, the *Daily Mail*, the newspaper that had received the vicar's strange account in the post—"The Whitechurch Murders: Solution of a London Mystery"—did grasp this alteration and said so. As we also see in the article of January 19, 1899, "Did Jack the Ripper Make a Confession?" the sidekick suspects helped muddy the waters—as was arguably their purpose:

> Certainly Major Arthur Griffiths, in his new work on "Mysteries of Police and Crime," suggests that the police believe the assassin to have been a doctor, bordering on insanity, whose body was found floating in the Thames soon after the last crime of the series; *but as the Major also mentions that this man was one of three known homicidal lunatics* against whom the police "held very plausible and reasonable grounds of suspicion," that conjectural explanation *does not appear to count for much by itself.* We thought at first the Vicar was at fault in believing that ten years had passed yet since the last murder of the series, for there were other somewhat similar crimes in 1889. But, on referring again to Major Griffiths' book, we find he states that the last "Jack the Ripper" murder was that in Miller's Court on November 9, 1888—*a confirmation of the Vicar's sources of information* [my italics].

As with the Griffiths revelation, the vicar received serious if brief attention in the national and regional press. For example, in the *Yorkshire Evening Post* of January 18, 1899, the article was fully reproduced from the *Daily Mail* with the headline: "The Ripper Mystery. A Vicar Says He Knows the Culprit's Identity. Died Shortly After the Last Murder." *The Coventry Evening Telegraph* of January 18, 1899, headlined the fact-and-fiction scoop as this: "Jack the Ripper. A Vicar's Strange Story." *The Evening Telegraph Angus Scotland* picked up the story on January 20, 1899: "Did Jack the Ripper Make a Confession?," and the *Daily Gazette for Middlesbrough* followed a day later: "Light on the Whitechapel Mystery." Six days afterwards the *Illustrated Police News*, a tabloid devoted to cops and crooks, made big play with the story and openly wondered if this was really it—the conclusive solution. It also added that the vicar "obtained his information from a brother clergyman *to whom the murderer made a full and complete confession*" (my italics). What this source left out entirely is the vicar's disconcerting claim to have mixed fact and fiction, presumably because it thoroughly sabotaged a good yarn. This is presumably why it dropped the vicar's parting clue; that the killer was "at one time a surgeon," because the tabloid had judged that a maniac who was handy with a knife because he was medically trained could not be just an afterthought. Even though this element would bring the gentleman suspect into alignment with Griffiths' "Mad Doctor," the newspaper dismissed it as one of the clergyman's bits of fiction. It hardly mattered, as the vicar's Ripper was body-slammed by Dagonet in "Mustard and Cress" in the January 22, 1899, issue of the *Referee*, just three days after first breaking in the *Daily Mail*. I think that in collusion with Macnaghten, the famous writer was determined to ruthlessly rewrite the vicar's Ripper as a better scoop (by eliminating not only the mix of fact and fiction but also the brother clergyman—now it is the vicar himself who hears the confession from a criminal lunatic on his deathbed). This is followed by Dagonet's torpedoing it on the basis that the real fiend had no time to confess anything to anybody, what his being a gibbering wreck with just enough demonic energy to stagger to the Embankment's edge:

> There are bound to be various revelations concerning Jack the Ripper as the years go on. This time it is a Vicar who heard his dying confession. I have no doubt a great many lunatics have said they were Jack the Ripper on their death-beds. It is a good exit, and when the dramatic instinct is strong in a man he always wants an exit line, especially when he isn't coming on in the little play of "Life" any more.

Claiming he is above interfering with all this tabloid grubbiness, as he has unimpeachable insider contacts with the top cops, Sims shows himself to be unrestrained and goes much further than the cautious major. The writer-criminologist consolidates "Mac's" myth that the police were about to arrest the "Mad Doctor," just like the forces of justice who were fast closing on a cornered Edward Hyde (and a shameless inversion of the Tumblety fumble in which the promising doctor suspect *was* arrested but jumped his bail): "I don't quite see how the real Jack could have confessed, seeing that he committed suicide after the horrible mutilation of the woman in the house in Dorset-street, Spitalfields. ... Almost immediately after this murder he drowned himself in the Thames. His name is perfectly well known to the police. If he hadn't committed suicide he would have been arrested." With this single column George Sims simply hit the reset button. All of his writings in 1888 to early 1891 about a clueless constabulary, the impenetrable mystery whose very nickname was a piece of journalistic exploitation, all were disposed of as so much "custard and mess" by the January 1899 column, as if written by a Sims' double in a parallel dimension. Comparing what Dagonet wrote in 1888 to his certainties of the 1900s—starting in 1899—show that of course he was shielding the late Sir Vivian Majendie, whose reputation may have been put at risk by his cousin's son-in-law (interestingly, Sims chose not to use the Jack-the-surgeon element, not yet, perhaps because he feared it would be a backhanded confirmation of the vicar's saying his suspect had been "at one time a surgeon"). How clever too of Sims to cannibalize his own short story from 1892, "The Priest's Secret," and overlay it onto the vicar's Ripper; he has this alleged "Jack" die in his bed after fooling a sincere but naive cleric with his last words—when the unidentified cleric had claimed no such thing. In fact, the clergyman carefully withheld the manner of the murderer's passing away, though it conveniently occurred after he made a full confession to a churchman. It suggests suicide, for surely the vicar would have wanted to deny the implication of this deceased gent having committed yet another mortal sin, if this was not how he died. Newspapers lost interest in the vicar's tale (the cleric was not talking, and the *Daily Mail* had no intention of outing him; plus Dagonet had assured his readers there was nothing to it) and he was swiftly forgotten. When rediscovered in the 1990s, the "North Country Vicar" was seen as nothing but a worthless tabloid curiosity. It was unappreciated that Griffiths and Sims, like encircling pincers, had snuffed out a source that was closer to the truth in its few facts about the drowned barrister than their own was.

In 1900, Vicar Charles Druitt died after a long illness. As if the coast were now clear Sims—in the *Referee* of February 16, 1902—began to elaborate on the "Mad Doctor" and for the first time revealed a highly incriminating fact never before mentioned: that the suspect had once been committed to an asylum as a potentially homicidal lunatic—perhaps twice (which meant the "Mad Doctor" was becoming more like the vicar's Ripper; he too was an ex-surgeon who had not worked since his mental breakdown and temporary seclusion). This premature release of the manifestly dangerous medico back in 1887 was evidence, Sims argued, that a penny-pinching state was regularly allowing the mentally deranged onto the streets (no doubt this was a true social concern; it is just that his example was fictitious). On July 3, 1902, Sims/Dagonet returned to the Whitechapel crimes to encourage the police to make more strenuous efforts in a recent murder investigation. Once more his example was not a real case but a reworking of the climax of Stevenson's classic via the "Aberconway Papers," as he writes of the "process of exhaustion which enabled them at last to know the real name and address of Jack the Ripper. ... The police were in search of him alive when they found him dead." While those words are technically true (CID detectives were indeed searching for information about Dr. Tumblety, including abroad, as Druitt's well-dressed corpse floated into view in Chiswick), they are also thoroughly misleading, and a boon for Scotland Yard's reputation as "Mac" took over as assistant commissioner.

On February 11, 1907, the chief dashed off a brief note to Sims as the latter prepared his largest article ever on "Jack the Ripper." Macnaghten has a go at Italians in London before providing a list of the victims' names, places they were killed and extent of the mutilations (repeating the "awful glut" mythos that Nichols was only slightly cut):

> Dear Sims, Yet another "light" in dark, & not generally known, metropolitan spots has flashed across my mind:—Eyre Street Hill—Clerkswell—when there is a large colony of Italians who are mostly ice-cream vendors by day, &, not infrequently, stabber & shootists by night. It may also save you the trouble of research if I give the times & places of Jack ye Ripper's pleasantries. ... & don't trouble to reply to this, Yours always M. L. Macnaghten.

The subsequent article by Sims may have been one of the most influential ever written on this subject, yet it lay totally forgotten until the mid 1990s. In the issue of *Lloyds Weekly* of September 7, 1907, Sims was provided with his own byline, "My Criminal Museum," and he used it to consolidate the image of the Ripper as a middle-aged, English gentleman-surgeon who strolled about the East End wearing fine clothes—minus a cape and top hat—and sporting a beard (a potentially satanic detail that did not catch on with illustrators, possibly because Henry Jekyll was always depicted as clean-shaven).[8] The affluent murderer and ex–asylum patient lived in a suburb "six miles" from the East End—which matches Blackheath—to which he returned, on foot, after each of his five homicides (that bit is likely to have been true too). The horror of what was done to Mary Jane Kelly, however, rendered it impossible for any man to go on living even "a single day" longer—the "awful glut" litmus at its most hilariously apocalyptic.

Consequently this physician who suffered from a "peculiar mania" killed himself immediately—in a big, stumbling rush—his body washing up no more than four weeks later ("Mac's" 1914 memoirs extend the gap between these two events by at least "a single day"):

> A month after the last murder the body of the doctor was found in the Thames. There was everything about it to suggest that it had been in the river for nearly a month. The horrible nature of the atrocity committed in Miller's-court pointed to the last stage of frenzied mania. Each murder had shown a marked increase in maniacal ferocity. The last was the culminating point. The probability is that immediately after committing this murderous deed the author of it committed suicide. There was nothing else left for him to do except to be found wandering, a shrieking, raving, fiend, fit only for the padded cell. What is probable is that after the murder he made his way to the river, and in the dark hours of a November night or in the misty dawn he leapt in and was drowned.

The article is almost a stand-alone piece of fiction, with mere slivers of fact permitted to peek through, but no reader could possibly know which was which (only a very devoted Dagonet fan would have noticed that the timing of the recovery of the body had shifted *backwards*). For significant witnesses, Sims claims there were only two: an unlucky bobbie who saw the sinister silhouette of a man emerging from the gloom of a crime scene but later, at some kind of official confrontation, could not positively identify that shape with the Polish-Jewish suspect (who now lived alone, worked in a hospital in Poland and was committed by state authorities).

A better witness, as expected by now from Sims, was a coffee-stall owner serving a stranger with suspicious blood-stained cuffs on the morning of the double murder (with not a jest about sausages in sight), and, once more, he brags about his 1879 pictorial resemblance to the best suspect. The Russian madman still brandishes his surgical knives and was reportedly "capable of any atrocity" despite Sims' seemingly knowing from Macnaghten that, at the time of the 1888 murders, the unnamed Ostrog was in France, the giveaway line being "when inquiries were afterwards set on foot he was found to be *in a criminal lunatic asylum abroad*" (my italics). The sidekicks are both cleared of complicity because they were alive and moving about among the public for a long time after the Miller's Court massacre—which again matches the known facts—while the real killer could be nothing but a mindless automaton: "a raving madman."

Most interestingly, a fictional variation of Dr. Tumblety was resurrected by Sims in his 1907 article—as a *young*, American medical student—who is no less than the leading alternate theory to the English doctor (no such American figure appears in either version of the Macnaghten report). But the strange Yank, who may have been stealing wombs to create some kind of "elixir of life," can be ruled out too because he did not instantly jump in a river; he was alive and well long after—which is true again.[9]

In 1917 George Sims published his own memoirs and repeated, for the final time, the coffee-stall customer story—"the redoubtable Ripper was not unlike me as I was at the time"—and also repeats the deceit about the doctor's rotting body recovered in early December 1888. Yet knowing that this might be the last time he ever wrote on this topic, Sims confronted head-on what he and Macnaghten seemingly had been doing for nearly twenty years; accusing a dead man who could not defend himself. Sims denied it: "But you can't try a corpse for a crime, however strong the suspicion may be. And the authorities could not say, 'This dead man was Jack the Ripper.' The dead cannot defend themselves. But there were circumstances which left very little doubt in the official mind as to the Ripper's identity."[10] Was this principled lament not rank hypocrisy? The dead Montague Druitt could, indeed, not defend himself—but then again he *did not need to* if he was rendered unrecognizable.

For all those years Sir Melville Macnaghten had been pointing *away* from the relevant dead man as much as towards the authentic fiend through the handy prism of "Jekyll and Hyde" (as George Sims was still doing in 1917).

By the Edwardian sunset, the image of "Jack the Ripper" as an English surgeon created by "Mac" and "Tatcho"—and not some poor, foreign nonentity—was no less than hegemonic (ironically, Macnaghten's later more factual memoirs made no headway against his own semi-fictional creation), thanks in large part to Robert Louis Stevenson's macabre classic. Instant icons of pop culture, Henry Jekyll and Edward Hyde had provided the indispensible template for the solution to "Jack the Ripper," one audaciously shoehorned into the 1888 investigation. Setting aside *The Strange Case of Dr. Jekyll and Mr. Hyde*, there were other pieces of popular literature written in the wake of the 1888 murders and the Dorset solution of 1891 that reveal Melville Macnaghten and George Sims must have been intimately aware of the true details about Montague John Druitt.

XIV

From Montague to Mortemer

Mr. Slade ... had a fine intellectual brow, and his face was pleasant in repose, but the smile was sinister, and he never laughed.—Illustrated Police News, 1905

Sir Melville's theory regarding the Whitechapel murders, corroborates to a large extent the theory cleverly elaborated by Mrs. BELLOC-LOWNDES in her last story, "The Lodger."—The New York Times Book Review, 1914

Evidence that the Montague Druitt solution, or at least its fictional variant "Doctor Druitt," had become common knowledge to members of the Garrick Club of London's writers and artists (whose membership included Sir Melville Macnaghten and George R. Sims) is that a minor comic writer named Frank Richardson must have known the Ripper's real name. Only discovered a few years ago by Chris Phillips this utterly mediocre book, *The Worst Man in the World* (London, Eveleigh Nash, 1908) contains an insider's jaw-dropping reference to the authentic Whitechapel murderer as the name Druitt becomes ... "Bluitt":

> Murder is practiced solely by the barbarous or the insane. What art could thrive with such exponents? Doctor Bluitt, whose fantastic ability was so strikingly exhibited in his admirable series of Whitechapel murders, flung himself raving into the Thames. If only he had been sane, he, I fondly fancy, might have founded a school. What the art requires is a sane Doctor Bluitt [58–59].

And later in the same text:

> Clearly the chords of sanity had snapped. Even as the medical man who will for ever be known as Jack the Ripper after the curious fantasies of his masterpiece in Miller's Court had flung himself, raving, into the Thames, so Sir Rupert, hopelessly insane, was now seized with homicidal mania [146].

To the average Edwardian reader, "Doctor Bluitt" was just a funny-sounding name—obviously fictitious; whereas to Macnaghten, Sims and the surviving members of the killer's family (including presumably William Druitt, who died the following year) and that of the late Sir Vivian Majendie, it surely could only have caused heartburn to see "Whitechapel," "Bluitt" and "Thames" in such discomforting proximity. Richardson may not have been conscious of potentially stamping on anybody's toes because all he knew was that Jack-as-Jekyll was the literal truth; the Ripper as middle-aged physician whose family and friends already knew the worst. To the presumed consternation of "Mac" and "Tatcho," this less-than-discreet wordsmith almost let the proverbial cat out of the bag.

(Or did Sims tell Richardson the whole story? Is that why the latter writes that the Ripper "might have founded a school"?) This chapter examines three pieces of popular literature from the Late Victorian and Edwardian eras that are pertinent to solving the mystery *inside* the mystery of "Jack the Ripper"; excerpts from a few of George Sims' short stories; Guy Logan's *The True History of Jack the Ripper* and *The Lodger* by Marie Adelaide Belloc-Lowndes—both of the latter authors being known to Sims and arguably influenced by him (who in turn was channeling Macnaghten). A few years before he launched the "Mad Doctor" solution, George Sims had likely exploited Montague Druitt in his "The Priest's Secret" of 1892. Another example is to be found in one of his stories of five years later featuring his female detective Dorcas Dene (she is in no sense a proto-feminist figure. Rather, she is a Victorian "New Woman," due to her intelligence, independence and multiple skills, but who had discovered a talent for deduction only after her husband had gone blind and they needed the income). She has a neighbor, Mr. Johnson, an avuncular, pipe-smoking, retired superintendent of the Yard who is clearly inspired by Macnaghten—"genial," "good-hearted" and "kind"—who has become a private eye, and he knows where all the bodies are buried. Mr. Johnson "was employed in many delicate family matters by a well-known firm of solicitors who are supposed to have *the secrets of half the aristocracy* locked away in their strong room" (my italics). She explains how the ex-cop has enlightened the budding detective about the world's inner and uglier workings:

> After my poor Paul lost his sight Mr. Johnson who was a widower would come in wherever he was at home—many of his cases took him out of London for weeks together—and helped to cheer my poor boy up by telling him about the latest romance or scandal in which he had been engaged.

Whereas Dorcas' appalled mother cannot bear to listen to the detective because

> she would soon begin to believe that every man and woman she met had a guilty secret, and the world was one great chamber of horrors with living figures instead of waxwork ones like those of Madam Tussaud's.

The literary conceit is that these "cases" are related to us by a writer, Mr. Saxon, a platonic admirer and "assistant" to the female sleuth—and an obvious stand-in for Sims. At one point the narrator warns her that he will feel compelled to publish his insider's account, despite her cases involving respectable upper class people who are fearful of a scandal if they go near the police—hence

Dr. Bluitt, Lord Helsham, Mortemer Slade and the Avenger—"His lips were thin ... his eyes placed rather close together in his head. He had a fine intellectual brow, and his face was pleasant in repose, but the smile was sinister" (Guy Logan, 1905). The picture is of Montague Druitt aged 15 in 1872 (courtesy Warden and Scholars of Winchester College).

their employing Mrs. Dene's discreet services. Dorcas is not the slightest bit perturbed at the idea of her V.I.P. clients' dirty linen being aired to the entire world because everybody, she demands of the Sims' proxy, will be impenetrably *hidden*:

> "And you don't object?"
> "Oh no, but with this stipulation, that you will use the material in such a way as not to identify any of the cases with the real parties concerned."[1]

This is exactly what is done with Montague Druitt, by the same author, and this disguise will later rupture post–World War II understanding of this subject. In a Dorcas Dene short story called "The Helsham Mystery" we find the intrepid detective retained by a Lady Helsham because her son has gone missing. Due to a note left for his actress-sweetheart, it sounds alarmingly to Dorcas as if the young aristocrat is contemplating suicide. A key dialogue exchange reads as if Sims has appropriated William Druitt's secretly mixed feelings about finding his missing Montie, as the mother in this story cannot hide a certain amount of relief at hearing that her son might be deceased. Dorcas reports that Lady Helsham "has seemed to me all along to be in a state of nervous terror as to something dreadful being likely to happen, and when I suggested suicide it seemed as though that was not the worst that she had contemplated. That's what I meant by its being a relief to her ... and she can only feel that relief for two reasons—either that his death would prevent his arrest for some crime, or would prevent the discovery of something which would bring terrible consequences to him."[2] Or to her, replies another character. A few days later the narrator is in Paris and reads in the *Daily Telegraph* that it seems that the young aristocrat has drowned—by accident. Consider how much this reminds us of the mysteries swirling around Montague John Druitt. A young man with everything to live for disappears, his relations are tortured by worry—but also by some dreadful secret and thus equally fear his return—and then, tidily, he is judged to have drowned. End of crisis. But this is not a story of homicide or suicide. Dorcas has herself arranged that Lord Helsham vanish due to a convoluted plot in which it turns out he is not the true heir, his aunt is really his mother, and to marry his actress-girlfriend he will have to emigrate, among other complexities.

In another Dorcas Dene story called "The Man with the Wild Eyes," there is the vivid description of the recovery of a drowned body in a lake found by a solitary rower. Again it reads as if it was adapted straight from a newspaper account of Druitt's reappearance in the Thames (and also involves not only attempted homicide but also the misleading of a coroner's inquest): "I found Dorcas standing at the edge of the lake, and Peters and two of the gardeners lifting the drowned body of a man into the boat which was alongside." Dorcas is anxious that the dead man's pockets be quickly searched before the police arrive, and that any compromising papers or letters be spirited away lest they embarrass a respectable family.[3] The deceased was Victor DuBois, who had been released from a private asylum, a ticking human bomb, exactly the same (false) criticism that Sims will later level at the state for prematurely releasing the Ripper. Victor tried to kill his fiancée while in a maniacal fit, only causing her to faint: "*Instantly* he became *furious*. Seized with a *sudden mania*, he grasped her by the throat.... The murderer, probably thinking that she was dead, must have waded out into the deep water and drowned himself"[4] (my italics). The intrepid sleuth makes sure that the subsequent inquest into his suicide is kept ignorant about the attempted homicide, which will be rendered easier by the non-attendance of the would-be victim: "Before she left Orley Park Dorcas advised the Colonel to let the inquest be held without any light being thrown on the affair by him.... We heard later that at the inquest an official from the asylum attended, and the local jury found that Victor Dubois, a lunatic ... drowned himself in the lake while temporarily insane.... The inquest ended in a satisfactory verdict."[5] Putting aside their value as textual evidence that George Sims and Melville Macnaghten had conferred in detail about the circumstances of Montie Druitt's life and death, the Dorcas Dene stories—despite their charming heroine—are marred by a tiresome lack of narrative ingenuity. But her chronicles are literary masterworks compared to the next piece to be analyzed.

As this book was being shaped into final form a sensational new source was found that further supports the theory of Macnaghten and Sims discreetly disguising Montie Druitt, if for no other reason than to protect their mutual friend Colonel Majendie. It is a tabloid serial called *The True History of Jack the Ripper* (1905) by Guy Logan, rereleased by Amberley Publishing as *The Forgotten 1905 Ripper Novel* (with commentary by Jan Bondeson) and involves the drowned "Mad Doctor" being *publicly semi-fictionalized.* This was known and understood by Edwardian readers because, obviously, the real names could not be used. The army deserter, failed actor-cum-writer and opportunistic journalist Guy Logan had become a regular contributor to the *Illustrated Police News*. He had a major hit with his serial novella, *Violet Kildare: A Romance of the South African War* about the Boer War (Logan had never been near South Africa) and the adventures of its titular character, spiced with generous dollops of sex and violence, and melodramatic twists. In an article for the same publication, Logan refers to George Sims.[6] Perhaps the famous crime writer was a source, even a quasi-mentor—in combination with Logan's lurid imagination—for his next serial, this time about the Whitechapel serial killer, as there was nobody else, apart from Macnaghten, who knew the nuts and bolts of the Druitt solution. The first installment in the 1905 *Illustrated Police News* of Logan's novella, titled "The Escape" (the entire serial was only published as a single book in 2013), begins by pointing out that the names of people and places have been altered in order to protect the innocent (and the guilty).[7] Just as with the drowned "Mad Doctor" being thought to be more accurate than the vicar's "honest lies," here we have a mixture of fact and fiction accepted as such by readers who do not know that Sims' writings in "Mustard and Cress" are the same kind of impenetrable confection. Logan has the proto-fiend make a daring escape from the asylum, which gives the writer a chance for him to kill (in this case a vigilant young doctor) before he even arrives in Whitechapel. Not all the names are simply conjured out of thin air either. George Sims must have known Montague John Druitt's real name and passed it along to Logan. We know this because the apprentice changed it into the very similar-sounding: *Mortemer*. One of the patients in Dr. Kent's rather attractive Home for the Mindless is Mr. Mortemer Slade; tall, slim, erudite, middle-aged, trained as a doctor but yet to practice, and quite insane in a high-functioning kind of way (Logan reverses Stevenson's Jekyll-and-Hyde equation; he makes Slade nine-tenths evil and only superficially one-tenth good). The novella's prose, it has to be said, is florid and cartoonish to the point of tedium, and may account for why this work had no staying power in pop culture (in terms of literary quality there is a Hyde-style devolution from Robert Louis Stevenson to George Sims to Guy Logan).

Unlike Druitt, Mr. Slade is clean-shaven, which is a shame because he sorely needs a moustache to twirl (later in the narrative he dons a false beard, becoming Sims-like). There is an unlikely subplot about Slade's ex-sweetheart—the upper class paragon of rectitude Phyllis Primrose—being haunted by the killer and his attempts to fiendishly sabotage her betrothal to a worthy gentleman (the Ripper pretends to be another doctor and diagnoses her fiancée with imminent heart failure, before trying to dispatch him with a knife). Whereas the description of the villain's features, minus the clichés about sinister smiles, is reminiscent of Druitt, suggesting that Logan sat down and had quite a long session with Sims—at some restaurant or pub, or his cluttered mansion—and the former took copious notes (a female detective, Mrs. Sarah Watts, turns up to be abducted by Slade so the story even has its own Dorcas Dene figure): "Mr. Slade smiled grimly. He had not a nice smile. His lips were thin, his teeth rather sharp and discolored, his eyes placed rather close together in his head. He had a fine intellectual brow, and his face was pleasant in repose, but the smile was sinister, and he never laughed."[8]

There are also examples in the text of Assistant Commissioner Melville Macnaghten's probable influence on Logan too. For example, the police chief in 1914 compares the unnamed Montie to Nero, and sure enough Logan has Mortemer Slade compare himself to the same ancient despot.[9] Another is that a witness to Martha Tabram (Logan uses her alternate name, Turner) on the fateful night later fails to identify two Coldstream Guards under arrest at the Tower. In his memoir chapter "Laying the Ghost of Jack the Ripper," Macnaghten had written—rather wistfully—of the chorus of newspaper boys in late 1888: "Even now I can recall the foggy evenings, and hear again the raucous cries of the newspaper boys: 'Another horrible murder, murder, mutilation, Whitechapel.'" In Logan this becomes, "The raucous cries of a newsboy attracted her attention.... AWFUL MURDER IN WHITECHAPEL, GHASTLY MUTILATION! NO ARREST! SPECIAL!"[10] One of the leading fictional characters—and Mortemer Slade's nemesis—is a gentleman private investigator, Edmund Blake, who is always way ahead of the flatfooted plods of the hapless commissioner, Sir Charles Warren (the latter's real name is used). On one level Logan rips off Conan Doyle's Sherlock Holmes; Blake even has his own Watson, though he soon drops out of the narrative. On the other hand, different from Holmes, Logan's description is of a shamus who hides a steel-trap mind behind an urbane flippancy, who loves to crack the most impenetrable mysteries while treating people as chess pieces to move around for his own amusement, reading like nothing less than Macnaghten's own lush fantasy version of himself.[11] The ending of Logan's book is nothing short of travesty: Edmund Blake heroically fights with Mortemer Slade on a Thames bridge during a fierce storm. Logan has taken literally—and he had no reason not to—Sims' frequent references in the 1900s to the fiend on the verge of being arrested. Sure enough, in the novella a posse of Scotland Yard men are also near the bridge, witnessing the titanic struggle, which has been shamelessly appropriated from the climax of the Sherlock Holmes story, "The Adventure of the Final Problem" (*The Strand*, 1893). Conan Doyle's detective wrestles with his arch-foe, Professor Moriarty, on the edge of the Reichenbach Falls, ending with the pair falling to their deaths in the raging waters beneath (irresistible public pressure forced the reluctant author to bring back Holmes a decade later; like Sims' Lord Helsham he had cleverly faked his own demise). By comparison Logan's finale is merely an anemic rip-off, despite Slade and Blake being killed by the same bolt of lightning.

Wading through this literary dross, we find there is also this gem to appreciate. In the "Aberconway Papers" Macnaghten had written, cryptically, that "the truth" lay at the bottom of the Thames. Here is what Logan writes of the deceased Slade (whose remains are disposed of in a "pauper's grave," shunned by his cousins—as perhaps the Majendie relations had done—unlike Druitt, who was buried in hallowed ground with some of his family in attendance) and the martyred Blake: "But the knowledge of the facts ... died with Edmund Blake. Only the great detective, now lying in a watery grave—for his body was never discovered—could have established the exact truth."[12] Combined with this earlier moment from Logan's confrontation between the disguised Druitt and the Macnaghten-inspired Blake, perhaps Macnaghten's meaning about something vital left behind in the Thames becomes clear as Slade *throws his knife* into the river before confronting Blake. One invented bit of business arguably does work. Mary Jane Kelly has met Slade several times and uses her single room on Dorset Street as a bolt-hole. In a genuinely macabre touch, the poor woman hosts him to a cold meal on the night he kills and mutilates her (unlikely as it sounds, Logan seems not to have seen Sims' copies of the postmortem stills of the Kelly murder, as Logan has Slade scooping out the woman's stomach and placing her boots inside her exposed abdomen).

There are also details that show Logan was briefed about some of Druitt's particulars, though the data has been distorted just enough to hide the young barrister. Suicide ran in Montie's family because, in addition to himself, and maybe Georgiana his older sister falling to her death when very aged, his grandmother had taken her own life. Logan's fictionalized version of a possibly inherited mental weakness is that Slade's uncle drowned himself in 1879. The year Logan chose is the very one that saw the publication of Sims' *The Social Kaleidoscope*, on whose cover the thinner-faced author bears a strong likeness to Druitt, even to the parting of the "sleek, black hair" in the dead center and a "fine intellectual brow" framed by "finely penciled eyebrows."[13] Druitt was a schoolboy athlete and, as an adult, a noted cricket player, while Slade "had been an athlete in his youth, had even now muscles of steel" and was a proficient boxer (another crib from Sherlock Holmes). Druitt was recorded to have "gone abroad" by his cricket club, and Slade uses the same cover with his landlady when he begins his final odyssey. At the inquest into the real Montie's suicide, Dr. Diplock had summarized a note about the dead man's fearing he was "going to be like mother," who had been permanently committed, and Slade too deplores ending up in the madhouse; "the worst that could happen to him then would be his incarceration in Broadmoor as a dangerous homicidal lunatic. The worst!" A mediocre graduate of Oxford, Druitt was, nonetheless, described in death as a "barrister of bright talent" while Slade is also an Oxonian, though graduating with "high honours," his peers predicting for him "a distinguished and honorable career."

The "Mac-Tatcho" axis wanted Dorset kept well away from the sweeping searchlights of the cruel tabloids. Consequently the middle-class Druitts in Logan's book are relocated to as far away as possible from the southwest (and promoted to the patrician rank) to Yorkshire in the north. The Slades are a truly noble family who traditionally service the sovereign (which was true of the Majendies). Geographically, these tally with the "North Country vicar" of 1899, a source openly engaged in deception and deflection for the same reasons: to shield the respectable from disaster. Even the young, aristocratic Tory member for West Dorset, Henry Farquharson, perhaps makes a cameo appearance, and he too has been transplanted *up north*: "Viscount Hardcastle was the elder son of the Earl of Dewsbury. He represented a Northern constituency in the Tory interests, and was regarded as somewhat of a political firebrand. 'A clever young man,' the Premier had pronounced him, 'but there is a little too much venom in his speeches.'"[14] Is the "venom" a veiled reference to the 1893 libel case Farquharson lost that seems to have tarnished his reputation, even in death?

Kosminski and Ostrog are here superfluous (as they will be in "Mac's" memoir). Logan reverts to the sighting in Mitre Square with the fictional addition that Slade has disguised himself as a man with a fake moustache (albeit not dressed as a seaman). This is a "fair moustache," a detail that goes all the way back to Joseph Lawende's 1888 sighting that both Macnaghten and Sims shy away from in all their Ripper writings (this is the only source that places Druitt, albeit fictionalized, as the man seen by the case's best witness). Having turned "Jack the Ripper" into a poor man's Professor Moriarty, Logan cannot have him exit Kelly's hovel and make a mad dash for the Thames, let alone "shrieking" and "raving." It is too ludicrous, even in a melodrama already straining credulity on a number of fronts. Logan the dramatist gives himself some breathing space by extending the gap between the final murder and the act of self-murder to a couple of days and nights. In these last scenes of Slade, who is broke, on the run and with no place to go, inexplicably the up-until-then cool-headed supervillain goes from Hannibal Lecter to hobo in the space of a few paragraphs. Logan tries to color the palate with some Christian angst, but his heart is clearly not in it: "[Slade] found that he loathed himself for being the thing he was. He cared little when the end came, or what form it took."[15] The Ripper's wandering out of London, to still be able to function, is nine years before Macnaghten will create exactly the same gap in *Days of My Years* (and Slade does not die near London's Embankment, as Druitt did not either). Despite being material soon to wrap fish-and-chips, Logan's work is only one of three "Jack the Ripper" primary sources that are closer to the historical Montague Druitt regarding the true timing of his suicide—the third being the "North Country vicar."

The year after Logan's potboiler, George Sims published *Mysteries of Modern London* and, as might be expected, the Ripper makes a walk-on appearance, this time exhibiting more features of Dr. Henry Jekyll: independent wealth and a lonely melancholia. The substantial checks found on the successful barrister's corpse have been exaggerated to make the physician so wealthy that he did not need patients—did not need to work at all. Similarly, the season rail pass has inspired Sims to write of "Jack" as a semi-invalid recluse who travelled aimlessly on London's public transport, until the next maniacal eruption. Echoing what he must have told Guy Logan, Sims dates the "Mad Doctor's" convalescence as ending twelve months before the murder of Polly Nichols. In the ninth chapter, entitled "Lunatics at Large," Sims, a touch sadistically, speculates about an unwary female passenger sharing a compartment with none other than the Ripper, then emphasizes the maniac's outward normality and upper class pedigree: "Some of us must have passed him in the street, sat with him perhaps at a cafes or a restaurant. He was a man of birth and education, and had sufficient means to keep himself without work."[16] By making his gentleman-murderer a rich, discharged patient from, presumably, a private asylum—with absolutely nothing to do, let alone working two jobs and playing teamsports—Sims here realigned his "Jack" with the one propounded by the forgotten "North

Country vicar" of 1899; now the drowned suspect was also an ex-surgeon (by the time of Macnaghten's 1914 memoirs, the suspect who committed suicide is not even referred to as a doctor at all). In "Laying the Ghost..." Macnaghten rather unconvincingly refers to a best-selling work of Whitechapel-inspired fiction not by Logan (or Sims) but by Maria Belloc-Lowndes (whom he does not name), which he simultaneously praises and dismisses. This is odd, because the "talented authoress" never touted her best-selling novel as a historical theory about "Jack."

> Only last autumn I was very much interested in a book entitled "The Lodger," which set forth in vivid colors what the Whitechapel murderer's life might have been while dwelling in London lodgings. The talented authoress portrayed him as a religious enthusiast, gone crazy over the belief that he was predestined to slaughter a certain number of unfortunate women, and that he had been confined in a criminal lunatic asylum and had escaped there from. I do not think there was anything of religious mania about the real Simon Pure, nor do I believe that he had ever been detained in an asylum, nor lived in lodgings.[17]

Either by direction from "Mac-Tatcho" or sheer coincidence, Belloc-Lowndes had some elements of the Druitt solution correct: a young, handsome, English gentleman, a renter of rooms, a thwarter of police, and a suicide but not a doctor. Yet the detail that was not a match, that the Avenger was only absent on the nights of the murders, is the one Macnaghten embraces and endorses. We will examine why a little further on. The core idea of working-class landlords suspecting that their gentleman/lodger of being a "Jack the Ripper"–type monster came from a dinner-party anecdote Belloc-Lowndes reportedly heard from a fellow guest: their servants once thought they rented a room to none other than the fiend.[18] There is also evidence from some newspaper accounts of 1888—including Sims—that the lodger suspect was genuine, though, as with Montague Druitt, it was based on a single incident of absence that was connected to a Whitechapel atrocity. It involved a foreign landlady (identified by a newspaper as a German named "Mrs. Kruer") and her blood-stained lodger, and a location, 22 Batty Street, that ran immediately parallel with Berner St., where Elizabeth Stride had been killed. To some in the media it seemed as if police might be on the verge of catching the fiend, as they were reportedly watching for the foreign lodger's return. However, competing newspaper sources from 1888 allege that this suspect was actually the German landlady's laundry client, and what's more *was* identified, arrested and allegedly cleared, as we see in the *Daily News* of October 18, 1888: "[The suspect] was taken to the Leman-street Police-station, where he was questioned, and within an hour or two released, his statement being proved correct."

On November 18, 1888, Dagonet weighed in with a characteristic "Custard and Mess" send-up, in which the laundress writes to complain to Sir Charles Warren (though German, she uses stage Cockney): "There is a stain on them which looks like blood. He is a queer-looking gentleman, my dorter says, as she has seen him when calling for the bill, and is wife is a inverlid. If he is not the Whitechapel murderer, please return, as I do not want to be mix up in the affair. P.S.—If the rewarde is pade, I hope I shall have my rites." Confirmation that the Batty St. lodger was still very much on Sims' mind in the Edwardian era is shown by an article he wrote for the *Yarmouth Independent* of February 25, 1911, yet the details do not match the newspaper accounts of 1888—nor that of his own parody. The suspect is now an American and a doctor, the laundress is back to being a landlady, one not identified as a German, flanked by a husband who is at home at the time of the incriminating incident. Another addition is a fearsome knife allegedly found along with the blood-stained clothing. He alludes to his 1907 article in *Lloyds Weekly* magazine, and the supposed in-your-face response of one particularly agitated fan that in 1888 she had an American lodger who hastily departed the morning after the night of the double murder, but not before her husband examined the doctor's black bag and found it contained blood-stained cuffs. Surely he must have been "Jack"! Investigation by police, however, found the man was in practice and quite innocent: "There was ample proof that the real author of the horrors had committed suicide in the last stage of his maniacal frenzy."[19] Sims had overlaid some Tumbletyesque features onto the Batty St. story. Exactly like Macnaghten would do in 1914, Sims' piece acts as both confirmation of a historical basis to Belloc-Lowndes at the same time as exposing it as dissimilar to the real killer—and yet Sims in 1915 would confirm her fictional element of the "Mad Doctor" being "absented" on the nights of his crimes.

First serialized in *McClure's* magazine in January 1911 (Macnaghten claims he only read the novelization two years later), *The Lodger: A Story of the London Fog* is full of shrewd insights into Victorian attitudes towards class rigidity and palpitating anxiety over looming poverty. Its serial killer—calling himself "The Avenger," and placing a calling card written in red ink beside each victim—is named Mr. Sleuth, a young, wealthy, well-spoken gentleman who lodges with an impoverished couple, the Buntings. It is as if an angel with deep pockets has come to deliver them from famine. Gradually their benefactor's solitary, nocturnal excursions, which always coincide with an Avenger horror (combined with his creepy piety), separately convince his landlords that the dreaded maniac is poring over his Bible in the room right above their very heads—yet the landlord harbors nagging doubts: "Surely it was inconceivable that this gentle, mild-mannered gentleman could be the monster of cruelty and cunning that Bunting had now for the terrible space of four days believed him to be!"[20] And there is another striking parallel with Druitt: the Avenger calmly and lucidly vanishes, having committed suicide, albeit offstage: "How pleasant it would be to take a flying leap over the balcony railing and find rest, eternal rest, below."[21] Close to a crack-up, the Avenger chooses to disappear— and unlike Druitt his *fictional* counterpart's body is never found—once he realizes that a police commissioner who some time before had had Mr. Sleuth committed as a dangerous madman has probably recognized him again. The top cop is named Sir John Burney and is obviously a thinly veiled Sir Melville Macnaghten. The resolution of the story even takes place at Madame Tussaud's Chamber of Horrors, which had so fascinated "Mac" as a boy: "[Burney] was a tall, powerful, handsome gentleman with a military appearance."[22] Just as Macnaghten frustratingly missed the Ripper, so Sir John does not recognize the escaped lunatic, Mr. Sleuth, as he passes right by him among the waxworks, let alone grasp that the psychologically imploding murderer has decided to do himself in. George Sims also appears, though as his unnamed self (along with his "Tatcho" remedy). The famous writer is noticed by a painfully anxious Mrs. Bunting as she discreetly attends a London inquest into the Avenger's latest atrocity, trying to confirm if her lodger is, or is not, the mad miscreant:

> Many of the gentlemen—they mostly wore tall hats and good overcoats—standing round and about her looked vaguely familiar. She picked out one at once. He was a famous jour-

nalist, whose shrewd, animated face was familiar to her owing to the fact that it was widely advertised in connection with a preparation for the hair—a preparation which in happier, more prosperous days [her husband] had had great faith in, and used, or so he always said, with great benefit to himself. This gentleman was the centre of an eager circle; half a dozen men were talking to him, listening deferentially when he spoke, and each of these men, so Mrs. Bunting realized, was a Somebody.[23]

At this inquest Mrs. Bunting harbors an almost unbearable secret—the likely identity of the fiend—but fears that the killer's exposure and apprehension will leave her and her husband social pariahs and thus unemployable and destitute. This private agony parallels William Druitt's at the 1889 inquest into Montie's death, and *his* self-interested need, due to class and economic pressures, to keep his mouth well and truly shut.[24] In his memoir three years after *The Lodger* debuted, Macnaghten appropriated the idea for multiplying Druitt's single absence three weeks after the final murder into an incriminating trend; a fictitious *deus ex machina* to explain family suspicion without the need for a confession to anybody. He needs *something*, as he also rejects the notion of the killer having been "detained" in an asylum, in which he could confess his maniacal desires. *The Lodger* provided the fictional shortcut, but Macnaghten had to be careful to simultaneously refute the novel, as Montague Druitt was a lodger. Sims repeated this "Avenger" motif a year later in *Pearson's Weekly*: "the case of the Mad Doctor who lived with his people at Blackheath, and who, during his *occasional absences* from home committed the crime which won his worldwide infamy as 'Jack the Ripper'" (my italics). Yet in reviewing "Mac's" book, *The New York Times Book Review* of November 15, 1914, was not remotely fooled by Macnaghten's attempts to distance the true murderer from Belloc-Lownde's fiction while simultaneously appropriating a central plot point. The reviewer easily saw that the Ripper was apparently identified by "his own people" in exactly the same way as his fictional alter ego: "Sir Melville's theory regarding the Whitechapel murders, corroborates to a large extent the theory cleverly elaborated by Mrs. BELLOC-LOWNDES in her last story, 'The Lodger.'"

Eleven years before he scanned the largely positive reviews in the press towards his memoirs, Melville Macnaghten had reached the pinnacle of his already distinguished policing career by being appointed assistant commissioner of CID. Free from the restrictions of his stern, unsympathetic "headmaster," Macnaghten could be the super-cop at long last. He would become noted for speaking of crime and horror in a "peculiarly flippant manner," which comes across to a 21st century reader as very modern and cool. As he wrote in his memoir about an odd case (the chapter is titled "Diurnal Oddments"):

When you are conscious of the fact that you have murdered your wife, and when a coroner's jury has recorded a verdict to this effect, the situation cannot fail to be unpleasant. But, when you happen to have been in jail at the time of the murder, and some two hundred miles away from the scene thereof, and the coroner still sums up dead against you, and the jury whole-heartedly agrees in returning a verdict of "willful murder," then the position does indeed become hopelessly embarrassing![25]

It reads as though Macnaghten was also musing about what he did, behind the scenes, to Michael Ostrog. The contrast with the chapter on the Ripper is again striking. "Laying the Ghost..." is missing his characteristic flippancy as he describes—in minimal detail—the fall of a fellow gentleman and master criminal whom the police of 1888 could not identify, catch, nor stop; a killer with many faces, virtually invulnerable to detection. "Mac" always believed, though, that had *he* been on the Force in 1888, he could have given "that fascinating criminal" a run for his money.

XV

DOUBLES AND DEFLECTIONS

Never was there a more ill-starred individual than Adolph Beck, and his case was indeed a "tragedy of errors"! ... When we met for the last time, one Sunday evening in Hyde Park, he bent over my hand and called me his "preserver"!—Sir Melville Macnaghten, 1914

A report circulated at the time, ... a student of surgery suffering from a peculiar form of murder-mania.... It has even been definitively reported that the student—long since dead—has been identified to the satisfaction of the police as the guilty man.— The Manchester Courier, 1903

On the occasion of Sir Melville Macnaghten's passing away in 1921, the *Sunday Post* of May 15 published an article (excerpted here for the first time) about the much admired Edwardian police chief. It was so over-the-top that his ghost could only have been well-pleased by this unnamed admirer's tribute ("By One Who Knew Him"): "Macnaghten of the Yard. Britain's Greatest Sleuth and the Mysteries He Solved." It said that "Mac" had single-handedly built the Yard to be "the finest detective system in the world" and was "the terror of wrong-doers even in the most remote corners of the world"; that he was better than any fictional sleuth, with his "mathematical brain" that could work out problems "which few men would be capable of solving."

The anonymous writer—more like a press agent—creates a swoony image of the former chief that is perfect for a movie, for a Hollywood Mac as he races to the scene of the most sensational crimes in a long, open, grey car flanked by detectives: "It was Mac of the Yard on the way to investigate a crime while the clue was warm." This "man of action" image was noted by no less than Sherlock Holmes' creator, Sir Arthur Conan Doyle, in the *Evening News* of February 8, 1908: "In London when a sensational mystery occurs Sir Melville Macnaghten, the Chief of the Criminal Investigation Department, often rushes to the spot in a motorcar, with a little band of assistants, comprising the keenest men at the Yard." Macnaghten's charm, accessibility and derring-do were all perfectly suited to the brief but jaunty years of Edward VII. The aging, overweight playboy-prince turned out to be an unheralded genius at global diplomacy; "Bertie" helped nudge his cautious ministers into an Entente Cordiale with France in order to strategically wedge his unstable, jealous nephew, Kaiser Wilhelm II. The jolly Macnaghten, somewhat stifled in the late Victorian era by killjoys such as Warren and Anderson, was a kind of premature Edwardian.[1]

Except that he was an American (from Michigan), Hawley Harvey Crippen, a.k.a. "Dr. Crippen" (though his credentials as a homeopathic doctor were not recognized in England), was the eponymous little man of George Orwell's *Decline of the English Murder*. Crippen had killed his shrewish wife, disarticulated her remains, burying some bits in his cellar, and taken off on a ship to the States with his young mistress. The pair of fugitives were disguised as father and son, causing Orwell to write, "No novelist would dare to make up…. Crippen's flight across the Atlantic with his mistress dressed as a boy." The captain of the ship sent a marconigram, a wireless telegram, of his suspicions about these two passengers, and it fell to Macnaghten to make the decision of whether to send the chief detective, Walter Dew, all the way to Canada to intercept and arrest Crippen. But what if it was not him? "Mac" knew such a public mistake would terminate his distinguished career, but so would a failure of nerve. (Did he also recall from the file, with a sinking feeling, the debacle over Dr. Tumblety's jumping his bail and some U.S. newspapers giving the completely false impression that Inspector Walter Andrews was *chasing* this prime Ripper suspect across the Atlantic to New York City—and failing to catch him?) Mac writes: "That night could not fail to be one of anxiety; but the die was cast, the Rubicon was crossed. If the coup happened to come off, well and good, but, if otherwise, why, then, the case would have been hopelessly messed up, and I didn't care to dwell on the eventualities of its future."[2] Only the commissioner, Edward Henry, to whom "Mac's" memoirs are dedicated ("The best all round policeman of the Twentieth Century"), backed his decision without equivocation; but it was enough, and Crippen and his girlfriend were arrested. He was hanged, while she was discharged. For the first time, wireless had been

The Proud Father—Sir Melville Macnaghten assists his daughter, Christabel, who was about to become Mrs. Henry Duncan MacLaren, July 19, 1910 (Christopher McLaren).

used to catch a criminal, and Macnaghten had been instrumental in the bold use of this cutting-edge technology.

A year into his tenure as assistant commissioner, Macnaghten had been one of the key players in the righting of a despicable miscarriage of justice that caused almost unprecedented public outrage. It involved a man who went to prison for the crimes of another. The tragedy of Adolph Beck exposed the British state as being utterly indifferent to the sufferings of a single, unjustly convicted foreigner—quite concerned only with never admitting a terrible error had been made—leading to the creation of the Court of Criminal Appeal. From 1907, the wrongly convicted could now challenge their convictions in an appellate court. Before this, lawyers and judges had acted as a phalanx against *ever* having their decisions overturned, no matter what new evidence was discovered.

The shocking core of the Beck injustice is that over a dozen lower-middle-class women *sincerely* mistook this down-at-heel entrepreneur, the hapless Beck, for another man, an unscrupulous swindler, as all but one separately picked Beck out of lineups without any promptings (a swindler whom some of them had met "up close and personal"). The real confidence man they later disastrously mistook Beck for pretended to be an aristocrat, charming his way into his targets' graces for an afternoon in their homes. He left behind checks that he knew would bounce while offering to sell some of their valuables (and pawn some other jewelry surreptitiously pilfered). This career criminal was a German whose real name was probably either Smith or Meyer, and who was of similar—but by no means identical—appearance to Beck. The German committed acts of larceny in 1877, 1895 and 1904. For the second spree of 1895, Beck was convicted (after being "recognized" on the street by one his double's victims), mostly on the devastating eyewitness testimony by a veritable harem of wronged women. Yet a policeman and the judge also believed they recognized him from the earlier conviction (the judge had been none other than the prosecuting counsel in 1877).

While Beck was doing hard labor, however, the Home Office discovered that he could not have been the earlier miscreant because he was not circumcised—as the earlier convicted felon had undoubtedly been—and this exculpatory evidence was suppressed, a fact that scandalized all classes when revealed by an official inquiry in 1905. The year before the inquiry the aged, embittered Beck, newly free from prison, had again been spotted by a recent victim of the other man and the tragedy repeated itself, almost exactly, resulting in another unsafe conviction. This time Beck's luck turned, for while incarcerated the genuine criminal was apprehended (under the alias William Thomas). None of the previous malice by the state is mentioned by Macnaghten, who claims virtually sole credit for getting Beck off the hook, while denying it to hardly anybody else—except the *compassionate* judge at the second trial: "Never was there a more ill-starred individual than Adolph Beck, and his case was indeed a "tragedy of errors"! ... No wonder that his wild cries of agony so impressed the learned judge that he put him back for sentence to the next Sessions."[3]

Another vital factor in the judge's caution, however, was none other than George Sims' valiant, stubborn advocacy on behalf of the accused—but this time "Mac" pointedly did not allow "Tatcho" to share the limelight. Sims had been the most prominent name who joined the campaign for a review of Beck's conviction of 1896, and he would receive a knighthood from the king of Sweden for his efforts (two years *ahead* of Macnaghten's from Edward VII, whose successor awarded him the King's Police Medal). Using a martial metaphor, Sims' friend Max Pemberton wrote: "An outcry arose, but it was George R. Sims who led the battalions."[4] Once Beck was pardoned—and compensated by the state with initially 2,000 pounds until a public outcry demanded it be more than doubled—we see the acclaim Sims received in other media, such as the *Manchester Courier and Lancashire General Advertiser* of August 13, 1904: "The Man with a Double. Was He Carelessly Convicted? Serious Charges by Mr. G. R. Sims.... Mr. George R. Sims who for years has championed Beck's cause says: '...a conspiracy of silence to cover up an official blunder.'"

In his memoir of 1917, Sims laments that the Beck affair caused a significant strain with the police, though whether this extended to his personal friendship with Macnaghten is left unclear. Whether out of pique over Sims' charges of police bungling or not, I surmise that Macnaghten wanted no revisiting of the mistakes of the government and Home Office. Characteristically, it may have been a concern over positive public relations that led "Mac" to airbrush his pal's role out of the story, as Sims' campaign was built upon the cover-up of the discrepancies between the first two convictions.

By contrast, the retired police chief narrowed his account to the parade of mistaken witnesses, which also allowed him to undercut Sir Robert Anderson's memoir of four years before and his spurious claim that a solitary witness had solved the Ripper case. (This point was made more directly by the *Jewish Chronicle* of March 4, 1910: "A more wicked assertion to put into print, without the shadow of evidence, I have seldom seen. ... Sir Robert [forgets] that such a case as that of Adolph Beck was ever heard of.") Macnaghten fires the same cannon at Sir Robert Anderson's massive ego without having to mention him by name: "An intelligent police officer will learn in every case something new, and the object lesson in this lamentable business was unquestionably the *extreme unreliability of personal identification*. All these women witnesses honestly believed they had picked out the right man" (my italics).

In 1904 Macnaghten headed off to find the contrary witness who could help establish Beck's innocence. This may parallel what he likely did with Henry Farquharson's "curious story" of 1891; he promptly and privately visited the M.P., following this with a similar interview with William and/or Charles Druitt, and of course with his close friend Colonel Majendie. According to "Mac," the most dyspeptic harlot melts before the urbane chief:

> The house was not the kind where one would be on the Sabbath. I had some little difficulty in obtaining my interview, and I when I had gained admittance to her presence I fear she was disappointed on learning my errand. But I flung down a sheaf of photographs in front of her, and she at once picked up one of Thomas, and said, "That's the scoundrel who robbed me nine years ago, and don't you forget it, Mr. Policeman!" After the ice was thus broken we got on capitally together, and I persuaded her to come up to Bow Street the next day and give evidence, although she was in wretched health at the time.

Earlier in his memoir account of this watershed case, Macnaghten's description of Beck's gratitude and of his being hardly affected after his nightmare reads like dialogue from U.K. television's *Black Adder*, starring Rowan Atkinson:

> I knew Beck only after his troubles were at an end and he had been discharged from Bow Street. Notwithstanding his awful experiences, he always struck me as being a lighthearted

lover of pleasure, and, mercifully for him, I do not think that the horrors of his wrongful imprisonment had weighed on him quite as heavily as they would have on most other men. He had the mercurial disposition of many of our continental friends. He was always touchingly and (as I thought) unnecessarily grateful for the assistance rendered to him at the time of Smith's arrest at his own release. When we met for the last time, one Sunday evening in Hyde Park, he bent over my hand and called me his "preserver"! I would have given a good deal (and so would many others) to have "preserved" him from his first sentence; but luck was dead against him at the time of his arrest and subsequent trial.[5]

It was not just a question of luck being "dead against him," however, as poor Beck had received a prolonged incarceration due to corrupt actions by officers of the state. Echoing Old Etonian Whitney Straight's nonsense about a dissipated and dying Guy Burgess looking "in the pink," Adolf Beck died a mere four years later, a broken man despite public exoneration, five thousand pounds' compensation and his foreigner's "light hearted, mercurial disposition."

In the history of sleuthing and the career of Melville Macnaghten it could be argued that far more important than Dr. Crippen, or Adolph Beck—or even Montague Druitt—was the Deptford Murder Case. This is because it established fingerprint identification as a successful tool for the identification and conviction of criminals. In his memoir's chapter 14, "Finger-Prints in General and the Deptford Murder Case in Particular," a modest Macnaghten gives the lion's share of the credit to his revered superior, Sir Edward Richard Henry—perhaps too much. Acceptance of this tool for crime-fighting had stalled in Britain since the 1890s. What the authorities needed was a test case to convince jurors that it was not some sort of hocus pocus. The murders of Mr. and Mrs. Harrow at Deptford in March 1905 provided what Macnaghten excitedly characterizes as a "supreme piece of good luck" that would entrench fingerprint identification as the D.N.A. breakthrough of the Edwardian era. The couple had been killed because it was falsely rumored that they had a load of cash hidden in their small shop. At the scene Macnaghten and his detectives found a "digital imprint" on a nearby tray that seated a cash-box. Information received pointed to two house-breaking brothers, the Strattons, as the likely killers. No confession was forthcoming and there were no witnesses. Culpability could only be established to a jury's satisfaction by the defendant's fingerprints: "Attempts to disparage the finger-print system were made at the trial of the Old Bailey, but they egregiously failed, and the brothers Stratton suffered the extreme penalty of the law."[6]

During his tenure as a capable, popular and even dashing civil servant, Melville Macnaghten also had to mount, with a compliant George Sims, a discreet, rear-guard action against several retired colleagues who challenged the drowned "Mad Doctor" solution created by the pair of gentleman to hide the connection to another prominent gentleman. Their dissent was fuelled by the famous writer's claiming that it was a monolithic Scotland Yard/Home Office solution and that it was a case resolved in 1888.

Twenty-two years after the horrific murder of Mary Jane Kelly, Sir Robert Anderson's reminiscences set off quite an imbroglio. He blithely revealed, for one thing, various underhanded machinations from 1889 by the Tory government against pro–Home-Rule, Irish politician Charles Stuart Parnell. Macnaghten alerted a retired and ill James Monro, who publicly denied Anderson's claim that he, as commissioner, had ever authorized anybody from his department to interfere in domestic politics. Similarly Anderson's confident assertion that the Ripper was a Jew identified by another Jew (who refused to testify) was almost certainly the result of a memory malfunction. In a 1908 interview the ex-chief had got himself into a hopeless muddle as he managed to confuse—and fuse—different pipes found at the Mary Jane Kelly and Alice McKenzie murders while claiming that William Harcourt was the home secretary during the Whitechapel crimes—he had in fact been the Liberal minister in the previous administration.[7] There was talk of denying Sir Robert his pension, but Home Secretary Winston Churchill excused the retired civil servant as nothing more than a conceited braggart.[8]

Despite his former boss's being treated as a laughing stock in the House of Commons, Macnaghten, the experienced survivor of the Whitehall jungle, may have observed all this with mixed feelings. Sir Robert Anderson's empty boasts about identifying the Ripper as a poor, foreign Hebrew handily protected the Majendies and the Druitts. On the other hand, his despised ex-boss was doing such a lousy job of it, he might make some in the press suspicious that this was a red herring to distract from the real story—which indeed it was. I think Macnaghten decided that Anderson needed some back-handed help. Consequently for the first and only time, "Mac" instructed "Tatcho" to reveal to the public that there was a "final" version of his internal report in which the Polish suspect was indeed considered to be as strong (or as weak) as the English and Russian doctor suspects. The following is from Dagonet's "Mustard and Cress" column of April 17, 1910, in which the latter mercilessly insults Sir Robert yet, simultaneously, tries to substantiate some elements of his outlandish claims:

> It was only the other day that the late esteemed head of the CID caused a storm of indignation among the King's Jewish subjects by stating that JACK THE RIPPER was a Jew, and that the Jews knew who he was and assisted him to evade capture. The statement went beyond ascertained facts. The mad Polish Jew, to whom Sir Robert refers, was only one of three persons who were each strongly suspected of being the genuine Jack. The *final official record*, which is in the archives of the Home Office, *leaves the matter in doubt* between the Polish Jew, who was afterwards put in a lunatic asylum, a Russian doctor of vile character, and *an English homicidal maniac*, one Dr.——, who had been in a lunatic asylum. In these circumstances it was certainly indiscreet of Sir Robert to plump for the Polish Jew, and to imply that many of the Jewish community in the East End were accessories after the fact. ... ANDERSON'S FAIRY TALES. There is no truth to the rumour that in the course of further romantic revelations to be expected from Sir Robert we shall learn.... The name of the eminent Jewish financiers who assisted Jack the Ripper to evade arrest [my italics].

With mounting strangeness the year 1910 saw Aaron Kosminski and William Grant once more colliding with each other. For example, in the *Ottawa Journal* of April 19, 1910: "Jack-the-Ripper Was Not a Jew. Lawyer Who Defended Him Says He Was an Irishman." George Kebbel gave interviews in which he said the unnamed Grant, once his client, was long deceased—and that the police were certain he was the fiend. The ex-seaman was no more pushing up daisies than Aaron Kosminski and, predictably offended, he sought redress in the courts (and help from the pushy celebrity doctor Forbes Winslow, who took him to see none other than Sir Melville Macnaghten).[9] Apparently Kebbel got the shock of his life when Grant ran up to him in the street to show he was very much alive and kicking; the lawyer fled and passed away the following year. Covertly undermining Sir Robert Anderson and George Kebbel probably cost

"Mac" no sleep at all, but he also had to be brutal with colleagues he liked yet whom he had, I believe, misled over the years.

The brutish-looking Severin Klosowski, alias George Chapman, was a Russian-Polish immigrant (nominally of the Catholic faith) who arrived in England around early 1887. An abusive spouse, he was convicted of poisoning his wife, Maud, on March 20, 1903, (and believed to have similarly dispatched two previous wives using the same m.o.), and hanged on April 7 of the same year.[10] Chapman had been in Whitechapel during the murders of 1888—might he be "Jack the Ripper"? As if to preemptively debunk such a superficial long-shot theory, somebody else still working at Scotland Yard, one "well versed in the annals of crime," spoke with a reporter from the *Westminster Gazette*, a mere four days after a jury took less than fifteen minutes to convict the wife-killer. I think this was Macnaghten, merging the drowned barrister with the insane medical student, John Sanders (who had been, however fleetingly, a Ripper suspect in 1888 and the subject of a Home Office report). He offers glimpses into the true killer, while also admitting that there other details he cannot divulge: "but I have every proof—of a circumstantial and private character—in my possession.... Some day the truth concerning these murders ... may be revealed." He then refers to a definitive report from 1888 that confirms the murderer was "a student of surgery suffering from a peculiar form of murdermania ... long since dead—[he] has been identified to the satisfaction of the police as the guilty man."

On the very same day the retired ex-inspector Frederic Abberline fell hard for the notion of George Chapman as "Jack." He was interrupted in his Bournemouth home by a reporter right in the middle of composing a letter to Macnaghten to let him know the good news that "Jack" was no more (while innocently assuring the same journalist, "We have never believed all those stories about Jack the Ripper being dead, or that he was a lunatic, or anything of that kind"). In his memoir Macnaghten is positive and complimentary towards the ex–field detective who had exhausted himself trying to bring the Whitechapel fiend to heel.[11] Nonetheless, Dagonet, as Mac's mouthpiece in his "Mustard and Cress" column of March 29, 1903, pushed equally hard for "Jack" as Jekyll. Macnaghten's internal report is played as an ace, albeit ambiguously because Sims simply claims it was written by the "Commissioner" (suggesting James Monro, but perhaps even more deliciously it refers to Mac's foe, Sir Charles Warren): "It is perfectly well known at Scotland Yard who 'Jack' was, and the reasons for the police conclusions were given in the report to the Home Office, which was considered by the authorities to be final and conclusive. How the ex–Inspector can say "We never believed 'Jack' was dead or a lunatic" in face of the report made by the Commissioner of Police is a mystery to me."

Frederic Abberline replied to Sims' salvo the following day with his own, again in the *Pall Mall Gazette*: "Scotland Yard is really no wiser on the subject than it was fifteen years ago. It is simple nonsense to talk of the police having proof that the man is dead.... Besides, the authorities would have been only too glad to make an end of such a mystery, if only for their own credit." Abberline was clueless that the shilling shocker being put about by Sims is the police—or at least "Mac"—making an end of the mystery for the credit of Scotland Yard. At the same time I think that Macnaghten's sly attempts to imply that the deceased suspect was the unnamed, insane student John Sanders, whom Abberline had handled (but remained unsure what had become of him) succeeded very niftily, as a *Pall Mall Gazette* reporter asked Abberline about a "young medical student" and the ex-detective replied, "I know all about that story. But what does it amount to? Simply this. Soon after the last murder in Whitechapel the body of a *young doctor* was found in the Thames, but there is absolutely nothing beyond the fact that he was found at that time to incriminate him. *A report was made to the Home Office* about the matter, but that it was 'considered final and conclusive' is going altogether beyond the truth" (my italics). Sims returned fire on April 5, 1903, claiming Major Arthur Griffiths had reportedly viewed the apparently unassailable "Home Office Report" and finishing this game of Ripper Ping-Pong with: "'Jack the Ripper' was known, was identified, and is dead. Let him rest."

In the same description of Abberline and Swanson (but not Anderson) attending a police reunion of giants, Macnaghten also commends John George Littlechild, the ex-chief of Special Branch who had retired in 1893 to become a private detective. His sleuthing had helped prove Oscar Wilde trawled the streets for homosexual liaisons: "Jack Littlechild ... retired more than twenty-one years ago.... His appearance is still refreshingly youthful, and his figure that of a light comedian."[12] In his letter to Sims in 1913 Littlechild wrote that he had "never heard of a Dr. D. in connection with the Whitechapel murders." Naturally he falls back on the doctor suspect he does recall who was vigorously pursued by Scotland Yard in 1888, Dr. Francis Tumblety, but then ends with this wildly inaccurate comment about the fleeing American, that "he shortly left Boulogne and was never heard of afterwards. *It was believed he committed suicide* but certain it is that from this time the 'Ripper' murders came to an end" (my italics). Actually, Dr. Tumblety had died peacefully in a Missouri nursing home as we see from the *New York Herald* of June 26, 1903: "DR. TUMBLETY DEAD ... LED AN EXCITING CAREER ... After a life which included in its multitude of exciting incidents an arrest on the suspicion that he was London's 'Jack the Ripper' ... probably because of his outspoken hatred of women ... came to this country followed by Scotland Yard men. He was also entirely cleared of this charge."

Suicide is a decidedly more satisfying resolution, at least for the image of the CID, and neatly eliminates the disappointing trip by Inspector Walter Andrews. Littlechild ends the letter perplexed over Sims' apparently quoting Major Griffiths as an authoritative source on this "Dr. D" and assumes—quite wrongly—that all this guff comes from Sir Robert Anderson whom, he cautions, "only thought he knew." Would Macnaghten have so bald-facedly misled a police chief he liked and respected? Here is a potentially relevant quotation from *Scoundrels and Scallywags and Some Honest Men* (1929), the memoirs of Tom Divall, an ex-chief inspector of CID, mentioning Macnaghten and the Ripper in the same paragraph. Here we have "Mac" caught talking out of the other side of his mouth, with Druitt (and Tumblety) quite unrecoverable yet dominating the "autumn of terror" timeline: "The much lamented and late Commissioner of the CID, Sir Melville Macnaghten, received some information that *the murderer had gone to America and died in a lunatic asylum there*. This perhaps may be correct, for *after this news* nothing was ever heard of any similar crime being committed"[13] (my italics). Such a tale, with its resolution on the other side of the Atlantic, certainly had the effect of distancing the crimes from the Majendie clan (later, "Mac" and "Tatcho" settled on the Jekyll-Hyde facade).

I also do not think Macnaghten would have hesitated at misleading a middle-class non–Old Etonian who expressed a belief that homosexuality was a dangerous perversion and who had helped ruin a literary genius. Another part of the 1913 letter to Sims is pertinent on this notion of Macnaghten maybe having settled a score. Littlechild describes in grotesque detail a despicable act of sadism towards a boy by the visiting American tycoon Harry K. Thaw. The latter really was an unscrupulous murderer and a notorious rapist of young men[14] (an abusive husband, Thaw shot the acclaimed architect Stanford White, the lover of his child-bride and ex-showgirl, Evelyn Nesbit, in Madison Square Garden, itself designed by the victim, complete with nude statuary based on his teenage mistress' luscious curves). Littlechild lumps the great writer Oscar Wilde and the harmless humbugger Dr. Tumblety with this truly vile creature. All three, to the retired cop, are examples of "contrary sexual instinct" and "degenerates." Are "Mac's" flirtatious words about Littlechild having a "youthful appearance" and a "light body" a subtle dig at the ex-chief's obsession with "the love that dares not speak its name"?

Even as a purely precautionary measure, Sir Melville Macnaghten would have been careful to scan every page of Sir Robert Anderson's book of 1910, no matter how distasteful, in order to be alert to any more potential gaffes from that quarter. He would have, therefore, come across the slander against himself, though he is unnamed (another of Swanson's 1910 annotations identifies Macnaghten as the hapless subject of this ugly put-down, again suggesting that all of the annotations are clarifications from Anderson, for how else could the ex-inspector know?) in which he mentions a lunatic named Townsend who aborted an attempt to shoot Gladstone because at the last minute the prime minister "smiled" at his would-be assassin. But then Anderson disparages a senior policeman (the unnamed Macnaghten) for having been unreasonably concerned about his own safety after receiving a threat in writing from the same nut. This had caused the former to throw the letter into the fire because, he said, "I felt so indignant and irritated at the importance he attached to it, and the fuss he made over it ... though no harm came of my act, I could not forgive myself for it."[15] Macnaghten makes no reference to the incident in his memoirs, yet how he must have blanched when he read that his allegedly "irritating" cowardice was so undignified that it blinded the assistant commissioner to the seriousness of an assassination threat against the head of government. While his former boss made such a fool of himself in 1910, Macnaghten could patiently keep his own powder dry until *his* memoir of 1914.

In 1911, as the assistant commissioner was preparing security for the coronation for Edward VII's son and successor—the gruffer and less glamorous former naval cadet George V—Macnaghten had experienced "the first premonitory symptoms of a breakdown." This must have been acutely distressing for an active person who had, he wrote, never known "a day's ill health." Fred Wensley wrote that his beloved chief bore his deteriorating health "gallantly." The following year, the assistant commissioner was prescribed six months' leave to recover his usually robust health. When his ship pulled out, all the men—*his* men—from CID touchingly came to the dock to wave farewell. Though he must have been in great pain, Macnaghten, accompanied by Dora, outwardly had a high old time, feted everywhere as a celebrity cop dropping in on the colonials from the Mother Country. He alighted, for example, from the R.M.S. *Mongolia* for a quick sortie in Perth, the capital of Western Australia. As covered back home by the *Western Mail*, on March 30, 1912, the charming chief extravagantly praised the constables on horseback: "He had never seen in all his experience seen finer mounted men."

In his memoirs he gushes about Australia and the generous welcome he received at every point of his six-week sojourn: "If Australia was the land of convicts once, it is the land of kindness now. In all I spent some three weeks on the continent, and the amount of hospitality which was crowded into those twenty-one days was overwhelming."[16] Upon returning to England, Macnaghten lasted nine more months before the doctors called time on the vocation he so loved. He received much laudatory mail upon the announcement of his enforced retirement, but the only letter he included in his book was from an ex-jailbird (whose name is withheld) that the chief had assisted to go straight: "I am emboldened to say to you how very grateful I feel towards you for all the kindness you showed to me." Macnaghten ends his book on the farewell dinner at Scotland Yard but without much detail.[17] To learn what he said, we need to turn to a newspaper report (yet another source that praises his incredible memory) reproduced from London in the *West Gippsland Gazette* of September 2, 1913. Macnaghten received an inscribed loving cup and "Lady Macnaghten, who was *accompanied by her daughter*, was presented with a handsome bouquet" (my italics). Though Macnaghten had two daughters this is likely to have been the younger girl, Christabel, to whom he was close. If it was, she would have absorbed how much her father was admired as a sleuth. There is also a subtle put-down, I think, towards Sir Robert Anderson, a police chief too conceited to ever concede an error: "[Macnaghten] admitted that he had made mistakes, but was of the opinion that the man who never made them, never made anything." The retiring chief's usual sangfroid touchingly crumbled on such a poignant occasion, surrounded by "my dear children"—as he calls his men on the last page of his book.

Among the expected thanks and compliments towards his men, about whom the journalist writes that not one "would refuse to extend himself to please his chief," is an unexpected reference to "Jack the Ripper," expressing a similar sentiment as he had at his farewell press conference a few months before: "Speaking with considerable emotion, Sir Melville said that when the clock struck twelve that night he would be officially dead. ... *Had he joined the force six months earlier he might have had a chance of catching Jack the Ripper;* and if that individual ever came back again he was afraid Chief Inspector Wensley would give him a bad time in Whitechapel" (my italics).[18]

In the opening preface of *Days of My Years* Sir Melville Macnaghten denies any hard feelings towards anybody: "It shall be my endeavor to tread on no corned toes, and to set down naught in malice. I have had my likes and dislikes, but, so far as I know, no enemies in the world, and I hope this state of things may continue to the end of the chapter."[19] Intense dislike of Anderson and Warren to one side (in the book the former does not exist, while the latter is pilloried, albeit unnamed, as a trampler of democratic rights), this was also, I postulate, a signal to reassure surviving members of the Majendie and Druitt families that he was not going to abandon them from retirement (at his press conference the year before he had already perjured himself about destroying any and all documentation that named their maniacal member). Sir Melville Macnaghten seems to have regretted his intemperate comments at his retirement press conference, and emotional CID farewell, about being "six months too late" to hunt the fiend, and so tried to take it back in the same preface—in which the only case mentioned is the Ripper. He tries to shift responsibility for the remark onto an "enterprising" journalist (in his memoir, Anderson had used the same adjective about the reporter who made up the hoax letter) for the bit about being dropped from Eton's elite cricket team (his *Times* obituary of 1921 suggested otherwise). He humbly asks the readers to make up their own minds as to whether he did have a go at this super-villain:

> It was said once *by an enterprising journalist* that ... I became a detective officer six months after the so-called "Jack the Ripper" committed suicide, and "never had a go at that fascinating individual." But the readers—if any take the trouble to peruse these pages—will be able to judge for themselves as to my "days," and how they have been spent[20] [my italics].

Every previous writer on this subject has misinterpreted these lines as meaning Macnaghten said he had these two regrets, whereas he is actually denying he had made any such comment. Nor have previous writers noticed that in the same paragraph, he cheekily juxtaposes championship cricket with the Whitechapel assassin, plus a preemptive apology for any inaccuracies: "I never kept a diary, nor even possessed a notebook, so that, in what I write, I must trust to my memory, and to my memory alone. Therefore, I crave indulgence if any inaccuracies shall be found to have crept into some minutes of my 'days.'"

Inside, readers found an entire chapter devoted to "Jack the Ripper" and saw that "having a go" meant investigating the "Protean" suspect "some years after" he had taken his own life (this put him neatly in opposition to Anderson, who in 1910 had implied that the killer was definitely identified by early 1889—at the latest—while still alive). Alone among the police memoirists, Sir Melville did not accuse an outsider to the British establishment but instead one of their own: an educated, English, Gentile gentleman and professional. He would assist the late Sir Vivian Majendie, but not to the point of claiming that they did not know who "Jack" was, nor that he was some lumpen nonentity—as Robert Sagar erroneously claimed in 1905. In "Laying the Ghost..." Macnaghten further gave Sir Robert nothing less than a swift kick in the posterior by reshaping the data involving the two murders on the same night, in order to absolutely clear the English Jewish community of any culpability in the Whitechapel horrors. The most obvious example of his doing this was to eliminate the Polish-Hebrew masturbator from existence as a Ripper suspect (and with one sidekick ditched, so went Ostrog—who *had* been cleared). This was unlike what he had Sims write in 1910, for now the gloves were off. In the "Aberconway Papers" Macnaghten had moved the unnamed Joseph Lawende and his two companions coming out of a club in Mitre Square across to sitting in a cart in Berner St. and interrupting the murderer before he could savage Liz Stride. He does so here too, but with an added polemical twist: "In this case there can be little doubt but that the murderer was disturbed at his demonical work by some Jews who at that hour drove up to an anarchist club in the street. But the lust for blood was unsatisfied. The madman started off in search of another victim, whom he found in Catherine Eddowes. This woman's body, very badly mutilated, was found in a dark corner of Mitre Square."[21] According to Macnaghten a trio of hard-working Jewish men almost *saved* a Gentile woman's life, and certainly protected her remains from desecration. Macnaghten follows by quashing his own fiction about a beat cop maybe seeing the Polish-Jewish suspect with the second victim that night. His beat cop now sees nothing useful—ergo, there was no super-witness in the whole saga: "On this occasion it is probable that the police officer on duty in the vicinity *saw the murderer with his victim a few minutes before*, but no satisfactory description was forthcoming" (my italics). It has been missed by previous researchers that Macnaghten is also more accurate here regarding his disguised Lawende sighting (the murderer and victim noticed together *before* the crime), starkly differentiating it from P.C. Thompson's near encounter with Frances Coles' killer and from Sims, who in 1907 has the fictional Bobbie sight the possible murderer, but only as a sinister silhouette emerging *after* committing the foul deed.

For the one and only time, Macnaghten not only mentions the graffiti, he elevates it as definitely written by the murderer. He does so, I believe, not because he actually thinks Druitt wrote it (though a schoolmaster is the kind of person who could be carrying chalk), but to debunk the notion of a Jewish "Jack" (for perhaps the only time, the ex-chief's memory genuinely fails him, slightly, as he writes "Goulburn" instead of Goulston St.; or was this deliberate, to avoid looking as if he is adapting written material?): "Hard by was a writing in chalk on the wall, to the effect that 'the Jews are the men who will not be blamed for nothing.' The apron gave no clue, and the chalk writing was obliterated by the order of a high police official, who was seemingly afraid that a riot against the Jews might be the outcome of this strange 'writing on the wall': This was the only clue ever left behind by the murderer."[22] In effect, Macnaghten has provided a particular meaning to the cryptic graffiti; the Gentile murderer was furious at being interrupted with Liz Stride and blamed the three Jewish men who pulled up in their cart and "forced" him to seek another harlot to slay. To make this work, Macnaghten cleans up the misspelling of "Jews" (as no English Ripper would get such a word wrong) while also indulging in some petty kicking of Warren's shin, the words "seemingly afraid" denying Sir Charles even the sincerity of his concern for public safety. The ambiguous graffiti appears in neither version of Macnaghten's report, nor in Sims' writings, yet is deployed here to crush Sir Robert Anderson's anti–Semitic bungle, becoming without doubt or qualification the "only clue left behind" by "Jack the Ripper." For the last time Macnaghten in 1914 wheels out the "awful glut" litmus test—except now it is not a test at all. It has become a poetic summary of the unnamed Montague Druitt's mental agony, with the added detail that his body was probably as riddled with disease as much as his mind:

> There can be no doubt that in the room at Miller's Court the madman found ample scope for the opportunities he had all along been seeking, and the probability is that, after his awful glut on this occasion, his brain gave way altogether and he committed suicide; otherwise the murders would not have ceased.[23]

In the next chapter we examine whether Sir Melville Macnaghten, the Old Etonian prankster, tried to propagate "substantial truth in fictitious form" about Montague Druitt even from beyond his own grave—and to keep the story diverted well away from Dorset and the Majendies.

XVI

RIPPER REMYSTIFIED

It shocks me greatly when you suggest that the actual name ... should be given. ... It would not be very pleasant to know that your uncle or great uncle was suspected of being "Jack the Ripper" would it?—Lady Christabel Aberconway, 1959

For an awful week it seemed.... Macnaghten must have been wrong altogether. No such doctor could be traced of that name.—Dan Farson, 1972

A curious and bright little girl who could read before she was taught how, Christabel Mary Melville Macnaghten (1890–1974) always seemed to be stumbling upon things her parents preferred her not to know. One day it was a sexually explicit translation of Balzac, which despite her father's surreptitious removal of it from a rectory's library the little girl had already finished—and had found quite "tedious."[1] When older she shocked her parents by quoting Dr. Samuel Johnson about his finding that going to the theatre aroused his "amorous propensities."[2] In another gem of intergenerational misunderstanding she told her parents she was reading about the Malthusian theory in "Progress and Poverty." The father glared while the mother restrained him with her arm and clarified the nature of this theory. Christabel relieved her parents when she replied it was arguing that the world's population was outstripping food supplies (they were worried it was about limiting the birth-rate via contraception).[3] Years before, Christabel had caused her father acute distress due to gazing upon the graphic autopsy photographs of the victims of "Jack the Ripper" (not publicly available in England until just two years before her death) while playing in his office: "As a child on Sundays always after church I walked with my father to Scotland Yard where he made various enquiries. On one occasion he found me looking at books of photographs of habitual drunkards, thieves, and the mutilated bodies of the victims of Jack the Ripper which somehow had been left in his room." To Christabel the photos looked neither revolting nor frightening, merely reminding her of "broken dolls." She wondered why anyone had wanted to photograph them, or why "my father was so greatly upset."[4]

Far more terrifying than any graphic photos was when Christabel Macnaghten was nearly sexually assaulted by a stranger. The little girl and her father were strolling on a country road near Ovingdean. He stopped to chat amiably with a farmer while she strolled along ahead. Suddenly a man whom Christabel describes in her 1966 memoir as an "old tramp" grabbed her and menacingly demanded, "I want a woman, I want a woman, and I'm going to have you. I'm full of fuck and I'm going to fuck you." Screaming for help only caused the filthy tramp to try to strangle her. The nick-of-time appearance of her father brandishing his walking stick was enough to frighten off this gross predator. A big hug and some soothing words from dad calmed her down. Later her mother tried to shield the sensitive Christabel from the full reality of her near-molestation (and her exposure to such crude language); "When I murmured that the tramp had said he was full of muck and was going to muck me, my mother said calmly muck was only another word for dirt, and of course he *was* dirty?"[5]

Christabel Macnaghten loved cats, found dogs tiresome and was wary of horses. She always seemed, as a little girl, to be in the company of middle-aged men strolling through isolated forests (Sir Edward Carson, who had vigorously prosecuted Wilde for perversion, asked what "dirty things" she would do to get money?) One of her more fearful woodland excursions inspired Rudyard Kipling to write the poem "The Way Through the Woods."

Lady Christabel Aberconway with feline companion—The attempts of Sir Melville's beloved daughter (shown here in 1950) attempts to secure her late father's legacy as the sleuth who solved the "Jack the Ripper" mystery met with mixed success (Christopher McLaren).

Thanks to her father's love of the theatre, Christabel mixed with thespian superstars such as Sir Henry Irving and Ellen Terry and with famous writers such as Kipling, Virginia Woolf, H. G. Wells (who, characteristically, made several unsuccessful passes at her), George Bernard Shaw (a nonstop talker, though always entertaining), and Evelyn Waugh (her circle of friends, the so-called "bright young things," were the inspiration for his novel *Vile Bodies*). Like her father Christabel had some aspirations to become a professional actor (Terry predicted she would one day positively *bloom* in the part of Lady Macbeth) and like Sir Melville's they came to nothing.

Aged twenty on July 19, 1910, her proud father beside her, Christabel married Henry Duncan McLaren in one of the year's great society events of the Edwardian sunset. A progressive aristocrat who was private secretary to future Liberal prime minister David Lloyd George, McLaren succeeded to the title Lord Aberconway the following year. Though wistfully missing treading the boards, Christabel adored being married to a man she actually loved and being a doting mother to her children. She was known by one and all as an amiable person, a wit and a free thinker. While visiting a dull flower-show she managed to make the notoriously bucolic King George V laugh (there were witnesses) with a risqué comment about monkeys' colorful rears. The person she "most disliked in my life" was Lord Alfred Douglas. Though she had never met the "horrid eccentric," Christabel despised the peer from afar for his betrayal of his lover, Oscar Wilde (her mother-in-law told her the *real* reason the writer was sent to prison). Once released, and with no possible future in England and having not seen his children, Wilde had died ill, alone, disgraced and penniless in Paris, in stark contrast to his younger aristocratic lover, who, purely due to the latter's higher social rank, had escaped the scandal virtually unscathed. Lady Aberconway's caustic opinion of the narcissistic peer got back to him (by then "Bosie" looked like something that had escaped from Dorian Gray's attic). From that moment Christabel became the unwilling recipient of menacing postcards every single day. Here is a representative example of what sounds like a Ripperish menace lurking in the shadows: "When you come back alone, late at night, to your great black marble hall, I shall be waiting for you, and when I leave you, your body, like bruised mulberries will not move." Alarmed, she contacted Scotland Yard, who promptly informed her that the culprit was probably Lord Alfred and, predictably, he was not charged, merely cautioned. The bizarre sequel to this cowardly harassment involved Christabel's arriving late to her seat at a theatre and, unknowingly, having to squeeze past the same Lord Alfred in the dark. Recognizing his postcard victim, he reached out and gave her "a fearful pinch on my left buttock" (she records that the same part of her anatomy suffered similar brutal treatment from a French porter and from an aged Thomas Hardy, who had lived near the Druitts).⁶

The king and queen—George V, Queen Mary and Lady Aberconway (to His Majesty's left) in 1933 (Christopher McLaren).

On May 12, 1921, Sir Melville Macnaghten died at Queen Anne Mansion in St. James, London. His death certificate records that he had progressive asthenia (chronic exhaustion) causing heart failure, having suffered paralysis agitans (uncontrollable shaking) for six years. He was barely sixty-seven. Was Sir Melville Macnaghten's memoir his last word on the Ripper case? As illness overcame his final years, did he try one last time to secure his place in posterity, yet still leave false trails that led away from the drowned barrister? Despite appearing to be tabloid hokum, the following article has tantalizing elements that argue in favor of its originating with Macnaghten. This is the eye-catching headline from *Reynolds's Weekly Newspaper* of May 15, 1921: "Dead Police Chief and 'Ripper' Murders. Man Who Solved Mystery of East End Horror." The author, though he had supposedly written a book—*Crime and the Criminal*—was left unnamed. By the end of his life Parkinson's probably impaired Macnaghten's speech, yet the article assures us that the writer heard the tale from the dead police chief's own lips, "and perhaps no more enthralling story could ever be told." It is possible that the famously discreet Macnaghten confided in this writer some *years* before he passed away in 1921, but made him promise not to publish until he had "joined the majority." But it is not very likely. Yet if it is bogus, the writer has, nonetheless, understood from some source that the late chief did take credit for solving the Ripper mystery, here outlandishly backdated to 1888: "The most remarkable piece of crime investigation was performed by the deceased *before he was connected with the police* at all. This was his solving of the "Jack the Ripper" mystery" (my italics). Macnaghten is correctly described as a true crime enthusiast and that reading up about the subject rendered him "wonderfully well equipped for his office." It could be surmised that the hack has extrapolated from *Days of My Years*. There comes, however, the startlingly inaccurate claim that not only did Macnaghten investigate the Whitechapel crimes in 1888, he did so because he was seconded by none other than Sir Charles Warren as a special, roving constable accompanied by a phalanx of detectives: "When Sir Melville came to London he obtained permission from Sir Charles Warren, the head of the Metropolitan Police, to undertake an investigation of the 'Ripper' crimes. Permission was readily granted, and he was also given the assistance of several uniformed men in case they should be required." And this is not the only aspect wildly at variance with the known facts or from even a cursory read of Macnaghten's memoirs. The victims are *all* old women, the unnamed Mary Kelly's severed hand is found fastened to the inside of her window, and a police surgeon faints upon seeing the gory spectacle in Miller's Court.

This is all very reminiscent of the vivid broad strokes of a silent film of the day; we just need suitably thunderous music as we read. For example, Macnaghten attends the scene of the most ghastly murder too, and our intrepid hero instantly formulates a theory as to the identity of the perpetrator which, as melodrama demands, proves to be absolutely correct. Yet in this account Macnaghten keeps his theory "entirely to himself," and this is, I think, broadly true. In another

"Jack the Pincher"—A desiccated Lord Alfred Douglas, Oscar Wilde's ex-lover, who menaced Christabel with postcards and, just once, his hand in the dark, c. 1940 (© National Portrait Gallery, London).

180-degree departure from "Laying the Ghost..." the killer is a "religious enthusiast," driven to remove morally soiled women from God's clean earth. Macnaghten meets a poor woman who used to wash dishes in a restaurant but is now thrown upon her own resources (shades of his Pinchin St. and Adolf Beck sorties). She tells him a "strange story" that corroborates his theory. While drinking gin alone in a bar—i.e., trawling for a client—a man chatted with her about the Whitechapel horrors. He carried a small black bag and made cryptic comments such as, "Truly in the midst of life we are in death." Discovering that she had lost her job because she was afraid of walking home after dark, the stranger offered to "kindly" escort her home, but, fortuitously for her, she did not keep the appointment. The lucky harlot also hands over to the not-yet-an-official-detective a tract ominously titled "Prepare to Meet Thy God." Macnaghten knows that this is "Jack the Ripper" as the tract functions as a confession of his homicidal mission. Yet the civilian-cop cannot overcome his unimaginative and "singularly inept" superiors, and more women needlessly lose their lives while public indignation reaches a fever pitch. Just as the indefatigable Macnaghten identifies the killer and prepares to arrest him, the aging zealot up and drowns himself in the Thames: "From certain evidence Sir Melville was able to convince the authorities that this was the man who had for so long terrorized the community. A few months later and he was made Chief Constable, and embarked upon a career of successful administration that raised the CID to the highest pitch of perfection." We just need "Mac" brandishing his spanking new badge while kissing Dora discreetly behind his top hat for the perfect fade-out (John Barrymore would have made a wonderfully athletic Macnaghten—see illustration). Yet there are features of this hokey account that perhaps *do* originate with Macnaghten, for who else could it be? The aged gentile-gentleman murderer—an utterly unrecognizable Druitt—is not portrayed as a "Mad Doctor," nor so shattered by Miller's Court that he has to commit suicide in a hurry (doing so only in about late 1889, having killed twice more). Both "Mac" and "Tatcho" had pilfered from Belloc Lowndes' Avenger in 1914 and 1915, respectively, and so does this author, but it is not the same element. Instead it is that of the one-man jihad "Jack," purging the East End of fallen women. Exactly as with the "North Country vicar" (and Sims), the suspect's culpability comes from his own words, in this case expressed in an incriminating document. Consider, finally, that the diabolical joke about Warren's being so desperate that he has to deputize an Indian planter/crime buff to catch the fiend reads like an overgrown schoolboy's idea of a sophisticated revenge against a man who had, in fact, temporarily blackballed Macnaghten from joining Scotland Yard.

If this strange and coincidental mish-mash has nothing to do with Macnaghten it shows, nevertheless, that there was some residual, short-term impact from Mac's memoirs; that *this* chief had stumbled upon the Ripper's identity and the latter, though an English gentleman, was neither a doctor nor a suicide the same night or early morning as Mary Jane Kelly's murder. Such basic understanding of the case was about to evaporate.

The following year Macnaghten's "partner in crime," George Sims, expired, aged 75. With the passing away of "Mac" and "Tatcho" there was now nobody around to refute, or debunk, any new upstart sleuths. It is appropriate then that the entire Jack the Ripper case should have been rebooted as an unsolved mystery by Sims' mirror opposite. With

Hollywood Mac—John Barrymore would have made a handsome, athletic Sir Melville in a movie of the police chief's life. This is exactly how the extraordinary article from *Reynolds Weekly Newspaper* of May 15, 1921, reads—like a cinematic melodrama. Was it the late police chief's last fact-and-fiction Ripper salvo, launched from the grave?

over one hundred books published, William Le Queux (1864–1927) was just as prolific as Sims yet was a right-wing, shamelessly jingoistic, anti-socialistic, alarmist-fantasist who was, in the Edwardian Era and after World War I, just as famous as the deceased Dagonet. It is also appropriate that it should be William Le Queux who first tried to bury the Sims-Macnaghten solution—of an English suicide—as he had been devastating in his critique of Major Griffiths' scoop about the drowned "Mad Doctor." It was nothing, Le Queux scoffed back in 1898, but transparent propaganda to enhance Scotland Yard's battered reputation.

For once Le Queux was accurate to the point of surgical precision (sometimes it takes one hustler to spot another). Journalist, author, spy, aviator, diplomat, world-traveller, radio pioneer, popular orator and all-round schmoozing celebrity William Le Queux was also, it has to be said, a truly terrible writer—compared to him, George Sims is Charles Dickens. The handsome, *pince-nez* adorned, name-dropping super-hack achieved his greatest commercial success with novels predicting a military assault on England's allegedly vulnerable shores. Le Queux did not care *who* was invading so long as foreigners were storming ashore to pillage and rape; in *The Great War in England in 1897* (1896) it was the French in coalition with the Russians (in that scenario, Germany was England's ally) while in his even bigger hit of 1906, *The Invasion of 1910*, it was the Hun himself who plays the part of the continental scourge.[7]

Of course a genuine war with Germany in 1914—which never involved England being invaded—confirmed Le Queux's credibility among his legion of worshipful fans. In 1917 he visited Russia after the February Revolution had ended monarchical-absolutist rule. In Petrograd the power vacuum was filled, shakily and temporarily, by a government of middle-class democrats ruinously committed to continue the fight against Germany, the very factor that had led to Nicholas II's downfall. That November, the same month as Lenin's Bolshevik coup, Le Queux published a book that proves he was as shameless a hoaxer as Dr. Tumblety and Tom Bulling: *The Amazing True Story of Rasputin the Rascal Monk*. In it he claimed to have viewed with his own "astounded" eyes documentary proof contained in the late Rasputin's safe that the alleged miracle-worker had been conducting a torrid affair with the czarina (who also pimped her own daughters to the monk) and, even more shockingly, that he had been the deep penetration agent of no less than the Kaiser's secret service: "German influence was eating the heart of Russia as a canker-worm—and that canker-worm was Gregory Rasputin himself."[8]

Surely Le Queux's book must show at least a few reproductions of this evidence of Teutonic espionage? Alas, no, for as the author sheepishly explains: "I had hoped to be able to reproduce many of the cipher telegrams and letters in facsimile, but the present shortage of paper has precluded this, and it could only be done if this book were issued in expensive form."[9] Such a pity. But for the miserliness of his publishers, we too could have seen the incriminating material for ourselves. He has, he assures us, diligently copied from the "dossier before me" all that exposes the true crimes of the "drunken, dissolute scoundrel from Siberia," material provided by sympathetic Russians who conveniently wish to remain anonymous. (Curiously, many of the telegrams between the Royal couple are, as he admits, written in English.) With sectarian fervor, Le Queux condemns the entire Orthodox faith, with its "malign influences and flighty practices," as responsible for the success of this "evil-minded libertine." He reveals that "the dastardly charlatan and poisoner" used secret narcotics to keep the hemophilia-afflicted boy-prince alive. As expected, the "money shot" is Rasputin's reported sexual mastery (Le Queux claims over *both* genders):

> [Rasputin] was abnormal.... His natural hypnotic influence was marked by the rare power he possessed of being able to contract the pupils of his steel-grey eyes at will.... It is a sign ... that the person is a criminal degenerate. ... He was a lunatic of an intensely erotic type; a satyr who possessed a truly appalling influence over women of all ages, and even at his word men in high positions did not hesitate to cast off their brilliant uniforms and decorations and mortify their flesh! ... The Cult of the Naked Believers rapidly spread everywhere.[10]

You can't say that Le Queux does not give the reader their money's worth! Who cares about boring questions of provenance when the gossip is this steamy?

When we turn, therefore, to the same source's Jack the Ripper revelations of 1923—and these involve Rasputin too, the gift that kept on giving for Le Queux—we should not be too troubled about taking any of it seriously. In his memoir *Things I Know About Kings, Celebrities and Crooks* (a blurb masquerading as a title), the author breathlessly

Rasputin with clothed *members of the "Cult of the Naked Believers"*—The best-selling alarmist William LeQueux claimed that the Ripper was really a Czarist assassin sent to discredit Scotland Yard. The English literary hustler also wrote that the murdered Rasputin (shown here in 1916) was his source—and that the "Rascal Monk" spoke French, slept with the Czarina (and her daughters) and worked as a deep penetration agent for the Kaiser.

explains that the provisional government led by Alexander Kerensky had handed to him a mountain of documents in confidence—now broken—that had allegedly been recovered from Rasputin's safe. The Russian democrats believed that only the fabulous Le Queux could possibly convey the truth of the mad monk to the world. Among the voluminous archive of letters, telegrams and "compromising correspondence from the Empress"— that to this day nobody else has ever sighted—the fearless writer hit the jackpot. Rasputin had dictated an account called "Great Russian Criminals"—in French! To Le Queux's "amazement" the work by the "rascal monk" covered the Ripper crimes because, according to Rasputin, while they were committed by a medical man, he was a Russian assassin! Why did the English writer hold this scoop back from inclusion in his earlier work? Apparently he could not verify the facts until 1923. He writes that he made a copy of this book before returning it to the revolutionary government, which meant that the Rasputin tome must have, by 1923, lain beyond reach in a Soviet archive. We are then privy to an excerpt that has only now been verified:

> The mysterious assassin was Doctor Alexander Pedachenko, who had ... gone to London, where he lived with his sister in Westmorland Road, Walworth. From there he sallied forth at night, took an omnibus across London Bridge and walked to Whitechapel, where he committed his secret crimes. ... [He] was aided by a friend of his named Levitski, and a young tailoress, called Winberg. The latter would approach the victim and hold her in conversation and Levitski kept watch for the police patrols, while the crimes and mutilations took place. Levitski, who had been born in London, wrote the warning post-cards signed "Jack the Ripper" to the Police and Press.[11]

Apart from being evil, why did these Russians on the payroll of the Czarist secret police, the fearsome Okhrana, commit these horrific crimes? What on earth were they trying to achieve, apart from blindly following orders? The mission of Dr. Pedachenko, "the greatest and boldest of all Russian criminal lunatics," was to humiliate Scotland Yard (in 1888 the improbable Triple Entente lay very much in the future)—what a shame "Mac" did not live to read this tosh. And the fate of this Dr. Pedachenko? Smuggled back to Moscow, he tried to murder and mutilate a local woman and—in a finale straight out of the Macnaghten playbook—he was sent to an asylum, where he expired in 1908. Le Queux writes, "Such are the actual facts of the 'Jack the Ripper Mystery' which still puzzles the whole world." There was open skepticism in the press towards Le Queux's Rasputin/Ripper solution—"not convincingly strong," as the *Empire News* of October 23, 1923, scoffs, as the motive, "to annoy and baffle Scotland Yard," was not only implausible, it was just plain silly. Assuming he made it all up, what gave Le Queux the idea of having the Ripper as a Russian assassin? It may have been from the writings of his deceased, leftist rival, George Sims, who had mused about just such a notion in "Mustard and Cress" on December 2, 1888: "The 'Russian' theory of the atrocities is worth thinking-out … a sensitive and excitable race … very apt to rush into extremes.… The [Russian] Vassili, who, about sixteen years ago, murdered a number of women in Paris, and who is reported to have been released from a lunatic asylum last January, may again have thought it his duty to work out the eternal salvation of the wretched East-end women."

Though William Le Queux had failed to convince almost anybody of his Russian secret service solution—and passed away four years later—his destructive legacy regarding popular understanding of the Jack the Ripper mystery was incalculable (and lasts to this day). He remystified what had been solved and was believed to have been solved by Edwardians. By the time, decades later, that Montie Druitt was finally found, it barely made a dent in the notion that the police had never really solved the case, and what's more never claimed to have done so at the time. (Macnaghten's revelatory press conference of 1913 was not rediscovered until the 1980s, and by then made no impact whatsoever.) Le Queux had sufficiently muddied the waters for the fiendish doctor element to become entrenched but detached from the Ripper as a tormented suicide. With the new paradigm of the Whitechapel crimes an unsolved case implanted in popular culture, it just needed somebody to take on the drowned "Mad Doctor" solution, head-on, and to debunk the literal existence of such a figure. Originally from my home city of Adelaide, South Australia, Leonard Warburton Matters (1881–1951) has the distinction of being the first person to author a book, *The Mystery of Jack the Ripper* (1929), devoted solely to the Whitechapel murders. An adventurer, Matters had fought in the Boer War, been a journalist in Argentina and was, for two years, a Labour member of Parliament (1929–1931, representing Kennington, the jobbing-hunting ground of Thomas Cutbush). For the first time here was a researcher, albeit one hostage to his own preconceived theory, making an effort to identify, by name, the "Mad Doctor" who drowned himself in the Thames. Like many before him, Matters read Major Griffiths' *Mysteries of Police and Crime* (1898) and absorbed his brief mention of a trio of alleged, prime police suspects—but where had it come from? ("I have to confess complete failure in the attempt to discover its origin.") Perhaps because he was an expatriate, Matters exhibits no knowledge of George Sims' many writings about the same suspect, and did not uncover all those "Mustard and Cress" columns in his research. Instead the novice's initial perplexity hardened into a sweeping skepticism after he had made an abortive attempt to find any reference to a medical man who was fished from that river after the Mary Jane Kelly murder, as can be seen in chapter 16 of his book:

> Furthermore, I have searched the columns of *the Times,* the *Daily Telegraph,* the *Daily News* and the *Star,* and have failed to find any reference between November 9th, 1888, and March 1889, to this sensational find in the Thames. Surely if the facts could have been substantiated such a discovery would have been a sensation—to say nothing of a great relief to the awestricken East End of London![12]

Like still-active mines that drifted around the world's oceans long after the conclusion of the Second World War, so the disguise Macnaghten and Sims had set up for short-term reasons of discretion (and that the police chief had tried to deflate in 1914, though Matters seems never to have learned of that source's existence either) continued to hide the Druitts more securely than ever.[13] Trapped by Major Griffiths' implied CID hunt for the doctor suspect while alive, Matters can only rhetorically moan: "The police are said to have missed this man at the time of the last murder. Why, if they knew him and strongly suspected him before it, they had not arrested him when they could get him, Major Griffiths does not explain."[14] Never fear, Matters provides his own solution: his own mad medico, "Dr. Stanley," who confessed on his deathbed while expiring in Argentina—that he had previewed two years before in an article reproduced in the *Syracuse Herald* on January 16, 1927 (Le Queux never made a known comment about it, and died the following October). The sub-editor of the New York paper has done a superb job of summing up Matters' entire theory in the headline: "Jack the Ripper, Famous London Surgeon, Dying, Pupil Says Revenge for Son's Death His Motive Claims Doctor, Dying, Confessed to Series of Crimes Baffled Authorities Killed Women Who Dragged Son Down to Death." His book confidently opens, "I have read that the body of 'Jack the Ripper' was taken out of the Thames. There is no warrant whatsoever for this assertion, and all the theories based on it, all the confident assurances that the police had found 'their man' are worthless." Also worthless is Leonard Matter's Dr. Stanley theory, as it was based entirely on word of mouth, as was another tall tale he swallowed whole, about trying to hunt a dinosaur, as he wrote in the *Scientific American* of July 1922: "AN ANTIDILUVIAN MONSTER. THE ARGENTINE PLESIOSAURUS … Whatever may be the opinion in scientific circles—and it is one of scornful scepticism—the fact remains that the report of the existence in Argentina of a living specimen of a race of mammoth reptiles, supposed to have been extinct for millions of years, has excited intense interest." Sir Arthur Conan Doyle, author of *The Lost World* (1912), should have sued for plagiarism.

What Lady Christabel Aberconway thought of the likes of William Le Queux (or Leonard Matters) rudely repudiating her father's solution is not known. At age 76 she wrote that when she stood before God's Great White Throne and had to account for her life she would say that on earth she had loved more than anything her friends and certain works of art. She also explained candidly that by "friends" she included her parents but not her siblings, from whom she seems to have been to some extent estranged (her oldest brother, Charles Melville Macnaghten, was a bona fide World War I hero).[15] It is a murky area, but it seems that her father's Ripper "memorandum" fell briefly into Christabel's hands around the time of her mother's death in 1929 (though it was owned by her sister, with whom relations may have been chilly). Maybe stung by Le Queux,

Christabel was determined to preserve the contents in order to protect her father's reputation. Discreetly she had a secretary make a typed copy while the suspects section was copied by her, in her own hand, to avoid any possibility of a leak to the press of "Dr. Druitt's" name. She sat on that copy for another generation, while the original would be lost, presumably destroyed, proving her correct that she was the only one of his children who could be relied upon to keep their father's Ripper legacy alive. Lady Aberconway gave her copy of the document a handwritten title: "Memorandum on articles which appeared in the Sun re JACK THE RIPPER on 14 Feb 1894 and subsequent dates. By my father Sir M. M."

One source that tried to defend the drowned "Mad Doctor" was Macnaghten's successor as CID chief, Sir Basil Thomson, who resigned in 1921 and dashed any hopes of being recalled as commissioner by getting himself arrested with a prostitute. He then compounded that scandal by trying to bribe the arresting bobbies with promises of promotion. In the American second edition of his memoir, *The Story of Scotland Yard* (Literary Guild, 1936, pp. 189–191), Thomson wrote of the Whitechapel murders. But he is clearly dependent on reading Major Griffiths' account of 1898. Consequently Thomson was quite fooled that the "Mad Doctor" was about to be arrested, and that the beat cop witness really was his tragic near-namesake (but that was from the 1891 murder of Frances Coles): "One was a Polish Jew reported by Police Constable Thomson, the one police officer who caught sight of the man in Mitre Court.... The third suspect was also a doctor on the borderland of insanity. His friends had grave doubts him, *but the evidence was insufficient for detaining him with any hope of obtaining a conviction* ... the medical evidence being that it had been in the water for a month" (my italics). Sir Basil Thomson's rewrite shows that he had no insider knowledge to offer on the Dorset solution and, as with all his Scotland Yard colleagues, had not been taken into "Good Old Mac's" confidence about Druitt. He had no idea, for example, that while he was assistant commissioner there was lying dormant in the Scotland Yard archive his predecessor's 1894 Ripper report. One can only imagine the shock if Thomson had read it, because he would have seen a name—"M. J. Druitt"—that the ex-chief might have recalled from when he had been a student at New College, Oxford, and had rubbed shoulders with a Montie Druitt.[16]

There is a very lonely example of a postwar researcher casting his experienced eye over Macnaghten's memoir, one uncontaminated by any of the Jack-the-Surgeon propaganda. Consequently it grasps, with remarkable ease, what the late chief was trying to communicate. An ex-inspector of the Australian police, Harry Mann, reviewed the Ripper mystery for the *Mirror* (Western Australia) on October 13, 1951. In a couple of paragraphs Mann is insightful, straightforward and, as we know from other sources, spot on: "In Sir Melville's opinion the man's brain finally collapsed and he brought about his own destruction. He does not say why that opinion was held, but there is a hint that maybe the Yard held a little more information in the end than has ever been released." Eight years before discovery of a version of Macnaghten's internal report would inadvertently derail understanding of this police chief, and with it, the entire Jack the Ripper subject, it is touching to see Mann come closer—in just a few lines—to the historical truth than entire shelves of books subsequently written on this mystery. The ex-cop's insightful summary of "Mac's" "Laying the Ghost..." would soon be obscured for over half a century: "Maybe the police found out after his death who he was; maybe *he came of a respectable family*, and after his violent end no good purpose would have been served and *a lot of suffering on innocent people* would have been inflicted by disclosing his identity. That dreadful secret is, I think, buried forever in a suicide's grave" (my italics).

By 1959 when yet another unscrupulous media fringe dweller, Donald McCormick, brought out his book *The Identity of Jack the Ripper*—unimaginatively resurrecting the Le Queux nonsense about the Russian sabotage agent—Lady Aberconway decided to act to defend her father's achievement. It is well known, now, that McCormick made sources up as easily as breathing, but about one aspect he was simply repeating, honestly and accurately, that there was no available evidence of a drowned surgeon:

> The simple test for the theory is to find out what doctor was found drowned in the Thames on the last day of December 1888. And as soon as the test is applied the theory is destroyed. For in none of the leading London morning or evening papers of the day is there any report of such an incident at any time between 9 November 1888, and the end of January 1889. Nor do the obituary columns of the newspapers, nor those of the Medical Directory for 1889 and 1890 provide any clues.[17]

I do not think that McCormick even realized that *this* even was the theory of the late Sir Melville Macnaghten. Nonetheless, a polite yet firm rebuttal letter by the miffed aristocrat was published in the November 7, 1959, edition of the left-leaning the *New Statesman*. In it Lady Aberconway deals with the claim about destroyed documents that McCormick had found in a book by crime writer Hargrave L. Adam, by conceding her father *might* have said this but only, she guessed, to get nosy members of the Garrick Club off his back.[18] For the first time, Christabel revealed some sort of unique documentation by this senior policeman that was still very much in existence: "I possess my father's private notes on Jack the Ripper in which he names three individuals 'against whom the police held reasonable suspicion' and states which of these three, in his judgment was the killer. None of these three names is mentioned by Mr. McCormick." This letter appeared five days before a television program would confirm her father had solved the case, yet it did not name the chief suspect: *Farson's Guide to the British*, hosted by Dan Farson. Just as Macnaghten had used the most successful writer of his time to disseminate his opinion, so his daughter would also tap a popular journalist, one with his own show on the new, all-pervasive medium of television. (Farson impressed Christabel enough that she agreed to appear on one of his other episodes of *Farson's Guide to the British* devoted to the English love of cats, about which the aristocrat had published a couple of charming books, broadcast on December 3, 1959.)

Daniel Negley Farson was born in Kensington, London, in 1927, the son of an American journalist, and died seventy years later, his private life, health and career in a somewhat disheveled state. As a boy he lived in Canada, holidayed in the United States, and regularly visited England, and it is the latter nation for which he renounced his dual citizenship. At the British public school of Wellington College, Dan Farson developed a lifelong antipathy towards the regimented, unquestioning ruling class—the diametric opposite of Sir Melville Macnaghten. He had two other qualifications to be the right person to reveal the truth about "Jack the Ripper." Firstly he was the great-nephew of Bram Stoker, the author of the classic vampire pot-boiler, *Dracula* (and the agent-manager of Sir Henry Irving, whom Christabel had known). Secondly, as a boy he had shaken hands with an honest-to-God mass murderer. Due to crisscrossing the world with his peripatetic, foreign correspondent father, little Dan had met Adolf Hitler. The Fuhrer patted the blonde-haired, blue-eyed child on the head and pronounced his Master Race blessing: "What a good, Aryan boy."[19] In a sense, Hitler had been fooled by the very surface quality that accounted for some of the discreetly homosexual Farson's initial success in 1950s television: he looked and sounded like a safe, clean cut, toffy-accented member of the British establishment. (Farson called his autobiography *Never a Normal Man*, a reference to his own father but which sounds like the perfect title for the Ripper's never-to-be-written memoir.) Actually his eclectic shows, such as *Out of Step*, were devoted to shining a light on outsiders: UFO buffs, vegans, nudists, interracial couples, disaffected youth, even bigots got to have their bigoted say (it has been noted before that, within a generation, Ripper buffs would have made an excellent subject for a Farson program). At the conclusion of his first television documentary series for 1959, ending in July, Farson had made a nationwide appeal for any information about the Whitechapel murders, as they were still within living memory. In his *Jack the Ripper* (History Book Club, 1972) Farson describes his fortuitous meeting with Lady Aberconway due to her daughter, Lady Rose McLaren, being his friend and fellow devotee of the Colony Club in fashionable Soho: "A few hours later at Maenan Hall, I explained my interest to Christabel Aberconway and she was kind enough to give me her father's private notes which she had copied out soon after his death."[20] As Dan Farson excitedly wrote thirteen years later about holding the bombshell document: "No one has known the name of the man whom the police suspected. Now, for the first time, this name lay in my hands." Although Farson had the name, "M. J. Druitt," he was woefully ignorant of the complex back-story as to the memo's creation—unknown to Christabel as well—to both reveal and conceal public knowledge about the drowned barrister via Griffiths and Sims. Nor did the reporter have time to find out.

Lady Aberconway had a stipulation for Dan Farson: the journalist was not to broadcast the suspect's name. Why did Lady Aberconway censor the identity of a police suspect who had been deceased thirteen years before the death of Queen Victoria? We need look no further than her reply to Ralph Partridge, who had reviewed the McCormick book. Partridge contacted Christabel hoping to also learn the name of the suspect in her father's notes. In a reply dated November 17, 1959, she demurred because it offended her sense of propriety; consideration must *still* be shown towards the Druitt family: "It shocks me greatly when you suggest that the actual name of the suspected 'Jack the Ripper' should be given. After all *he might have a nephew or a niece*, born about 1890, who would not yet be 70: they in turn might have a child about to get married. It would not be very pleasant to know that *your uncle or great uncle* was suspected of being 'Jack the Ripper' would it?"[21] (my italics). C. Ward-Agius noticed what nobody before had noted about Lady Aberconway's stricture: her father must have been aware that Mr. Druitt had no children of his own, and to know that he must have been well-informed about his suspect's correct details.

What neither Dan Farson nor Lady Aberconway considered was that her reticence, motivated by compassion and decency, perfectly encapsulated her father's comparable reticence about revealing Druitt's identity (despite all the writers she mentions hobnobbing with in her book, George Sims is not among them). This was due to not knowing that the notes were created for public consumption and *ipso facto* by the ethical standards of father and daughter could not contain enough information to embarrass the Druitts, nor of course the Majendies (and this while the suspect's siblings and cousins were still alive).

Needing to swiftly verify the details of this "Dr. Druitt," Farson and his team immediately hit the same wall as previous writers: the "Mad Doctor" disguise that was still acting as a shield against uncovering the Dorset solution. His chief researcher, Jan Matos, could find no such person in the records of births and deaths held at Somerset House (because she was looking for a Druitt who died aged 41 in 1888). By October, Farson was in full panic that his scoop was nothing but a mirage, a fear he shared with readers in 1972: "For an awful week it seemed that there was no such person as M. J. Druitt, that Macnaghten must have been wrong altogether. No such doctor could be traced of that name. No such body had been found in the Thames that month."[22] Back in 1959 Dan Farson publicly moaned about his dilemma in the November 1–7, 1959, issue of the *TV Times*: "At the moment of writing we are on the last lap, and still do not know what we shall find. I expect we shall label our theory 'The Strange Case of the Man who never Died.'" Yet "Team Farson" had a crucial advantage over all previous researchers—they had the *name* of Macnaghten's suspect. Via telephone enquiries Matos located a couple of Druitt descendants—just like the ones Lady Aberconway had been so concerned about being spared the awful truth—who had predecessors who were medical men related to Montague. On October 16, 1959, at Somerset House these other Druitts led a relieved Farson to the correct death certificate of maybe the authentic "Jack the Ripper"—Montague John Druitt.[23]

Yet his death certificate unambiguously showed that Druitt was a "barrister at law," and furthermore was not middle-aged—not 41—but in fact 31, and thus born in 1857. Everybody in the Druitt family seemed to be a doctor *except* Montague! How to explain these discrepancies between what the late assistant commissioner had written and the raw, immovable facts? Knowing almost nothing about Christabel's father and his acclaimed memory, or George R. Sims, or that Macnaghten's memoir did not repeat that the unnamed Druitt was middle-aged or a doctor, Dan Farson assumed that the police chief must have had a defective memory. It was a reasonable theory, yet one easily refuted by more extensive research—research beyond the time and resources of a T.V. reporter working on a limited budget and to a tight schedule. As the two programs were being edited, Farson suffered an unusual and—he believed—devastating reversal. Some unknown man—perhaps another Ripper researcher—had entered his place of work and brazenly walked off with all of Farson's voluminous correspondence, from eager viewers, about their knowledge of the Whitechapel crimes. Despite that setback, *Farson's Guide to the British*, "The British as Murderers—Jack the Ripper" was broadcast on November 5, 1959, at the very late time of 10:45 p.m. and ran for a stingy 13 minutes and 30 seconds. The second episode, broadcast on November 12, 1959, ended with a *tour de theatre* as Farson held up Montie Druitt's death certificate. Acceding to Lady Aberconway's wishes, Farson had blacked out the deceased's name. Viewers had to settle for just the suspect's initials: M. J. D.[24]

Yet Farson was left with a frustrating sense of a lack of completion, that the jigsaw contained too many missing pieces to be called a closed case. The celebrity-reporter decided to launch a further search for a bridging source: something that would incontrovertibly link the drowned not-a-doctor with the Whitechapel murders, and thus render irrelevant Sir Melville's seemingly bizarre biographical mistakes about his own chief suspect. What Farson needed, of course, was to stumble upon the "West of England" M.P. sources from 1891 and 1892. These are the "missing link" or "Rosetta Stone" primary sources that span the chasm between the 1889 positive obituaries about Mr. M. J. Druitt and his seemingly inexplicable reemergence, a few years later, as a prime Ripper suspect in Macnaghten's memorandum (they establish that belief about Montie's culpability originated, rightly or wrongly, with "his own people" in Dorset, and not later with a seemingly confused police chief). While Daniel Farson's dissatisfaction with the "Aberconway Papers" was sound, his subsequent line of inquiry was anything but, as he embarked on a delusional quest worthy of Don Quixote jousting at windmills. Instead of taking the time to methodically trawl at least British newspaper articles from the Late Victorian and Edwardian eras, it was he, rather than the late Macnaghten, who suffered a self-defeating memory lapse.

Shortly after the broadcast Farson had what he thought was nothing short of an epiphany: he remembered perusing a certain letter in his brazenly stolen dossier that mentioned the Druitt name *before* he had read the Macnaghten memo. The letter pointed to a primary source viewed decades before in the Australian state of Victoria, apparently titled: *The East End Murderer—I Knew Him* by none other than a Lionel Druitt—a cousin of Montie's who had emigrated Down Under in 1886. It is a measure of Farson's utter desperation that he could have entertained such a ridiculous idea: a family member who revealed for publication a secret that could only bring disaster to all concerned—which, conversely, hardly anybody apparently took any notice of. It is a very convoluted quest whose ins-and-outs need not detain us.

In brief, Dan Farson came to Australia in 1961 to do his show, this time exploring ex-colonial manners and mores (local women's magazines forlornly swooned over the Brit's magnetic, blue-eyed good looks[25]). For hundreds of miles beneath the unforgiving Australian sun the reporter tramped from one obscure and dusty town to another, trying to find evidence of this tell-all document by the murderer's relation—that never could have existed. What had become garbled in Farson's mind was that the stolen correspondence almost certainly referred to an 1892 pamphlet about another vile murderer named Frederick Bailey Deeming, an English migrant who had been executed that year in Melbourne. This psychopath had murdered his second wife in Australia, having already slaughtered his entire family back in England. There was empty press speculation, at the time, about Deeming also being the Ripper—or even confessing to the Whitechapel murders. When broadcast, "Farson in Australia" (1961) was a critical and commercial success (the reporter's last; the more radical Sixties began to leave him behind as his initial clean-cut hipness dated quickly), but the titular host was left disappointed and frustrated because of his "bridge too far."[26] For the public to finally learn the likely Ripper's name it would take the brashness of an American writer-hustler to elbow to one side anachronistic English etiquette about pleasing upper-class sensibilities. Enter stage left, Tom Cullen.

XVII

Jack the Oxonian

Some independent genius ... by murdering and disemboweling four women, converted the proprietary press to an inept sort of communism.—George Bernard Shaw, *The Star*, 1888

Overwhelmed by a sense of hopelessness and futility, might he not have conceived it as his mission to call attention to these evils, even to the extent of committing murder?—Tom Cullen, 1965

It was an American exiled in England, and not local boy, Dan Farson, who would have the distinction of being the first author to publish Montague John Druitt's name as the man likely to have been "Jack the Ripper" (Farson did not publish his book until 1972). There is no record that the American had spoken with the Lady Aberconway, let alone been admonished as to what he should and should not reveal. It would not have mattered if he had been, as he was not one to tug his forelock.

Born on May 16, 1913, in Oklahoma City, Thomas Alden Cullen grew up in California, where he studied political science and economics at the state university. With mass unemployment engulfing the nation in the 1930s, Cullen became a socialist, working as a journalist for the left-leaning United Progressive News. In 1934 Cullen actively campaigned for Upton Sinclair, a progressive writer and the Democratic Party's candidate for governor. The latter's platform was to End Poverty in California (E.P.I.C.) by the radical redistribution of wealth. Sinclair was defeated by the Republican, who branded his opponent a communist traitor. A disgusted Cullen, by now deeply cynical about how ordinary Americans could be scared into voting against their own economic interests, subsequently served in Europe and North Africa during the Second World War, as a reporter for the army. Despite proving his patriotism on the frontline, by the 1950s Cullen had become one of the millions of victims of the McCarthyite witch-hunts. While abroad in London, he was branded a potential subversive and his passport was confiscated. Fortunately, Cullen was allowed to work in the U.K.—so long as he promised to resist overthrowing Her Majesty's government on behalf of the international proletariat.[1]

Published in 1965 as "Beatlemania" was cresting, Tom Cullen's *Autumn of Terror* (a.k.a. *When London Walked in Terror*) is arguably the finest book written on this subject; it is a neglected literary/historical masterpiece albeit in a minor key.[2] This is in spite of errors by Cullen, some of which he could not have avoided as he was constrained by a lack of time and resources. Yet it has to be said that he made a number of significant, unforced errors too. Of the second variety, he has the Ripper writing the original letter that coined the killer's nickname, even though *all* the senior police figures (and George Sims) agreed it was a fake created to increase newspaper circulation. These deficiencies are dwarfed, nevertheless, by Cullen's vivid prose and his dazzling vision of a rotten-to-the-core class system that deserved the Ripper. Discussed a little further on is this socialist's compelling polemic as to why Druitt killed only in Whitechapel-Spitalfields, a theory refracted, admittedly, through the narrow lens of Cullen's leftist, ideological bias. Even Lenin, who was in London in 1902, makes a walk-on appearance in Cullen's book, among notables who visited an East End center for hands-on Christian charity, Toynbee Hall.

The living dead—This was the cover of George Sims' influential 1883 work on systemic poverty in London, one that inspired other leading writers and reformers in the late Victorian era.

This American journeyman-wordsmith may have been as unscrupulous as he was talented. Apparently Dan Farson believed that it was *Cullen* who had fast-talked his way into his office and walked off with his bulging dossier on "Jack the Ripper." Farson's private accusation was based on Cullen's book making a passing reference to one of the interviews on his television show that had in fact not been aired—a transcript of the interview existed only in the purloined dossier. Yet surely a much more incriminating aspect is that Cullen had possession of a copy of Sir Melville's "memorandum," which Lady Aberconway had only provided to Farson. Don Rumbelow, an ex-policeman and crime writer, recalls that in a conversation with Cullen, the latter said that he was waiting for Farson to "put his head above the parapet and publicly accuse him of stealing the memorandum ... when he would sue him for libel"—which is not quite the same as a protestation of innocence. A third possibility is that Cullen was not the thief but that the contents of Farson's missing attaché found their way into his eager hands.[3] For all their bitter rivalry, accusations and counter-threats, Tom Cullen did not challenge Dan Farson's assumption that Sir Melville Macnaghten had an unreliable memory. Thus a fundamental misinterpretation based on limited research cemented itself as a "definitely ascertained fact." The American did read Macnaghten's memoir but decided that the ex-chief was quite mistaken in asserting that the murderer's identity only became known to him "some years after" he killed himself: "It is perhaps unfortunate that the CID chief did not keep a notebook, for, relying upon his memory concerning events which had occurred many years earlier, he has allowed a number of errors to creep into his discussions of the Ripper case, both in his notes which he made in 1894 and in his memoirs published in 1914."[4] It is excruciating to see such a brilliant writer back himself into the equivalent of a Whitechapel cranny, having mused just a few lines earlier that *Days of My Years* is significantly different from the so-called memorandum ("But this time there is no mention of the Polish Jew or of the Russian doctor"), but still judge both accounts to be riddled with "errors."

Why did Cullen, eyes wide open, step into this booby-trap? Mostly it was due to the "West of England" M.P. sources remaining dormant (they would do so for another quarter of a century). Partly it was because the American exile thought he had found, or at least been handed, the elusive "missing link" source that made the case for Druitt's guilt irresistible. This allegedly clinching source claimed that Scotland Yard quietly disbanded their special patrols after the barrister washed up at Chiswick. To disabuse the reader that this might have been due to some other reason, such as budget cuts, Cullen offers us a genuine if minor figure from 1888: Mr. Albert Backert. The latter was a self-appointed busybody, the head of a Whitechapel Vigilance Committee. Worried that police attention was suddenly slackening, Backert bitterly complained to the authorities and was reportedly taken into their confidence to shut him up: "It was then suggested to me that the Vigilance Committee and its patrols might be disbanded *as the police were quite certain that the Ripper was dead*.... He was fished out of the Thames two months ago and it would only cause pain to his relatives if we said any more than that"[5] (Cullen's italics).

This was, potentially, a tremendous discovery, confirming as it did Macnaghten's later opinion about Druitt. The "Backert" source, however, cannot withstand the slightest scrutiny and should never have been taken seriously by the wily Cullen. A mass of contemporaneous sources prove that the police patrols were by no means quietly disbanded in early 1889 (a point made by Frederic Abberline in his 1903 interview). Essentially, the Backert "revelation" is a reworking of the "Mad Doctor" hustle about the fast-closing but too late police dragnet. The final nail in the coffin regarding Cullen's scoop is its total lack of credible provenance; it had been conveniently "discovered" in the papers of a Dr. Thomas Dutton. Though this English physician had existed, his allegedly voluminous crime archive has never been sighted by anybody except its "executor"—none other than inveterate hoaxer Donald McCormick. In a footnote, Cullen admits that his source for the Backert "bridge" is McCormick, "who got it, apparently, from Dr. Thomas Dutton's papers." This is the same Dr. Dutton who—according to McCormick—proved that Le Queux's 1923 supposedly Rasputin-derived theory was *kosher*. Elsewhere in the body of the text Cullen shows that he seems all too aware what a weak foundation this is on which to build any theory: "In the absence of better proof, Dr. Dutton's statements that Pedachenko and the Ripper was one and the same person must be treated with great reserve."[6] Determined to provide a definite textual link between "Sad Death of a Local Barrister" and "I have always held strong feelings about No. 1," Cullen allowed this pathetic hoax to trump the 1914 memoirs: "Macnaghten's memory is clearly at fault, as attested by Albert Backert's statement."[7] The American should have paid greater attention to the dowager aristocrat's 1959 letter refuting McCormick, as it revealed that her father was quite capable of fibbing when the occasion suited.

Tom Cullen's book suffered a body-blow just the following year with the publication of Britisher Robin Odell's fine book *Jack the Ripper: In Fact and Fiction*, which argued that Druitt was never a major suspect, of Macnaghten's or anybody else at Scotland Yard. An unknown person acting on Odell's behalf gained access to the police archive. Among the surviving bits and pieces about the Whitechapel crimes was found the Macnaghten report that had never gone to the Home Office (and had lain there, undisturbed, for seventy-two years). Odell argued that the lines "no shadow of proof" and that "any one" of the three suspects could have been "Jack" thoroughly deflated Cullen's red balloon. None of these early researchers, however, had found the Sims sources from the *Referee* and were therefore totally in the dark about the Macnaghten report(s) having been composed and utilized as part of a complex game of media manipulation. Robin Odell's background was science, not history, and this perhaps too-literal approach shows in his crude misreading of Macnaghten's memoir: "Sir Melville Macnaghten's published memoirs do not carry any reference to this "very reasonable suspicion," [about Montie] nor is there any reference to a Mr. M. J. Druitt."[8]

International events were unwittingly to influence public perceptions of the Ripper mystery, specifically the Watergate scandal of 1972–74. In July and August of 1973, against a backdrop of daily headlines of conspiracy and cover-up slurping out of the White House like a sickening oil spill, a very unusual program was broadcast in Britain to a huge and receptive audience: *Jack the Ripper*, a BBC semi-documentary in six prime-time episodes. The show proposed a new and jaw-droppingly despicable reason for Macnaghten's "inaccuracies": he was posthumously framing Druitt as a Ripper *decoy*! The makers of the show built towards the 'scoop' that the case was in reality a *royal* Watergate, though with the truth emerging too late to topple the current occupant of the British throne. After hours of typically polished and plummy recreations of various sources (among which we get to see Montie pulled from the river and a reserved William testify at the inquest), the program revealed its own much more impressive bridging source than any musty document—a living witness! This was the aged picture restorer Joseph Gorman, who had legally changed his name to Sickert as he claimed to be the illegitimate child of the famous painter Walter. With his full beard and owlish spectacles, he certainly looked the part of a Cockney street prophet.[9] In a five-minute insert in the last episode, Gorman-Sickert revealed what his father had supposedly told him: his mother was really the "love child" of a secret marriage between a dirt-poor woman and none other than Prince Albert Victor, Victoria's grandson and heir. This attention-seeking old faker said the conspiracy involved the entire terrified Victorian establishment, including Her Majesty, the prime minister, and the heads of the constabulary, all deciding to murder Mary Jane Kelly. This harlot knew the truth of the unacceptable liaison. So they could make her death look like she was merely the final, random victim of a serial killer, four other "unfortunates" had to die first. Joseph Gorman-Sickert was claiming royal lineage while simultaneously accusing the same dynasty of resorting to common murder. This was pathetic, penny-dreadful stuff that in any other era except the 1970s "Age of Paranoia"—of charlatans such as Uri Geller; claims of extra-terrestrials mutilating cattle, and the Jonestown mass suicide—would never have made it to the screen, small or large.[10] The idea of a royal cover-up had been first spread around by the cranky Dr. Stowell, who had been making this his conversation piece since even before Dan Farson aired his first Ripper program. Stowell had died three years before the hit program, never knowing the enormity of what he had unleashed; the vice-like, clammy embrace by mass culture of some kind of sinister royal connection to the Whitechapel horrors. The real Queen Victoria had been concerned for the poor women's plight and exasperated at the lack of progress by her police.

The peculiar conceit of this British television series was that it was narrated—and the sources and crime scene locations analyzed—by two fictional detectives from very popular British television shows. Detective superintendents Charlie Barlow (portly, baritone-voiced Stratford Johns) and John Watt (tall, fair and vinegary Frank Windsor) had appeared in hard-hitting, gritty crime shows such as *Z-Cars* and *Softly Softly*, and other spin-offs (though these dramas were more realistic and brutal than previous dramatizations of British policing, both Barlow and Watt were still just as incorruptible as the sentimentalized bobbies of *Dixon of Dock Green* in the 1950s). However brilliant the acting, this use of *faux* detectives was still the tip-off that this show was no more to be taken seriously than any other work of fiction on "the tube." The American equivalent might have been the buddy-cops *Starsky and Hutch* investigating the controversial 1892 Lizzie Borden axe-murder case, or zooming around Dealey Plaza in their red Gran Torino trying to find witnesses to the Grassy Knoll shooter whom C.I.A. goons had neglected to bump off. A year before Macnaghten was accused of framing Druitt, Lady Christabel Aberconway may have realized that the efforts to guarantee her father's place in history—as the man who likely solved the Ripper case—were receding. A friend of her late nephew, the one who had lost the original notes, pestered her for clarification. Belatedly she drew his attention back to Sir Melville Macnaghten's published account, forgetting (or pretending to forget) that her relative was deceased and that she *had* seen the original "memo" to make her copy: "My elder sister, ten years older than myself, took all my father's papers when my mother died, which is why Gerald has them: I have never seen them. But in my father's book, *Days of My Years*, he talks of 'Jack the Ripper.' ... That is, alas, all the information I can give."[11] Three years after the Jack the Ripper television balderdash, journalist Stephen Knight wrote the blockbuster *Jack the Ripper: The Final Solution* (George G. Harrap, 1976), the literary version of the Gorman/Sickert hoax. Don Rumbelow had published a very fine book the year before, but had unwisely regurgitated the McCormick-Dutton-Backert nonsense as a possible missing link. By the late 1980s serious researchers such as Martin Fido and Paul Begg had wrenched the subject back to planet Earth, but still could not reconcile Macnaghten's "inaccuracies" with his reputation for competence. Consequently both attempted the herculean task of rehabilitating Sir Robert Anderson as the critical and reliable contemporaneous police source. It is a measure of the fragility and ambiguity of this line of revisionist argument that this pair of incisive, judicious and entertaining analysts ended up advocating two entirely different Polish-Jewish suspects as the Ripper (while still producing two of the very best historical works on this subject).

To return to Tom Cullen, let us examine his forgotten theory as to why Montie Druitt would have killed and mutilated poor prostitutes in the East End, despite how dangerous this location had become for a man, no matter how fit and athletic, who lodged six miles away in Blackheath. In chapter 16 of *Autumn of Terror* Tom Cullen begins by quoting a facetious 1888 letter by playwright George Bernard Shaw (whom Christabel Aberconway found never shut up).[12] The 34-year-old firebrand was full of disgust for the indifference of the so-called better classes towards systemic suffering. Shaw's letter was published in the *Star* of September 24, 1888. As with other newspapers, this tabloid's circulation was being stimulated, almost daily, by the Whitechapel murders, and anything to do with them. They eye-catchingly titled Shaw's provocative letter linking the Ripper with the Social Question, that is, systemic poverty:

BLOOD MONEY TO WHITECHAPEL.

> SIR,—Will you allow me to make a comment on the success of the Whitechapel murderer in calling attention for a moment to the social question? Less than a year ago the West-end press, headed by the *St. James's Gazette*, the *Times*, and the *Saturday Review*, were literally clamoring for the blood of the people—hounding on Sir Charles Warren to thrash and muzzle the scum who dared to complain that they were starving—heaping insult and reckless calumny on those who interceded for the victims—applauding to the skies the open class bias of those magistrates and judges who zealously did their very worst in the criminal proceedings which followed—behaving, in short as the proprietary class always does behave when the workers throw it into a frenzy of terror by venturing to show their teeth.

The Irishman laments all the failed efforts by well-meaning reformers to convince a reactionary state to help the poor, rather than bludgeon them for *being* poor, by remonstrating, marching, and issuing pamphlets and articles; and yet the upper classes and their media organs were still for muzzling the scum—"Now all is changed." The seismic shift Shaw had noticed was the complete about-face in the media in *sympathetically* reporting the social background to these terrible crimes by bluntly informing their readership that the victims had turned to selling their bodies and risking the knife of this maniac because they had *nowhere to live and nothing to eat*! A madman was drawing attention to the horrors of the East End more effectively than all the well-meaning but ineffectual social reformers:

"*Some independent genius*"—The socialist and playwright George Bernard Shaw in 1888, the year he wrote a satirical letter that may have uncovered the Whitechapel murderer's true motive (© National Portrait Gallery, London).

> Private enterprise has succeeded where Socialism failed. Whilst we conventional Social Democrats were wasting our time on education, agitation, and

organization, some independent genius has taken the matter in hand, and by simply murdering and disemboweling four women, converted the proprietary press to an inept sort of communism.

George Bernard Shaw jokes, tastelessly yet bitingly, about the good that might come if the madman switched targets and eviscerated, say, a more up-market target: "Indeed, if the habits of duchesses only admitted of their being decoyed into Whitechapel backyards, a single experiment in slaughterhouse anatomy on an aristocratic victim might fetch in a round half million and save the necessity of sacrificing four women of the people."[13]

Yet Shaw in 1888 *was* being satirical. He did not mean, literally, that social improvement was the actual motive of the unknown killer, just a beneficent byproduct of insanity. By contrast, Tom Cullen examined other Victorian sources and saw some of them openly wondering, with trembling trepidation, whether revulsion at human suffering might be the *true* motive—before hastily pulling back from such a disturbing idea ("Too horrible to contemplate"). Cullen quotes the Reverend Samuel Barnett, who ran the charitable Toynbee Hall, as saying, "The murders were bound to come.... The Whitechapel horrors ... will not be in vain if at last the public conscience awakens to consider the life which these horrors reveal." His activist wife backed this sentiment by writing, "Verily, it was the crucifixion of these poor lost souls which saved the district." The socialist newspaper *Commonweal* agreed that "in our age of contradictions and absurdities, a fiend-murderer may become a more effective reformer than all the honest propagandists in the world." In volume 27 of the *Survey of London* is the acknowledgment that the "Whitechapel murders undoubtedly gave a further impetus towards the rebuilding of the Flower and Dean St area." In the wake of the killing of Annie Chapman, the *Daily Telegraph* repeated the same theme with heavy sarcasm:

> She has effected more by her death than many long speeches in Parliament and countless columns of letters to the newspapers could have brought about. She has forced innumerable people who never gave it a serious thought before to the subject to realize how it is and where it is that our vast floating population—the waifs and strays of our thoroughfares—live and sleep at night and what sort of accommodation our rich and Enlightened Capital provides for them, after so many acts of Parliament passed to improve the dwellings of the poor, and so many millions spent by our Board of Works, our vestries.... "Dark Annie" will effect in one way what fifty Secretaries of State could never accomplish.[14]

In the *Referee* of September 23, 1888, George Sims as Dagonet made the same link between the abyss and the murders in "Mustard and Cress," though he did not for a moment consider it a motive: "A great many letter writers in the daily papers are pointing the lesson of the Whitechapel horrors, and endeavoring to attract public attention to the conditions under which the East-end poor live. Under any civilized conditions it would have been impossible for these monstrous crimes to have been committed one after the other in the heart of a densely-populated neighborhood. ... In 'How the Poor Live,' these murders which are now horrifying London were clearly foreshadowed.'" The murders happened, however, not *only* in the East End, Tom Cullen points out, but specifically in the "evil quarter mile"; the worst of the worst, according to reformers. As the progressive *Lancet* wrote, "It is worthy of note that the crimes have been committed in precisely the same district where, as sanitary reformers, we have often demanded the intervention of the authorities."[15] The weekend assassin, furthermore, chose the time when the East End would be most congested. He left his victims to be found in the street for maximum shock effect and, with Mary Jane Kelly, turned her hovel into a charnel house on the very morning of the Lord Mayor's Parade, blighting the show. All just a coincidence? To Tom Cullen, whether Montague Druitt was a doctor or a barrister was quite immaterial. What counted for this Marxist polemicist was that Macnaghten's suspect was an Oxonian. The Reverend Samuel Barnett visited Oxford frequently when Montague Druitt was there, exhorting the privileged young men to help those who lived in Whitechapel and Spitalfields "without knowledge, without hope, and often without help." A number of Druitt's generation answered this call by spending their holidays at Toynbee Hall trying to do good works. Cullen speculates how this might have affected an already mentally disturbed Montie:

> Might not someone of Druitt's education and refinement whose mind was delicately balanced, at best, have been pushed to the edge of insanity by the sights around him in London's East End? The nightly spectacle of women selling their bodies for tuppance or a stale crust of bread had sickened Jack London on his brief visit to Spitalfields. What might it have done to a Montague John Druitt, whose mind had become unhinged? Such a man, overwhelmed by a sense of hopelessness and futility, might he not have conceived it as his mission to call attention to these evils, even to the extent of committing murder?[16]

In an anthology of pieces about the metropolis in 1901, *Living London* (Cassell and Company), George Sims is both a contributor and the editor. One of the essays is "London's Social Settlements" by Howard Angus Kennedy (pp. 267–272), who offers a positive view of Toynbee Hall and this invasion of educated men to help the underprivileged classes:

> You think of Whitechapel as the prowling ground of Jack the Ripper, as a labyrinth of reeking slums, or a Ghetto crowded with foreign Jews chaffering in Yiddish over piles of old clothes. Yet when you have passed through the arched entry of Toynbee Hall you might imagine yourself in the "quad" of some old college at Oxford or Cambridge. ... As you listen to the talk you soon discover that these Oxonians and Cantabs have become naturalized and enthusiastic Londoners—for London's sake.

Kennedy mentions that one Oxonian is running classes in his room for "pupils." In Balliol Hall, another center of busy charity work, the author writes that in a common room are "young professional men, medical students, schoolmasters, clerks, and so forth." (There is also mention of a "Poor Man's Lawyer.") A tour guide to the abyss informs the author of the significance of where they are walking: "If you had come here one night before the place was bought and christened, you might have stumbled over the mutilated corpse of a murdered woman. On this very stone one of Jack the Ripper's victims was done to death."

Unbeknownst to Cullen, potential confirmation of Druitt as a charity worker in the East End is found within the "North Country vicar" article in the *Daily Mail* of 1899: that the maniac had gone to Whitechapel to help fallen women who became his victims, due to this "man of good position" suffering from "epileptic mania." Something else that Cullen should have realized is that the Emma Smith and Martha Tabram murders were almost as sensational as the ones supposedly committed in their aftermath by a single killer (with the press happily acquiescing in adding them to the Ripper's list, even though they had almost certainly been killed by separate gangs). I think these earlier horrific crimes, committed by multiple perpetrators, potentially provided the Oxonian Druitt with a blueprint for savagery: how to *keep* throwing a spotlight onto the "evil quarter mile." Charity work, either with Toynbee Hall or some other reformist organization, would certainly have provided the barrister-teacher with knowledge of the topography of his killing zone, as Cullen summarizes with dazzling literary virtuosity:

> He knew the short-cuts between the streets, which alleys were blind, which streets led to dead-ends. ... He also knew which lodging-houses had inter-connecting doors, and how to run the maze of their courts without being detected. He had studied the terrain as a general might study a situation map.
> For his life depended upon his knowledge of the area. On the night of the double murder, for example, when the police were hot on his heels, one false turning, one mis-step would have landed him in the arms of the law. He knew the habits of the local police patrols intimately. He had evidently timed their rounds, trained himself to recognize their measured tread, noted their wooden lack of perception.
> If Jack the Ripper was not actually of the East End and all indications are that he was not, he was certainly omnipresent there. He hovered over this slum-ridden, crime-infested area like some evil genius.[17]

It remains a thought-provoking theory that does at least provide a rational reason why a murderer of strangers would keep returning to the same, increasingly risky killing zone—a location that had already suffered two eerily similar crimes with which *he was not connected* but by which he may well have been inspired. We picture Montie Druitt changing into his seaman's garb after an evening serving the poor at Toynbee Hall, walking through the dimly lit streets congested with human flotsam, timing the police patrols at every corner, choosing a drunken, staggering, toothless hag as the next sacrifice, reassuring her with his gentlemanly manners, quickly strangling her in a dark nook, cutting her open with indecent speed and melting back into the maelstrom. After walking back to Blackheath, Druitt cleans up, plays cricket, and then scans the *Times* at his leisure about the latest Whitechapel horror, one that also causes anguished reappraisals and thunderous editorials regarding the "evil quarter mile." Mission accomplished?

"Jack the Ripper" as a deranged social reformer is a diabolical theory that nobody at the time—not Macnaghten, not the Druitt family, not Major Griffiths, not George Sims—seems to have entertained about Montague Druitt. (Farson rejected it outright in his book, without deigning to mention Tom Cullen's name.) The upper limit of Melville Macnaghten's moral imagination may have been reached in the reluctant acceptance that a fellow gentleman, a teacher of boys, an athlete and an Oxonian, could be a "Protean" murderer. Further than that the affable sleuth could not go, and it did not matter as he had other concerns to deal with, such as how to both reveal and conceal the solution and in doing so enhance the reputation of his Scotland Yard while protecting the Majendies and the Druitts (and keep everybody out of the libel courts).[18] He succeeded brilliantly, but sadly placed too much faith in "Laying the Ghost of Jack the Ripper" being considered the final and definitive word on the subject, as Stevenson's Jekyll and Hyde—at least via Sims' down-market rip-off—were far too strong as pop cultural icons of the macabre to be displaced by such an austere portrait of a mere "Simon Pure" (especially as "Mac," the acclaimed raconteur, does not even include the unforgettable finale in the river).

It must have been tempting for Sir Melville to protect the Majendie and Druitt clans by simply never breathing a word about their monstrous Montie. It is hard to imagine that either clan would have disabused him, though they, and he, may have been all too acutely aware that on the tenth anniversary of the tragic barrister's burial a vicar (who may have also straddled both clans) was going to put them all in potential jeopardy with his "substantial truth under fictitious form." "Mac" could have undercut the vicar by deflecting public attention towards a different suspect entirely; that despite his justified antipathy about pandering to his conceited, puritanical boss, the chief constable could still have headed off this reemergence of the Druitt solution by promoting as the likeliest "Jack" a fictional variant of the harmless self-abuser or, even more temptingly, pushed that Russian deadbeat to the fore as the "Mad Doctor." Instead Macnaghten, an *anti*-anti–Semite, judged that the so-called better classes—of which he was a leading member—must be forced to confront an unpalatable truth. The Ripper had been one of their own and not some alien: Jack the Cricketer, not Jack the Jew. The murderer had in fact been just the sort of gentleman who would have liked to have been invited to the memorable dinners thrown by Melville Macnaghten, as fondly remembered by George Sims in his often hilarious 1917 memoir:

Christine Ward-Agius—The author's partner and researcher, who found the short story "The Priest's Secret" by George Sims and, even more critically, Sir Vivian Majendie. This close friend of Sir Melville Macnaghten, and Sims, had a previously unknown familial link with Vicar Charles Druitt—the first cousin of barrister and Ripper suspect Montague Druitt (Christine Ward-Agius).

> Until a year or two ago I used to attend these fistic causeries de lundi [boxing matches] regularly and in excellent company. *My friend of many long years, Sir Melville Macnaghten*, late Chief of the CID at Scotland Yard, had the charming idea of giving little Corinthian dinners on Monday nights at his house, 32 Warwick Square. The little party generally consisted of Sir Melville, *Colonel Vivian Majendie*, Mr. B. J. Angle, Mr. Tom Anderson, Mr. Charles Moore, an old Indian friend of Sir Melville, *and myself.* After dinner we drove to the National Sporting [Club], and many a fine contest was a fitting finish to the Corinthian night's entertainment. That pleasant little party of sportsmen meets on Monday nights, alas, no more. Eheu ! fugacts [my italics].

This regular soiree by boxing aficionados also, frankly, reads like a Whitechapel Grand Central Station. We have Melville Macnaghten, the discover of the "secret" about the late Mr. Druitt; George R. Sims, who would propagate the drowned barrister as Henry Jekyll; the head of the Central News, Charles Moore, who was none other than the alleged originator of the hoax letter that coined the fiend's nickname; and the heroic Col. Majendie, who simply had the bad luck to be distantly related to the bloody maniac.

Sims has abbreviated a line from the Roman poet Horace, and the full translation is: "Alas, the fleeting years glide on." Before *another* hundred years glide on, we might consider that "Jack the Ripper" *was* identified in the Late Victorian era, and that two friends protected a completely innocent third by both concealing that solution yet simultaneously revealing just how pitch black could be the dark side of an English gentleman.

Chapter Notes

Introduction

1. George Orwell was haunted his whole life by the guilty fear that he had committed homicide at Eton College—via amateur voodoo. Orwell biographer Gordon Bowker (*George Orwell* [London: Little, Brown, 2003]) interviewed an Etonian contemporary, the late Sir Steven Runciman, and the latter confided for the first time that he and Eric Blair were bullied at Eton in their first year by an older boy, Phillip Yorke. Inspired by their mutual love of ghost stories, Orwell molded a figurine of their tormentor from the wax of a melted candle. They disagreed over the severity of the supernatural ambush; Orwell wanted to pierce its heart with a pin but Runciman convinced his chum just to break off a leg. To the fledgling occultists' astonishment, it appeared to work, for within days Yorke broke his leg. Then as if Blair and Runciman had been sucked into the pages of a supernatural thriller, their tormentor died—though of lymphatic leukemia, from which he had long suffered. Other boys learned of Orwell and Runciman's black magic prowess and treated them respectfully, even warily. Orwell was so deeply affected by the tragic coincidence that he never spoke or wrote of it. Runciman only unburdened himself about the "murder" on his deathbed. At Eton, after his murder-by-voodoo, Blair cultivated the cool persona of the aesthete and outsider, while in adult life, as Orwell, he exploited his Etonian contacts to get published. A number of Tories helped a socialist without the slightest reservation, because it was about coming to the aid of a fellow member of the "Old Boy" network.

2. John Le Carre's espionage bestseller *The Honourable Schoolboy* (London: Hodder & Stoughten, 1977) is the second of his classic George Smiley/Karla trilogy. The titular character, however, is the heroic and tragic sometime-operative of Smiley's, the big-hearted, sports-mad journalist Jerry Westerby. I think the nickname also perfectly suits Sir Melville Macnaghten.

3. To take but two examples of the low regard in which Sir Melville Macnaghten is held by today's would-be sleuths: In the entertainingly bombastic *Jack the Ripper: Anatomy of a Myth* by William Beadle (Dagenham: Wat Tyler, 1995) the author exonerates the suspect who committed suicide by excoriating Macnaghten. According to Beadle, Macnaghten was bereft of "outstanding capabilities." He produced a report that was "thoroughly mediocre, haphazard and badly researched." To take a second example, Patricia Cornwell in *Portrait of a Killer: Jack the Ripper, Case Closed* (New York: Berkley, 2003) damns Macnaghten for "derailing" the investigation and for lacking firsthand information. She dismisses Macnaghten's memoirs, along with two others by ex-policemen, as worthless.

4. Stewart P. Evans and Keith Skinner in their laudable *The Ultimate Jack the Ripper Companion* (New York: Carroll & Graf, 2000) painstakingly transcribed all the relevant primary material, including internal police accounts, contemporaneous newspaper articles, medical reports, Home Office files, and reminiscences by senior policemen—all except the relevant sections from Macnaghten's memoirs, which are absent (as are the "draft" version of his internal report, coverage of his 1913 press conference, the "West of England" M.P. articles, and any of George Sims' columns about the "Mad Doctor" suspect). This is also true of another fine book, *Jack the Ripper: Scotland Yard Investigates*, by Evans, this time teamed up with veteran Ripper writer Donald Rumbelow, which is a beautifully written and illustrated account of the police investigation between 1888 and 1891. In a chapter of excerpts by various police figures regarding who each thinks was the likeliest "Jack," Macnaghten's 1913 press comments make it in but not, sadly, *Laying the Ghost of Jack the Ripper*.

5. T. Cullen, *Autumn of Terror: Jack the Ripper, His Crimes and Times* (London: Bodley Head, 1965), 221. Otherwise this book is rich in vivid prose and arguably has a firmer grasp of the class dynamics of the subject than any other.

6. In Patricia Cornwell's 2002 bestselling *Portrait of a Killer*, she argues unpersuasively—if passionately—for her suspect, the brilliant and dissolute German-born English painter, Walter Sickert. He was certainly fascinated by the Whitechapel crimes (and everything squalid and seedy, often the subject of his work). She interprets his painting *Jack the Ripper's Bedroom* (1907) as the egocentric killer "hiding in plain sight," while ignoring medical evidence, and

other accounts of the time, that Sickert was neither homicidally enraged by impotence (he fathered several illegitimate children) nor even in London at the time of the crimes. Millions of dollars of the author's own money were invested in DNA testing to prove the artist may have written several of the Ripper hoax letters to the police—but not the original. (Since when does a sick sense of humor make a person as a serial killer?) Nor for all her praise of the detective Frederic Abberline did she discover that in 1903 he advocated the executed wife killer (by poison, not by knife) George Chapman as the Whitechapel murderer.

7. In 1976 the British journalist Stephen Knight produced the biggest bestseller on this subject prior to Cornwell: *Jack the Ripper: The Final Solution* (Book Club Associates, by Arrangement with George Harrap, 1976). It reads like a tabloid: Sir Melville Macnaghten was a minor figure in a cover-up of the Duke of Clarence's inappropriate marriage to a commoner. This is based on the word of one old faker, Joseph Gorman-Sickert, that he was not only the famous painter's progeny, but the true heir to the British throne. Nobody took it as more than a good yarn and Gorman later admitted it was a hoax. In 1992 it was announced with much fanfare that a "diary" had been found, allegedly written by Liverpool cotton merchant, James Maybrick, who confessed to being none other than the Ripper. The following year, however, publication proved to be something of a fizzer. Though the artefact was Victorian, the text did not match samples of the merchant's handwriting. Worse, the document had no credible provenance: some old guy, by then conveniently deceased, gave it to some other ordinary joe who, lo and behold, "discovered" its significance, both historically and commercially.

8. Paul Begg in his incisive *Jack the Ripper: The Facts* (London: Robson, 2006), writes: "That [Macnaghten's suspect] continued to carry out his responsibilities ... destroys the suggestion that his brain gave way immediately or soon after the murder in Miller's Court, as Macnaghten asserted, showing that he was wrong or at the very least should not be interpreted literally" (325). This was very influential on my thinking: that the police chief not only twisted the data though exaggeration but went a step further by deliberately fictionalizing it—depending on the intended audience.

9. *Amazon Women on the Moon* (Universal, 1987), written by Michael Barne and Jim Muholland, directed by Carl Gottlieb, Joe Dante, Peter Horton, John Landis and Robert K. Weiss. Costing $5 million, it barely made more than half a million at the North American box office. It must have been seen by many more people on video (including this author) judging from the number of people I have met who can quote at length one or two sketches.

Chapter I

1. Major Arthur Griffiths, quoted in Stewart P. Evans and Paul Gainy, *The Lodger: The Arrest and Escape of Jack the Ripper* (London: Century, 1995), 158.

2. The journeyman academic Martin Fido wrote a superb book on this subject, *The Crimes, Detection and Death of Jack the Ripper* (London: Weidenfeld & Nicolson, 1987), though I disagree with his provisional conclusion that the fiend was a violently insane, local Polish immigrant named David Cohen. Nevertheless, I salute his attempt to make the incomplete, contradictory bits and pieces fit together. I also agree with Fido when he writes that Macnaghten was "the most strikingly gentlemanly of all the police chiefs" (144–45). He also writes: "Indeed, as becomes a gentleman, Macnaghten was neither a liar nor a boaster" (145). I agree that the chief was not corrupt or a boaster, but out of necessity for a fellow gentleman and close pal, who was distantly related to the chief suspect, "Mac" was economical with the truth to protect the killer's respectable relations.

3. M. Macnaghten, *Days of My Years* (London: Edward Arnold, 1914), 5, 7.

4. This is from the Oxford University Press (http://global.oup.com/): "In his book *The Lion and the Unicorn* (1941), the novelist George Orwell wrote: 'Probably the battle of Waterloo was won on the playing-fields of Eton, but the opening battles of all subsequent wars have been lost there.' The original statement (in the form 'The battle of Waterloo was won on the playing fields of Eton') is attributed by oral tradition to the Duke of Wellington, but is probably apocryphal. The earliest version of it, recorded in 1856, said to have been uttered by the Duke when revisiting Eton, is 'It is here that the battle of Waterloo was won!'"

5. N. Fraser, *The Importance of Being Eton* (London: Short, 2006), 19. O. R. Thorpe in *Eden: The Life and Times of Anthony Eden* (London: Chatto and Windus, 2003), 144, adds the detail that Hitler accused Eden of "duplicity" for denying that Eton was nothing less than a paramilitary training corps. The Old Etonian bluntly replied that this was a "grave misapprehension." Military field-days were not taken seriously by students, except as a chance to smoke a "clandestine cigarette." Hitler nonetheless may have gained this notion of a supposed Etonian edge from World War I general and "Old Boy" Sir Henry Rawlinson, who remarked that it was the school virtue of "playing the game" that had defeated the Hun in 1918.

6. Early in 2012 George Osborne was caught out admitting that he could not recall the last time he had eaten a humble pasty (whose price he had just scandalously upped via a value-added tax). Despite staunchly supporting the Tories at the 2010 election, the *Sun* and the *Daily Mirror* crucified Osborne for being so elitist and insensitive, a gaffe also seized upon by a gleeful *Telegraph*: you can cut British citizen's services, but you can "never—on pain of death—mess with their snacks."

7. An account of Guy Burgess' appalling (yet funny) misbehavior, from his Russian "controller," Yuri Modin, reads like an out-of-control schoolboy

being reported on by his long-suffering valet: suitcases bulging with Foreign Office documents exploding all over the floor of a bar; meetings with his KGB handler in gay nightclubs vigilantly watched by the police; the English spy driving so fast that his Russian passenger went completely numb ("Never again did I get into a car with Guy Burgess"); regularly getting pinched by motorcycle cops for speeding; propositioning male hitchhikers; representing his country at an ultra-conservative military academy; and criticizing American imperialism while advocating the diplomatic recognition of Red China. See Y. Modin, *My Five Cambridge Friends: Burgess, Maclean, Philby, Blunt, and Cairncross by Their KGB Controller* (New York: Farrar Straus Giroux, 1995).

8. C. Aberconway, *A Wiser Woman? A Book of Memories* (London: Hutchinson, 1966), 21–22.
9. Macnaghten, *Days of My Years*, 5.
10. *Ibid.*, 6.
11. G. Orwell, *Inside the Whale and Other Essays* (London: Penguin, 1969), 37–38.
12. Hargrave L. Adam, quoted by Martin Fido in *The Crimes, Detection and Death of Jack the Ripper* (London: Weidenfeld & Nicolson, 1987), 143.
13. Macnaghten, *Days of My Years*, 4.
14. *Ibid.*, 5.
15. *Ibid.*, 10.
16. *Ibid.*
17. Aberconway, *A Wiser Woman?* 21–22.
18. Orwell, *Inside the Whale*, 177.
19. *Ibid.*, 179.
20. Macnaghten, *Days of My Years*, 33–34.
21. *Ibid.*, 25.
22. *Ibid.*, 35–37.
23. *Ibid.*, 42.
24. P. Begg, *Jack the Ripper: The Facts* (London: Robson, 2006), 339.

Chapter II

1. N. Fergusson, *Empire: How Britain Made the Modern World* (London: Penguin, 2002), 163.
2. M. Macnaghten, *Days of My Years* (London: Edward Arnold, 1914), 45–48.
3. C. Aberconway, *A Wiser Woman? A Book of Memories* (London: Hutchinson, 1966), 22.
4. Macnaghten, *Days of My Years*, 51.
5. *Ibid.*, 52.
6. S. P. Evans, and D. Rumbelow, *Jack the Ripper: Scotland Yard Investigates* (Stroud, UK: Sutton, 2006), 24.
7. *Ibid.*, 10–31.
8. Macnaghten, *Days of My Years*, 220.
9. *Ibid.*, 221.
10. Evans and Rumbelow, *Jack the Ripper*, 24–27.
11. Macnaghten, *Days of My Years*, 53.
12. *Ibid.*, 202–03.
13. *Ibid.*, 7.

Chapter III

1. P. Begg, *Jack the Ripper: The Facts* (London: Robson, 2006), 4–5.
2. *Ibid.*, 14.
3. D. Rumbelow, *The Complete Jack the Ripper* (London: Virgin, 2013), 4–5.
4. C. Bloom, *Victoria's Madmen: Revolution and Alienation* (New York: Palgrave Macmillan, 2013), 153.
5. The *Times* obituary makes no reference to the Ripper case, but there is such a connection made in another contemporary tribute, this time by a fellow Liberal and journalist, T. P. O'Connor. As reproduced in *The Gloucester Journal*, September 9, 1922, O'Connor writes: "So poor George Sims is dead! It is like the disappearance of Temple Bar or the Monument, or something else that every Cockney regards as an immutable and indestructible fact of his city.... Whenever London was startled and puzzled by mysterious crimes—such as the murders by Jack the Ripper—Sims was sure to be one of the first of the amateurs on the scent. There was the additional reason for Sims' interest in this criminal, that many people saw a likeness between Sims and the supposed murderer, a likeness which Sims admitted. Sims was one of the journalists who claimed to have discovered the name of the murderer—he declared that he was an insane doctor, who, after the murders, drowned himself in the Thames...."
6. W. J. Fisherman, *Into the Abyss: The Life and Work of G. R. Sims* (London: Elliott & Thompson), 24.
7. S. Wade, *Conan Doyle and the Crimes Club: The Creator of Sherlock Holmes and His Criminological Friends* (Stroud, UK: Fonthill, 2013), 76.
8. Rumbelow, *Complete Jack the Ripper*, 20.
9. G. R. Sims, *My Life: Sixty Years' Recollection of Bohemian London* (London: Eveleigh Nash, 1917), 136.
10. M. Macnaghten, *Days of My Years* (London: Edward Arnold, 1914), 277–78.
11. G. R. Sims, *My Life*, 175.

Chapter IV

1. T. Cullen, *Autumn of Terror: Jack the Ripper, His Crimes and Times* (London: Bodley Head, 1965), 28–29.
2. M. Macnaghten, *Days of My Years* (London: Edward Arnold, 1914), 55–56.
3. *Ibid.*, 57.
4. *Ibid.*, 57–58.
5. *Ibid.*, 58.
6. S. P. Evans and D. Rumbelow, *Jack the Ripper: Scotland Yard Investigates* (Stroud, UK: Sutton, 2006), 51.
7. Cullen, *Autumn of Terror*, 27.
8. Macnaghten, *Days of My Years*, 58.
9. P. Begg, M. Fido and K. Skinner, *The Complete Jack the Ripper A to Z* (London: John Blake, 2010), 373–76.
10. Macnaghten, *Days of My Years*, 273.
11. *Ibid.*
12. M. Fido, *The Crimes, Detection and Death of Jack the Ripper* (London: Weidenfeld and Nicolson, 1987), 156–59.

13. Cullen, *Autumn of Terror*, 47.
14. Begg, Fido and Skinner, *Complete Jack the Ripper*, 87–90.
15. Macnaghten, *Days of My Years*, 58.
16. Evans and Rumbelow, *Jack the Ripper*, 71–72.
17. Dagonet (George R. Sims) in his "Mustard and Cress" column in the *Referee*, September 23, 1888: "That statement that the police believe the Whitechapel murders to have been committed by a baboon which recently escaped from a ship in the East India Docks is authoritatively denied, but Sir Charles Warren is understood to have said that it wanted Edgar Allan Poe at the yard to give them something to work on."
18. P. Begg, *Jack the Ripper—The Facts* (London: Robson Books, 2006), 105–107.
19. P. Sudgen, *The Complete History of Jack the Ripper* (London: Constable & Robinson, 2006), 155.
20. *Ibid.*
21. Begg, Fido and Skinner, *Complete Jack the Ripper*, 535–36.
22. *Ibid.*, 417.
23. Macnaghten, *Days of My Years*, 59.
24. Cullen, *Autumn of Terror*, 116–17.
25. Macnaghten, *Days of My Years*, 59.
26. Evans and Rumbelow, *Jack the Ripper*, 128.
27. Begg, Fido and Skinner, *Complete Jack the Ripper*, 186–88.
28. D. Rumbelow, *The Complete Jack the Ripper* (London: Virgin, 2013), 125.
29. Macnaghten, *Days of My Years*, 58.
30. *Ibid.*, 59–59.
31. *Ibid.*, 59.

Chapter V

1. P. Begg, M. Fido and K. Skinner, *The Complete Jack the Ripper A to Z* (London: John Blake, 457–59). A number of modern researchers favor another (probably) Jewish witness as the critical one whom police believed had seen a man, perhaps "Jack"—described as a stout prole—in the act of striking a victim that night. But the woman in question was Elizabeth Stride, not Catherine Eddowes. These books even put forward the theory that it was this witness, Israel Schwartz, who was later used by Dr. Robert Anderson to confront the Polish-Jewish suspect but who refused to testify against a fellow Hebrew (or so Anderson claimed in his 1910 memoirs, without naming either the suspect or the witness). The problem of Schwartz, a Hungarian with very limited English, is that he gave two very different accounts of what he saw that night. In the version taken down by Inspector Donald Swanson he provided a bizarre and self-serving account in which he too was nearly a victim, though of sectarian intimidation. Perhaps Schwartz, frightened of the police, said this to excuse his seeing a Ripper victim accosted by a drunken client and doing nothing to help. In the second version, an interview with the *Star*, Schwartz seems more honest as he mentions another man with a knife, and says that this, understandably, caused him to flee. This second, allegedly armed man is a better fit for the sailor-like figure seen a little later conversing with Eddowes by Joseph Lawende. On the other hand, the *Star* in a subsequent issue also wrote, "In the matter of the Hungarian who said he saw a struggle between a man and a woman in the passage where the Stride body was afterwards found, the Leman-street police have reason to doubt the truth of the story. They arrested the man on the description thus obtained, and a second on that furnished from another source, but they are not likely to act on the same information without additional facts." Schwartz was not called to testify at the inquest into Stride's murder, circumstantial confirmation that the police may have cleared the man he saw openly bashing the prostitute. A Jewish witness was reportedly used to confront Gentile suspects, Tom Sadler in 1891 and William Grant in 1895, and though unnamed he is clearly Joseph Lawende and not Israel Schwartz—because he is referred to as the witness to the *Eddowes* murder. Finally, Sir Melville Macnaghten, by implication, dismissed Schwartz as offering nothing of value as he, arguably, favored the testimony of Lawende probably because the latter had described a man who was a generic fit for Montague Druitt—a witness sighting that the police chief went to great lengths to obscure from the Late Victorian and Edwardian public.
2. *Ibid.*, 285.
3. *The Times* (London), November 7, 1888.
4. Begg, Fido and Skinner, *Complete Jack the Ripper*, 540.
5. M. Macnaghten, *Days of My Years* (London: Edward Arnold, 1914), 60–61.
6. T. Cullen, *Autumn of Terror* (London: Bodley Head, 1965), 172–73.
7. Begg, Fido and Skinner, *Complete Jack the Ripper*, 533.

Chapter VI

1. Frederick Porter Wensley's memoirs, *Forty Years in Scotland Yard* (Country Life, 1931) as excerpted in the *Dallas Morning News*, October 18, 1931; by Frederick Porter Wensley formerly Chief Constable CID New Scotland Yard, *Chapter 4 Sir Melville Macnaghten*.
2. *Ibid.*, *Dallas Morning News*, October 11, 1931, Chapter 1, *A Constable in Whitechapel*.
3. *Ibid.*, October 18, 1931.
4. *Ibid.*
5. *Ibid.*
6. M. Macnaghten, *Days of My Years* (London: Edward Arnold, 1914), 211.
7. F. P. Wensley, *Dallas Morning News*, October 18, 1931.
8. M. Macnaghten, *Days of My Years*, 292.
9. F. P. Wensley, *Dallas Morning News*, October 18, 1931.
10. N. Connell, and S. P. Evans, *Edmund Reid—Victorian Detective: The Man Who Hunted Jack the Ripper* (Stroud, UK: Amberley, 2009), 110.
11. Macnaghten, *Days of My Years*, 140.
12. F. P. Wensley, *Forty Years of Scotland Yard*, ex-

cerpt from Wensley's 1931 memoirs, *Casebook: Jack the Ripper*, Jonathan Menges, http://www.casebook.org/ripper_media/rps.wensley.html.
   13. P. Begg, M. Fido and K. Skinner, *The Complete Jack the Ripper A to Z* (London: John Blake, 2010), 321.
   14. Macnaghten, *Days of My Years*, 54.
   15. *Ibid.*, 211.
   16. *Ibid.*, 222.
   17. S. P. Evans, and D. Rumbelow, *Jack the Ripper: Scotland Yard Investigates* (Stroud, UK: Sutton, 2006), 245–46.
   18. Found by Chris Phillips in the U.K. National Archives, HO 144/985/112737 (105).

Chapter VII

   1. P. Begg, *Jack the Ripper: The Facts* (London: Robson, 2006), 340–41.
   2. M. Macnaghten, *Days of My Years* (London: Edward Arnold, 1914), 63.
   3. *Ibid.*
   4. *Ibid.*, 64.
   5. *Ibid.*, 68–69.
   6. S.P. Evans, and D. Rumbelow, *Jack the Ripper: Scotland Yard Investigates* (Stroud, UK: Sutton, 2006), 206–208.
   7. Macnaghten, *Days of My Years*, 56–57.
   8. Evans and Rumbelow, *Jack the Ripper*, 216–217.
   9. Macnaghten, *Days of My Years*, 270–71.
   10. P. Roland, *The Crimes of Jack the Ripper* (London: Arcturus, 2006), 100–01.
   11. Macnaghten, *Days of My Years*, 71–76.
   12. P. Sudgen, *The Complete History of Jack the Ripper* (London: Constable & Robinson, 2006), 402.
   13. N. Connell, and S. P. Evans, *Edmund Reid—Victorian Detective: The Man Who Hunted Jack the Ripper* (Stroud, UK: Amberley), 115.
   14. Evans and Rumbelow, *Jack the Ripper*, 218–22.
   15. F. P. Wensley, "Forty Years of Scotland Yard," excerpt from Wensley's 1931 memoirs, *Casebook: Jack the Ripper*, Jonathan Menges, http://www.casebook.org/ripper_media/rps.wensley.html.
   16. P. Begg, M. Fido and K. Skinner, *The Complete Jack the Ripper A to Z* (London: John Blake, 2010), 450.
   17. Evans and Rumbelow, *Jack the Ripper*, 251.
   18. Macnaghten, *Days of My Years*, 54.

Chapter VIII

   1. M. Macnaghten, *Days of My Years* (London: Edward Arnold, 1914), 62.
   2. *Ibid.*, 54.
   3. A. Spallek, "The West of England M.P.—Identified," *Ripperologist* 88 (February 2008), 31–34.
   4. Discovered by Paul Begg in late 2011 and passed on to the author in a private communication.
   5. A. Spallek, "The West of England M.P.—Identified," 31–34.
   6. *Rethinking Pitt-Rivers: analyzing the activities of a nineteenth century collector*, http://web.prm.ox.ac.uk/rpr/.
   7. Further research by C. Ward-Agius discovered that in 1880 Col. Majendie's sister Mary married Sir Fleetwood Isham Edwards the assistant keeper of the Privy Purse and Assistant Private Secretary to the Queen—another incentive for Macnaghten and Sims to disguise the Druitt solution. Winchester College also hosted a nexus of suggestive associations. Col. Majendie's cousin (and Isabel Majendie Druitt's uncle) the Reverend J.T.H. Du Boulay, was a Master (of Du Boulay House 1862-93 named in his honor) and Chaplain of the school at the same time that Montie Druitt held the high ranking position of Prefect of the Chapel. Rev. Du Boulay was close to the Rev. William Hough and his wife Georgiana (nee Druitt—Montie's brother-in-law and sister) Isabel's brother, the Reverend Arthur Du Boulay Hill, was an Assistant Master at the school at the same time Montague was a student and prefect and another brother, Charles Sydney Hill, also attended Winchester at the same time as Rev. DeBoulay and A.H. Evans. As mentioned in the body of the text Evans, married Isabel's cousin in 1888 in a wedding attended by Col. Majendie, *and* was likewise a Master at Winchester, and an English cricketer (who had played against Montie). Two years after the probable Ripper graduated in 1876, Colonel Majendie entrusted his only son (and only surviving child) Henry Grylls Majendie to Winchester College in the knowledge that fellow family members were already ensconced. Also, Sir Melville's beloved nephew, Hugh Macnaghten, became a Master at the School in 1885. The nephew shared his uncle's adoration for Eton and the life of the public school. Hugh later returned to Eton as a House Master and then Vice-Provost and was frequently visited at Eton by his uncle, Melville. Tragically the nephew committed suicide in 1929 aged 67. In a sad irony Hugh Macnaghten was found drowned, a suicide in the Thames attired in his cricket whites.
   8. Macnaghten, *Days of My Years*, 80.

Chapter IX

   1. T. Cullen, *Autumn of Terror: Jack the Ripper, His Crimes and Times* (London: Bodley Head, 1965), 223–27.
   2. *Ibid.*
   3. *Ibid.*
   4. S. Heard, "Mr. Valentine's School," *Ripperologist* 32 (December 2000): *Casebook: Jack the Ripper*, Jonathan Menges, http://www.casebook.org/dissertations/dst-valentine.html.
   5. P. Begg, *Jack the Ripper: The Facts* (London: Robson, 2006), 322.
   6. *Ibid.*
   7. P. Sudgen, *The Complete History of Jack the Ripper* (London: Robinson, 2006), 394–95. Phillip Sudgen argues that the case for Montague Druitt as the Ripper is terminally weak, as it is totally reliant on Macnaghten's allegedly poor memory. The author seems to know nothing about the "West of England" M.P. breakthrough of 1991 (the reissue of his excel-

lent book came out two years before Henry Farquharson was identified) and only gives a cursory glance at the Sims articles—e.g., he does not absorb the implication of "family" being disguised as "friends" for public consumption. Although Sudgen thinks that Druitt's busy schedule makes him very unlikely to be hiking all the way to the East End to kill women and then return, on foot, for his sporting matches, he concedes, "Nothing we have learned categorically rules Druitt out of the picture." In an example of how the same data can be interpreted in the opposite fashion, Don Rumbelow argued that the cricket matches were circumstantial evidence *in favor* of Druitt's guilt because they placed the suspect in London: "There is again the confirmatory evidence from the cricketing records that [Druitt] was playing in a match at Canford on the same day that [Polly] Nichols' body was found, 31 August" (*The Complete Jack the Ripper* [London: Virgin, 2013], 165).

8. M. Macnaghten, *Days of My Years* (London: Edward Arnold, 1914), 62.

9. Macnaghten knew that Sir Charles Warren's resignation, though offered in writing on November 8, was only accepted by the Home Secretary on November 10, 1888. I think that Macnaghten was hoping that if the loathed ex–Commissioner perused his 1914 memoirs the latter could not help but observe that—irony of ironies—he had exited on the very same day as "Jack the Ripper" reached his use-by date too! Sir Charles had, supposedly, stormed off in a huff at the very moment he had triumphed over the Terror. If this speculation is correct it again shows that the dating of Druitt's suicide is, for "Mac," polemical and plastic, and not to be taken literally.

10. Macnaghten, *Days of My Years*, 101.

11. *Ibid.*, 61.

12. *Ibid.*, 100–101.

Chapter X

1. D. Rumbelow, *The Complete Jack the Ripper* (London: Virgin, 2013), 211.

2. *The Daily Northwestern*, May 26, 1890.

3. D. J. Leighton, *Ripper Suspect: The Secret Lives of Montague Druitt* (History Press, 2007), 112.

4. P. Begg, M. Fido and K. Skinner, *The Complete Jack the Ripper A to Z* (London: John Blake, 2010), 147.

5. P. Begg, *Jack the Ripper: The Facts* (London: Robson, 2006), 326.

6. G. Logan, *The True History of Jack the Ripper: The Forgotten 1905 Ripper Novel* (with additional material by Jan Bondeson; Stroud, UK: Amberley, 2013), 142.

7. *Ibid.*

8. P. Begg, *Jack the Ripper*, 328.

9. D. Farson, *Jack the Ripper* (History Book Club, 1972), 125.

Chapter XI

1. "The 1844 Report of the Metropolitan Commissioners in Lunacy," http://studymore.org.uk/xmad1844.htm.

2. *Birmingham Daily Post*, February 21, 1889.

3. "The Druitt Papers," National Archives, http://www.nationalarchives.gov.uk/A2A/records.aspx?cat=182-druitt&cid=0#0.

4. G. Logan, *The True History of Jack the Ripper: The Forgotten 1905 Ripper Novel* (with additional material by Jan Bondeson; Stroud, UK: Amberley, 2013), 42.

5. "The Druitt Papers," National Archives, http://www.nationalarchives.gov.uk/A2A/records.aspx?cat=182-druitt&cid=0#0.

6. There was also another cousin, Philip Druitt, born 1865, who was a curate at St. Bartholomew's Armley in Leeds—which *is* in the north of England—though he was never a vicar. The Reverend William Hough also had a brother, James, who ministered in Worcestershire, which is in the midlands. Another tantalizing clerical figure potentially close to Montague was a non-family member, John Henry Lonsdale, born in 1855, who died of acute septicemia in 1903. The Reverend Lonsdale is a kind of weird doppelganger for Montague: he was also a young barrister who worked a few doors down from Druitt's address in the city. In 1888 he gave up the law and was ordained an Anglican minister, becoming a curate in Wimborne, Dorset. (He also nearly drowned!) Perhaps they never met, though this seems implausible. We know from a newspaper source (the *Salisbury and Winchester Journal and General Advertiser*, May 14, 1887) that Lonsdale did know well the Reverend Charles Druitt because a burglary at the former's residence included the theft of some possessions belonging to the vicar. He married a captain's daughter on December 18, 1888, while Montie's body was beginning its slow ascent back to the air-breathing world. Could John Henry Lonsdale have been the priest to whom the repentant killer turned in his despair? It is possible, though he was a no-show at Montie Druitt's funeral (though Lonsdale may have been on his honeymoon). If he was the clergyman who heard the confession, Lonsdale may have then confided in a friend who was also the killer's cousin, Vicar Charles, who concealed/revealed the truth in 1899. There is another aspect of Lonsdale's resume that needs to be mentioned: he was an Old Etonian. Here we have another Old Boy, who graduated *the same year* as Macnaghten. Could this former-barrister-turned-cleric have learned the secret from Charles Druitt and passed it on to Henry Farquharson, who briefed Macnaghten? Was this an example of the "Old Boy Network" trumping all other loyalties?

Chapter XII

1. M. Macnaghten, *Days of My Years* (London: Edward Arnold, 1914), 164–72.

2. P. Sudgen, *The Complete History of Jack the Ripper* (London: Robinson, 2006), xviii.

3. P. Begg, M. Fido and K. Skinner, *The Complete Jack the Ripper A to Z* (London: John Blake, 2010), 118–25.

4. C. Aberconway, *A Wiser Woman? A Book of Memories* (London: Hutchinson, 1966), 111.

5. Macnaghten, *Days of My Years*, 145.
6. *Ibid.*, 139.
7. Sudgen, *Complete History*, xix.
8. A descendant of Donald Swanson's sold these annotations to a British newspaper in the late 1980s. Regarding the Polish suspect, the entire primary source reads: "Because the suspect was *also a Jew* and also because his evidence would convict the suspect, and witness would be the means of the murderer being hanged which he did not wish to be left on his mind. And after this identification which suspect knew, no other murder of this kind took place in London." On the back endpaper Swanson had also penciled, perhaps years later, "Continuing from page 138, after the suspect had been identified at the Seaside Home where he had been sent by us with difficulty in order to subject him to identification, and he knew he was identified. On suspect's return to his brother's house in Whitechapel he was watched by police (City CID) by day and night. In a very short time the suspect with his hands tied behind his back, he was sent to Stepney Workhouse and to Colney Hatch [asylum] and died shortly afterwards—Kosminski was the suspect—DSS." If he is expressing his own opinion, Swanson is wrong not only about Kosminski being long deceased, but also about no more murders of this kind having taken place in London; Frances Coles was killed within days of the real Aaron Kosminski's incarceration. Or, it could be just Swanson repeating what Dr. Anderson had told him in retirement, a time when his revered ex-chief's memory was very unreliable (as also noted in the body of the text, a 1908 interview shows Anderson capable of all sorts of confusions and conflations). Why would the suspect and witness have been taken to the Seaside Home, a police convalescent hospital built at Hove in early 1890? In their excellent 2006 work, *Jack the Ripper: Scotland Yard Investigates* (Stroud, UK: Sutton, 2006), Stewart P. Evans and Donald Rumbelow came up with an ingenious theory to explain this bizarre locale: Dr. Anderson and/or Swanson is merging "Kosminski" with the Tom Sadler fiasco of 1891, as the latter had been involved with a *Seaman's* or Sailor's Home, from which a witness positively identified him as selling a potentially incriminating knife (plus far from being certain that the killer was long deceased Swanson, at the time of the Coles murder, was apparently telling a reporter in 1891 that he might be disguising himself as a woman). Nicknamed the "Swanson Marginalia," this source is characterized as reliable—even definitive—because people would not lie to themselves. This is a double-edged sword, as you can write what you like to yourself, knowing you will never be held to account for any of it.
9. A. P. Moore-Anderson, *Sir Robert Anderson and Lady Agnes Anderson*, ch. 3, "London. The Home Office and Secret Service," 1947, http://www.casebook.org/ripper_media/rps.apmoore.2.html.
10. P. Begg, M. Fido and K. Skinner, *The Complete Jack the Ripper A to Z* (London: John Blake, 2010), 27.

Chapter XIII

1. J. Campbell, "The Beast Within," *Guardian*, December 13, 2008.
2. R. L. Stevenson, *Vintage Stevenson: Dr. Jekyll and Mr. Hyde, and Other Stories* (London: Vintage, 2007), 48.
3. D. Sharp, "The Strange Case of Dr. Jekyll and Saucy Jack," *Ripperologist* 55 (September 2004), Casebook: Jack the Ripper, Jonathan Menges, http://www.casebook.org/dissertations/rip-alan-sharp.html.
4. M. Fido, *The Crimes, Detection and Death of Jack the Ripper* (London: Weidenfeld & Nicolson, 1987). Though I disagree with Fido's conclusions, we do not completely disagree on every aspect. The author also postulates that the Aberconway version was probably written after the official version: "But that additional material ... shows that Lady Aberconway received her father's further thoughts on the matter after he had deposited in Scotland Yard ... and come to the definite conclusion that M. J. Druitt was Jack the Ripper" (149). Fido also speculates that Macnaghten's cryptic comment about the "truth" lying at the bottom of the river *might* refer to the killer's knife: "What the evidence he conjectured once lay at the bottom of the Thames may be, we do not now know. Possibly the Ripper's knife, fallen from Druitt's pocket" (151). In 1975, ex-policeman and true crime writer Donald Rumbelow had also regarded the Aberconway Papers as being written after the official version, a position left unaltered in the 2013 reprint and update of his classic work: "The statement [in the Aberconway Papers] was made some years after his original notes when he was not so sure" (*The Complete Jack the Ripper* [London: Virgin, 2013], 161). However, in Rumbelow's superb book with Stewart P. Evans, we read, "The account of Macnaghten's suspects published by Major Griffiths ... appears to be taken from Macnaghten's draft version" (*Jack the Ripper: Scotland Yard Investigates* [Stroud, UK: Sutton, 2006], 255).
5. In *The Complete History of Jack the Ripper* (London: Robinson, 2006), Philip Sudgen wrote an excellent account of the Whitechapel murders of 1888 but is on much shakier ground in his confident debunking of Macnaghten and Sims and the veracity of their Druitt solution. It has to be said, however, that the late, much admired author at least makes some effort, however superficial, to analyze *Days of My Years* along with a few of the "Mustard and Cress" columns (strangely, Sudgen seems unaware of the existence of the "West of England" M.P.). This incisive source nonetheless repeats the discredited conventional wisdom that this affable police chief knew little accurate information about the drowned barrister, and amateurishly and callously squeezed his weak suspect into his "awful glut" paradigm. On page xxi of his revised introduction, an affronted Sudgen wrote that Michael Ostrog's exoneration was just about the last nail in Mac's coffin as a credible source on the Ripper: "Considerable doubt [is] thrown upon the value of Macnaghten's

report. ... Macnaghten comes out of the Ostrog evidence very badly. His characterization of Ostrog was grossly unfair. ... Even when writing of events within his personal knowledge Macnaghten was extremely misleading. ... Macnaghten was well aware, too, that there were serious doubts about Ostrog's insanity." One reads these denunciations and with a shameful grin completely agrees; Macnaghten *was* being "grossly unfair," and "extremely misleading," while being "aware" of Ostrog's feigned insanity. That "Good Old Mac" could be deliberately, even impishly reshaping Ostrog for his own indulgent propagandist purposes had not been previously considered.

6. P. Begg, M. Fido and K. Skinner, *The Complete Jack the Ripper A to Z* (London: John Blake, 2010), 367–68.

7. S. P. Evans, "Arthur Griffiths, Dr. Robert Anderson and Jack the Ripper," *Casebook: Jack the Ripper*, 1998, Jonathan Menges http://www.casebook.org/dissertations/dst-spe.html.

8. Sims writes: "Various witnesses who had seen a man conversing with a woman who was soon afterwards found murdered said that he was a well-dressed man with a black moustache. Others described him as a man with a closely-trimmed beard." In perhaps another example of Macnaghten's extraordinary powers of recall, there *was* a minor witness who so described a hirsute suspect (though not a Gentile nor so well-dressed) as reported in the *Evening Standard* of September 10, 1888: "The police attach importance to the statement of the woman ... Emily Walton, is a lodger in the common lodging houses of Spitalfields. And says she was with the man at half-past two. ... Scotland Yard authorities had come to a definite conclusion as to the description of the murderer ... rather dark beard and moustache."

9. The American suspect of Sims' 1907 article appears to be a fusion of Dr. Tumblety with the innocent, American specimen hunter: "The other theory in support of which I have some curious information, puts the crime down to a young American medical student who was in London during the whole time of the murders, and who, according to statements of certain highly-respectable people who knew him, made on two occasions an endeavour to obtain a certain internal organ, which for his purpose had to be removed from, as he put it, 'the almost living body.'" This is very similar to the *Chicago Tribune* of October 7, 1888, in which Dr. Tumblety is probably juxtaposed with a creepy theory about some madman taking his Shakespeare a little too literally: "An American who used to live in New York keeps a herb shop now in the Whitechapel district. A detective called at his place this week and asked him if he had sold any unusual compound of herbs to a customer since August. Similar inquiries were made at other shops in the neighborhood. The basis of this investigation has a startling Shakespearean flavor. An eminent engineer in London suggests to the police the theory that the murderer was a medical maniac trying to find the elixir of life and was looking for the essential ingredient in the parts taken from the murdered bodies; that, like the witches in 'Macbeth,' he spent the time over a bubbling caldron of the hellbroth made from the gory ingredients looking for the charm." This 1888 article then chides the police for wasting their time on such "wild theories." If this comes from Macnaghten, once again his powers of recall are awesome (the police chief should have considered a carnival career; "Mr. Mac and His Marvelous Memory"). He seems to have remembered an article—or he kept it in a private file—that mentioned the American herb doctor suspect and then a separate, and patently ludicrous theory about an elixir-of-life dabbler and, characteristically, welded the two together for "Tatcho."

10. G. R. Sims, *My Life: Sixty Years' Recollection of Bohemian London* (London: Eveleigh Nash, 1917), 141–42. Researcher Chris Phillips has recently found that in Sims' "Mustard and Cress" column, in *'The Referee'* of October 13, 1907, the author made another implausible mention of the "Mad Doctor" suspect; as an asylum patient who was incurably maniacal and yet released back onto the streets (in this article he also equates the disguised Druitt once more with Neil Cream, as he will do in a column excerpted from Macnaghten's memoirs of 1914 and the following year in a 1915 article for "Pearson's Weekly"): "I sat down the other day to make out a list of the world-shocking tragedies which had during the last twenty years been the result of releasing uncured lunatics from lunatic asylums and insane criminals from gaols ... Neil Cream was released from gaol, where he was undergoing penal servitude for life, and he murdered seven or eight women. Jack the Ripper was released from a lunatic asylum, and then committed five of the foulest and most horrible murders to be committed in the annals of crime. I could name fifty similar instances if this were a book and not a newspaper...."

Chapter XIV

1. G. R. Sims, *Dorcas Dene, Detective: Her Adventures* (London: F. V. White, 1897; reprint, British National Library, General Historical Collection, digitized by Microsoft), 23.

2. *Ibid.*, 14.

3. *Ibid.*, 40–41.

4. *Ibid.*, 42.

5. *Ibid.*, 43.

6. G. Logan, *The True History of Jack the Ripper: The Forgotten 1905 Ripper Novel*, with additional material by Jan Bondeson (Stroud, UK: Amberley, 2013), 25.

7. *Ibid.*, 37.

8. *Ibid.*, 38.

9. *Ibid.*, 39.

10. *Ibid.*, 66.

11. *Ibid.*, 47.

12. *Ibid.*, 185.

13. *Ibid.*, 63.

14. *Ibid.*, 63.

15. *Ibid.*, 173.

16. G. R. Sims, *Mysteries of Modern London*, http://www.casebook.org/ripper_media/rps.sims1.html.

17. M. Macnaghten, *Days of My Years* (London: Edward Arnold, 1914), 62.

18. This might be a variation on the young, insane student suspect, John Sanders, at least as told by the brilliant if dissolute German-born English painter Walter Sickert. The following is a fragment of Sickert's anecdote about a consumptive veterinary student, as recorded by Osbert Sitwell in the latter's 1950 memoirs, as reported in Tom Cullen's *Autumn of Terror* (London: Bodley Head, 1965): "The landlord and landlady would hear him come in about six in the morning, and then walk about in his room for an hour or two until the first edition of the morning paper was on sale, when he would creep lightly downstairs and run to the corner to buy one. Quietly he would return and go to bed; but an hour later, when the old man called him, he would notice, by the traces in the fireplace that his lodger had burnt the suit he had been wearing the previous evening" (155). The landlords were going to alert the authorities when his mother appeared to whisk the ill young man back to Bournemouth—and sure enough, the Whitechapel murders ceased. In a lovely end to the yarn, apparently Sickert wrote the name of the young medical student into a copy of the memoirs of Giacomo Casanova belonging to Sitwell. But when he went to search for the penciled name he discovered that his book had been a victim of the Nazi Blitz. The anecdote reads like some kind of Victorian version of Norman Bates and his mummified mum (Osbert Sitwell is Christabel Aberconway's source for Margot Asquith claiming that her mother was the most beautiful woman of her generation). Sickert's tale, accessible here only at one remove, may simply be a plagiaristic lift from *The Lodger*. Yet details such as "Bournemouth" and the focus on a living, widowed mother might point to Macnaghten as Sickert's source.

19. G. R. Sims, *Casebook:* February 25, 1911, http://www.casebook.org/press_reports/dagonet.html.

20. M. Belloc Lowndes, *The Lodger: A Story of the London Fog* (New York: Pocket, 1940), 287.

21. *Ibid.*, 297.

22. *Ibid.*, 291.

23. *Ibid.*, 202.

24. *Ibid.*, 117.

25. Macnaghten, *Days of My Years*, 238.

Chapter XV

1. The best book to argue for the playboy Edward VII as a pushy, ambitious, Francophile politician is Ian Dunlop's excellent *Edward VII and the Entente Cordiale* (London: Constable, 2004).

2. M. Macnaghten, *Days of My Years* (London: Edward Arnold, 1914), 189–202.

3. *Ibid.*, 96–97.

4. S. Wade, *Conan Doyle and the Crimes Club: The Creator of Sherlock Holmes and His Criminological Friends* (Stroud, UK: Fonthill, 2013), 78.

5. Macnaghten, *Days of My Years*, 92–99.

6. *Ibid.*, 144–159.

7. P. Sudgen, *The Complete History of Jack the Ripper* (London: Robinson, 2006), xvi.

8. P. Begg, *Jack the Ripper: The Facts* (London: Robson, 2006), 366.

9. L. Forbes Winslow, *Recollections of Forty Years*, 1910, as excerpted on *Casebook: Jack the Ripper*, Jonathan Menges, http://www.casebook.org/ripper_media/rps.winslow.html.

10. P. Begg, M. Fido and K. Skinner, *The Complete Jack the Ripper A to Z* (London: John Blake, 2010), 264–66.

11. Macnaghten, *Days of My Years*, 273.

12. *Ibid.*

13. S. P. Evans and P. Gainey, *The Lodger: The Arrest and Escape of Jack the Ripper* (London: Century, 1995), 231.

14. "Whipping of Boy Starts Hunt for Harry K. Thaw: Indicted Here for Kidnapping and Offences Recalling Old Murder Trial Charges," *The New York Times*, January 10, 1917.

15. R. Anderson, *The Lighter Side of My Official Life* (London: Hodder and Stoughton, 1910), 224–25.

16. Macnaghten, *Days of My Years*, 284.

17. *Ibid.*, 293.

18. Sir Melville saying the Ripper was still alive was just a rhetorical flourish. Yet writers have accepted that he had a living suspect before fixing upon the late Mr. Druitt. Whilst perfectly plausible in theory this sub-theory is based on a single and rather startlingly anomalous source that may be flawed: Douglas G. Browne's *The Rise of Scotland Yard: A History of the Metropolitan Police* (Edinburgh: George C. Harrap, 1956). Browne writes, "A third head of the CID, Sir Melville Macnaghten appears to identify the Ripper with the leader of a plot to assassinate Mr. Balfour at the Irish Office" (207). There was a plot by Irish terrorists to kill the chief secretary for Ireland (and future prime minister and Old Etonian) Arthur Balfour, which was foiled by Special Branch. In the 1950s Browne apparently had access to files that were confidential and/or have since been lost. At some point did Macnaghten seriously entertain the notion that the Ripper was a political assassin? If the entire page is viewed from which the quotation is taken, Browne is actually commenting on *senior policemen's books*: "[The Ripper's] identity is unknown to this hour, though definite claims to the contrary have been made, and numberless theories propounded. Sir Robert Anderson, who succeeded James Monro as Assistant Commissioner, CID, just after the second Whitechapel murder, says that the murderer was a low-class Polish Jew. According to Basil Thomson, 'in the belief of the police he was a man who committed suicide in the Thames at the end of "1888,"' and who 'had probably been at some time a medical student,' *a third head of the CID, Sir Melville Macnaghten, appears to identify the Ripper with the leader of a plot to assassinate Mr. Balfour at the Irish Office*. Where experts disagree, there is a fine opening for fancy; others have held that the Ripper was a sailor, a mad West

End doctor, and even a midwife.... The only points on which there is very general agreement are that the murderer lived close to the scene of his crimes, and that since these ceased as unaccountably as they had begun, either he was dead by the end of the year, or a few months' dreadful madness had suddenly spent itself." Browne is demonstrably wrong: Macnaghten *and* his successor, Thompson, were *not in disagreement* about the Ripper being a suicide. What I postulate is that Browne, perhaps in a rush to finish a book he had not started, took *literally* the last lines of Mac's memoir chapter about how "[Jack] *had knocked out a Commissioner of Police, and nearly settled the hash of one of Her Majesty's principal Secretaries of State.*" I think he assumed, mistakenly, that this hyperbolic line referred to the aborted Balfour plot of 1888. Confirmation that Browne has skimmed *Days of My Years* is shown by a footnote at the bottom of p. 207 quoting the "I'm not a butcher" ditty that opens "Laying the Ghost...." For Browne to so hopelessly misrepresent Macnaghten's opinion also shows that Macnaghten's 1894 report remained unknown and undisturbed in the Scotland Yard file."

19. In Sir Melville Macnaghten's chapter on "Jack the Ripper" he is uncharacteristically tart towards *another* police chief of 1888, City Commissioner Major Henry Smith (although he does not name him). In "Laying the Ghost...," Macnaghten writes, "Only two or three years ago I saw a book of police reminiscences (not by a Metropolitan officer), in which the author stated that he knew more of the 'Ripper murders' than any man living, and then went on to say that during the whole of August 1888 he was on the tiptoe of expectation. That writer had indeed a prophetic soul, looking to the fact that the first murder of the Whitechapel miscreant was on 31st August of that year of grace." Why is he so hard on Major Smith, especially as the latter absolutely rejects Sir Robert Anderson's claims of a low-life, low-level Jewish conspiracy as insulting rubbish? Possibly because Macnaghten wanted to assert his own primacy as the police authority on the case and this was a way of pushing back both Smith and Anderson without directly mentioning the latter. It may also have been because Smith's memoir, alone, reminded Edwardians about Joseph Lawende (though unnamed) and his sighting of a Druitt-like figure: "One a sort of hybrid German ... saw them distinctly. This was, without doubt, the murderer and his victim. ... The description of the man given by the German was as follows: Young, about the middle height, with a small fair moustache, dressed in something like navy serge, and with a deerstalker's cap—that is a cap with a peak both fore and aft. I think the German spoke the truth, because I could not 'lead' him in any way. 'You will easily recognize, him, then,' I said. 'Oh no!' he replied; 'I only had a short look at him.' The German was a strange mixture, honest apparently, and intelligent also. He 'had heard of some murders,' he said, but they didn't concern him." Smith is apparently ignorant of the supposedly diffident Lawende later being used by the Met to confront *two* suspects, and to have allegedly affirmed to the second. The retired chief has the suspect's hat quite wrong too, with the deerstalker inadvertently upping the class of the suspect closer to the real Druitt.

20. *Ibid.*, viii–ix In *The Sheffield Evening Telegraph*, June 2, 1913, in its coverage of Macnaghten's chatty retirement press conference, the reporter speculated on the date of the suspect's demise: "The head of the Criminal Investigation Department at Scotland Yard, Sir Melville Macnaghten, who retired on Saturday, has one great regret—that he joined the Department *six months after* 'the Whitechapel murderer committed suicide, and I never had a go at him. As Sir Melville joined the force on May 24, 1889, Jack the Ripper apparently ended his life in *the previous December*, at the close of the year in which he murdered seven women in the East End of London.'" [My Italics] The 1913 newspaper has the timing of Druitt's suicide essentially correct. In his memoir Sir Melville claims the actual date of his belated debut on the Force was June 1, 1889. In fact, this was *exactly* six months after Montague Druitt killed himself. Hence his need, I argue, to assert in his book's preface that he had never said this, because if he had then he could not have claimed in *Days of My Years* that the chief suspect *probably* died in early November 1888.

21. *Ibid.*, 59.
22. *Ibid.*, 60.
23. *Ibid.*, 61.

Chapter XVI

1. C. Aberconway, *A Wiser Woman? A Book of Memories* (London: Hutchinson, 1966), 39–40.
2. *Ibid.*, 109.
3. *Ibid.*
4. *Ibid.*, 40.
5. *Ibid.*, 33.
6. *Ibid.*, 128–30.
7. William Le Queux had many imitators, such as Erskine Childers with *The Riddle of the Sands* (1903) and Hector Hugh Munro (under his pseudonym Saki) with *When William Came* (1913), both far superior novels. All this wallowing in national violation inspired P. G. Wodehouse to write his marvelous send-up *The Swoop, or How Clarence Saved England* (1909), in which the British are invaded by nine countries simultaneously including the Germans, the Russians, the Swiss (who deploy their *navy*), Turkey, Moroccan brigands, the Mad Mullah of Somalilhand and the Chinese, led by Prince Ping Pong Pang. The reaction of the local citizenry hovers between amusement and apathy (a newspaper places the line "German Army Lands in England" *beneath* the Cricket news: "Surrey Doing Badly") but the day is saved by Clarence Chugwater—a resourceful boy scout.
8. W. Le Queux, *The Amazing Story of Rasputin the Rascal Monk* (Melbourne: Melville & Mullen, 1918), 148.
9. *Ibid.*, 5.
10. *Ibid.*, 9–10.

11. W. Le Queux, *Things I Know About Kings, Celebrities and Crooks* (London: Eveleigh Nash & Grayson, 1923), 271.

12. L. Matters, *The Mystery of Jack the Ripper* (London: Hutchinson, 1964), 114.

13. *Ibid.*, 115.

14. It is possible that Leonard Matters' anti-discovery of no drowned medical man in any London newspapers in late 1888 inadvertently soured Guy Logan on Sims. Logan no doubt felt he had been led down the garden path—which he had been—as he sourly wrote in his *Masters of Crime* in 1928: "The late George R. Sims was fond of declaring that, in the end, the murderer's identity was known to the police, that he was a doctor who had become insane, and that his body was found in the Thames soon after his last exploit, but nothing to establish this story was ever put forward, and I regard it as pure myth." No mention is made by the disgruntled Logan that a quarter of a century before, he had written a serial for a newspaper built around Sims' tale. For Macnaghten and Sims, once Guy Logan had served his purpose he was discarded (*The True History of Jack the Ripper: The Forgotten 1905 Ripper Novel* [Stroud, UK: Amberley, 2013], 207).

15. Aberconway, *A Wiser Woman?* 149.

16. Noel Rutherford, Thomson, Sir Basil Home (1861–1939), *Oxford Dictionary of National Biography*, Oxford University Press, January 2008, http://www.oxforddnb.com/.

17. T. Cullen, *Autumn of Terror: Jack the Ripper, His Crimes and Times* (London: Bodley Head, 1965), 222.

18. *Ibid.*, 218.

19. D. Farson, *Casebook: Jack the Ripper*, http://www.casebook.org/authors/obituaries/farson.html; R. Carmody, "Daniel Farson," on Farson's television programs and their impact, http://www.transdiffusion.org/tv/tvheroes/daniel_farson.

20. Farson, *Casebook*, 15–16.

21. Lady Aberconway's concern about the potential anguish of the suspect's descendants may have been well-meaning but overblown. When finally writing his own book eleven years later Dan Farson contacted such a Druitt—yet another medical man—the great-grandson of Montie's uncle, Robert, who far from feeling mortified was tickled pink at the infamous connection: "I wrote to Dr. Druitt in the first place because I was anxious not to distress his family, and received this welcome reply: 'I do assure you that the subject causes me no distress whatever. In a macabre way it livens up an otherwise dull, though very worthy, ancestry.'"

22. Farson, *Casebook*, 111.

23. *Ibid.*, 112.

24. Cullen, *Autumn of Terror*, 218.

25. I am indebted to Adam Neil Wood and his detailed article about the history of the "Aberconway Papers," Lady Aberconway's correspondence with newspapers, and Dan Farson's machinations in the U.K. and Australia over Druitt and his cousin's alleged clincher document, as detailed in the online magazine *Ripperologist* 124 (February 2012).

26. Farson, *Casebook*, 138. In the *London Times* October 5, 1972, we have this extraordinary story of the Farson's 1972 book running into legal trouble in Australia; it reads like the imbroglio that might have happened in Macnaghten's day—just seventy or so years too late: "Daniel Farson's book 'Jack the Ripper,' which identifies Montague John Druitt as the Whitechapel murderer, has run into unsuspected legal snags in Australia, the country where Farson believes that 'the final pieces of evidence ... which will close the file forever' may still exist. The peculiar libel laws of the state of New South Wales have dissuaded the Sydney Sun Herald from giving Druitt's name in their preview of the book, and have restricted the Australian Broadcasting Commissions to references to a 'Mr. D.' The difficulty is that in New South Wales it is, in effect, possible to libel the dead, and family descendants offended by Farson's allegations would be in a position to sue. Michael Joseph, the book's publishers, who have a consignment bound for Australia at the moment, are seeking advice from their agents there before deciding whether to risk a writ. Farson's book does make it clear that Montague Druitt's cousin, Dr. Lionel Druitt, who had a surgery in the Minories at the time of the murders, did emigrate to Australia, and probably has untraced descendants still living there."

Chapter XVII

1. *The Telegraph*, August 3, 2001, obituary.

2. Tom Cullen also wrote fine books on Dr. Crippen, the relationship between Queen Victoria and John Brown, and the hustler of noble titles, Maundy Gregory.

3. A. N. Wood, "The Aberconway Version," *Ripperologist* 124 (February 2012), 5–15.

4. T. Cullen, *Autumn of Terror: Jack the Ripper, His Crimes and Times* (London: Bodley Head, 1965), 221.

5. *Ibid.*, 215–16.

6. *Ibid.* Even more execrable is that on 206 Cullen swallowed whole, or appeared to, the ludicrous claims by McCormick citing the Dr. Dutton archive that the latter had *photographed* the Goulston St. graffiti: "Dr. Thomas Dutton, amateur criminologist and expert in microphotography ... claims that he actually photographed the wall-writing at the request of the police, and that the prints were destroyed on Warren's orders. 'The microphotograph which I took definitely established that the writing was same as that in some of the latter's,' the doctor adds" (111). That Cullen made this a footnote is still no excuse for trying to subliminally turn a silly, unreliable source into a credible one in order to make the Backert "bridge" work later.

7. R. Odell, *Jack the Ripper in Fact and Fiction* (Edinburgh: George G. Harrap, 1966), 180–81.

8. T. K. Martin, and E. Jones, *Jack the Ripper*, BBC, 6 episodes, July 1973.

9. F. Wheen, *Strange Days Indeed: The Golden Age of Paranoia* (London: Fourth Estate, 2009) 185–200.

10. A. N. Wood, "The Aberconway Version." Lady Aberconway's dismissive response maybe understood as the last gasp of possible rivalry within the family about Macnaghten's Ripper legacy being continued by a proxy/crony of her nephew, a man named Philip Loftus. The latter claimed in a letter to the aged aristocrat that he had been shown by her nephew, the late Gerald Donner, the original "Macnaghten memo" and that it differed significantly from his aunt's copy. For example, Druitt was called "Michael," and the other two were a Pole nicknamed "Leather Apron" and a "jobber" named "Thomas Cutbush." Despite the total lack of provenance for this claim, the illogic that Sir Melville Macnaghten would have included Cutbush—when the document was partly created to refute this "suspect"—and the fact that Major Griffiths' suspects section is almost exactly the same as the "Aberconway Papers," this tidbit has been eagerly embraced by many writers on this subject as the ur-version of the "memorandum." In actual fact the third, final and arguably definitive version is the memoir chapter "Laying the Ghost..," which is the *only* account by the author for public consumption under his own name. In it the sidekick suspects are removed altogether and the Druitt "conclusion" is based on information received years later, and not on the "awful glut" three-card-trick timing.

11. Cullen, *Autumn of Terror*, 208.

12. If he really were the Ripper then it is ironic that in his 1889 interview in New York, Dr. Francis Tumblety responded to a pointed question about his notoriety as a misogynist by providing an unconvincing anecdote of a gushing duchess composing a poetic tribute—of stunning awfulness—to her bouquet-bearing breakfast companion: "'I don't care to talk about the ladies, but I will show you one little evidence that I am not regarded with aversion by the sex. I will first explain how it came to me. I had received a letter of introduction to a lady of rank, a duchess, who was then at Torquey, which is several hundred miles from London. I presented my letter and was invited to breakfast with her. When I came I presented her with a bouquet of flowers and she picked up a quill which was lying on the table near by and dashed off the following stanzas extempore: 'To Dr. Francis Tumblety, M.Ed./Thanks for the lovely rosebuds sent./Its beauty may be fleeting,/But not its sentiment./And its charming beauty/Nor colour cannot last,/It will be a pleasant duty,/In memory of the past,/To guard the faded flower,/ When you have gone from me,/ In memory of the hour/You came to sweet Torquey (pronounced Torkee)./ Mary. 'Now that doesn't look like a woman-hater, does it?' said the doctor, with a look of pride."

13. D. Farson, *Jack the Ripper* (History Book Club, 1972), 100.

14. Cullen, *Autumn of Terror*, 210.

15. *Ibid.*, 235.

16. *Ibid.*, 213.

17. In the seventh chapter of his memoirs, "Railways Tragedies," Sir Melville recounts the horrific blitz-murder of a barmaid, Elizabeth Camp, on a train in 1897. Nobody was charged, but the ex-chief believed he had identified the killer. Unfortunately the line-up failed to produce the desired result. In the press appeared a leak about another police suspect; a young barrister who briefly went into an asylum (researcher Chris Phillips has established that this second man had an iron-clad alibi). In writing about the Camp murder for his book—a case he spoke of in the same breath as the Ripper at his 1913 retirement press conference—Macnaghten recalled *both* suspects, and arguably fused them together. He used details about the barrister to partly fictionalize the real killer, who was himself disguised on the fateful day (with a cheap false moustache). Yet in this safely composite account Macnaghten also slides into details that were not true of *either* suspect in the 1897 crime but were probably inspired by another young barrister, one who was a maniacal murderer: Montague Druitt: "Two or three years later the police at *Blackheath* found a man *wandering* about in pitiable plight. He was much travel-stained; he had evidently been sleeping out for some nights, and possessed no overcoat. He appeared half-witted, and though unshaved for many days had very little hair on his face... His home he stated was on the *River Thames*, some forty miles from London... Some months after the man was *ajudged insane* and confined in a lunatic *asylum*, and as far as I know, *died there*" (my italics). To further back this argument there is, in the *Illustrated Police News* of February 27, 1897, an article regarding the Elizabeth Camp murder, which also overlaps with a soon-to-be disguised Druitt. An unnamed police officer claimed that the bar-maid's killer may have instantly drowned himself in the Thames: "Filled with horror, the repentant murderer escaped from the dreadful contact with his awful work at the earliest moment, and then sacrificed his own life in a frenzy of remorse. ... The Thames, which flows not far from Wandsworth Station, offered what seemed to him, if the suggestion be correct, the easiest means of atonement." No other source from 1897, or afterwards, remotely suggests such a line of inquiry by the constabulary. This is, I postulate, Macnaghten's "dress rehearsal" for disguising Montie Druitt at the end of the following year, perhaps to create a precedent for instant self-destruction in a river. This was the fictional element of the tale first communicated by M. P. Henry Farquharson that Macnaghten relentlessly propagated through George Sims—that the murderer had no time to confess to anybody—before pointedly easing the throttle off the "double bang" of murder and self-murder in his memoir chapter "Laying the Ghost of Jack the Ripper." The Camp tragedy may have been a dry run for this propaganda campaign, one that did not catch on with the media, but it stayed on his mind in the following years. It is arguably further textual evidence that Sir Melville Macnaghten knew that Montie Druitt was a young lawyer and not a middle-aged doctor.

18. G. R. Sims, *My Life: Sixty Years' Recollection of Bohemian London* (London: Eveleigh Nash, 1917), 175–6.

BIBLIOGRAPHY

Nonfiction

Aberconway, Christabel Mary. *A Wiser Woman? A Book of Memories.* London: Hutchinson, 1966.
Anderson, Robert. *The Lighter Side of My Official Life.* London: Hodder & Stoughten, 1910.
Begg, Paul. *Jack the Ripper: The Facts.* London: Robson, 2006.
Begg, Paul, Martin Fido, and Keith Skinner. *The Complete Jack the Ripper A to Z.* London: John Blake, 2010.
Bloom, Clive. *Victoria's Madmen: Revolution and Alienation.* New York: Palgrave Macmillan, 2013.
Browne, Douglas G. *The Rise of Scotland Yard: A History of the Metropolitan Police.* London: George C. Harrap, 1956.
Card, Tim. *Eton Renewed: A History from 1860 to the Present Day.* London: John Murray, 1994.
Connell, N., and S. P. Evans. *The Man Who Hunted Jack the Ripper: Edmund Reid—Victorian Detective.* Stroud, UK: Amberley, 2009.
Cullen, Tom A. *Autumn of Terror: Jack the Ripper, His Crimes and Times.* London: Bodley Head, 1965.
Dunlap, Ian. *Edward VII and the Entente Cordiale.* London: Constable, 2004.
Evans, Stewart P., and Donald Rumbelow. *Jack the Ripper: Scotland Yard Investigates.* Stroud, UK: Sutton, 2006.
Evans, Stewart P., and Paul Gainey. *The Lodger: The Arrest and Escape of Jack the Ripper.* London: Century, 1995.
Farson, Daniel. *Jack the Ripper.* History Book Club, 1972.
Fergusson, Niall. *Empire: How Britain Made the Modern World.* London: Penguin, 2002.
Fido, Martin. *The Crimes, Detection and Death of Jack the Ripper.* London: Weidenfeld & Nicolson, 1987.
Fisherman, W. J. *Into the Abyss: The Life and Work of G. R. Sims.* London: Elliot & Thompson, 2008.
Fraser, Nicholas. *The Importance of Being Eton.* London: Short, 2006.
Leighton, D. J. *Ripper Suspect: The Secret Lives of Montague Druitt.* Stroud, UK: History Press, 2007.
Macnaghten, Melville L. *Days of My Years.* London: Edward Arnold, 1914.
Meyers, Jeffrey. *Orwell: Wintry Conscience of a Generation.* New York: W.W. Norton, 2000.
Odell, Robin. *Jack the Ripper in Fact and Fiction.* London: George G. Harrap, 1966.
Orwell, George. *Inside the Whale, and Other Essays.* London: Penguin, 1969.
Roland, Paul. *The Crimes of Jack the Ripper.* London: Arcturus, 2006.
Rumbelow, Donald. *The Complete Jack the Ripper.* London: Virgin, 2013.
Shelden, Michael. *Orwell: The Authorized Biography.* New York: HarperCollins, 1991
Sims, George R. *Dorcas Dene, Detective: Her Adventures.* London: F. V. White, 1897. Reprint, British National Library, General Historical Collection, digitized by Microsoft.
———. *My Life: Sixty Years' Recollection of Bohemian London.* London: Eveleigh Nash, 1917.
Sims, George R., ed. *Living London.* London: Cassell, 1901.
Sudgen, Philip. *The Complete History of Jack the Ripper.* London: Robinson, 2006.
Thorpe, D. R. *Eden: The Life and Times of Anthony Eden.* London: Chatto & Windus, 2003.
Wade, Stephen. *Conan Doyle and the Crimes Club: The Creator of Sherlock Holmes and His Criminological Friends.* Stroud, UK: Fonthill, 2013.

Fiction

Belloc Lowndes, Marie. *The Lodger: A Story of the London Fog.* New York: Pocket, 1940.
Martin, T. K., and E. Jones. *Jack the Ripper.* BBC, 6 episodes, July 1973.
Le Queux, W. *Rasputin the Rascal Monk.* Melbourne: Melville & Mullen, 1918.
———. *Things I Know About Kings, Celebrities and Crooks.* London: Eveleigh Nash & Grayson, 1923.
Logan, Guy. *The True History of Jack the Ripper: The Forgotten 1905 Ripper Novel.* Additional material by Jan Bondeson. Stroud, UK: Amberley, 2013.
Matters, Leonard. *The Mystery of Jack the Ripper.* London: Hutchinson, 1964.
Stevenson, Robert Louis. *Vintage Stevenson: Dr. Jekyll and Mr. Hyde, and Other Stories.* London: Vintage, 2007.

INDEX

Numbers in ***bold italics*** indicate pages with illustrations.

Abberline, Frederick 48, 50, 58–59, 107, 171–72, 194
Aberconway, Lady Christabel 20, 27, 129, ***166***, 177, ***178***, ***179***; father's memorandum 144, 159, 174–75, 177, 186–91, 196
Aberconway, Lord Henry 178
Adam, Hargrave L. 21, 70, 87–88, 188
Alexander II 37
Amazon Women on the Moon 2, 8
Anderson, Sir Robert 48, 51–52, 62, 71, 73, 76, 78, 131–32, 137–39, 165, 169–70, 172–76, 196
Andrews, Walter 61, 71
Angle, B.J. 201
Asquith, H.H. 131–32, 134–35
Asquith, Margot 27, 131
Atkinson, Rowan 168
Australia 174, 191

Backert, Albert 194–95
Balfour, Arthur 20
Barnett, Joseph 57, 198
Barnett, Rev. Samuel 60
Barrymore, John ***144***, 181, ***182***
Baxter, Wynne 47, 58, 61, 84
Beck, Adolf 40, 42, 123, 165, 167–169, 181
Belloc-Lowndes, Marie 154, 155, 161–63, 181
Bertillon, Alphonse 131
Black, Peter 99
Blackadder 168
Blackheath 12, 14–15, 98, 101, 110, 112–13, 151, 200
Blunt, Anthony 20
Bond, Dr. Thomas 58, 76
Booth, Charles 36
Borden, Lizzie 1, 196
Bowyer, Thomas 57–58
Bradford, Sir Edward 132
Bulling, Tom 53, 79, 183
Bundy, Ted 104
Burgess, Guy 20, 169
Byrnes, Thomas 72

Cambridge 20, 118, 199
Cameron, David 20
Carroll, Lewis 8
Carson, Sir Edward 178
Chapman, Annie 49–50, 120, 137, 198

Chapman, George 87, 171
Chiswick 7, 12–14
Churchill, Lady Randolph 106
Churchill, Sir Winston 106, 170
Clarence, Duke of 106–07, 195
Clarke, Alan 19
Coleridge, Lord 13, 93, 100
Coles, Frances 15, 69, 82–84, 115, 124, 130, 135, 145–46, 176
Colocott, John 129
Conan Doyle, Sir Arthur 73, 158, 165, 186
Connolly, Cyril 21
Conrad, Joseph 95, 143
Conservative Party 3, 11–13, 19, 56, 59, 91, 97, 100, 102, 106–07, 109
Corpus Christi College Mission 119
Crawford, Henry 55
Cream, Dr. Thomas Neil 103–04
Crippen, Dr. Hawley 166, 169
Cullen, Tom 191–95, 197–98, 200
Cutbush, Charles 133
Cutbush, Thomas Hayne 129, 131, 133, 135–36, 185

Dagonet *see* Sims, George R
Days of My Years see Macnaghten, Sir Melville
Deeming, Frederick 191
Deptford Murder 169
Dickens, Charles 1, 40, 182
Diemschutz, Louis 51
Diplock, Dr. Thomas 14, 108–09, 112, 159
Divall, Tom 172
Dorset 102; Bournemouth 94, 100, 108, 110, 141, 171; Christchurch 12, 100; Whitchurch Canonicorum 116, 120; Wimborne Minster 13, 15, 97, 99, 102, 106, 108–09
Douglas, Lord Alfred 179, ***180***
Druitt, Ann 14, 97, 99, 106
Druitt, Arthur 109, 119
Druitt, Rev. Charles 10, 15, 94, 96, 105–08, 116, 118, 120–21, 125–26, 133, 149–151, 187, 191, 194, 199
Druitt, Edward 119, ***120***, 124
Druitt, Emily 99
Druitt, Isabel Majendie (née Hill) 94, 120, 207*ch*VIII*n*7

Druitt, James, Jr. 109–10, 121
Druitt, James, Sr. 3, 94, 102, 109, 121
Druitt, Katherine 99
Druitt, Lionel 191
Druitt, Matilda 109
Druitt, Montague John: alleged confession 10, 105, 114–16, 125; athlete 9, 13, 15, 94, *97*, 98, 101, 110, 159, 200–01; barrister 7, 9, 13, 15, 98–99, 100–01, 110; early years 9, *13*, 97–98, *108*, *147*, *155*, 207*ch*VIII*n*7; Ripper suspect 86–88, 94, 101–03, 105, 112–14, 133–34, 145–46; suicide 12, 14–17, 94, 98, 100, 103, 106–13, 115–16, 147, 151, 156, 159–60, 194–95; teacher 98–99, 101, 109, 111
Druitt, Dr. Robert 99
Druitt, Dr. William 13–14, 97, 99, 134
Druitt, William Harvey 12–15, 100, 105, 108–14, 212, 125, 154, 156, 163
Du Boulay, Isabel Aimee Houssemayne 94, 207*ch*VIII*n*7
Du Boulay, Rev. J.T.H. 207*ch*VIII*n*7
Dutton, Dr. Thomas 194

Eddowes, Catherine 51–56, 101, 122, 175
Eden, Sir. Anthony 19–20
Edjalji, George 73
Edward VII, King 16, 107, 165, 173
Edward VIII 107, 137
Edwards, Sir Fleetwood Isham 207*ch*VIII*n*7
Eton College 3, 5, 17–26, 29, 32, 34–35, 45, 62–65, 91, 95, 175, 207*ch*VIII*n*7
Evans, Alfred Henry 94, 207*ch*VIII*n*7

Farmer, Annie 59–60, 74, 122
Farquharson, Henry Richard 82, 86, 89, 90–91, *92*, 93–94, 100–06, 113–19, 121, 126–28, 130–33, 135, 146, 159–60, 168
Farson, Daniel 106, 113, 177, 188–96
Fleet, H.L. 106, 112
Forbes-Winslow, Dr. Lyttleton 170
Ford, Ford Madox 148–49
Fry, Stephen 19

Gacy, John Wayne 104
Garfield, Pres. James 72
Garrick Club 154, 188
Gatty, C.T. 92–93, 100, 135
Gellar, Uri 196
George V, King 107, 173, 178, *179*
Gladstone, William 19, 32, 132–33, 173
Goldsmith, Sir James 19
Gorman-Sickert, Joseph 195–96
Goulston St. Graffiti 176
Grant, William 137–39, 170
Griffiths, Maj. Arthur 17–18, 108, 115–17, 131, 137, 140, 144–50, 172, 182, 185–86, 200
Guiteau, Charles 72

Harcourt, William 170
Hardy, Thomas 97, 179
Henderson, Sir. Edmund 31–32
Henry, Sir Edward 166, 169
Hill, Rev. Arthur Du Boulay 207*ch*VIII*n*7
Hill, Charles Sydney 207*ch*VIII*n*7
Hill, Maria Elizabeth 94

Hitler, Adolf 19, 188–89
Home, Sir Alec Douglas 20
Hough, Georgiana (née Druitt) 118–20, 207*ch*VI-II*n*7
Hough, Rev. William *118*, 119–20, 207*ch*VIII*n*7
Hutchinson, George 58–59

Irving, Sir Henry 178, 188

James, M.R. 19, 88
Johns, Stratford 196
Johnson, Boris 20
Juettner, Dr. Otto 118

Kebbell, George 137, 170
Kelly, John 51
Kelly, Mary Jane 14, *57*, 58–60, 82, 87–88, 101–05, 115, 117, 133–35, 149, 151, 159, 169–70, 180–81
Kennedy, Howard Angus 199
Kerensky, Alexander 184
Keynes, John Maynard 19
Kingston Park Cricket Club 109
Kipling, Rudyard 178
Kosminski, Aaron 9, 80–82, 135–39, 146, 160, 170

Labouchere, Henry 131–32
Lancing College 27
Laurie, Hugh 19, 22
Lawende, Joseph 55–56, 60, 75, 83, 137–38, 145, 160, 175–76
Lawless, H.W. 84
Le Carre, John 5
Lenin, V.I. 183, 193
Leo XIII, Pope 119
Le Queux, William 148, 182–86, 194
Liberal Party 12, 56, 101, 106, 131, 170, 178
Lincoln, Pres. Abraham 71
Littlechild, John George 53, 61, 73, 79, 172–73
Llewellyn, Dr. Rees 47–48
Lloyd George, David 178
The Lodger A Story of the London Fog see Belloc-Lowndes
Logan, Guy 100, 111, 121, 154–60
London, Jack 45
Long, Alfred 52
Lucan, Lord 19

Macdonald, Dr. Roderick 58
Mackenzie, Alice 76–78, 91, 122, 135, 146, 170
Maclean, Donald 20
Maclean, James McKenzie 130
Macmillan, Sir Harold 20
Macnaghten, Charles Melville 186
Macnaghten, Dora 27, *28*, 128, 131, 173–78
Macnaghten, Hugh 207*ch*VIII*n*7
Macnaghten, Sir Melville Leslie *19, 166*; *Days of My Years* 7–8, 45–47, 51–53, 57–58, 85–88, 102–104, 175–76; early years 5, 17–19, 21–24; friendship with G.R. Sims 6–7, 11, 41, 44, 151, 201–02; friendship with V.D. Majendie 2, 10–11, 95, 101, 121, 124, 129, 137, 157, 201–02; memorandum 86–88, 94, 101–03, 105, 112–14, 133–34, 145–46
Madame Tussaud's 22, 75, 101, 155, 162
Majendie, Mary 207*ch*VIII*n*7

Majendie, Henry 95
Majendie, Henry Grylls 207*ch*VIII*n*7
Majendie, Maj. John Routledge 95
Majendie, Col. Sir Vivian Dering *2*, 4, 10, 15, 94–96, 101–03, 112, 115, 117, 120–22, 126, 130–34, 136, 138, 143, 150, 172, 175, 201, 207*ch*VIII*n*7
Mann, Harry 187–88
Mansfield, Richard 143
Matos, Jan 190
Matters, Leonard 185–86
Matthews, Henry 33–34, 50, 56–60, 103
McCarthy, John 57–58
McCormick, Donald 188–89, 194–95
McLaren, Lady Rose 189
Mearns, Andrew 36–37
Monro, James 29–34, 48, 62, 67, 71, 76–79, 122, 169, 171
Monty Python 5, 20
Moore, Charles 79, 201
Morden Cricket Club 98
Moulson, George 12, 111
Mylett, Catherine Rose 71

National Sporting Club 201
Nichols, Mary Ann "Polly" 47–50, 99, 101, 143
Nicholas II, Czar 183
Nimoy, Leonard 9
North Country Vicar *see* Druitt, Charles

O'Connor, T. P. 132
Odell, Robin 195
Orwell, George 2–3, 17–19, 23, 45, 166
Osborne, George 20
Ostrog, Michael 25–26, 63, 75, 129, 136–137, 146, 152, 160, 163, 175
Oxford 9, 13, 26, 94, 98–99, 119–120, 159, 187, 199

Parnell, Charles Stuart 169
Partridge, Ralph 189
Pearcey, Mary 80, *81*
Peel, Sir Robert 30
Pemberton, Max 168
Philby, Kim 20
Phillips, Dr. Bagster 76
Pitt, William 19
Pitt-Rivers, Gen. M. P. 93
Pizer, John 50, 135
Poe, Edgar Allan 49
Poll, Pearly 46–47

Race, William 131, 133, 145
Rasputin, Gregory 183, *184*, 194
Reid, Edmund 46
Richardson, Frank 154–55
Ripon, Lord 28
Roberts, Leslie M. 29
Ruffell, Fred 74

Sadler, James "Tom" 83–85, 91, 124, 135, 146
Sagar, Robert 42–43, 175
Salisbury, Lord 20, 59–60
Sanders, John 49–50, 91, 135, 171
Sanders, Laura 49
Seaman, William 65
Shaftesbury, Lord 106, 117

Shaw, George Bernard 178, 192, *197*, 198
Shelley, Percy 19
Sickert, Walter 195
Sims, George Robert 2, 6–11, 15–17; *Dagonet* columns 12, 15, 37, 41, 43, 49–50, 53–54, 56, 59, 77–78, 84, 122–23, 132, 150–151, 161, 170–172; *Dorcas Dene* stories 40, 155–157; early years 38–39; friendship with M. L. Macnaghten 6–7, 11, 122–124, 157, 201–02; friendship with V. D. Majendie 2, 10–11, 201–02; *How the Poor Live* 39, 198; *In the Workhouse-Christmas Day* 39; memoirs 38, 152–53, 168, 201–202; *The Priest's Secret* 124–126, 150
Sinclair, Upton 192
Smith, Emma 45–48, 125, 199
Smith, Maj. Henry 52
Stevenson, Robert Louis 5, 141–43, 147, 157
Stillwell, Osbert 27
Stoker, Bram 88
Stowell, Dr. Thomas 196
Straight, Whitney 20, 169
Strange Case of Dr. Jekyll and Mr. Hyde 6, 43, 140–41, *142*, 143–48, 150–51, 153–54, 157, 160, 171–72, 200
Stride, Elizabeth 51, 74, 101, 122, 161, 175–76
Swanson, Donald 48, 56, 83, 138–139, 172

Tabram, Martha 46–48, 158, 199
Tatcho *37*, 40, *41*, 163
Teck, Princess May of 107
Thaw, Harry K. 173
Thompson, Ernest 82, 145, 176, 187
Thomson, Sir Basil 6, 187
The True History of Jack the Ripper see Logan, Guy
Tumblety, Dr. Francis 8, 55, 61–62, 71–73, 76, 135, 166, 172, 183

Valentine, George 14–15, 98, 108–112
Van Gogh, Vincent 8
Victoria, Queen 29–32, 60, 99, 102, 106, 132, 195–196, 207*ch*VIII*n*7
Violenia, Emanuel 50

Walpole, Sir Robert 19
Warren, Sir Charles 27, 32–34, 48, 50, 52, 56–57, 59–60, 62, 67, 79, 102–03, 122, 158, 161, 165, 171, 174, 176, 189–81
Watkins, Edward 52, 55
Waugh, Evelyn 178
Weld, Sir Frederick 119
Wellington, Duke of 18, 32
Wells, H.G. 178
Wensley, Frederic Porter 64, *65*, 66–67, 69–70, 173–74
Whitchurch Canonicorum 116
Whitechapel 13, 36–37, 45–47, 56, 70
Wilde, Oscar *129*, 130–132, 179
Williamson, Adolfus 67, 75
Wilson, Gordon Chesney 29
Winchester College 9, 13, 23, 94, 98, 207*ch*VIII*n*7
Windsor, Frank 196
Winslade, Henry 12, 62, 108–09, 111
The Wizard of Oz 36, 148
Wodehouse P.G. 5
Woolf, Virginia 178

www.ingramcontent.com/pod-product-compliance
Ingram Content Group UK Ltd.
Pitfield, Milton Keynes, MK11 3LW, UK
UKHW050529150426
5217IPUK00026B/1861